CHRISTIAN
HOME
LEARNING
GUIDES

The Christian Companion to Zane Publishing's Home Library Titles

CHRISTIAN HOME LEARNING GUIDES

The Christian Companion to Zane Publishing's Home Library Titles

By *Marshall Foster* and *Ron Ball*
With a Foreword by *Paul Zane Pilzer*

Zane Interactive Publishing, Inc. • Dallas, Texas 75207 • 214-800-6000

PowerCD is a registered trademark and *PowerCD Explorer* and *American Concise Encyclopedia* are trademarks of Zane Interactive Publishing, Inc.

ISBN: 1-57573-132-0

Published by Zane Interactive Publishing, Inc.
1950 Stemmons, Suite 4044
Dallas, Texas 75207-3109

Phone: 214-800-6000
Fax: 214-800-6090
Website: http://www.zane.com

Printed in the United States of America

The views expressed herein are exclusively those of the authors and do not reflect the position of the publisher.

CONTENTS

FOREWORD

Today's Heresy is Tomorrow's Dogma
By Paul Zane Pilzer

THROUGHOUT HISTORY HUMANKIND has formulated theories to explain the mysteries of the universe, oftentimes theories that appeared valid at the time but ones that we now believe to be completely false.

Worse still, humankind has not been receptive to even hearing, let alone tolerating, a view alternative to the mainstream. The early Christians were persecuted by the Romans for their monotheism, a view now universally accepted by virtually all peoples of the world. Similarly, sixteen hundred years later Galileo was tried by the Inquisition for supporting the Copernican theory that the planets revolve around the sun instead of the earth, a view that contradicted the longheld Ptolemaic belief but one that is now accepted worldwide.

Today we like to think of ourselves as living in an information age where we know all the answers. And yet, a close examination of present-day theories shows that we are perhaps even further from the truth than were Ptolemy and Galileo. In physics, we have contradictory theories to explain things big (Newtonian) and things small (quantum mechanics), both of which cannot be simultaneously correct, yet both of which are used every day in the development of space travel and semiconductors. In biology, we classify our world of living creatures based on a system of evolution that we now know, thanks to the benefits of DNA research, may not be correct. It seems that the more we learn the less we know—something my father always taught me was the beginning of true knowledge.

To resolve such chaos, many of us have looked to our spiritual origins, most of which were developed at a time when religion and science were the same discipline.

The *Christian Home Learning Guides*, written by Marshall Foster and Ron Ball, is designed to present the evangelical Christian view of the mainstream subjects taught in school today and featured on Zane Home Library CD-ROMs. It is designed for the parents of Christian homeschoolers, as well as the parents of children in public and private schools, who wish to provide their children with the Christian view of world history, science, and literature.

Zane is proud to be a leader in electronically publishing mainstream school curricula—secularly preparing our children and our world for the twenty-first century. Zane also is proud to be publishing the *Christian Home Learning Guides*, which offers a Christian perspective of the humanities and sciences. Zane is most proud, however, to be publishing both together—preparing children today for success in the secular world in which we live, while also providing them the framework to reconcile this secular knowledge with their religious beliefs.

EDITOR'S PREFACE

ZANE PUBLISHING WAS extremely fortunate to have two best-selling authors, Marshall Foster and Ron Ball, combine their talents and expertise in the writing of the *Christian Home Learning Guides.*

Marshall Foster's outstanding analysis of world history set forth in the six acts of *God's Historical Drama* brings the past to life. His experience training students and families in a biblical worldview is reflected in his essays *A Biblical Worldview for Success, Geography: Setting the Stage, Worldview Expression in Art, Worldview Expression in Literature, Myths & Legends, Preparing the Christian Student for College,* and *A Magnificent Optimism.*

Ron Ball's experience as a leading evangelist and educator has enabled him to communicate the impact of Christian leadership within these pages. His ability to incorporate education and a biblical perspective is evident in his essays *Faith amd Music, Faith and Science,* and *Leaders in Christian History.*

Goals of the Text

The goal of this book is twofold: It is designed to (1) give the student a providential timeline of Christian history that highlights the people and events that have shaped our world from ancient times to the present, and (2) offer the student the instruction and encouragement needed to face the next century.

Pedagogical Features

Timeline: The Timeline of Christian History gives the dates and major events that have occurred in history.

Essays: Written by Dr. Foster and Mr. Ball, these essays examine the Christian history of the world from ancient times to the present, including a look at how the humanities and science have reflected world events.

Sidebars: Biographical highlights of notable people covered in the essays can be found in the sidebars of the chapters.

CD-ROM Analyses: Chapters include analyses by Dr. Foster or Mr. Ball of the Zane CD-ROM titles related to the subject material.

Review Questions: Questions that help the student strengthen his or her understanding of the subject material can be found at the end of most chapters. Answers to the questions can be found in Appendix P.

Related Scripture: Scriptural verses that relate to the material can be found at the end of the chapters.

Suggested Reading: A list of recommended books that can supplement a student's study of the chapter material can be found at the end of the chapters.

Glossary: Terms found in small caps within the text can be found in the glossary at the back of the book.

Historical Documents: Documents such as the Declaration of Independence and the Ten Commandments can be found in the appendix.

Acknowledgments:
I would like to thank my assistant editor, Peter Tepp,
for his help in proofing this book,
and Dana Bilbray for the book's layout and design.
— JUDITH M. EMMERT

ABOUT THE AUTHORS

Marshall Foster

DR. MARSHALL FOSTER is the founder and president of the Mayflower Institute, a nonprofit educational foundation started in 1976 that is dedicated to teaching the biblical and historical foundations of liberty.

A nationally recognized historian, best-selling author, keynote speaker, and syndicated radio host, he speaks at business conventions, statewide homeschool conventions, seminars, and churches. He has written three books, numerous syndicated articles, and is the editor of the monthly *Mayflower Institute Journal*, which addresses current cultural dilemmas. He also is the Director of Education for *American Christian Tours*, overseeing and leading Christian heritage tours worldwide.

A former Bible College professor who was the founder and director of both the Los Angeles Rams chaplain's program and the Campus Crusade ministry at the University of Southern California, Dr. Foster has been featured on the Trinity Broadcast Network and numerous radio and television programs such as *The 700 Club, Focus on the Family, Point of View,* and *Duffy & Co.*

Foster graduated from the University of California at Santa Barbara with a bachelor of arts in economics. His graduate work was accomplished at Talbot Theological Seminary and the California Graduate School of Theology. He earned his doctorate of divinity from Cathedral Bible College.

Foster and his wife of twenty-seven years, Trish, reside in Southern California with their two children.

Ron Ball

SINCE DELIVERING HIS FIRST seminar at the age of fifteen, Ron Ball has presented dynamic messages of biblical success to over three million people in America, Europe, Australia, and Asia.

As president of the Ron Ball Association, he has spoken over 12,000 times at business conventions, civic rallies, and Christian crusades. He received the honor of Financial Researcher of the Year (1990) by the Financial Research Institute of America. He has appeared on television and radio broadcasts in forty states and has contributed to magazines in four countries.

Ball has shared the platform with such noted leaders as Dexter Yager, Zig Zigler, Dr. Charles Stanley, Art Linkletter, Ronald Reagan, Denis Waitley, Pat Robertson, and Paul Conn.

He has co-authored with Dexter Yager five best-selling books that have now sold more than one-half million copies worldwide and have made best-seller lists throughout the United States.

Ball was born in Paintsville, Kentucky. He graduated with a bachelor of arts degree from Asbury College in 1973 and with a master of divinity from Asbury Theological Seminary in 1976. He did his postmaster's work at Emory University in Atlanta.

Ball and his wife, Amy, reside in Tennessee with their daughter, Allison, and son, Jonathan.

ACKNOWLEDGMENTS

Marshall Foster

I AM DEEPLY INDEBTED to the millions of forgotten, faithful believers who have laid down their lives for the spiritual and political liberty we enjoy. Without these precious liberties this book would not have been possible.

A project of this magnitude required the faith and commitment of many individuals. Years ago, my friend Don Held, together with Paul Pilzer, spearheaded the vision of this project. Don has diligently worked to restore America since I first met him in 1980.

My sincere thanks also to Paul Pilzer, Dexter Yager, Billy Florence, Craig Holiday, and my co-author Ron Ball for perceiving the great educational crisis and being willing to bring the biblical principles of this book back home to the American family where the solution lies.

My wife, Trish, has always been my writing inspiration. Her tireless research, editing, and ideas can be seen on every page I have written. Douglas Brown deserves special thanks for months of intelligent input and long hours. Judith Emmert, our chief editor, was a consistent source of encouragement and labored unceasingly for excellence. Coby Turner also contributed in many ways to this project.

It is not possible to thank all of those who have been so generous with their help and their prayers. However, special thanks to Dr. John Chacko, Dan and Corinne Allen, Jim Halcomb, Marlene Mitchell, and Lois Herman for their support, suggestions, and insight.

Most importantly, I am grateful to God for His indescribable gift, His Son, Jesus Christ, who is the center of all history, the foundation of all learning, and our Savior and Redeemer.

Ron Ball

I AM IMMEASURABLY GRATEFUL to my wife, Amy, and her commitment to the education and spiritual growth of our children, Allison and Jonathan. Her commitment to create Godly excellence in them has always been a thrilling challenge for me.

Allison and Jonathan, I further dedicate this work to you and your future, that you will become powerfully effective in influencing your world for Jesus Christ.

I am further grateful to Dexter Yager and his organization of distributors around the world who are engaged in the process of educational excellence everywhere.

This project would not have existed without the two men who championed it from the beginning: Billy Florence and Paul Pilzer. Their support and commitment have been essential.

My thanks as well to Marshall Foster, my valuable, intelligent partner in this endeavor, and to Judith Emmert for her help as an effective and always encouraging editor.

INTRODUCTION

By Ron Ball

SINCE THE BEGINNING of Western Christian civilization, the positive goal of God's glory has infused every part of life.

The truly ultimate questions and perplexities of our world—death, suffering, human connections, and the significance of our lives—have been examined through the arts, which reach deep into the human heart and fly upward to face God and receive His answers. Whether painting, sculpture, theater, or literature, the arts have traditionally sought to understand God, the workings of His world, and our place in it.

History has provided a roadmap through the tangled confusion of past events. It has taught lessons, provided warnings, and stubbornly reminded us that only God's laws work and bring blessing to the human race. We have been witnesses to the lives of those men and women who chose not to obey God. The wreckage of their lives serves as a glaring reminder that God's laws cannot be broken—you only break yourself in the attempt.

Throughout the centuries, education has been a formidable factor in art, literature, political leadership, and spiritual growth. This is not to say that education alone is primary in importance. The relationship of the individual to God through Jesus Christ, of course, supersedes every other element of life. Biblically directed spiritual life is the dynamic core from which all other aspects radiate.

The leaders of the twenty-first century must be equipped and prepared to follow in the spiritual footsteps of our ancestors, those people who challenged and changed the world through their love, service, and obedience of God. Christian leadership should be an honor to God by its intellectual discipline and its spiritual depth and excitement. We should outteach, outwork, and outlove the rest of the world! We know that the mind can be a terrible instrument of selfish pursuit, manipulation, and savage cruelty, or it can be a means to godly study, beautification and enrichment of life, and ongoing blessing for other people. It can be the birthplace of new horizons and fresh ideas, full of excitement and endless possibilities.

It is our conviction that when the intellect, the emotions, the will, and the spirit are in the right balance with God, the whole person becomes an expression of excellence for the glory of God.

The Bible itself stresses the importance of the mind in spiritual growth: "Do your best to present yourself to God as one approved, a workman who does not need to be ashamed and who correctly handles the word of truth." (2 Tim. 2:15 *New International Version*) "All Scripture is God-breathed and is useful for teaching, rebuking, correcting and training in righteousness, so that the man of God may be thoroughly equipped for every good work." (2 Tim. 3:16-17 *NIV*)

**CHRISTIAN HOME
LEARNING GUIDES**

Zane Publishing's educational program and this book offer you and your children two critical requirements for future influence: (1) solid grounding and factual education; and (2) a biblical Christian perspective and application of the program.

Zane has done an outstanding job in its CD-ROM titles. Your children will go beyond the threshold of basic information; they will become *educated*—a precious commodity in today's society. They will learn the foundation for a rich, full, productive life; they will learn to reason, to think, to create.

The Christian application of the Zane material will keep your children grounded in biblical leadership and authority. It will guide them and mold them as they learn to seek God for themselves and enjoy their relationship with Jesus Christ.

At times, you will encounter secular interpretations of events in the CD-ROMs. There is, for example, a clear evolutionary bias in the material in the *Biological Sciences* series. Do not be alarmed! It is our conviction that students should know and understand positions outside of evangelical Christianity. We are confident that their faith will be stronger when they know both sides and understand why we believe the biblical view of the world is correct both intellectually and spiritually.

God bless you. You are beginning an adventure in learning, a journey into the hearts and minds of your children.

Together, assisted by this excellent program and humbly dependent on the blessing and help of God, you can build godly men and women who will lead us into the twenty-first century.

What are you waiting for? Let's go!

CHRISTIAN HOME LEARNING GUIDES

The Christian Companion to Zane Publishing's Home Library Titles

PART ONE

A Biblical Plan for Godly Education

A BIBLICAL WORLDVIEW
FOR SUCCESS

If we work upon marble, it will perish; if we work upon brass, time will efface it; if we rear temples, they will crumble into dust; but if we work upon immortal minds, if we imbue them with principles, with the just fear of God and love of our fellow men, we engrave on those tablets something which will brighten to all eternity.

—DANIEL WEBSTER

THE HISTORY OF CHRISTIANITY has been the history of the growth of excellence in education. The ancient world had no conception of education for the common man. Scholarship was the sole property of the class-conscious elite of Greece, Rome, and Egypt. Our Lord rent the veil of educational elitism when He said, "Let the little children come to Me, and do not forbid them; for of such is the kingdom of heaven."[1] He taught that everyone, including children, must know Him through His written Word (John 8:31). Christians spearheaded the cause of literacy from the time of the early Church through the Middle Ages. Monasteries and schools were established and eventually the first universities were started for the purpose of Christian and classical training at Cambridge, Paris, and Bologna.

With the invention of the printing press and the start of the Protestant Reformation, a PARADIGM shift took place in education. The Bible, for the first time in history could be purchased and read by the average family, and reformers like Martin Luther and William Tyndale made certain it was available in the common language of the people. For the purpose of scholarly study of the Bible, schools and universities were founded throughout Europe. For the very first time books by Shakespeare and Milton, and books on science and civil government, could be found in thousands of homes, being read by candlelight.

For twelve years, a small banished congregation of English believers studied together next to the leading university in Europe, the University of Leiden. In the fall of 1620, these Pilgrims braved a sixty-six day voyage to settle the untamed wilderness of New England. According to their own diary, they came for three major purposes. They desired to be free to pursue family-directed education apart from the corruption and tyranny of Europe. They hoped to be materially prosperous through free enterprise in order that others would be drawn to join their colony and their faith. And they wanted to help advance the Christian faith "to the remotest parts of the world."

These three ideals were the underlying foundations of America's success for more than two hundred years. From this precious seed unprecedented prosperity and liberty have flourished, and the world missionary movement has grown worldwide. But perhaps the most amazing result of the intelligent biblical faith of our forefathers was the quality of education that it produced.

See the appendix for
The Westminster Shorter Catechism

Harvard historian Perry Miller said, "In contrast to all other pioneers, they made no concessions to the forest, but in the midst of frontier conditions, in the very throes of clearing the land and erecting shelters, they maintained schools and a college."[2] Only four people out of one thousand in New England were illiterate in the early 1800s, according to John Quincy Adams.

Moses Coit Tyler, historian of American literature, indicated the colonists' "[f]amiliarity with history. . .extensive legal learning. . .lucid exposition of constitutional principles, showing, indeed, that somehow, out into the American wilderness had been carried the very accent of cosmopolitan thought and speech."[3] From this fertile intellectual soil came the world's foremost political documents and cultural prosperity.

Millions of Americans still share this common vision of our forebears. But in the nineteenth and twentieth centuries many Christians were persuaded to withdraw from the "SECULAR" world and two hundred years of educational leadership. This left a vacuum that was quickly filled by a new breed of secular intellectuals. Historian Paul Johnson explained: "With the decline of clerical power in the eighteenth century, a new kind of mentor emerged to fill the vacuum and capture the ear of society. The secular intellectual might be deist, skeptic or atheist. But he was just as ready as any pontiff or presbyter to tell mankind how to conduct its affairs."[4] As a result of this secularization, the original American dream is withering, choked by a cacophony of sound bites and superbowls, government regulations and educational misinformation.

THE BATTLE FOR IMMORTAL MINDS

Today, the pressures on American students to reject the Christian faith are greater than ever. What has been the result of the removal of Christian faith and values from education? From 1960 to 1990, violent crime increased 560 percent, teenage suicide rose more than 200 percent, and SAT scores dropped almost 80 points.[5] Another study found that, among other things, "nearly one-third of American seventeen-year-olds do not know that Abraham Lincoln wrote the Emancipation Proclamation,. . . nearly half do not know who Joseph Stalin was, and. . .about thirty percent could not locate Britain on a map of Europe."[6] As the fruit of education without God and the Bible has become evident, the twentieth-century illusion of "Happy Days" and a secular "Camelot" has slowly died. But from the ashes of these misguided dreams has come a new passion burning in the hearts of godly parents all across our nation. Their realistic dream is to give their children the moral, traditional Christian education they need and deserve.

The present generation of Christian parents is beginning to prepare children not only to survive, but to succeed in the twenty-first century. They are realizing that the unbelieving world has little interest in presenting the central, positive impact of Christianity to our children. They are simply reasserting their God-ordained role as the primary, if not only, teacher to their children. They are claiming this jurisdiction whether their children are in public, private, or home school. This movement toward parental involvement is a national phenomenon.

Already, young people who are being taught the truth of God in history, science, free enterprise economics, law, government, and the arts are stepping back into leadership. They are assuming these roles in a culture that was built through the intellectual sweat, the spiritual tears, and the life's blood of their Christian forebears. The most important preparation for this pivotal generation of Christians is a comprehensive biblical worldview.

WHAT IS A WORLDVIEW?

Everyone—including teachers, textbook writers, and the authors of this book—has a set of conscious or unconscious presuppositions that guide all thoughts and actions. Dr. Francis Schaeffer, the eminent twentieth-century Christian apologist, defined "presuppositions" this way: "By presuppositions we mean the basic way an individual looks at life, his basic world view, the grid through which he sees the world. . .presuppositions also provide the basis for [his] values, and therefore the basis for [his] decisions."[7] An individual's presuppositions make up his or her worldview. Professor Ron Jenson emphasized the importance of developing the proper world view when he said, "Our world view may be conscious or unconscious, but it determines our destiny, and the destiny of the society we live in."[8]

Worldviews are not inherited; they are learned. If a parent does not reinforce a biblical worldview at home, students will probably absorb a secular worldview from the classroom. Many modern historians, scientists, philosophers, and educators have attempted to claim objectivity in their chosen field of study. Most Americans have adopted this myth of neutrality. They have been convinced that basic education skills and facts can be taught without a religious or philosophical bias. This has resulted in the unspoken but ironclad separation of a Christian worldview from education. R. L. Dabney explained the impossibility of neutrality in education:

> The instructor has to teach history, cosmogony [study of origins], psychology, ethics, the laws of nations. How can he do it without saying anything favorable or unfavorable about the beliefs of evangelical Christians, Catholics, Socinians [Unitarians], Deists, pantheists, materialists, or fetish worshipers, all who claim equal rights under American institutions? His teaching will indeed be 'the play of Hamlet, with the part of Hamlet omitted.'[9]

A person's worldview will shape every conclusion he draws. A Marxist historian will choose and interpret the facts of history to portray religion as the "opiate of the people." An unbelieving scientist will welcome a theory such as spontaneous evolution to avoid his accountability to a holy God and His immutable laws. And a Christian will (or should) interpret life based upon the Word of God and Jesus Christ. One worldview is right and other worldviews are wrong. But no worldview is neutral. [For more on worldviews, see *Preparing the Christian Student for College. Ed.*]

WHAT IS THE IMPACT OF A BIBLICAL WORLDVIEW?

A Christian world and life view is at the core of the great accomplishments of Western civilization. Christian historian Philip Schaff illuminated the significance of Christ and Christianity:

Jesus of Nazareth, without money and arms, conquered more millions than Alexander, Caesar, Mohammed and Napoleon; without science and learning, He shed more light on things human and divine than all the philosophers and scholars combined; without the eloquence of the school, He spoke words of life such as were never spoken before, nor since, and produced effects which lie beyond the reach of orator or poet. Without writing a single line, He has set more pens in motion and furnished themes for more sermons, orations, discussions, works of art, learned volumes, and sweet songs of praise than the whole army of great men of ancient and modern times. Born in a manger and crucified as a malefactor, He now controls the destinies of the civilized world and rules a spiritual empire which embraces one-third of the inhabitants of the globe.[10]

In our secular age, textbooks and news reports often fail to report the central role of Christianity in building civilization. But a biblical worldview has blessed mankind as no other. It cannot be denied that the greatest universities, as well as literacy and education for the common man, were a product of Christianity. The Christian work ethic was the foundation of the free enterprise system and CAPITALISM, which have geometrically increased the wealth of the world. Representative constitutional government had its roots in the Old and New Testaments, not in ancient pagan cultures, and found its fullest expression in the Christian experiment in colonial America. The biblical worldview of a created universe of order and design provided the basis for modern science, and a reasonable faith for most of its pioneers. The Christian legal structure, centered in the Ten Commandments, provided a basis for justice and peace that is still the wonder of the world. Christian conscience, preaching, and the Bible were central in the abolition of slavery, both in antiquity and in more modern times. With Christianity came a high regard for all human life, since it was destined for eternity, and the elevation of women as joint-heirs in God's kingdom, not servants of men. Christ's Samaritan example and Christian love produced hospitals, homes for the insane and orphans, and food banks for the hungry. Christianity brought an end to human sacrifice, POLYGAMY, IDOLATRY, and the elevation of leaders to "god" status that is so common in non-Christian cultures.

It is impossible to consistently hide the overwhelming impact of Christianity throughout history. Even Napoleon himself, one of the great tyrants of history, had to admit, "I search in vain in history to find the similar to Jesus Christ, or anything which can approach the gospel. . . nations pass away, thrones crumble, but the Church remains."[11]

Not only must we emphasize that great accomplishments have been the result of a sincere biblical Christianity, but that those who have performed these deeds lived lives of hope and optimism. Believers, "with a firm reliance on Divine Providence," have dared to act in the face of impossible odds, knowing that God would be their rewarder.

Faith in the fact that covenant keepers win and covenant breakers lose has led believers throughout history to persevere and win: Moses and Pharaoh, David and Goliath, Deborah and the Canaanites, Paul and the Roman Empire. Christopher Columbus battled against the skepticism of men. Isaac Newton fought the ignorance of the Middle Ages. George

Washington warred against the British Empire. George Washington Carver struggled against ingrained racism. All are examples of God building His kingdom through the faithful service of His people. Against incredible odds, they transformed their world by seeing beyond the circumstance to a biblical worldview.

TIMELESS BIBLICAL BLUEPRINT

In our media world of fantasy and hype, being an NBA forward or a rock star is the dream of millions. But the real world changing occupation—and the most satisfying—is the parental challenge of preparing their young to serve God in the next generation. "Behold, children are a heritage from the Lord, the fruit of the womb is His reward. Like arrows in the hand of a mighty warrior, so are the children of one's youth."[12]

The Bible makes it clear that the authority and responsibility to educate children rests with parents. We may have assistance in the form of teachers or a curriculum, but we are accountable to train and point God's "immortal arrows" into the next generation. Obedience to this task brings great reward. "Train up a child in the way he should go, and when he is old he shall not depart from it"[13]

What is the Bible's strategy for successful child training? Most biblical scholars, both Jewish and Christian, would agree that the most complete and powerful statement in all the Bible concerning children's education is in the five-step strategy of Deuteronomy 6:4–12. This passage is called the Shema, which relates God's vital declaration to the Hebrew people as they prepared to enter the Promised Land. God began His vital declaration with the wake-up call, "Hear [Shema], O Israel!" It means "Listen! Attention! Wake up!"

It is not an overstatement to say that obedience to the principles laid down in the Shema is pivotal to the success of any family, education program, and, ultimately, for the success of any nation. Here are those principles.

1. Know God: His Character and Attributes

> Hear, O Israel; The Lord our God, The Lord is one.[14]

A knowledge of the true character and nature of God is the first and most important truth to be comprehended by any parent or child. Without this knowledge of our Creator from the Bible, we would be left groping for false gods and idols like much of the world. The Westminster Catechism is an ideal means of educating children about the nature of God.

2. Love the Lord: Personal Relationship and Faith

> You shall love the Lord your God with all your heart, with all your soul, and with all your might.[15]

As parents, we must do more than exhibit an intellectual knowledge of God. We are admonished to love the Lord with our whole being. In doing so, we are responding in obedience to the love God already displayed for us: "But God demonstrates His own love toward us, in that while we were still sinners, Christ died for us"[16]. Christian educator Douglas Wilson said, "The command to teach children all the time is not limited to religious instruction. If our children do not think like Christians when they study history, math, or science, then they are not obeying the command to love God with all their minds."[17] As a result of obedience to the first two commands of the Shema, parents themselves are prepared to share God's view of the world, and through their sincere love for Him, exhibit a real faith to their children.

3. Teach God's Truth to Your Children

> These words which I command you today shall be in your heart and you shall teach them diligently to your children, and shall talk of them when you sit in your house, when you walk by the way, when you lie down, and when you rise up.[18]

This commandment tells us that God's Word and truth should be in our memory so that as parents we can naturally take advantage of every opportunity, throughout the day or night, to teach our children. Here we see the importance of consistent training. We are told in Isaiah 28:10, "For precept must be upon precept, precept upon precept, line upon line, here a little, there a little." Even fifteen or twenty minutes a day of consistent teaching can transform a child. It is clear that a home library and CD-ROM curriculum could be a great complement to this training.

4. Mark Yourself, Your Home, and Your Business with Obedience to God's Law

> You shall bind them as a sign on your hand, and they shall be as frontlet between your eyes. You shall write them on the doorposts of your house and on your gates.[19]

Like the Jews who visibly displayed their obedience to God on their persons and homes, we should show our obedience to the world—first in our own lives, then in our homes, and then through the works of our hands. This command graphically documents God's internal-to-external strategy for changing His world—from the heart, to the home, to the society. The Bible affirms this strategy in both the Old and New Testaments: "This is the covenant that I will make with them after those days, says the Lord. I will put my laws into their hearts, and in their minds I will write them."[20] This is how the New Testament believers were able to permeate and eventually subdue the pagan Roman Empire.

5. Expect Blessings for You and Your Children for 1,000 Generations

> And it shall be, when the Lord your God brings you into the land of which He swore to your fathers. . .to give you large and beautiful cities which you did not build, houses full of all good things, which you did not fill, hewn-out wells which you did not dig, vineyards and olive trees which you did not plant. . . . Beware, lest you forget the Lord.[21]

Here we see the promise of blessing which follows obedience to the Shema. Those who, by faith, obey God can be the greatest optimists because they know God is going to reward them regardless of their temporary situation.

Later in Deuteronomy God details how long this generational blessing can reach: "Know that the Lord your God, He is God, the faithful God who keeps covenant and mercy for 1,000 generations with those who love Him and keep His commandments."[22]

We know that God's plan centers on the fulfillment of the Shema, for He blessed the nations through Abraham, who trained his children and household:

> And the Lord said: Shall I hide from Abraham what I am doing? Since Abraham shall surely become a great and mighty nation, and all the nations of the earth shall be blessed in him? For I have known him, in order that he may command his children and his household after him, that they keep the way of the Lord, to do righteousness and justice, that the Lord may bring to Abraham what he has spoken to him.[23]

ESSENTIALS OF HOME EDUCATION

The Christian education that occurs in the home cannot do without three simple elements, which in combination can enhance a child's education and produce godly leaders of future generations.

All real, effective education is rooted in God's infallible Word. Noah Webster said, "The Bible was America's basic textbook in all fields."[24] Verna Hall, one of America's foremost Christian educators, said, "We, as a people, must return to the Holy Bible as our American political, economic, social, educational and civic textbook."[25] It is the textbook of textbooks. The cause of the poor success rate of modern education has been the erosion of these biblical foundations. The Bible speaks of the way of success in Joshua 1:8, when God says to Joshua:

> This Book of the Law shall not depart from your mouth, but you shall meditate in it day and night that you may observe to do according to all that is written in it. For then you will make your way prosperous, and then you will have good success.

Jesus said, "You shall know the truth, and the truth shall make you free."[26] The liberating truth of which he spoke is the Bible, the Word of God. Paul said to Timothy, "All Scripture is given by inspiration of God, and is profitable for doctrine, for reproof, for correction, for instruction in righteousness, that the man of God may be complete, thoroughly equipped for every good work."[27]

In an educational environment, the Bible provides unity in the midst of a diversity of subject matter. The Bible gives truthful order, which eliminates the chaos of modern relativism. To help develop a consistent biblical worldview, we recommend that the Bible verses in each section be read and analyzed, aloud if possible, before the CD-ROMs are studied. Then, the biblical worldview essay, at the beginning of each section, should be read to glean further principles that apply to the specific academic subject. By following this procedure, before studying the CD-ROMs, the specific facts that are learned can be placed within the context of their biblical purpose. Note that Zane's CD-ROMs come equipped with a complete King James version of the Bible.

The godly parent is the ideal educator. Christian parents should not be intimidated by the plethora of educational philosophies that dominate the field of learning. The Lord never gives us a task to do without empowering us to do it. He also gives us clear instructions in Scripture for accomplishing the task.

The Shema gives us the most successful educational plan of all time. It centers upon the teaching of children naturally, throughout the day's activities. This consistency of training in the home enables the parent to integrate the academic data with a biblical worldview. The result is a wise child who is able to discern right from wrong—one who, "by reason of use, [has his] senses exercised, to discern both good and evil."[28]

Over time the student will become increasingly self-disciplined and capable of independent thinking. It is the self-starting individual who will lead the twenty-first century. Samuel Adams said the goal of education is, ". . .to renovate the age, by impressing the minds of men with the importance of educating their little boys and girls,. . .of instructing them in the art of self government, without which they can never act a wise part in the government of societies, great or small."[29]

The final element in home education is knowledge of and access to the facts. The *Christian Home Learning Guides* can assist the teacher greatly in this process of self-learning by helping the parent organize and summarize the meaning and purpose of the facts being learned and by providing a suggested reading list for further study. The combination of the *Christian Home Learning Guides* and Zane's CD-ROMs gives the parent/student team a combination of knowledge for twenty-first-century living and the ability to analyze facts and their interpretation through a biblical perspective. The interplay between the CD-ROM curriculum and the Guides enables the student to compare and contrast the worldviews and see the strength of God's truth in all academic fields. In most cases, the information presented on the CD-ROMs is portrayed in an excellent factual manner, with great interactive capability. In those areas where a biblical worldview would be especially helpful, the contrast is presented clearly in the worldview essay.

We believe that all Christian students should be aware of the alternative ideologies that are vying for their allegiance. They must be ready to defend their biblical worldview in a marketplace of ideas.

With the exciting combination of tools and technology that have been made available through Zane Publishing, a parent and student will be equipped to defend a biblical view of Creation, our representative government, the free enterprise system, the Christian ethic, history, private sector solutions to the welfare state, law, crime, the environment, and many other crucial questions. Our hope is that strong, biblically centered, intelligently trained families will lead the way back to a restored "One Nation Under God."

"FOR SUCH A TIME AS THIS"

We are a privileged generation. Not only do we and our children have the great legacy of what has been done in Christ's power through the ages, but we also live in the last decade of the second millennium after Christ. Historically, the ends of centuries, and especially millennial years, have signaled great changes.

As we stand poised at the dawn of the twenty-first century, another great transformation of the world is occurring all around us. The 1990s have seen the explosion of the computer age. God has unleashed the invention of the microchip at this time in history. Its impact may be even greater than the world-changing inventions of the past like the printing press, sea compass, and nuclear power. Its potential for the family is just now being discovered.

Futurists like John Naisbitt, John Dale Davidson, and Lord William Rees-Mogg agree that the microcomputer and its spin-offs are going to devolve power back to the individual and the family, and away from the secular state, as no invention since gunpowder. Naisbitt, quoting George Gilder, said:

> 'Rather than pushing control to Big Brother at the top, as the pundits predicted, the technology by its very nature pulled power back down to the people,' writes George Gilder. 'All the world will benefit from the increasing impotence of imperialism, mercantilism, and statism.' People in our day possess, 'powers of creation and communication far beyond those of the kings old.'[30]

Paul Zane Pilzer was one of the great visionaries in the 1970s who saw this trend and has converted his dream into the reality of the Zane CD-ROM titles. Now the coming generation has a high-quality CD-ROM educational tool that can enlighten and inform in the home, with parental supervision. With the addition of the *Christian Home Learning Guides*, the parent and the student can study not only the factual details, pictures, and drama of a twenty-first-century classroom in the home, but they also will be empowered to approach the learning process from a biblical world and life view.

RELATED SCRIPTURE

Deuteronomy 6:4–12; 7:9   Isaiah 28:9–10
Joshua 1:7–8   Colossians 2:8
Psalm 1; 127:3–4   1 Timothy 3:16–17; 4:2–3
Proverbs 22:6   Hebrews 5:14

SUGGESTED READING

Samuel Blumenfeld, *Is Public Education Necessary?* (Boise, ID: Paradigm Company, 1981).

Marshall Foster and Mary-Elaine Swanson, *The American Covenant: The Untold Story* (Thousand Oaks, CA: Mayflower Institute, 1992).

Greg Harris, *The Christian Home School* (Brentwood, TN: Wolgemuth, 1988).

Linwood Laughy, *The Interactive Parent: How to Help Your Child Survive and Succeed in the Public Schools* (Kooskia, ID: Mountain Meadow, 1988).

CHRISTIAN HOME
LEARNING GUIDES

Francis A. Schaeffer, *How Shall We Then Live?* (Wheaton, IL: Crossway, 1976).

Paul C. Vitz, *Censorship: Evidence of Bias in Our Children's Textbooks* (Ann Arbor, MI: Anchor, 1986).

Douglas Wilson, *Recovering the Lost Tools of Learning: An Approach to Distinctively Christian Education* (Wheaton, IL: Crossway, 1991).

PART TWO

God's Historical Drama

TIMELINE OF CHRISTIAN HISTORY

Beginning of civilization in Fertile Crescent after God creates the earth	c. 4000 B.C.
Great kingdom of Egypt	c. 3100–1085
Abraham migrates by God's calling to the Promised Land	c. 2000
Jacob's family migrates to Egypt during great famine	c. 1750
Twelve tribes of Israel are brought out of Egypt by Moses through the Red Sea	c. 1250
Joshua and the Hebrew people conquer the Promised Land	1200
David makes Jerusalem Israel's capital and unites Israel	1000
Solomon builds the temple	960
The Kingdom of Israel divided (Israel and Judah)	925
Ahab and Jezebel exposed for the worship of false gods by Elijah	842
Assyrians defeat Northern Kingdom of Israel and Jews taken away into slavery	721
Nebuchadnezzar besieges and captures Jerusalem and Judah falls into captivity	598
Age of Socrates, Plato, and Aristotle in Greece	410–322
Alexander the Great begins his conquest of the known world, reaching as far as India	335
Alexander dies of a fever after carousing in Babylon	323
Rome destroys Carthage	146
Julius Caesar assassinated, marking the end of the Roman Republic	44
Octavius (Augustus Caesar) establishes the Roman Empire and the worship of himself	31
Jesus of Nazareth, the Savior, is born in Bethlehem, as the prophets foretold	4 B.C.
Jesus Christ, the Son of God, is crucified and rises from the grave three days later	A.D. 29
The Apostle Paul is executed in Rome after evangelizing the Roman world and starting churches	64
Persecution and martyrdom of Christians in the Roman Empire	64–306

70	Romans kill millions of Jews in Jerusalem and destroy the Jewish temple
135	The Jews are defeated again by Romans and expelled from Palestine
250	Emperor Decius forces Christians to sacrifice to the gods for a certificate or die
313	Edict of Milan brings absolute toleration of Christians as Emperor Constantine is converted
325	Council of Nicea confirms the doctrine of Christ's divinity
405	Jerome's Latin translation of the Hebrew Bible is completed
410	Barbarians (Visigoths) sack Rome
426	Augustine of Hippo completes his great work *The City of God*
432	St. Patrick sees the conversion of much of Ireland through a forty-year mission
451	The Council of Chalcedon confirms Christ's deity and lordship over heaven and earth as the God-man
476	The last real Roman emperor is deposed by barbarian Odoacer
600	Augustine evangelizes the Anglo-Saxon kingdoms (England)
610	Mohammed starts Islam in Mecca (spreads especially through the sword in the seventh century)
700	The advanced but pagan Mayan civilization is at its peak
716	Boniface sets out as a missionary to pagan Germany
731	The great monk Bede completes his ecclesiastical history of England
732	Charles Martel defeats the Arab onslaught at Tours, saving Christendom
754	Boniface is martyred after evangelizing southern Germany
800	Pope crowns Charlemagne emperor as Church and State align
800–1000	Vikings terrorize and plunder western Europe
1000	Leif Ericson voyages to Canada, Greenland; but colonies are wiped out
1020	Viking King Olaf declares Christianity to be the law of the land
1066	William II of Normandy defeats the Anglo-Saxons and restructures England
1095	Pope calls for first crusade to take back the Holy Land from Moslems
1150	Universities of Oxford and Paris founded
1113	Peter Waldo founds the Waldensians, ancient evangelicals who have lasted for eight hundred years
1212	Children's Crusade sets out for the Holy Land; thousands are slaughtered
1215	King John signs the Magna Carta under threat from nobles
1260–1500	Great cathedrals rise in Europe
1280	Marco Polo spends more than twenty years in China, opening trade and exploration
1300	Gunpowder revolutionizes the art of warfare

The Plague (Black Death) kills one-third to one-half of the European population	1345–83
The Hundred Years' War begins ravaging Europe	1337
The Renaissance brings a revival of the arts and a move back to classical humanism	1350–1600
The Great Schism: two popes claim power and weaken faith in the Roman Church	1378
Wycliffe stands against Pope and translates the Bible into English	1381
Columbus discovers the Americas, thinking he has reached the Indies	1492
Martin Luther nails his Ninety-five Theses to the door at Wittenburg, starting the Reformation	1517
John Calvin completes his *Institutes of the Christian Religion,* systematizing a knowledge of the Bible and spreading the Reformation throughout northern Europe and to America	1536
John Knox leads Scotland to overthrow Queen Mary and establish Protestant republic	1560
St. Bartholomew's Day Massacre kills thousands of French Huguenots	1572
Dutch miraculously withstand the Spanish siege of Leiden	1574
The Spanish Armada is defeated by the English fleet and providential storms	1588
Pilgrims begin their secret church in Scrooby, England	1603
The first successful English settlement begins in Jamestown, Virginia	1607
Pilgrims escape from England to Holland and settle in Leiden	1608
The Authorized Version of the Bible completed by Puritan Divines (King James Bible)	1611
The Thirty Years' War, plague, and famine ravage Europe	1618–1648
The pioneers at Jamestown start the first representative assembly called the House of Burgesses	1619
Pilgrims sail to Plymouth and sign the Mayflower Compact before landing	1620
First official Thanksgiving celebrated on 29 November in Plymouth	1623
John Endicott leads the first Puritans to Salem	1628
John Winthrop leads a thousand Puritans to settle in Boston	1630
Harvard College founded to train ministers in the Bible	1636
Most people in Scotland agree on a National Covenant and are subsequently persecuted for their faith	1638
The Connecticut Constitution is written as the forerunner to the United States Constitution	1639
English Civil War leads to the beheading of Charles I in 1649	1642
The Westminster Assembly creates the Westminster Confession, a classic statement of Protestant doctrine that was widely taught in America	1646

1650s	John Eliot translates first Indian Bible as missionary to the Indians in America
1660	Charles II is recalled by the English to reestablish the monarchy
1666	Great fire devastates London and helps to stop the great plague of 1665
1675	King Philip's War ends a fifty-year peace with New England Indians
1682	William Penn is given a grant to start a new colony now called Pennsylvania
1685	Louis XIV revokes the Edict of Nantes, ending religious liberty in France
1688	The Glorious Revolution brings religious liberty to England and dethrones James II
1700s	The Enlightenment enshrines human reason and then escapes into romanticism
1734	The Great Awakening begins under the influence of George Whitefield and Jonathan Edwards
1738	John Wesley is converted in England and leads a great revival there; founds the Methodist church
1754	Benjamin Franklin calls for unity among the thirteen colonies
1760	The English defeat the French in the French and Indian War
1765	The Stamp Act is passed by Parliament and enforced upon the colonies
1775	The British march on Lexington and Concord on 19 April; the American Revolution begins
1776	The Declaration of Independence is read to the people of the colonies on 4 July
1776	Washington crosses the Delaware River on Christmas night to win the Battle of Trenton
1777	The American army suffers and regroups at Valley Forge, Pennsylvania
1781	Lord Cornwallis surrenders at Yorktown, Virginia, on 19 October, ending the American Revolution
1783–87	The Articles of Confederation fail to produce a workable national government
1785–1850	Unitarian cult comes to America and makes inroads in the intellectual community
1787	The Constitutional Convention meets in Philadelphia and writes a new Constitution
1788	Eleven states ratify the Constitution
1789	George Washington is elected and inaugurated as first president
1789	The French Revolution begins; it ends with the Reign of Terror in 1794 and the dictatorship of Napoleon
1790s	The Second Great Awakening sweeps America, beginning in colleges and rural towns
1793	William Carey arrives in Calcutta and starts the first organized missionary movement

Eli Whitney invents the cotton gin, which revives slavery in the south	1793
Washington's Farewell Address sent to the nation	1796
George Washington dies 14 December and the nation mourns for three years	1799
American missionary movement begins with Presbyterians and Baptists	1800–06
Louisiana Purchase doubles America's land mass for fifteen million dollars	1803
Lewis and Clark expedition to the northwest	1804
The British Parliament votes to abolish the slave trade	1807
The United States ends the African slave trade	1808
The War of 1812 (British defeated in 1815)	1812
Napoleon defeated at Waterloo by Wellington and is exiled	1815
The African Methodist Episcopal Church is established	1816
The first railroads and steam locomotives start crossing America	1820s
Charles Finney, the Father of Revivalism, is converted and begins fifty years of preaching and educating	1821
John Adams and Thomas Jefferson both die on 4 July, exactly fifty years after the revolution	1826
Noah Webster publishes *An American Dictionary of the English Language*	1828
Federal reserve banking is developed; doctrinal weakness leads to the founding of numerous "Christian" cults	1830s
Samuel Morse invents the telegraph	1835
Medical missionaries Marcus and Narcissa Whitman forge the Oregon Trail; she is the first white woman to cross the continent	1836
At the Alamo, in San Antonio, Texas, 187 Texans hold off 5,000 Mexicans for 12 days before being annihilated	1836
Horace Mann, a Unitarian, becomes the first secretary of the public schools in Massachusetts	1838
Karl Marx and Friedrich Engels write *The Communist Manifesto*, calling for worldwide revolution	1848
Gold is discovered in California and the rush to the west begins	1848
National depression and the beginning of the Third Great Awakening, especially among Civil War troops	1857
Dwight L. Moody first starts preaching in Chicago to the poor underclass	1858
Charles Darwin publishes *On the Origins of Species*, developing the theory of evolution	1859
A devastating civil war kills 600,000 Americans	1861–65
The South is ravaged by carpetbaggers; the slaves are freed	1865
American law, led by Harvard Law School, jettisons 900 years of Christian legal theory for the evolutionary concept of positivism and case law	1870s

1892	Charles Haddon Spurgeon, called the "Prince of Preachers," dies in London
1914–18	The First World War destroys a generation of Europeans and Americans; ten million die
1925	The Scopes trial opens the door for widespread dissemination of the evolutionary hoax into American culture
1929	J. Gresham Machen, the last great orthodox theologian at an Ivy League school, resigns to start Westminster Seminary
1920–33	Prohibition, the failed experiment at stopping the consumption of alcohol, is in effect
1929	The great stock market crash marks the beginning of the ten-year Great Depression
1933	The founding of the American welfare state under Franklin Delano Roosevelt
1939–1945	The Second World War
1941	The Japanese attack Pearl Harbor on 7 December
1945	Two atomic bombs are dropped on Japan, forcing a Japanese surrender and ending World War Two
1945	The evangelical and charismatic movements gain momentum among believing Protestants and Catholics
1945	The United Nations founded in San Francisco with the dream of world peace
1948	The World Council of Churches is established, moving toward ecumenical church unity at the expense of orthodox Christian doctrine
1948	The Cold War begins as communism takes China, and Russia becomes the "evil empire"
1949	Billy Graham holds his first crusade in Los Angeles, California
1950–53	The Korean War ends in a stalemate as China enters the war
1950	Great evangelistic outreach for Christianity, especially in Asia and South America
1955	Rock 'n' roll exemplifies a generation of institutional decline
1962	The Supreme Court removes voluntary prayer from public schools
1962	Second Vatican Council begins and deeply affects Roman Catholicism
1963	Martin Luther King Jr. leads a march on Washington, D.C., for equality
1963	The American Camelot ends with the assassination of President John F. Kennedy
1964–69	The Beatles lead the psychedelic/drug revolution as they venture into Eastern mysticism
1964–75	The Vietnam War tears at the fabric of American culture
1973	The Supreme Court creates a right to abortion and forces it on all states
1978	The Christian right becomes a political force in American politics and culture, spearheaded by Jerry Falwell and Pat Robertson

Francis Schaeffer dies after giving his life to exposing modern culture to biblical Christian answers	1984
The Berlin Wall comes down as eastern Europe breaks from communism	1989
The Soviet Union disintegrates under the failed communist system	1991

Material covered in the Geography: Setting the Stage chapter can be found in the following Zane Publishing Home Library titles:

U.S. Geography: The Land & Its People
U.S. Geography: The Northeast
U.S. Geography: The Southeast
U.S. Geography: The Midwest
U.S. Geography: The Rockies
U.S. Geography: The Southwest
U.S. Geography: The West
U.S. Geography: Alaska & Hawaii
World History: European History: Columbus and the Age of Discovery

GEOGRAPHY: SETTING THE STAGE

Where were you when I laid the foundations of the Earth?
—The Lord speaking to Job

WHEN THE CURTAIN RISES for the first act of a play, everything that has been in preparation for weeks is ready—hopefully. The actors have committed their lines and movements to memory and are ready to go the full five acts. Their costumes have been measured, made, and adjusted, and now the actors wait in the wings dressed as the characters they will portray. And do they walk out onto a stage that has useless and inappropriate props scattered about haphazardly? Hardly. The stage is as ready for the actors as the actors for the stage.

Since we as Christians understand history as the plan of God, we know that the Earth is the stage on which the drama of life is enacted. The earth has been providentially prepared for the unfolding of God's will in much the same way that the stage has been prepared for the actor. Not only its general layout, but its specific features are the work of God.

Psalm 24:1–2 declares:

> The earth is the Lord's, and all it contains,
> The world, and all who dwell in it.
> For He has founded it upon the seas,
> And established it upon the rivers.

And in Numbers 14:21, God declares to Moses that He will fill the earth with His glory. He did not simply create it and leave it to follow His natural laws; He is actively working to fill it with His glory. The planet is therefore not to be considered an end unto itself, but as a part of the whole of God's grand design.

But did God really arrange the minute features of the earth? Acts 17:26–28 tells us that:

> . . .He made from one, every nation of mankind to live on all the face of the earth, having determined their appointed times, and the boundaries of their habitation, so that they should seek the Lord, in the hope that they might grope for him and find him, though He is not far from each one of us. For in Him we live and move and have our being. . .

The coming into being of nations and their geographical extent are the concern of God, who uses these to fill the earth "with the glory of the Lord." The fact that God led Abraham and Jacob to specific places to settle their families, who were to number like the stars of the heaven, rather than simply telling them to find a nearby spot and begin His nation, shows that He is interested in the details of geography.

MOSES

Thirteenth century B.C.
Hebrew prophet and lawgiver

Claim to fame:
Moses led the children of Israel out of bondage in Egypt and received the Ten Commandments from God.

Did you know?
The biblical books of Genesis, Exodus, Leviticus, Numbers, and Deuteronomy, collectively called the Pentateuch or Torah, are called the Books of Moses, and the Law he proclaimed is called the Mosaic Law.

So it is literally true that all the world is a stage. Arnold Guyot, an eminent Christian geographer of the nineteenth century, said that the earth must be regarded primarily "as the abode of man, and the theatre for the action of human societies."[1] The idea is that the world is a place designed specifically for the unfolding of a Divine drama with human figures playing major roles. The elements of geography are not limited to landmasses and bodies of water, or to the boundaries of nations and cities, but also include the natural regions of the continents, and the plants and animals that are common in each region. These are the props that are placed throughout the vast stage of the earth by the perfect mind of the Sovereign Creator.

GEOGRAPHY AND THE HAND OF PROVIDENCE

On Zane's CD-ROMs, the beautiful montage of God's geographic order is laid out before the student. As Christians, we know that there is a planned created order for all things. We can therefore study how the geography of the earth has been used to fill it with God's glory. It will not take much brainstorming to think of times in biblical history when the elements of geography played an important role in the history of God's plan. The parting of the Red Sea (Exodus 14) and the GOURD and worm from Jonah 4:5–7 are instances that quickly come to mind. In the New Testament, we see the fig tree withered by Christ (Matthew 21:18–20) and, looking from a broader geographical perspective, the course of Paul's missionary journeys as examples of the Providential arrangement of geographical features.

Nor was the Providential plan for the planet complete at the end of the events recorded in the Bible. The mountain BOWERS, endless valleys, and varied climates of Europe gave great impetus to cultural diversity, intellectual innovation, and trade. Thus, in Europe, the Reformation, the Bible, and the great universities provided a solid foundation of truth and a platform for discipling the nations (Matthew 28:18–20).

The English Channel set England, Scotland, and Ireland apart from the rest of Europe, and preserved the British Isles as a haven from much of the religious and political turmoil of continental Europe. It allowed true believers to survive the inquisitions of the Counter-Reformation. It facilitated the English victory over the Spanish Armada, which was trying to destroy the seedbed of the Reformation. Had Adolf Hitler not faced the English Channel, his *blitzkrieg* would have annihilated England in 1940.

In a similar way, America was preserved for five thousand years until a Bible-believing remnant of persecuted Europeans settled its shores in the seventeenth century. Three thousand miles of ocean on one side and five thousand miles on the other protected the continent from the development of any significant civilization until the arrival of the Christian Pilgrims. The French philosopher Alexis de Tocqueville said, "Although the huge territories [of North America] were inhabited by many native tribes, one can fairly say that at the time of discovery they were no more than a wilderness. The Indians occupied but did not possess the land."[2]

ABRAHAM

Hebrew patriarch
of the second millennium B.C.

Claim to fame:

He was the recipient of the Abrahamic Covenant and the founder of Judaism.

Did you know?

Abraham began the Jewish and Christian practice of blessing children.

JACOB

Ancestor of
the people of Israel

Claim to fame:

Jacob fathered twelve sons, the ancestors of the twelve tribes of Israel.

Did you know?

Jacob wrestled with an angel and received the name of Israel.

God's control of the weather has been a major factor in war after war. Napoleon was defeated at Waterloo by Wellington during a sudden storm that bogged down his artillery. George Washington's artillery managed to arrive at the crucial battle at Princeton because the rain-soaked roads froze the very hour his wheels needed to roll. The Japanese lost the flower of their navy and four aircraft carriers when clouds parted just as twenty American dive-bombers flew overhead at the Battle of Midway. The storm of 5 June 1944, gave the Allies cover and the advantage of surprise for their invasion of France; the D-day operation the following day succeeded and Hitler was eventually defeated.

God, who knows all and created all, has a plan and purpose for everything in His Creation. History bears out this conclusion as the seemingly inconsequential elements of geography take on new significance as nations rise and fall, men war with each other, and the Gospel is spread to the world.

HOW SHOULD CHRISTIANS RELATE TO GOD'S CREATED ORDER?

> And God blessed them, and God said unto them, 'Be fruitful, and multiply, and replenish the earth, and subdue it: and have dominion over the fish of the sea, and over the fowl of the air, and over every living thing that moveth upon the earth.[3]

The greatest inspiration for the exploration, settlement, and development of God's earth has been His original Gospel purpose. Adam was given the commission in Genesis 1:26–28 to be fruitful and multiply, and to fill the earth. His first acts included the classification of plants and animals. Noah had the commission repeated to him while he was still on the ark after the Flood. Jesus gave the full spiritual as well as physical breadth of the command to reach the world when he gave the Great Commission:

> All authority has been given to me in heaven and on earth. Go therefore, and make disciples of all the nations, baptizing them in the name of the Father, and of the Son, and of the Holy Spirit, teaching them to observe all things that I have commanded you; and lo, I am with you always, even to the end of the age. [4]

How does this commission relate to the American Christian student who is studying geography? We providentially live in the nation from which most of the missionaries and money for missions have come for two centuries. God has placed us here for a purpose. Approximately four billion of the six billion people living today have never heard the good news of the Gospel.[5]

The chain of Christianity moved westward across America in the nineteenth century. Now as we face the twenty-first century, we have the exciting challenge of reaching the burgeoning nations of Asia. The upcoming generation of believers face geometrically expanding opportunities to change God's world. We must not only reach these unreached people with the message of salvation through Christ, but also help them improve their

---

PAUL
Born: c.A.D. 10
Died: c.A.D. 65

Claim to fame:
Paul was the author of many books of the New Testament, including Romans, I and II Corinthians, Ephesians, Galatians, Philippians, Colossians, I and II Thessalonians, I and II Timothy, and Philemon.

Did you know?
Paul, a Jewish pharisee, persecuted Christians before Jesus appeared to him in a blinding light. He became the apostle to the gentiles.

standard of living (since 800 million people live in absolute poverty), and develop literate, moral, and then free societies.

There are students reading this book who may live to invent the solution to the world's critical water shortage, or the solution to soil degradation and a way to increase agricultural output, or a new energy source to supplant fossil fuels and their pollution, an urban blight. The needs are many, but we serve a great God. If we will learn about God's world and the people in it, we can be prepared to hear God's voice when He directs us into our special mission field and purpose that He has planned uniquely for each one of us.

J.C. Ryle, a great theologian of the last century, left us these encouraging words that should inspire us to spread the truth of the Gospel to the geographic corners of the world:

> The world before and the world after the introduction of Christianity were as different worlds as light and darkness, night and day. It was Christianity that starved idolatry, and emptied the heathen temples— that stopped gladiatorial contests, elevated the position of women, raised the whole tone of morality, and improved the condition of children and the poor.[6]

THE "FLAT EARTH"

In the nineteenth century, Washington Irving, who is famous for his fantastic *Tales of Sleepy Hollow*, invented another tall tale that eventually became not only widely known, but widely believed. According to Irving, Christopher Columbus was the first European to come up with the idea that the earth was a sphere. When he presented the idea to the public, he became the object of the scorn of the ignorant people and the opposition of the leaders of the Church, who claimed that the Bible taught that the Earth was flat.

The truth of the matter is that in the fifteenth century, *everyone* knew that the earth was a sphere. To have suggested that the earth was a four-cornered flat mass would have provoked the same response as it would now. Why has this obvious falsehood been perpetuated in the last two centuries? Perhaps because it appeals to those who like to view Christianity as irrelevant to the facts of natural and social sciences like geography.

The truth is that Christians historically have nearly always been found in the avant-garde of discovery. Centuries before Columbus attempted to find a westward route to India, a Christian theologian with an unusual name, the Venerable Bede, wrote, "the earth is a globe that can be called a perfect sphere because the surface irregularities of mountains and valleys are so small in comparison to its vast size." He continued to say that "it was not without reason that the Sacred Scriptures and secular letters speak of the shape of the earth as an orb."[7]

Many ancient religions have unusual ideas about the shape of the earth. They imagine it to be hollowed out in the back of a turtle or resting on top of elephants' backs. JUDAISM, though it is one of the world's oldest religions, is remarkably accurate in its descriptions of the earth's form. In Job 26:7, God is said to have hung the earth upon nothing, and the earth

28

is described in Isaiah 40:22 as a "circle," or, translated differently, a sphere. These insights may seem unusual for a civilization centuries before the discoveries that established these things as known facts. But these are no mere stabs in the dark made by a pre-scientific culture; they are the revelation of the Creator. Through the inspired reading of His inspired Word, Christians through the ages have consistently arrived at true conclusions about God's created order.

CONCLUSION

The study of geography should teach students to have an awed reverence for God's power and judgment. God prostrated Job by simply declaring his geographic marvels:

> Where were you when I laid the foundations of the earth? Tell me, if you have understanding. Who determined its measurements? Surely you know! Or who stretched the line upon it? To what were its foundations fastened? Or who laid its cornerstone, when the morning stars sang together, and all the sons of God shouted for joy? Or who shut in the sea with doors, when it burst forth from the womb; when I made the clouds its garment, and thick darkness its swaddling band; when I fixed My limit for it, and set bars and doors; when I said, 'This far you may come, but no farther, and here your proud waves must stop!'. . . Then Job answered the Lord and said: 'Behold, I am vile; what shall I answer you? I lay my hand over my mouth. Once I have spoken, but I will not answer; Yes, twice, but I will proceed no further.'[8]

Arnold Guyot further explained the meaning of geographic study:

> . . .it is not enough to have seized. . .the functions of the great masses of the continents. . . . To understand and appreciate them at their full value, we must rise to a higher position. We must elevate ourselves to the moral world to understand the physical world: the physical world has no meaning except by and for the moral world. . .[9]

From this perspective, Christian families can study the globe and all of its geographic wonders and perceive the unseen hand of God everywhere present, as He uses His world and His people to spread the Gospel to the nations until "the earth shall be full of the knowledge of the Lord, as the waters cover the sea."[10]

CD-ROM ANALYSES

• It is encouraging to see that the authors of Zane's CD-ROMs about geography have avoided the kind of earth-worship that is far too common today. This is a remarkable feat considering the degree to which the concerns of geography are environmental. While discussing the environmental problems that come with human populations in rebellion against God and His command to be the earth's caretakers, the authors do not accept the entire environmentalist agenda.

• The *U.S. Geography: The Land & Its People* CD-ROM begins with an unbiblical timeline that sets the age of the earth at 4.5 billion years. (In the

Timeline at the front of this book, students can find the true Christian perspective on the age and the origin of the universe.) At the beginning of this CD-ROM, the presentation also seems to somewhat diminish the significance of individuals and of America as a nation. It is true that a man is insignificant apart from God. What makes him significant is that the God of all Creation takes an interest in him.

> When I consider thy heavens, the work of thy fingers, the moon and stars, which thou hast ordained; What is man, that thou art mindful of him? And the son of man, that thou visitest him? For thou hast made him a little lower than the angels, and hast crowned him with glory and honour. Thou madest him to have dominion over the works of thy hands; thou hast put all thing under his feet. . ." (Psalm 8:3–6)

This CD-ROM also suggests that the underlying principle of America is Greek democracy rather than the biblical principles of godly self-government acknowledged by the Founders. The student can refer to the comments on ancient Greece in the *Drama of the Ancient World* chapter, and study the biblical principles of our founding liberties that are detailed in the *The American Expression of Liberty* chapter to find the Christian history of our constitutional republic.

• On three *Earth Science* CD-ROMs—*Ecology I*, *Ecology II*, and *Earth's Natural Resources*—watch for the assumptions made about evolution and environmentalism. As Christians, we cannot allow ourselves to dismiss environmental problems as unimportant, nor can we permit alarmists to frighten us into buying warnings of imminent environmental apocalypse. Some will object to references to environmental concerns, particularly on the *Earth's Natural Resources* CD-ROM, but the *Ecology* series is mostly very fair in its description of environmental issues—remarkably fair considering how popular it is in our politically correct society to make environmental problems out to be on the verge of cataclysm.

REVIEW QUESTIONS

1. What is God's ultimate plan for the earth according to Numbers 14:21?

2. Give some instances in history when geography has influenced the outcome of events.

3. What are some of the problems facing us today that can be solved through proper Christian stewardship?

4. What does the Bible say about the earth's shape?

RELATED SCRIPTURE

Genesis Ch. 1–2	Matthew 6:10
Psalm 24:1–2	Matthew 28:18–20
Job Ch. 38–42	Acts 17:26–28

SUGGESTED READING

Rosalie J. Slater, *Teaching and Learning America's Christian History* (San Francisco, CA: Foundation for American Christian Education, 1987).

Frank Kaleb Jansen, *Target Earth* (Pasadena, CA: Global Mapping Int'l, 1989).

GEOGRAPHY:
SETTING THE STAGE

Material covered in the Drama of Ancient History chapter can be found in the following Zane Publishing Home Library titles:

Elementary World History: Cradles of Civilization
Elementary World History: Exploring Ancient Egypt
Elementary World History: The Greek and Roman World
Prentice Hall: Discovering World History
History through Art: Ancient Greece
History through Art: Ancient Rome
World Literature: Women in Literature: Heroines, Sirens, Shrews
World Literature: European Literature: The Ancient World—The Renaissance
Religious Studies: Christianity and Civilization
Religious Studies: Religions of the World

ACT ONE:
THE DRAMA OF ANCIENT HISTORY

The mighty heroes of the world. . .conquered nations for themselves and made them miserable; the apostles conquered them for Christ and made them happy.

–MATTHEW HENRY

SHAKESPEARE PERCEPTIVELY SAID, "All the world's a stage." Knowingly or not, each of us is an actor on the stage. Most American students, however, know little either of the part they must play or of what has already been enacted on the stage of history. Ask the average American student what he remembers about ancient history and visions of Hollywood classics will dance in his head: Ben-Hur in the chariot race; Spartacus holding off the Roman legions; Pharaoh sending his doomed chariots into the watery tomb of the Red Sea.

The true play of history is not a series of monologues competing to drown each other out. There is a script, an author, a cast, and a stage manager smoothly orchestrating the events that pass before the eyes of a "great cloud of witnesses." Those who perceive chaos in this historical drama have closed their eyes to the role of the lead character, Jesus Christ. Rising from obscurity in a rural town to cause controversy and division in society (Matthew 10:34–35), His part in history has continued long after His seeming exit from the stage. He is the hero of history. Though He does not appear in every scene, His influence is felt throughout.

The purpose of this chapter is threefold. First, we will clarify the biblical view of history, which is vital in order to establish an unchanging epistemology (basis of truth). Without the Bible as the anchor to reality, any self-proclaimed expert or scientist could lead us to believe his own biased interpretation. Secondly, we will survey the history of God's redemptive remnant in biblical history from Adam through Jesus Christ. Contrary to secular history curricula, we perceive the providence of God in His dealings with His people as central to understanding all ancient cultures. Thirdly, we will analyze the universal failings of ancient pagan cultures. It is hoped that this analysis will help the student to find a balanced and insightful view of the ancient world. Our aim also is that the faith of the reader will increase as biblical religion is compared and contrasted with the idols of man's creation. A proper understanding of the events, places and people who have played their parts on the stage of history will prepare us to face the twenty-first century.

See the appendix for
The Ten Commandments

HEROES AND VILLAINS

History has its great Hero, Christ, and its heroes, those who follow Him. It also has its villains, from Lucifer to modern-day atheistic world leaders.

The fact that man is disposed by his innate sinfulness to join the ranks of the villains is evident in history as hordes of men joined the vanguard of immoral empire-builders who promised the riches of the world and free rein to their ungodly desires. The fact that the victories of the "bad guys" are only temporary, while the triumph of the Hero is inevitable and eternal, is etched in every scene of the great, unfolding drama.

The study of antiquity brings us face to face with the supernatural forces behind this cosmic conflict. The ancient world, from the time of the Garden of Eden through the coming of Christ, was engaged in a volitional rebellion against God's created realm. Men and nations have for the most part sought to be free from the true God through the worship of other gods, the breaking of God's law, and the establishment of a new world order, usually centered in the worship of man and the state.

ACT ONE, SCENE TEN: CURSES! FOILED AGAIN!

The first unified skirmish in man's rebellion against God followed the Flood. Before this time, every man followed his own will—which set all people except Noah and his family against the plan of God. After the waters of the flood subsided and the world was again populated, mankind united under the banner of Nimrod.

The Bible teaches that all civilization after the universal flood came from Noah's sons: Shem, Ham, and Japheth. Their descendants migrated southeastward from Mount Ararat to the plain of Shinar (Sumer).

Originally, the people had been told by God to go forth and fill the earth (Genesis 9:1–3). And Genesis 10:5 says that for a time this did happen: "From these the coast land peoples of the Gentiles were separated into their lands, everyone according to his own language, according to their families, into their nations."

But Nimrod, one of Noah's great-grandsons and the founder of NINEVEH, "began to be a mighty one on the earth."[1] He built many cities and was able to coerce or entice all of the other families to come under him and his worship of pagan idols, such as Baal and Ashtaroth. In direct rebellion against God's command to multiply and fill the earth, all the people of the earth set out with one language to build a tower into heaven. God thwarted their efforts and scattered the people by confusing their languages.

In Genesis 11:1–6, in Nimrod's Tower of Babel, we see man's first attempt at salvation through a counterfeit Messiah— state worship disguised as religion. God did not tolerate man's assault on His sovereignty. By confusing the languages of the masses, He forced a dispersion of the people into various nations worldwide, thereby preventing a centralized, one-world government.

Throughout the centuries, numerous attempts have been made by men and nations to establish a new world order without God. Each of these attempts has met with failure. Like the withering weeds that Isaiah speaks of in Isaiah 40:23–24, these powermongers have found some real obstacles as they lunged for the golden ring of world power. This knowledge that God knows how to handle the evil conspirators and tyrants of our day, just as He has in the past, should encourage our families.

All civilizations from Mesopotamia to Egypt, Greece, and Rome, as well as our modern cultures, have faced the same challenges when attempting to overthrow God's moral order. They have faced the scriptural truth that it is God who has set the boundaries and the times of habitation for every people on earth (Acts 17:26). No one overrides God's will for men and nations.

They also have faced the historic reality that since Nimrod, numerous drives at world power have been attempted and all have been thwarted by God. Nebuchadnezzar was turned into a hairy beast eating grass on all fours. On the verge of world conquest, Alexander the Great self-destructed before his death at the age of thirty-three. Julius Caesar met his fate in the Roman Senate. Napoleon met his on the mud-drenched fields of Waterloo. Adolf Hitler faced off with God, and then committed suicide in a Berlin bunker in April 1945.

Additionally, all idolaters, according to the First and Second Commandments, have faced a generational curse to the fourth generation.

> You shall have no other gods before me...you shall not bow down to them nor serve them. For I, the Lord your God, am a jealous God, visiting the iniquity of the fathers on the children to the third and fourth generation of those who hate Me.[2]

Another great obstacle faced by all tyrannies is the penetration of the Gospel and the Word of God into all the world. Two billion people now profess Christian faith worldwide.[3] They acknowledge God's sovereignty and man's sinfulness, and are hard to convince when the United Nations or any new order offers the deceptive bait of the false promise of world-wide peace and unity.

We and our children can learn from the Tower of Babel the great truth expressed by Isaiah that we should fear God, not those who conspire for world conquest:

> Do not say, 'A conspiracy,' concerning all that this people call a conspiracy, nor be afraid of their threats, nor be troubled. The Lord of hosts, Him you shall hallow; let Him be your fear, and let Him be your dread.[4]

At the same time, the Tower of Babel gives us ample warning that we should shun any movement that calls for world unity or the blurring of national or familial identities. The Bible calls for local accountability in the family, church, and local civil government to restrain man's sinful nature.

OUR ROLE AS SPECTATORS AND AS PLAYERS

Unless you lived in Elizabethan England, the language of Shakespeare's incomparable plays is foreign to you—sometimes you might even feel that it is literally a foreign language. Yet once you learn to understand the language, everything makes perfect sense. In the same way, we must first understand the proper attitude to history before it will really begin to make sense.

D.W. Billington, in his book *Patterns in History*, explained the historical view held by the apostles:

The earliest Christians retained the attitudes to history found in the Old Testament. They continued to believe in divine intervention, to conceive of the historical process as a straight line and the panorama of world events as moving towards a goal.[5]

History from a Christian perspective is not just the accumulation of millions of events over time and in space, but the outworking of the plan of an omnipotent, perfect sovereign God. What is this plan? In 1876, Reverend S. W. Foljambe, historian and pastor, put it this way:

> It has been said that history is the biography of communities; in another and profounder sense, it is the autobiography of Him 'who worketh all things after the counsel of His will' (Eph. 1:11), and who is graciously timing all events after the counsel of His Christ, and the kingdom of God on earth.[6]

Notice that history is not merely the act of a distant, uninvolved God—He is a participant, its most important character.

Where can this proper view of history be acquired? Only through the Bible, the only infallible history book. It is the Word of God. It contains sixty-six books, and was written in three languages—on three continents over a period of more than 1,500 years—by more than forty authors, yet there is a complete unity of thought and historical detail. The Masoretic text, which is the standard Hebrew text today, and which is known to Christians as the Old Testament, is the most accurate and well-documented history of the ancient world. No other ancient document was copied by TALMUDISTS who dedicated their entire lives to preserving the accuracy of the text. Renowned archaeologist William Allbright said, "There can be no doubt that archaeology has confirmed the substantial historicity of Old Testament tradition."[7]

As Christians, we often emphasize the spiritual and devotional lessons to be learned from reading the Bible. However, we can become so familiar with the basic stories of the Bible that we forget these events actually happened and were ultimately the central theme of world history. "For we did not follow cunningly devised fables when we made known to you the power and coming of our Lord Jesus Christ, but were eyewitnesses of His majesty."[8]

The Judeo-Christian thread weaving through all of the ages is no legend, myth, or fairy tale, like Hesiod's depiction of the Greek gods in 1500 B.C. It is the history and the truth to which all peoples must come if they are to understand the past and find hope for the future. For this reason, we begin this study of the ancient world with a narrative of the biblical history of redemption. The Scriptures are the interpreter of all history and are of special importance in the study of the ancient world since they unveil God's redemptive plan to reach out in love to the rebellious human race.

ACTING LESSONS:
HOW TO APPROACH YOUR ROLE IN HISTORY

Imagine taking the stage to act in a play without knowing what the play itself is about, without even knowing your part. It would be a disaster!

But many Christians assume that if they love the lead Actor enough, everything else will fall into place. We have a role in history, and we need to know our lines. By understanding the play, as we discussed above, we gain insight into where it is going. By understanding that God has a purpose for us individually and by devoting ourselves to it, we gain insight into where to go.

> For the Lord giveth wisdom: out of his mouth cometh knowledge and understanding…He keepeth the paths of judgment, and preserveth the way of his saints. Then shalt thou understand righteousness, and judgment, and equity; yea, every good path.[9]

God accomplishes His purpose in history by providentially superintending His creation. This is called the Providential view of history and it was the predominant view of Christians from all ages, including our American founders. Noah Webster, the great educator and LEXICOGRAPHER who compiled the first American dictionary in 1828, defined providence as

> The care and superintendence which God exercises over His creatures. . .some persons admit a general providence, but deny a particular providence, not considering that a general providence consists of particulars. A belief in divine providence is a source of great consolation to good men. By divine providence is understood God Himself.[10]

As you might have surmised, Noah Webster was a devout Christian holding to the Providential view of history. Note that in his definition of providence, Webster said that it is "a source of great consolation to good men." In this statement, he alluded to the peace that comes from knowing that a just God presides over nations and that His plan cannot be thwarted. The opposite is also true. If one is fighting the God of history and then learns of His Providence, it can be very disconcerting!

Eighteenth-century historian Charles Rollan reflected on the predominant view of early America and Christendom all the way back to Saint Paul when he wrote:

> Nothing gives history a greater superiority to many branches of literature, than to see in a manner imprinted, in almost every page of it, the precious footsteps and shining proofs of this great truth, viz. that God disposes all events as supreme Lord and Sovereign; that He alone determines the fate of kings and the duration of empires and that He transfers the government of kingdoms from one nation to another because of the unrighteous dealings and wickedness committed therein.[11]

Has the great God of the universe unveiled to us His cosmic plan for the ages? Yes! The Scriptures reveal His will. The Godhead (trinity) before time began planned the redemption of His people and His world (Rev. 13:8; Titus 1:2). Jesus Christ—through His death, resurrection, ascension, and eventual second coming—provides the center focus and meaning for history. As I Corinthians 15:24 says, at the end of time as we know it, "Then comes the end, when He [Christ] delivers the kingdom to God the Father, when He puts an end to all rule and all authority and power." All of God's created order is destined to bow before Jesus Christ: "For He must reign till He has put all enemies under His feet."[12] The Lord Himself tells us what will happen at the end of history, "For it is written: 'As I live, says the LORD, Every knee shall bow to Me, and every tongue shall confess to God.'"[13]

THE CREATION

The curtain rises and the play of history begins at the book of Genesis—the book of beginnings. Here God clearly answers the deepest philosophical questions of the human heart: From where did I come? What is my purpose? What is the meaning of life?

Ancient history following the biblical chronology does not allow for Darwin's evolutionary scheme of amoebae crawling out of the primordial slime to invent fire and the wheel. In fact, history and modern archaeological findings are confirming that man's intelligence and ability to build complex, modern civilizations was evidenced as recorded history began c.3000 B.C. The myth of man's evolving capacity first to speak, then to write and build cultures, directly contradicts the Bible's declaration and the historical fact of highly developed cities that were built immediately after the flood (e.g., Babylon). The Bible, in Genesis 1, says that the world began with a six-day creative act of God, wherein God created all things in their full and completely developed state: "In the beginning God. . ." In the science section of this book, the biblical account of creation is defended as opposed to spontaneous evolution. God's inerrant Word unequivocally teaches that His direct act of special Creation (initiated and completed through God's spoken word) was the beginning of His working with the world and man. Creation was not the beginning of God. He existed from eternity past into eternity future. God is not a captive of His own history. He transcends time. He has no beginning.

All history since creation should focus on God as the proactive prime mover directing his world and his cultures. Man knows that he is created by God and is responsible to Him because God has placed this knowledge in him (Romans 1:19). Throughout history we see man and nature responding to God's blessing or judgment through either repentant faith or willful rebellion.

THE PERFECT SCENE MARRED BY SIN

The Garden of Eden (probably near the Fertile Crescent) was a place of perfect communion with God, and man was in an innocent state. He was given dominion over the earth and its creatures, and was called to subdue the earth and govern it under God (Genesis 1:28). But Adam and Eve sinned against God. They disobeyed his orders and succumbed to the temptation of Satan to eat of the tree of the Knowledge of Good and Evil for the chance to be "as gods," to discern right and wrong for themselves (Genesis 3).

Because of their sin, Adam and Eve were driven from the garden. Sin, rebellion, and death became the universal inherited nature of the human race. The story of history from this time forward is the story of two powerful forces vying to control history: the Kingdom of God versus the Kingdom of Satan (Colossians 1:12), Christ versus Antichrist.

ADAM AND EVE

The first man and woman created by God

Claim to fame:
Succumbed to the temptation of Satan.

Did you know?
"Adam" comes from the Hebrew word adamah, *meaning "earth," the substance from which Adam was formed.*

All men and women are caught up in this struggle, and so are all civilizations. Either they fall back on the grace of God, accepting God as sovereign, or they continue their rebellion, which leads to their destruction and, ultimately, the deterioration of their cultures. This is the meaning of history. All of our studies of world history should focus upon this conflict and the inevitable victory of Christ through His death, resurrection, and imminent return. The study of world history is a story of a loving, holy God reaching out to save rebellious human beings who were building ziggurats (pyramids) for human sacrifices, and idols of animal gods, and worshipping other men. Romans 1:18–32 documents this pattern of idolatry that is still prevalent in our day:

> For the wrath of God is revealed from heaven against all ungodliness and unrighteousness of men, who hold the truth in unrighteousness; because that which may be known of God is manifest in them; for God hath shown it unto them. For the invisible things of Him from the creation of the world are clearly seen, being understood by the things that are made, even His eternal power and Godhead; so that they are without excuse: because that, when they knew God, they glorified Him not as God, neither were they thankful; but became vain in their imaginations, and their foolish heart was darkened. Professing themselves to be wise, they became fools, and changed the glory of the incorruptible God into an image made like to corruptible men , and to birds, and four-footed beasts, and creeping things.

The Bible teaches that after the Fall, but before the Flood, the residual blessing of man's former perfect state was still perceptible as his life span exceeded nine hundred years (Genesis 5–6). Contrary to evolutionary theory, history records that mankind developed technological civilizations almost immediately after the first record of man on earth. According to one account of life before the Flood:

> Indications are that civilizations before the flood was very well advanced. Certainly, after the flood great cultures quickly appeared, and evidence indicates a higher level of attainment for man around 2000 B.C. than in 800 B.C. The pyramids appeared very early in Egypt; the great developments in Minoan culture surpassed those of Greek states, and ancient Ur seems closer to us than cultures which succeeded it centuries later. To read history merely as development is to distort it; the development is there, but decline and degeneration are also present.[14]

THE FLOOD

Except for Noah and his family, God destroyed all of mankind through the flood because He saw "that every intent of the thoughts of [man's] heart was only evil continually."[15] After 120 years of preparing the ark, Noah, his family, and the animals in pairs entered the boat. God flooded the world for forty days and nights. The ark came to rest on Mount Ararat and all the human race was destroyed.

Most ancient cultures tell stories of the universal flood. Such stories of the flood have been found in CUNEIFORM documents excavated in the near East. An Akkadean story of the flood is in the Atrahase Epic made c.1630.

NOAH

Hero of the biblical flood

Claim to fame:
At divine direction, Noah built the ark over a 120-year period.

Did you know?
The story of Noah has similarities with other Near Eastern accounts of the deluge in the Gilgamesh epic and the Babylonian myth of Atrahasis.

Another story of the flood and the building of the ark has been found on a Sumerian tablet in southern Babylonia. In another Babylonian story of the flood, discovered in 1872 by George Smith, great detail is given. It is part of the longer Epic of Gilgamesh and it actually states that the boat came to rest on a mountain in northwestern Persia, and that birds were dispatched from the ark to determine when to disembark. Although these many accounts are not in complete agreement on every detail of the true biblical history, they manifest the universal knowledge of all civilizations that this judgment did occur.

After the Flood, Noah and his family were once again given the dominion mandate to be fruitful and multiply and fill the earth (Genesis 9:1–3). For the first time, civil government was instituted to restrain evildoers, and capital punishment was established. But Noah's descendants quickly reverted to their self-worshipping ways, even after the Flood. The life expectancy of man quickly went down from approximately nine hundred years to its current three-score and ten, or seventy years.

CIVILIZATIONS IN REBELLION

Not long after the Flood, the people of the earth gathered to build the Tower of Babel. As we noted earlier in this chapter, God dispersed the people to destroy their one-world dreams and to fill the earth. Soon after, we see the Sumerian civilization growing in the Fertile Crescent, the Egyptian civilization, and, by 2000 B.C., cultures developing throughout Europe and Asia. Each of these groups of people denied the one true God and created POLYTHEISTIC religions or nature cults (the worship of nature).

ENTER ABRAHAM

God has always had a human witness to the world of His reality and grace. From the beginning, there was always a faithful remnant who shared and lived the reality of the one true God. The Lord also gave in the hearts of men and in the creation a constant witness of His existence, character, and plan of salvation (Romans 1:18–20).

About 2000 B.C., God called out a man named Abram from Ur of the Chaldeas. He made a covenant with Abram, changing his name to Abraham. This unconditional agreement was that all the nations of the earth would be blessed through his seed.

> Now the Lord had said to Abram: "Get out of your country, from your kindred and from your father's house to a land that I will show you. I will make you a great nation; I will bless you and make your name great; and you shall be a blessing. I will bless those who bless you, and I will curse him who curses you; and in you all the families of the earth shall be blessed.[16]

Abraham and his family followed God's instruction and journeyed to Canaan to become the first of the Hebrew people.

After Abraham and two generation of his descendants had lived in the promised land for 240 years, they were transferred by God's providence to Egypt, where they grew from a large family of seventy to several million in a few hundred years. The Egyptians, fearing this blessed, multiplying

---

ABRAHAM

*Hebrew patriarch
of the second millennium B.C.*

Claim to fame:

He was the recipient of the Abrahamic Covenant and the founder of Judaism.

Did you know?

Abraham began the Jewish and Christian practice of blessing children.

new nation, enslaved and mistreated the Jews. God used Moses, a formerly adopted son of pharaoh and an eighty-year-old exiled Jew, to deliver His people by divine intervention, c.1250 B.C.

FROM FREEDOM TO BONDAGE

The story of Israel's rise and fall as a force and witness in the ancient world is central to world history. Throughout our study of ancient and modern history we will allude to the many principles, commandments, and governmental structures ordained by God and given to Israel to model and propagate. These truths are applicable to every nation in every time.

After leaving Egypt, the Hebrews spent forty years of unbelief in the wilderness, and only their children were brought into Canaan by Joshua and Caleb to found the Hebrew republic. God gave them favor and success, but they soon turned from dependence upon "the God of their salvation" to a desire to be like all the other nations (I Samuel 8). God made plain the consequences of their rejection of His rule over them and gave them a king who would enslave them, tax them oppressively, and take their children.

Under King David and his son, Solomon, (1050–980 B.C.), Israel reached its greatest extension of power and influence. But after Solomon's death, Israel was divided into two kingdoms. Ten tribes seceded to form the northern kingdom, Israel; Judah and Benjamin remained in the line of MESSIANIC hope in the southern kingdom, called Judah.

Despite the warnings of her many prophets, the nation of Israel was doomed by repeated generational APOSTASY. Israel fell to the Assyrians in 721 B.C. The Assyrians then fell to Babylon in 607 B.C. Babylon then proceeded to destroy Judah between 606 and 586 B.C.

After 536 B.C. and the defeat of Babylon by the Medo-Persian power, a limited number of Jews were allowed to return and rebuild the walls and the temple in Jerusalem (see the books of Ezra and Nehemiah). A period of Greek and Roman conquests of Palestine followed, allowing only a brief period of Jewish independence from 167–63 B.C.

CHRIST ENTERS A DYING WORLD

The Roman legions ruled Israel with an iron fist from 63 B.C. through the destruction of Jerusalem in A.D. 70, when millions of Jews were massacred and the temple was destroyed. By the time Jesus Christ entered the ancient world, it was dying and under the most pervasive tyranny the world had ever known. Historian Richard Frothingham explained the importance of Christ's coming:

> This low view of man was exerting its full influence when Rome was at the height of its power and glory. Christianity then appeared with its central doctrine, that man was created in the divine image, and destined for immortality; pronouncing, that, in the eye of God, all men are equal. This asserted for the individual an independent value. It occasioned the great inference, that man is superior to the state, which ought to be fashioned for his use. This was the advent of a new spirit and a new power in the world.[17]

KING DAVID
Born: *1004 B.C.*
Died: *965 B.C.*

Claim to fame:
King of Judah and Israel, who, as a youth, slew Goliath.

Did you know?
Was given the Davidic Covenant.

SOLOMON
Born: *965 B.C.*
Died: *928 B.C.*

Claim to fame:
Built a great temple in Jerusalem, the Temple of Solomon.

Did you know?
Began his reign with wisdom, bringing Israel to the height of power.

There is no greater landmark in all of history than the birth of Jesus of Nazareth (c.4 B.C.–c.A.D. 29). In fact, this one event marks the dividing line of all history. All events prior to the miraculous incarnation in Bethlehem lead up to this moment and all subsequent history looks back to it as the foundation for all good and the hope of eternal life. That is why history is divided into B.C. (Before Christ) and A.D. (anno *Domini*—in the year of our Lord). After the Savior came all of history was seen as moving forward, founded on the incredible love of God who "became flesh and dwelt among us." In this generation, we celebrate two millennia (2,000 years) since His birth.

We still must stand in awe of the angel's declaration to Joseph, Mary's husband:

> Joseph, son of David, do not be afraid to take to you Mary your wife, for that which is conceived in her is of the Holy Spirit. And she will bring forth a Son, and you shall call His name Jesus, for He will save His people from their sin.[18]

God personally entered human history in the form of His Son, and died to pay for our rebellion and sin. He then rose from the dead, giving us the real hope of eternal life if we place our faith in Him. Then Jesus sat down at the right hand of God to take his place of authority "over heaven and earth."[19] He is the true ruler of the earth.[20]

The resurrection of Jesus Christ is the most well-documented event of the ancient world, a fact attested to by historian Thomas Arnold:

> I have been used for many years to study the histories of other times, and to examine and weigh the evidence of those who have written about them, and I know of no one fact in the history of mankind which is proved by better and fuller evidence of every sort…than the great sign which God hath given us that Christ died and rose from the dead.[21]

The polytheism of the Sumerian civilizations had failed. The animism (nature-worship) of Egypt had been exposed. The humanism and philosophy of Greece had proven itself incapable of building lasting liberty, peace, or prosperity. And the Roman Empire, with its series of godless emperors, had proven itself to be brutal, perverse, and decadent.

Into *this* world came the Messiah. To document the impact of this holy event on world history would take more volumes than the world could contain (John 21:25). Perhaps the most powerful narrative detailing God's plan to defeat His enemies through Christ is expressed in the words of Mary, Jesus' mother, in the MAGNIFICAT, from Luke 1:46–55:

> My soul magnifies the Lord, and my spirit has rejoiced in God, my savior, for he has regarded the lowly state of his maidservant; for behold, henceforth all generations will call me blessed. For He who is mighty has done great things for me, and holy is His name, and His mercy is on those who fear Him, from generation to generation. He has shown strength with His arm; He has scattered the proud in the imagination of their hearts. He has put down the mighty from their thrones, and exalted the lowly. He has filled the hungry with good things, and the rich He has sent away empty. He has helped His servant Israel, in remembrance of His mercy, as He spoke to our father; to Abraham and to his seed forever.

Theologian William F. Arnatt said, "The Magnificat teaches that through the Messiah, God will dethrone all enemies." And so he did! After Christ died and was resurrected to the right hand of power on high, Colossians 2:15 explains what happened: "having disarmed principalities and powers, he made a public spectacle of them, triumphing over them in it." He is now "far above all principality and power and might and dominion, and every name that is named, not only in this age, but also in that which is to come."[22] No wonder the commission Christ gave to His disciples rocked the world to its foundations:

> All authority has been given to me, in heaven and in earth. Go, therefore, and make disciples of all the nations, baptizing them in the name of the Father, and the Son, and the Holy Spirit, teaching them to observe all things that I have commanded you, and lo, I am with you always, even to the end of the age.[23]

CHRIST VS. CAESAR

The climax of the first act of history is the challenge of the Roman caesars to the dominion of Christ. The greatest Hero of all time was born into a world ruled by a mere man who declared his own godhood, usurping the rightful place of Christ alone. Augustus Caesar (27 B.C.–A.D. 14) provides the archetypal contrast to King Jesus: Caesar, the ultimate Roman dictator who ruled his temporal kingdom by the point of a sword, and Jesus, the King who established His universal rule from a manger and a cross.

Although these rulers never met, the collision of their kingdoms was inevitable. They gave historical expression to the battle that has been raging since the beginning of time. Who is Lord: God or Satan? Is salvation through the finished work of Christ or through the largesse and wisdom of man? Let us examine the legacies of these opponents: Jesus of Nazareth and Octavius, who subsequently took the title of Augustus.

AUGUSTUS'S LEGACY

Octavius, the adopted son and heir of Julius Caesar, was rightly portrayed by Shakespeare as a cold fish in *Antony and Cleopatra*. He anticipated Machiavelli's ideal prince in his ability to manipulate the masses. After defeating Mark Antony and Cleopatra's force at the sea battle at Actium in 31 B.C., Octavius became the ruler of a united Rome. He endeared himself to the Romans by acting and dressing humbly in public. To buy the allegiance of his subjects, he pacified them with bread and circuses. He verbally proclaimed his faith in representative government, but his actions proved otherwise. He quietly gutted the old republic of any power and solidified his absolute power through the ancient proven method of the short sword buried up to the hilt in the chest of his enemies. Using such tactics, he founded the Roman Empire. He declared himself to be God, or *pontifex maximus*, the priest of the gods. In 17 B.C., he led the pagan priests in a celebration, offering sacrifices and declaring all past sins of the people of Rome forgiven.

What was the fruit of Octavius's life? His accomplishments were many. Ably assisted by Macaenes, an administrator and patron of the arts,

AUGUSTUS
Born: *63 B.C.*
Died: *A.D. 14*

Claim to fame:

First Roman emperor who enshrined the practice of emperor worship.

Did you know?

He was the grandnephew of Julius Caesar, who adopted him as his son and heir.

Octavius extensively rebuilt Rome and created the Pax Romana, or "peace of Rome," which was protected by Roman legions who reigned over the Mediterranean. In his personal life, however, Octavius could not escape the generational curse that inevitably follows all those who give themselves to idolatry. (See Exodus 20:5–6)

He had three wives in a continual search for a male heir. His only daughter, Julia, had two boys, but the boys were killed before he could groom them for power. He finally had his stepson, Tiberius, marry his daughter Julia, and named Tiberius his successor before his death at the age of seventy-six.

Augustus Caesar's tragic familial dynasty ended in the fourth generation. Tiberius was smothered to death by one of his generals and the vicious Caligula stole the throne and then killed Tiberius's young grandson, Gemellus. After four years of total debauchery and a reign of terror, Caligula himself was stabbed to death. Rome celebrated with three years of parties after his death. The feeble-minded Claudius then ruled Rome until his fourth wife, Agrippina, was able to use murder and deceit to make her son, Nero, Rome's new emperor. Incest, murder and torture were a way of life for Octavius's last descendent. Nero tortured Christians by putting tar on their bodies and using them as torches at his dinner parties. He took believing children to the Colosseum, dressed them as sheep, and unleashed wild dogs to eat them. Nero finally committed suicide, thus ending the family dynasty of Augustus Caesar.

CHRIST'S LEGACY

What is the fruit of the brief earthly life of Jesus of Nazareth? One purpose of this book is to expound the centrality of the person of Christ in all of history. To measure His impact upon His world is a herculean task. In the last verse of his gospel, the Apostle John said, "And there are also many other things that Jesus did, which if they were written one by one, I suppose that even the world itself could not contain the books that would be written."[24]

Napoleon Bonaparte, more notorious for his butchery than for his devout Christianity, nevertheless said of Christ:

> I know men, and I tell you that Jesus Christ is not a man. Superficial minds see a resemblance between Christ and the founders of empires, and the gods of other religions. That resemblance does not exist. There is between Christianity and whatever other religions the distance of infinity…. Everything in Christ astonishes me. His spirit overawes me, and his will confounds me. Between Him and whoever else in the world, there is no possible term of comparison.[25]

Suffice to say that the transforming power of the Gospel of Jesus Christ unleashed an unknown liberty to the spiritually dead ancient world. Unlike Caesar, and all other powermongers, kings, and religious gurus, Jesus is not in the grave but rules from on high. His followers, beginning with the twelve apostles, brought the mighty Roman Empire to its knees by A.D. 312 through the conversion of the Emperor Constantine. Through them, He continues to transform lives and nations today.

Matthew Henry, the great Bible commentator of the colonial era, described Christ's impact plainly:

> [T]he mighty heroes of the world…conquered nations for themselves and made them miserable; the apostles conquered them for Christ and made them happy.[26]

Through this brief comparison of Christ and Caesar, the reality of the conflict between the two battling spiritual kingdoms in this world becomes obvious. Our children must know of this battle as it rages in our day, and be prepared to stand and defend the Kingdom of God in the classroom and the boardroom, seeing through the subtle deceptions of our modern-day caesars to the victorious, reigning Christ, who won the victory over Satan and all other principalities and powers at the cross.

WORLD CULTURES IN PERSPECTIVE

Zane's CD-ROM titles concerning the ancient world gives an excellent overview of the accomplishments and cultural uniqueness of several of the societies that rose and fell before the Christian era.

As Christians, we can appreciate the wonders of the ancient world, the wisdom of Socrates, and the administrative genius of the Romans. These accomplishments show the image of a Creator who has made mankind different from the animals. We, the human race, have been given the commission to subdue the earth (Genesis 1:28). Many of the ancient civilizations exhibited incredible sophistication, energy, and ambition as they attempted to subdue their world.

But an honest assessment of the success of the classical world must conclude that every civilization, without exception, failed and ultimately collapsed because of a false view of God, man, government, and law.

In regard to ancient cultures and their accomplishments, most classical scholars in our day have placed a flattering lens over the ancients. Today's historians are enamored with the "grandeur that was Rome and the glory that was Greece." Often, their writings focus only on the marvel of Egyptian architecture in the building of the pyramids, or the greatness of Greek democracy, or the stability of Roman law and the Pax Romana. The frequent assumption is that societies are ever evolving, becoming better and better. Historian Otto Scott broke the silence that is PANDEMIC among liberal scholars when he highlighted the real foundation of the grandeur of antiquity: "that 'grandeur' was based on slavery, used torture as an instrument of the courts, and human sacrifice as part of religion and politics. Such sacrifices, said renowned Cambridge historian Lord Acton, 'were the turning-point at which paganism passed from morality to wickedness.'"[27]

Five glaringly ungodly practices stand out to the honest student of all antiquity:

1. Religious idolatry and human sacrifice went hand in hand in all of the major cultures.

The Greeks, for all their talk of man's greatness, sacrificed their own people to their gods. Euripides described the sacrifice of Iphigenia. On the LINTEL of the Parthenon was a relief of a Greek ruler sacrificing his two daughters to ensure victory in battle. Plato said that human sacrifice was a common "custom." Herodotus described human sacrifices in Egypt. Rome is well-known for its barbaric sacrifices for religious and political purposes.

False religion always leads to violence and death, whether it is based on the worship of a golden calf or covered in the cloak of humanistic atheism. Human sacrifice was brought to an end only with the Christianization of Europe through widespread missionary efforts and the unleashing of the Bible. The Saxons of England sacrificed humans up to the time of Charlemagne. The Franks (Germans) practiced burning men at the stake in honor of Odin into the eighth century. The Scandinavians were renowned for their human sacrifice until their conversion in the middle of the eleventh century. What would the world be like today if Christianity had not come?

2. *Tyranny (rule without the sanction of God[28]) and the worship of political leaders were universal in the ancient world.*

The Egyptian and Sumerian civilizations developed the deceptive art of politically controlling the people through a series of man-created vengeful gods who intimidated the people into accepting their dictatorial rule.

Greece was guilty of the same debauchery, but in a more sophisticated HELLENISTIC package. We learn of Greek democracy, but, as Zane's *The Greek and Roman World* CD-ROM points out, it was short-lived and limited to a small minority of the population. The CD details that the age of democratic rule lasted no more than seventy years out of twelve hundred years of Greek history! The CD-ROM also details the fact that Athenian democracy was sustained through coerced military subjection of the neighboring city-states to Athens.

The Roman experiment with the republic was for a limited few and died forever with the assassination of Julius Caesar. In fact, "by the last days of the Roman republic, in the middle of the first century B.C., approximately three out of seven persons in Italy were slaves. In that slaves were overwhelmingly men rather than women and children, it is possible that the majority of men in ancient Rome were not just poor, they were slaves."[29]

Too often students today are taught that the foundation for America's republic is to be found in the democracy of Athens and the republic of Rome. This assumption is a grand exaggeration of the influence of classical antiquity upon our founding fathers.

Where did the founders get their ideas? Professors Donald Lutz and Charles Hyneman reviewed 15,000 items and read 2,200 books and materials of our founding period. They documented the sources cited by our founding statesmen. *In the 1770s, 44 percent of all citations were from the Bible.* In contrast, 18 percent of the writers cited were from the Enlightenment (most of whom were Christians), and only 11 percent were from the classical period of Greece and Rome.[30]

Our educated founders read the classical writings, but as law professor John Eidsmoe stated, "The founding fathers cited the classics illustratively rather than demonstratively."[31] In other words, classical references were used as illustrations of already developed political theories rather than as proofs of those theories.

John Adams, in a letter to Thomas Jefferson after they had both seriously studied Plato, said concerning the subject of their study, "My disappointment was very great, my astonishment was greater, my disgust shocking. . . His *Laws*, and his *Republic*, from which I expected most, disappointed me most."[32]

James Madison evaluated the democracies in antiquity he had studied and said,

> . . . such democracies have ever been spectacles of turbulence and contention; have ever been found incompatible with personal security and private property; and have in general been as short in their lives as they have been violent in their deaths."[33]

It is intellectual dishonesty for modern scholars to fail to teach the unmistakable bond between Christianity and our constitutional republic. The founders, because of their depth of understanding of the Bible, the nature of man, and God's plan for liberty under law, were far advanced from the days of unrealized dreams of justice and representation that dominated the governments of antiquity.

This book will document, in later chapters on the founding of America, how the biblical foundations of American society were the central cause of our advanced governmental structure and the only hope for the maintenance of political and religious liberty into the coming century.

The ancient world demonstrates Lord Acton's axiomatic truth that power corrupts and absolute power corrupts absolutely. But it is not just the leaders who were to blame for the spread of tyranny. All people are universally born in sin. They naturally tend to follow demagogues who promise them freedom while delivering the slave collar and burdensome taxation. Note that in the twentieth century we have seen a resurgence of such demagogues, exemplified in men like Stalin, Hitler, Tojo, and Mao Zedong. False religion always leads to tyranny, regardless of the century.

The ancient Hebrews gave the only true light to antiquity concerning the hope for liberty, both spiritual and political. By following the biblical pattern they experienced this freedom, blessing, and a constitutional republic for brief periods during the time of the Judges (c.1375–c.1025 B.C.). But soon they, too, chose to resist God's authority over them and sought asylum in the enslaving bonds of a king so they could be like all of their neighbors (I Samuel 8). Twenty-six hundred years later a Christian remnant would cross the Atlantic Ocean and adopt the covenants and republican principles of the Bible. They were called the Pilgrims, and we will learn much more about them in coming chapters.

3. The enslavement or execution of enemies was a practice of antiquity and of the barbarian cultures of Europe and Asia.

The study of Zane's CD-ROMs shows the constant rise and fall of empires and kings who fought almost nonstop wars. Their armies, which were not restrained by God's laws or faith in Him, became raping, pillaging hordes who were paid by plunder and the fulfillment of their lusts.

Hollywood and most modern texts tend to romanticize the conquests of the ancients. It was not just the Hittites and Assyrians who were characterized by extreme barbarity. The Romans, who are known for their enlightened rulership of the world, actually killed more people than all other nations combined over an 800-year period. They annihilated entire civilizations, such as Carthage during the third Punic War, and the Jewish civilization at Jerusalem in 70 A.D. Roman armies besieged Jerusalem for four years, starving the people to the point of sheer insanity. Josephus, a Jewish historian of the time, recorded conditions during the last days of the siege:

> Refuse which even animals would reject was collected and turned into food. In the end they were eating belts and shoes, and the leather stripped off their shields. Tufts of withered grass were devoured, and sold in little bundles for four drachmas.[34]

4. The ancient world neglected God's law and developed codes and methods of enforcement that were humanistic and preferential, and brought misery and destruction to millions.

God gave Moses and the people of Israel His written laws called the Ten Commandments right after they left Egypt. God Himself wrote them on stone tablets and gave them to a humbled Moses, indicating their divine source. These laws were quite different than those of Hammurabi, ruler of Babylon, some two hundred years earlier.

The Scriptures say that all people from the beginning of time were aware of God's laws because of their innate conscience, even though it was distorted after the Fall.

> For when Gentiles, who do not have the law, by nature do the things contained in the law, these, although not having the law, are a law unto themselves, who show the work of the law written in their hearts, their conscience also bearing witness, and between themselves their thoughts accusing or else excusing them.[35]

This is why it should not be surprising that a pagan king would compile laws two hundred years before Moses. Contrary to most of modern evolutionary historiography, the civilizations did not begin with nature worship and evolve to polytheism, then MONOTHEISM, and in the modern era to reason and finally to science. The Christian view of history understands that the nations, in rebellion to the monotheism of Noah, created polytheism, animism, and humanism as alternatives. They then used reason and science in the Enlightenment to enable modernity to continue its rebellion against God's unchanging laws.

Hammurabi, a ruthless but shrewd tyrant, united all of Mesopotamia under his rule in c.1800 B.C. Using an elaborate bureaucracy, he ruled for forty-one years. He had almost three hundred laws carved in stone under his image and that of Shamash, the sun god. The carved image shows Shamash giving the laws to Hammurabi. However, since the Babylonian gods were understood to be corrupt and unjust, Hammurabi's laws were corrupt and unjust as well. Some of his laws were practical and brought

HAMMURABI

**Ruler of Babylon
from 1792 B.C. to 1750 B.C.**

Claim to fame:
Wrote the Code of Hammurabi, one of the greatest of the ancient codes of law.

Did you know?
A stone slab containing the Code of Hammurabi was discovered in Susa, Iran, in 1901.

order, but without a knowledge of the true God, they were much less humane, equitable, merciful, and respectful of the rights of women, slaves, and the poor. The king, the rich, the men, and the army had special rights and little or no punishment for their crimes.

On the other hand, the DECALOGUE given to Moses was a perfect reflection of the character of the one true God. These laws, stated as prohibitions, were given to protect the sanctity of God (the first four Commandments), the sanctity of life and property (the Sixth, Eighth, and Ninth Commandments), and the sanctity of the family (the Fifth, Seventh, and Tenth commandments).

In the wilderness of Sinai the Creator Himself gave to the Jews His holy laws. Later, after the death of Moses, God told Joshua as he went into the promised land how he and the people could be successful:

> This Book of the Law shall not depart from your mouth, but you shall meditate in it day and night, that you may observe to do according to all that is written in it. For then you will make your way prosperous, and then you will have good success.[36]

The Ten Commandments, contrary to popular secular interpretation, are not just one of many codes of conduct developed in antiquity. They were not just for the Hebrews, but were intended to be taught to all nations (Matthew 28:18–26). Obedience to the commandments destroyed polytheism as an option; set the standard of worship; forbade idolatry; gave authority to vows and holy speech; set aside a day of rest and worship each week; established the authority of parents in the family over generations; protected innocent life from violence; established the holiness of the marriage contract and relationship; established private property as a right as opposed to communal ownership; commanded truth telling, especially as it relates to bearing a faithful witness; and established the need for a clear conscience by dealing with the evil desires to covet.

As a part of this study of the ancient world, we recommend that the parent direct and lead the family in the memorization of the Ten Commandments. [See also the Westminster Catechism in the Appendix. *Ed.*]

5. The persecution of believers in the true God was a standard rule of all ancient cultures.

We see this persecution as far back as the ridicule of Noah by all the people. After the Flood, true believers like Abraham had to flee pagan cultures. In Sodom, Lot's house was surrounded by a city full of homosexuals (Sodomites) who demanded to have relations with the two angels that had come to his home (Genesis 19:4–11). In Egypt, Joseph was persecuted for his religious stand. In Persia, Daniel was thrown to the lions for his faith. Near Jerusalem, Christ was crucified, as man's hatred of God found its fullest expression. In Rome, Paul was beheaded. It is no wonder that God judged each of these ancient cultures. To this day there is little left all around the Mediterranean of these cultures except for signs of God's past judgment.

The Scriptures make it clear, however, that God takes "the wrath of men to praise Him."[37] Joseph said it well in the last chapter of Genesis: "You meant evil against me, but God meant it for good."[38] A concluding example may help illustrate this point.

About A.D. 284, after two and a half centuries of Roman persecution of the Christian church, the Emperor Diocletian inaugurated the last great empire-wide genocide of believers. At that time there was a Roman legion of soldiers called the Theban Legion, which consisted of six thousand men, all of whom were Christians. The legion had been stationed in the eastern part of the empire, where they had been safe; however, at the time of the persecution, Maximian, who had been made Caesar and the Augustus by Maximian, ordered them to Gaul (modern France). He ordered them to sacrifice to Caesar rather than to Christ and to kill all the Christians in the region.

The legion refused, so Maximian decimated its ranks by killing every tenth man. Still the legion refused, so every tenth soldier of those who remained was killed. The remnant of the legion drew up a remonstrance and presented it to Maximian. It read:

> Our arms are devoted to the emperor's use, and shall be directed against his enemies; but we cannot stain our hands with Christian blood; and how, indeed, could you, O emperor, be sure of our fidelity, should we violate our obligation to our God, in whose service we solemnly engaged before we entered the army? You command us to search out and to destroy the Christians; it is not necessary to look any farther than ourselves; we ourselves are Christians, and we glory in the name. We saw our companions fall without the least complaint, and thought them happy in dying for the sake of Christ. But nothing shall make us lift up our hands against our sovereign; we would rather die wrongfully, and by that means preserve our innocence, than live under a load of guilt. Whatever you command, we are ready to suffer: we confess ourselves to be Christians, and therefore cannot persecute our brothers nor sacrifice to idols.[39]

Maximian was enraged by their stand. He ordered his army to turn on the Theban Legion and kill them at once. The legion was slaughtered to a man. The Christians had lost another battle at the hands of Roman barbarians. But, in the long run. who won the war for the world?

Maximian's vengeful victory was short-lived. He was deposed almost immediately, and Constantine was chosen emperor in A.D. 306. Zane's *The Greek and Roman World* CD-ROM speaks of Constantine's conversion, which is called the Vision of Constantine. This vision is detailed by the ancient historian Eusibius, who relates how Constantine, while heading toward a battle against his rival Maxentius, saw a cross of light hanging in the sky. He immediately put crosses on his shields and declared Christianity the favored religion of the empire. The children of the Theban Legion were then free to worship Christ. To this day, their descendants share in this great legacy of liberty.

CONCLUSION OF ACT ONE

Even as the ancient empires of the Middle East and the Mediterranean illustrated the futility of rebellion against the sovereign God, they were used by God to accomplish His will. As the great traders and colonizers of the ancient world, the Greeks took their beautiful and rich language wherever they went, so that Greek was spoken everywhere. Here was the language that would articulate the Gospel to millions in succeeding centuries. The Romans contributed the roads, commerce, and freedom of travel, enabling the Gospel to reach the whole world in the first century. And the ancient Jews, God's chosen people, were the great instruments of God to reveal His word, His law, His covenants, and even His only begotten Son. All of history—every event in the past and in our lives in the present—has great importance, for it is leading up to the fulfillment of God's plan for the ages.

As the curtain falls on the first act, the stage is set for the action to resume to the north and west, centered no longer around the Mediterranean Sea, but around the northern European nations where the Gospel of Christ blossoms among primitive barbarian clans.

CD-ROM ANALYSES

• The *Cradles of Civilization* CD-ROM is an overview of the development of ancient civilizations. Much can be learned here about the cultures, religions, governments, and architecture of Egypt, Mesopotamia, Greece, and Rome.

Christian parents should be aware, however, that the theory of evolution is woven into the beginning of this teaching. Using our introductory essay on the drama of the ancient world and the science section of this book, the parent or student can recognize this evolutionary bent and correct it with the biblical alternative.

• *The Greek and Roman World* CD-ROM is packed with good information concerning the classical cultures. Along with the great accomplishments of both societies, a subtle emptiness of purpose is conveyed by this overview. Christian parents can teach their children the reasons why these great civilizations crumbled. A good place to start this critical analysis would be to teach the five universal failings of ancient cultures that are in this chapter.

The CD-ROMs also do a good job of introducing Christianity and stating that it gained dominance in the latter part of the Roman Empire. Parents should apply the instructional material in this chapter to greatly expand the student's understanding of Christianity's influence.

• Ancient Egypt comes alive in the *Exploring Ancient Egypt* CD-ROM, especially her architecture and religion. The CD-ROM shows how, for most Egyptians, life was dominated by tyranny and a fixation on death which kept them in bondage to evil spirits. A good project would be to compare the religion of Egypt with Christianity. In this comparison, the centrality of religious faith and doctrine to the development of culture and politics can be highlighted.

• *Discovering World History* makes great use of the medium, including a wide array of instructional materials. In addition, it is a valuable overview of world history, showing in parallel chronology the development of cultures on every continent. With the history chapters of the *Christian Home*

Learning Guides as a companion, this CD-ROM will provide a wealth of knowledge, and can stand alone as well as any classroom history text. The absence of a Christian worldview only shows occasionally, as when the authors make reference to the theories of social and biological Darwinism, or when humanism is said to maintain a Christian worldview.

• The *History through Art: Ancient Greece* CD-ROM is a detailed description and pictorial presentation of the art and architecture of Greece. The pictures of sculptures are excellent, but parents need to be aware of the substantial nudity. With young children, selective viewing may be best.

The presentation also compares Greece and Egypt, placing Egypt and its tyranny in the bad light it deserves. But as Christians, we should view Greece with the same critical eye, revealing that despite the greater sophistication of its pagan religion, it was nevertheless a corrupt society in deep need of a knowledge of the one true God.

At one point the claim is made that the U. S. Constitution is based upon the Greek democracy. This is only marginally true. The American history section of the Learning Guides recounts the full history of America's constitutional roots, tracing them back to the Hebrew republic and Christian principles—not those of Greek democracies.

• Through the art and architecture of Rome, the practical and worldly Romans are realistically portrayed in the *History through Art: Ancient Rome* CD-ROM. Many suggestions are also offered as to why the empire collapsed. Christianity is depicted as the only religion that challenged the personality cult of the emperor. A student can perceive the conflict between Christ's leadership and the counterfeit leadership of Caesar, a contrast brought out in this chapter of the *Guides*. The causes underlying the fall of Rome would be a good project for the student, especially if America's decline is studied, showing the parallels.

• Because of the incredible breadth of its topic, *Christianity and Civilization* functions primarily as an overview of church history, rarely addressing the profound effects of Christianity in world civilization. For further in-depth study, see the history chapters of this book and the other suggested titles. The inclusion of the history of Christian heresies and cults necessitates some parental assistance in distinguishing between these and orthodox Christianity.

• As a brief survey of four dominant world religions, *Religions of the World* is admirably even-handed. Why it does not feature the constant caveats of the *Christianity and Civilization* CD-ROM is unclear, but with the guidance of parents, students can learn a great deal about the religions of people in distant nations and local communities. This knowledge is important for everyone—from missionaries to high school students—who are witnesses to members of other religions. Students ought to be reminded of the often oppressive teachings of Hindu and Islam, which are not mentioned in this presentation.

REVIEW QUESTIONS

1. Name some major rebellions against God from history and the Bible, other than the ones mentioned in the chapter.

2. Name some of the achievements of ancient civilizations.

3. What are some differences between the Greek gods and the God of Christianity?

4. Who was the Roman emperor when Christ was born? Who was the Roman emperor when Christ died?

5. Name the Ten Commandments.

6. List the five ungodly characteristics of ancient cultures mentioned in this chapter.

7. Who is the most important person in ancient history?

8. What is the only perfect history book?

RELATED SCRIPTURE

Genesis 11:1–9	Psalm 78
Exodus 20:1–17	Romans 1:18–25
Psalm 2	Ephesians 1:9–11

SUGGESTED READING

D. James Kennedy and Jerry Newcombe, *What if Jesus Had Never Been Born?* (Nashville, TN: Nelson, 1994).

Henry M. Morris and John C. Whitcomb, *The Genesis Flood* (Phillipsburg, NJ: Presbyterian & Reformed Publishing Company, 1995).

Francis A. Schaeffer, *How Should We Then Live?* (Wheaton, IL: Crossway, 1996).

Joseph A. Seiss, *The Gospel in the Stars* (Grand Rapids, MI: Kregel Publications, 1978).

Material covered in the the Middle Ages and the Renaissance chapter can be found in the following Zane Publishing Home Library titles:

History through Art: The Middle Ages
History through Art: The Renaissance
History through Art: Great Works of Art Explained, Part I
History through Art: Great Works of Art Explained, Part II
Prentice Hall: Discovering World History
Art & Music: The Medieval Era
Art & Music: The Renaissance
European Literature: A Literary History: Beowulf—Hamlet

ACT TWO:
THE MIDDLE AGES
AND THE RENAISSANCE

Yes, it is a press, certainly, but a press from which shall flow in inexhaustible streams the most abundant and most marvelous liquor that has ever flowed to relieve the thirst of men. Through it, God will spread His Word; a spring of pure truth shall flow from it; like a new star it shall scatter the darkness of ignorance, and cause a light hithertofore unknown to shine among men.

–JOHANNES GUTENBERG,
INVENTOR OF THE MOVEABLE TYPE PRINTING PRESS

A CHRISTIAN ANALYSIS of the centuries leading up to the founding of the American republic is a vital study that can prepare us for the great challenges awaiting us as Christians in the twenty-first century. From history we also can learn the lessons that prepare us for individual achievement. By properly studying history, you can make your life truly a command performance!

History, however, is no longer taught as a discipline of lessons and principles, despite the fact that, as economists James Dale Davidson and Lord William Rees-Mogg point out,

> ...the study of history has essentially been a self-help project. That it no longer holds such value for the current generation of students, who shun history for more practical disciplines, is evidence of a failure among historians. They have abandoned the old-fashioned notion that history has lessons...[1]

Parents and students can approach this subject with great anticipation if they see their study from a providential perspective. History does not cause itself. It is written and directed by the Creator of the universe. President James Garfield (1831–1881), one of our last truly Christian presidents, illustrated a knowledge of providence worth emulating when he stated:

> The world's history is a Divine poem, of which the history of every nation is a canto, and every man a word. Its strains have been pealing along down the centuries, and though there have been mingled the discords of warring cannon and dying men, yet to the Christian philosopher and historian—the humble listener—there has been a Divine melody running through the song which speaks of hope and halcyon days to come. [2]

As we act our proper roles for our Lord in the time we have been appointed, there is an audience, a great "cloud of witnesses" who are rejoicing in the heavens and glorifying God. That great cloud of witnesses is defined in Hebrews 12:1–2, 22–24. These witnesses include (1) countless multitudes of angels in festal, or celebratory, gathering, (2) the church in heaven and the righteous who have been made perfect—all the believers who set the stage for us, (3) the God who is the judge of all, and (4) Jesus, the Mediator of a new covenant. Every day we rise to put on

See the appendix for
The Apostle's Creed
The Magna Carta
The Ten Commandments

our spiritual armor and fight the good fight of faith (1 Timothy 6:11–12); these are the "cloud of witnesses" whom we will meet face to face some day.

In the life of a Christian, the most important goal is to find and do the will of God. God's will is found through prayer and the study of His Word, through the individual insights given by the Holy Spirit, and through wise counsel. There is yet another important way to help direct our lives, and that is to discern and learn from history.

The apostle Paul wrote of the importance of learning from the victories and failures of past generations. He said:

> Now all these things happened to them as examples, and they were written for our admonition, on whom the ends of the ages have come. Therefore let him who thinks he stands take heed, lest he fall.[3]

Sir Winston Churchill, former British prime minister, said, "If you look far enough back in history, you may be wise enough to see far ahead into the future." He knew very well of what he spoke. Imagine the great tragedy the British people could have avoided if they had heeded the historical follies of past English monarchs. If they had remembered Queen Elizabeth I's foolish optimism concerning Spain's promises never to send an armada, they would have been more cautious of Hitler's assurances to Neville Chamberlain in 1938.

SEEING ORDER IN APPARENT CHAOS

Most modern historians neither understand nor present the historical purpose and vision of history that is made clear by biblical Christianity. The result is that they often become bogged down, becoming experts in minutiae, but can no longer play the prophetic role of projecting trends into the future or calling a nation back to unchanging principles.

Famous historian Arnold Toynbee described most modern historians by saying that they see "only as a horse sees between its blinders or what a U-boat captain sees through his periscope.[4] They approach history not with an open mind, but with IDEOLOGIES that allow them to see only what supports their private agendas. No wonder students have lost interest in history in recent generations.

But from a Christian perspective, the history of nations leads us to an obvious conclusion: they who keep covenant with the God of the Bible and its laws and principles live longer, deeper, richer, freer lives, as a general rule. Sharon Camp and Joseph Spiedel, in *Target Earth*, documented that of the top twenty-five nations in quality of life and standard of living, twenty-four have Christian foundations.[5] The other is Japan, whose success is partially due to the adoption of biblical principles of liberty and free enterprise, in imitation of the Western nations following the Second World War. Historians often recoil from drawing this inescapable conclusion because it indelibly stamps history with God's name and law, and they would prefer to write their own scenarios.

The following historical narrative is a summary of the great beneficial effect of biblical Christianity in Western civilization. The authors admit that we see through a mirror darkly (1 Corinthians 13:12), and do not share fully in God's cosmic perspective of all events. But we are called as Christians to use our sound mind (2 Timothy 1:7), and because "we have the mind of Christ" (1 Corinthians 2:16), we can perceive the hand of God working out His plan for the world.

THE CHRISTIAN IMPACT
IN THE DEVELOPMENT OF EUROPE

Historian Otto Scott summarized well the premise that we will document in this chapter on the medieval march of Christendom. He said:

> For the first time, an entire civilization mired in decay was lifted and transformed into an entirely new condition, against the will of its government and many of its leaders. Christians did this despite persecution, torture and humiliation for nine generations. Then, after Constantine, Christians converted a savage Europe from human sacrifice to the faith, and created the richest, most diverse, most successful civilization the world had ever known.[6]

In this chapter, we are going to portray the Middle Ages, or Dark Ages, as the age of faith and pioneering evangelization. During this period, Christianity became the dominant force in Europe as a continent was transformed from BARBARISM.

We will see how God used FEUDALISM (self-governing local rule) to keep emperors in check, and how the Church and family played a predominant role in community life.

We will observe the much-heralded rise of the Renaissance, which reintroduced classical paganism to Europe. We will see how the renewed humanistic faith in the goodness of man, a pagan doctrine, brought on a rebirth of tyrannical government among the nation-states and empires of Europe.

Throughout our survey of the development of Europe, we will be highlighting the unseen hand of God and His remnants in each generation, from the early missionaries and converted barbarians like Patrick and Boniface to the persecuted purifiers of biblical doctrine like John Wycliffe, John Hus, and Martin Luther.

The stage has been set. Let us now introduce the players.

THE DARK AGES: NOT SO DARK

In modern textbooks, it is fashionable to use the term "Dark Ages" to describe the period from the Fall of Rome (fifth century) to the rediscovery of classical culture in the Renaissance (fourteenth century). The reason for this classification is philosophically—not historically—based. There is a definite bias today against teaching the unifying theme of Western civilization during this era, which was the Christianization of barbarian Europe.

Historian James Thompson spoke of the Dark Ages as the "age of pioneers." Just as surely as the American pioneers moved west, the Christians from the Mediterranean moved west and established a new way of life for the pagan tribes of Europe.

SAINT PATRICK

Born: c.A.D. 385
Died: A.D. 461

Claim to fame:

He brought Christianity to Ireland.

Did you know?

He was born to a Christian family in Britain who were Roman citizens.

AUGUSTINE

Born: Middle of the sixth century
Died: A.D. 604

Claim to fame:

The first archbishop of Canterbury.

Did you know?

Augustine of Canterbury is called the "Apostle of the English."

BONIFACE

Born: 675
Died: 754

Claim to fame:

Called the "Apostle of Germany"; later sainted.

Did you know?

His given English name was Wynfrid.

These new pioneers were spearheaded by missionaries like Saint Patrick. Patrick traveled from England to Ireland, where he spent his life preaching the gospel of hope in Jesus Christ to a people lost in the worship of the gods of darkness. No fires were allowed at night in Ireland for fear of the "gods'" displeasure. Patrick defiantly lit huge bonfires on hilltops and invited the people to worship the one true God. In A.D. 432, Patrick introduced a Latin book, *Liber Ex Legi Moisi* (i.e, *The Book of the Law of Moses*), to converted Irish leaders. They established the Ten Commandments as the foundation of Britain's civil law. Much of Ireland was converted by the time Patrick died in 461. Ireland went on to become a great center for evangelical Christianity and missionary zeal for three centuries.

In the sixth century, Augustine (not the Bishop of Hippo) arrived in Britain to reignite the torch of Christianity that had been lit there in the first century.

In the eighth century, an English Benedictine missionary was given permission by Pope Gregory II to organize a church in Germany. Boniface, known as the Apostle of Germany, found people worshipping under a great oak tree upon entering the city of Geismar. Upon learning that they were praying to Thor, the German god of thunder, Boniface began to preach against the Anglo-Saxon's heathen god. Seeing that his efforts were in vain, he decided to teach the people an object lesson. He approached the tree with an ax. His biographer Willibald recorded that as he struck it, a gust of wind blew the tree into four parts, which Boniface then ordered cut up for use in building the first church in Germany. The people's faith in false gods was broken.

In 754, Boniface and the converts he was baptizing in a river were ambushed and slaughtered by a barbarian tribe. His work was not in vain, though, for Christianity had permeated Germany and would continue to do so through the work of Martin Luther during the Reformation.

The nomadic life of European tribes during the Middle Ages was not the romantic romp through the woods that is portrayed by Hollywood. It was a brutal life, characterized by plunder, pillaging, and widespread destruction. One by one, however, through much Christian sacrifice and faith, these barbarian tribes—including the Vandals, Visigoths, Angles, and Saxons—began to be converted. The Franks in Gaul (France) moved toward Christianity under Clovis (481–511). Charles Martel (714–741), a converted Frankish ruler, held off and defeated Muslim invaders at the crucial battle of Tours in 732. And the tribes of northern Europe, such as the Vikings and the Danes, would find their faith in the one true God, though it would not be until several centuries later.

KING ALFRED THE GREAT & ENGLISH CIVIL LAW

King Alfred (871–899) was the first Anglo-Saxon ruler to successfully resist the invading pagan Danes. He united southern England and set the stage for a united nation.

Alfred legitimately earned the title "the Great," not only through military prowess, but by using the Bible to interpret and codify English Common Law (A.D. 890). He was a devout believer who built churches, founded schools, and invited foreign scholars to teach and translate important works. He divided his realms into shires (counties), which were governed by officials called shire-reeves (sheriffs). This strengthened the Anglo-Saxon practice of local self-government.

In the reign of Alfred the Great, we see the seed of American Christian liberty. English Common Law, based upon the law of God, became the foundation of the Magna Carta (1215), the English Bill of Rights, and the Mayflower Compact; it is even mentioned in our Constitution.

Though surrounded by pagan tribes—the Danes and the Scots—Alfred clearly demonstrated the superiority of a biblically based society. However, the struggle for religious and political liberty would go on another eight hundred years before it would be fully realized in America's constitutional republic.

KINGS, VASSALS, AND SERFS

Until A.D. 1000, roving barbarian tribes like the Vikings made life miserable for the far more peaceful and civilized Christians of Europe. The people, faced with certain death from these invading tribes, gave up some of their freedom and land rights to nobles and kings in order to obtain security. A hierarchical structure was established, descending from the king to the lord to the vassal, or SERF. This was the beginning of feudalism. During this period, Europe was divided into numerous fiefdoms (small kingdoms). The result was a reciprocal local accountability, which made it difficult for empire-building tyrants to control large areas.

In 1020, the Norwegians (Vikings) held the first national assembly in their history. King Olaf declared Christianity to be the law of the land, and the former practices of blood sacrifice, black magic, the sale of infants, slavery, and polygamy were banned.

After the barbarian invasions were eliminated by Christian evangelization, the need for the feudal system diminished; however, it remained in place for many years. Many things—crusades, plagues, church scandals, and wars among nations—distracted people from the need to protect their God-given rights from the ever-increasing royal power of such monarchs as John Lackland, the brother of Richard the Lion-Hearted and enemy of the legendary Robin Hood, who took advantage of this power and ignored the common law of the land.

THE MAGNA CARTA

England endured much after the death of Alfred the Great. The Danes invaded again, pillaging the land and attempting to destroy Christianity's hold on the people. The Normans attacked and defeated the Anglo-Saxons at Hastings in 1066, bringing a new aristocracy to the land. But the people never forgot English Common Law, its biblical foundations, and its limitations on the power of tyrants.

When Richard the Lion-Hearted, who had spent his entire reign fighting in the Crusades and foreign wars, was killed in France, his unscrupulous brother John became king. He squandered the royal treasury and taxed his English subjects and barons to the breaking point. Finally, in

KING ALFRED THE GREAT
Born: *849*
Died: *899*

Claim to fame:
Alfred, after repelling several Danish invasions, became the first king to be considered overlord of all England.

Did you know?
According to legend, Alfred, in hiding and in disguise after a defeat at the hands of the Danes, was scolded by an old woman for letting her cakes burn.

KING JOHN
Born: 1167
Died: 1216

Claim to fame:

He was forced to sign the Magna Carta at Runnymede in 1215.

Did you know?

John's nickname was Lackland, because he was left out of his father Henry II's division of territory among his sons.

1215, the barons rebelled and raised an army. They defeated John at Runnymede on 15 June and forced him to sign the Magna Carta, or Great Charter, which describes the fundamental principles of just government based on centuries of English legal tradition, which has its ultimate foundation in biblical law.

The influence of this great charter on Western civilization cannot be overestimated. The colonists in America argued that as they were Englishmen by birth, they were guaranteed the personal and political liberty defined in the Magna Carta. In 1779, John Adams, defending the right of the Americans to stand against the king's tyranny, appealed to its rights and privileges:

> Where the public interest governs, it is a government of laws, and not of men; the interest of a king, or of a party, is another thing—it is a private interest; and where private interest governs, it is a government of men, and not of laws. If, in England, there has ever been such a thing as a government of laws, was it not *magna charta*? And have not our kings broken *magna charta* thirty times? Did the law govern when the law was broken? Or was that a government of men? On the contrary, hath not *magna charta* been as often repaired by the people? And, the law being so restored, was it not a government of laws, and not of men?[7]

In the Magna Carta, we see the principles of our Declaration of Independence, particularly our Bill of Rights. The charter guaranteed (1) the perpetual freedom of the Church, (2) the protection of property from government theft, (3) no taxation without representation, and (4) a trial by a jury of peers. The last of the sixty-three clauses in the charter states:

> It is accordingly our wish and command that the English Church shall be free, and that men in our kingdom shall have and keep all these liberties, rights, and concessions, well and peaceably in their fulness and entirety for them and their heirs, in all things and all places forever.[8]

Today, one of four copies of the original charter still in existence is available for viewing at our national archives. We, as American Christians, must go back and remember the great Christian reasoning and sacrifices that have resulted in our 220 years of unprecedented liberty and prosperity. If we continue to forget these precious Christian foundations and documents, our liberties will be gone and a new age of barbarism and tyranny will wipe away the protection of our Christian legal foundations.

A FAITH IN CRISIS

After the conversion of the barbarians, European cities began to grow and national identities took shape. During the centuries that followed, Christianity was the central binding societal institution. The medieval cathedrals built from 1040 into the fifteenth century illustrate a deep-seated faith in a sovereign God.

But the battle of the ages continued to rage. Even though the faith was growing, the Church hierarchy was becoming increasingly corrupt, especially in Rome, where the pope began to demand worldwide allegiance.

Most of the histories of Europe in the Middle Ages focus upon the external political struggle and scandals of powermongers, kings, and popes. Seldom is the emphasis placed on what God was doing with His sincere saints to set the stage for the Reformation and the spiritual freedom and missionary activity that would follow.

Several events opened the eyes of the people to the truth. The Crusades, although a corporate failure in their attempt to regain the Holy Land, did open trade and help advance the economies of Europe as never before. The papacy was captured by the French kings, and from 1309 to 1376, the popes resided in Avignon instead of Rome. This, along with the Great Schism in which two competing popes vied for power from 1378 to 1417, did much to break the people's faith in the infallible Church.

During this same time, a plague called the Black Death swept across Europe, killing between one-third and one-half of the population (1345–1353). Europe was being tested through this time. Many, unable to cope with the plague, lost their faith. Others, however, saw God's hand in this tragedy and repented.

JOHN WYCLIFFE: THE MORNING STAR OF THE REFORMATION

The real reformation began 150 years before Martin Luther hammered his famous theses onto the church door at Wittenberg. It began in England with John Wycliffe, who is rightly called "the Morning Star of the Reformation." Wycliffe was educated at Oxford University, where he became a professor of divinity. He first gained prominence by his efforts to reform the Church in England, which had become corrupt and riddled with superstition. He was persecuted for his attempts but was saved from death through his friendship with a powerful nobleman.

Wycliffe was expelled from Oxford and retired to a country pastorate. He began to see that efforts at external reform of the Church were doomed to failure, for the people could begin to reform their lives—and then the life of the Church—only if they had the Word of God. However, the Bible could be read only by the educated clergy and nobility for it was in Latin. Without waiting to gather a committee of scholars to tackle the immense task of translating the Bible into English, Wycliffe began the task alone, finishing his translation in 1381.

As he translated the Scriptures, Wycliffe pondered the pressing problem of how to get God's Word to the people despite the opposition of court and clergy. He was led of God to found an order of Poor Preachers who took his tracts and translated portions of the Bible and distributed them to the people throughout England. The people flocked to meetings on village greens, in chapels, and in halls, where the preachers read aloud to them from the Bible. But now the preachers were confronted by another serious hurdle: few of the common people could read.

Undaunted, the preachers set about to teach the people to read, instructing men, women, and children, so that they could understand the Scriptures for themselves. One observer who disapproved of God's Word being put into the hands of the common people wrote that

JOHN WYCLIFFE
Born: *1330*
Died: *1384*

Claim to fame:
He initiated the first translation of the Bible from Latin into English.

Did you know?
He is considered the forerunner of the Protestant Reformation.

61

Wycliffe's Bible had "become more accessible and familiar to laymen than it had...been to the most intelligent and learned of the clergy."

Such opponents called his Poor Preachers and their followers Lollards, a scornful name meaning "idle babblers." But Lollardy penetrated deeply into English life, so much so that soon followers of Wycliffe were everywhere and among all classes of people, from poor farmers and artisans to noblemen. One panic-stricken opponent claimed: "Every second man one meets is a Lollard!"

Through Wycliffe's Bible, an entire nation was awakened out of religious torpor and given a new sense of purpose. Eventually, the Pope summoned Wycliffe to Rome to undergo trial before the papal court for heresy. He was too old and ill to go, however, and died 31 December 1384, while ministering to his parish church. Lollardy continued long after his death as a sort of underground movement, emerging into full light again in the time of the Pilgrims and Puritans.

His enemies' hatred followed Wycliffe beyond the grave. In 1425, forty-one years after his death, the Church ordered his bones exhumed and burned, along with some two hundred books he had written. His ashes were cast into the River Swift, which flows near Lutterworth and "the little river conveyed Wycliffe's remains into the Avon, the Avon into the Severn, Severn into the narrow seas, they to the main oceans.... And thus the ashes of Wycliffe are the emblem of his doctrine, which is now dispersed all the world over."

In the next two hundred years, many of God's finest would give their lives for the furtherance of His purpose, not seeing the full fruition of Christian liberty, but heralding its coming.

THE RENAISSANCE: THE REBIRTH OF ANTIQUITY

As the fifteenth century approached, God was preparing to bring before the people of the world a clear distinction between real Christianity and the cultural patchwork called Christendom. The Crusades brought increasing trade between the East and West and, in the thirteenth century, led to more prosperity and exposure to the literature of the great pagan classical civilizations. Under the renewed influence of Greco-Roman thought, millions of Europeans succumbed to the old Greek religion that made man the measure of all things. This new philosophical revolution came to be known as the Renaissance.

Without the Word of God as the absolute standard for conduct, corruption was inevitable. In the Renaissance, external refinement and sophistication was the standard, not the development of internal character. In this atmosphere, new means of torture were developed just as quickly as the practical inventions and artistic innovations for which the Renaissance is famous. An emphasis on aesthetics, the love of beauty, replaced the Christian emphasis on ethics and morality; form took precedence over content.

During this period, the Roman church came under the complete sway of the humanistic revival. Pope Alexander VI (1492–1503), a wealthy Borgia (prominent Italian merchant family), bought the papacy and lavished upon himself every pleasure and extravagance known to man. It was this blatant sin, duplicated by Leo X a few years later, that appalled a young Martin Luther when he came to Rome.

In this licentious atmosphere, the Church was corrupt, the people were antinomian (without moral law), and civil government followed suit. Niccolo Machiavelli, an influential Florentine public official and political thinker, wrote several works on government. In a political treatise entitled *The Prince*, he stated that for a ruler to be successful he had to be expedient and not governed by principles of right and wrong. He said, "It is safer to be feared than to be loved." Of the wicked Pope Alexander VI, he said:

> He did nothing else but deceive men, he thought of nothing else, and found the occasion for it; no man was ever more able to give assurances or offer more things with stronger oaths, and no man observed them less; however, he always succeeded in his deceptions, as he well knew this aspect of things.[9]

The new god-kings of the fifteenth to the seventeenth centuries would embrace the Machiavellian political philosophy by enslaving the people and taxing them into poverty to fund their wars, gardens, and villas. Gone were the days when kings would ride into battle in front of their troops to defend the honor of their God and country. Shakespeare's Hamlet accurately described a politician in the Machiavellian tradition as "one that would circumvent God."

PROVIDENTIAL PURPOSE IN THE RENAISSANCE

There is no doubt that God used the age of the Renaissance to prepare western Europe for the coming age of the Reformation. God took the "wrath of men to praise Him" by:

1. Using the Renaissance to revive an interest in the classical languages and in the searching out of early manuscripts. Many early Christian sources were recovered from monasteries in Constantinople and other eastern cities. The result was a renewed study and translation of the Bible;

2. Provoking a spirit of inquiry and the questioning of the authority of the Roman church. This drove men back to see the simplicity of the New Testament Church and its doctrine of grace through Christ;

3. Popularizing the use of movable-type printing. Johannes Gutenberg was the man who brought this invention to Europe. His greatest achievement was the printing of the first Bible in 1455. Now, for the first time in history, thousands of copies of the Scriptures and great works could reach the hands of the common man;

4. Providing in the Renaissance an obvious contrast to the biblical faith declared in the Scriptures. For the next 150 years, Europe would be torn asunder on the central issue of who is sovereign: God or Man; God or the Church; God or the State.

Europe had been brought out of the darkness of the barbarians into the light of the Gospel in the Middle Ages. But, with few people having a

NICCOLO MACHIAVELLI
Born: *1469*
Died: *1527*

Claim to fame:

He wrote The Prince, *in which he states that politics by nature is amoral and that any means, however unscrupulous, can justifiably be used in achieving political power.*

Did you know?

The adjective Machiavellian, derived from Machiavelli's theory of politics, means marked by cunning, duplicity, and bad faith.

Bible or knowing how to read, whole countries were susceptible to the siren cry of liberty with no accountability, as exemplified in the man of the Renaissance.

The foundations for a lasting liberty had not yet been laid. But, as we will see in the next chapter, geography, literature, inventions like gunpowder, the printing press, and the sea compass, and above all, a stalwart remnant of believers, were going to be used in a master plan that only God could have devised.

God was not losing in the cosmic battle for His world. On the contrary, He was doing it His way in His time. He was following the strategy He gave to Israel through Isaiah:

> But the word of the Lord was to them, 'precept upon precept, precept upon precept, line upon line, line upon line, here a little, there a little,' that they [their enemies] might go and fall backward, and be broken and snared and caught.[10]

CD-ROM ANALYSES

• Two CD-ROMs in the *History through Art series* are dedicated to the study of the medieval and Renaissance history of Europe. Other than this, there are resources only for the art and music of this period. Students wishing to study this period in greater depth should refer to the suggested reading list for this chapter to find good sources of information on this important and interesting era.

• *Discovering World History* makes great use of the medium, including a wide array of instructional materials. In addition, it is a valuable overview of world history, showing in parallel chronology the development of cultures on every continent. With the history chapters of the *Christian Home Learning Guides* as a companion, this CD-ROM will provide a wealth of knowledge, and can stand alone as well as any classroom history text. The absence of a Christian worldview only shows occasionally, as when the authors make reference to the theories of social and biological Darwinism.

• *History through Art: The Middle Ages*
This CD-ROM focuses on the symbolic art and rugged, primitive life of the period. The student should focus also on the great progress of this age (A.D. 500–1500). The barbarian tribes were converted, modern nations formed, the Magna Carta and English Common Law developed, and great art and literature were produced. It was Christianity that brought about these triumphs.

• *History through Art: The Renaissance*
The art of the Renaissance reflected a combination of the Christian appreciation for human potential and the newly rekindled false hope in the centrality of men in all things—a hope borrowed from the ancients. The CD-ROM presents the fact that much of Renaissance art was religious in nature and reflected a biblical view of God, man, and man's

purpose on earth. The parent should be aware that some of the art portrays nudity. With young children, selective viewing may be best.

• *History through Art: Great Works of Art Explained*
The titles in the *Great Works* series are best suited to older students as they contain detailed studies of important works of art. *Great Works of Art Explained, Part I* focuses on three important works of religious art with an impressive degree of detail. Because it deals with art produced in the Middle Ages, the theology it embodies is Catholic, and, and Protestant parents will want to explain Catholic doctrines such as the veneration of Mary to their children.

In *Great Works of Art Explained, Part II*, three works on military themes are examined, again in great detail. Of special interest to Christian parents are the latter two, which depict the tragedy of tyranny.

REVIEW QUESTIONS

1. What are the five ways to know God's will?

2. What caused the need for feudal society? What eliminated this need?

3. What important document was signed at Runnymede? What later documents were influenced by it?

4. Name three events that preceded the Renaissance and prepared the way for the Reformation.

5. Who was called the "morning star of the reformation," and what was his most important achievement?

6. What idea from classical times was revived in the Renaissance?

7. In what four ways did the corruption of the Renaissance prepare the world for the Reformation?

RELATED SCRIPTURE

Isaiah 28:10	1 Timothy 6:11–12
Isaiah 58:12	2 Timothy 1:7
1 Corinthians 10:11–12	Hebrews 12:1–2, 22–24
Ephesians 6:10–17	1 Peter 3:14

SUGGESTED READING

Charles Coffin, *The Story of Liberty* (Gainesville, FL: Maranatha, 1987).

David Fountain, *John Wycliffe: The Dawn of the Reformation* (Southampton, England: Mayflower Christian Bookshops, 1984).

Philip Schaff, *History of the Christian Church* (Grand Rapids, MI: Eerdmans Publishing, 1976).

Caroline Stoel and Ann Clarke, *Magna Carta: Liberty Under Law* (Portland, OR: Magna Carta in America, 1986).

Material covered in the European Foundations of Liberty chapter can be found in the following Zane Publishing Home Library titles:

World History: European History: Columbus and the Age of Discovery
World History: European History: The Thirty Years' War
World History: European History: The Rise & Fall of the British Empire
World History: European History: The French Revolution
Prentice Hall: Discovering World History
European Literature: Shakespeare's London

ACT THREE:
THE EUROPEAN FOUNDATIONS OF LIBERTY

Lord, I die in the faith that Thou wilt not leave Scotland, but that Thou wilt make the blood of Thy witnesses the seed of Thy church, and return again and be glorious in our land. And now, Lord, I am ready; the Bride, the Lamb's wife, hath made herself ready.

— JAMES RENWICK,
LAST OF THE SCOTTISH COVENANTING MARTYRS

WE ARE POISED on the brink of the third MILLENNIUM A.D. It is a time of great change, when the very premises of culture, government, family, and religion are being challenged. It is a time of gripping apocalyptic fear on the one hand, and on the other, a time of hope as we anticipate a new millennium.

Our present study is directed at providing the Christian family with the essentially biblical foundations of American liberty and prosperity. These foundational truths, such as the sovereignty of God over all human institutions, the covenantal, or compact theory of government, the sin nature of man, the Christian work ethic and principles of free enterprise, the Ten Commandments as the foundation of JURISPRUDENCE, and many others, were ingrained in the first settlers of America. An understanding of these principles will help the student discern the meaning of the history portrayed in Zane's CD-ROM series.

Why is such a study needed? For many years there has been a conscious attempt by many in our secular culture to ignore, distort, and censor the study of Western civilization as it has been known and taught for three hundred years. Political correctness and historical REVISIONISM have silenced most academic dissenters who dare to reassert the Christian foundations of our Eurocentric national history. The reason we will focus on the state of the Church throughout this study is that the theology of any nation will ultimately determine the nature of the rest of its institutions.

If it is true (and it is) that obedience to the biblical blueprint brings blessing, both in this life and the life to come (see Deuteronomy 8), then there is great hope for the future. Our future is independent of the rise and fall of those who oppose the faith. Rather, our success rests upon our willingness to recommit ourselves to covenant with God and His cosmic purposes. As we will see in the following chapter, our forefathers built the world's foremost republic from a desolate wilderness in 150 years by walking in covenant—in relationship with their God.

Deuteronomy 7:9 says, "Therefore know that the Lord your God, He is God, the faithful God, Who keeps covenant and mercy for a thousand generations with those who love Him and keep His commandments." Only twelve generations have passed since our forebears penned their first civil and religious compact. By God's grace, the skeleton of our constitutional republic remains intact. Prayerfully, the study of the sacrifice

See the appendix for
The Apostle's Creed
The Westminster Shorter Catechism

67

MICHELANGELO

Born: 1475
Died: 1564

Claim to fame:

Great Italian painter and sculptor who painted the ceilings of Rome's Sistine Chapel.

Did you know?

He was one of the architects of Saint Peter's Church in Vatican City, the principal and largest church of the Christian world.

RAPHAEL

Born: 1483
Died: 1520

Claim to fame:

He painted the School of Athens.

Did you know?

At his death, a false rumor persisted that Pope Leo had intended to make him a cardinal.

COPERNICUS

Born: 1473
Died: 1543

Claim to fame:

He proposed the heliocentric theory, in which the earth and other planets revolve around the sun, and so displaced the geocentric system, which placed the earth at the center of the universe.

Did you know?

By liberating astronomy from a geocentric viewpoint, Copernicus paved the way for Kepler's laws of planetary motion and Newton's theory of universal gravitation.

and legacy of those who have gone before can lead us to a restoration of the covenants of our fathers and God's renewed blessing on our land.

LIFE IN 1500

The hopes and fears of the early sixteenth century were much like those we are experiencing today. It was an exciting era, the day of Michelangelo, Machiavelli, Raphael, Copernicus, and Columbus. Institutional structures that had not changed for centuries were under critical review, and, especially in religious aspects, found wanting.

But this free-thinking revolution, brought on partially by the Italian Renaissance, was not the experience of most Europeans. For the vast majority of people who were feudal vassals or poor farmers in the valleys of northern Europe, there was little news of Columbus's discovery of America or Michelangelo's painting of the Sistine Chapel's ceiling. These people were faced with the constant struggle to eat the next day. Droughts, pestilence, and floods often drove thousands of people to begging for food. Maimed war veterans and the insane and mentally retarded wandered the streets and were periodically marched into the forest to die of exposure. Plague continued to devastate Europe in 1500. In Strasbourg alone, it took the lives of 16,000 of the 25,000 residents, and left 300 deserted villages in the region.

It was an age of death contrasted with humanistic hope in the pleasures of Italy. It was an age of great religious pomp and external show, but the heart of the Church was rotting with HYPOCRISY and lawless living. In this age of crisis, two great events shaped the future of liberty more than any other.

THE CHRIST-BEARER

On 12 October 1492, a mapmaker and seaman from Genoa opened the door of the world forever. Christopher Columbus had fulfilled his vision of twenty years to bring the light of Christ to the undiscovered heathen lands to the west. Thus, he fulfilled the promise of his name, which means "Christ-bearer."

Most people do not know that Columbus was a self-taught student of the Bible with a magnificent library. From reading his journals and his *Book of Prophecies*, written in 1502, his fundamental motive for exploration is easily discernible.

In his famous letter to Santangel in 1493, just after returning for the first time from the "new world," he wrote:

> So, since our Redeemer gave this victory to our most illustrious King and Queen, and to their famous realms, in so great a matter, it is fitting for all Christendom to rejoice and make celebrations and give solemn thanks to the Holy Trinity with many solemn prayers for the great exaltation which it will have in the turning of so many peoples to our holy faith, and afterwards for the temporal benefits which henceforth will bring great refreshment and gain, not only to Spain, but to all Christians.[1]

In his *Book of Prophecies*, which are predominantly Scriptures and their application, Columbus wrote:

I have already said that for the execution of the enterprise of the Indies, neither reason, nor mathematics, nor world maps were profitable to me; rather the prophecy of Isaiah was completely fulfilled.[2]

These words from Isaiah 49:16, recorded in the *Book of Prophecies*, are exemplary of the Scriptures that inspired this missionary-minded discoverer:

> Listen to me, O coastlands, and hearken, you peoples from afar. The Lord called me from the womb, from the body of my mother he named my name...I will give you a light to the nations, that my salvation may reach to the end of the earth.

On his second voyage, Columbus brought seventeen friars to evangelize the native population.

Yet there were failures and greed along the path to liberty. Columbus, following the common practice of his day, enslaved the natives in his desire to bring riches back to his sovereigns. Many CONQUISTADORS followed, most of whom did not share in Columbus's missionary purpose. But the Franciscan and Dominican friars also came. Most of these soldiers of the Cross attempted to bring the light of the Gospel to the once Gospel-barren Americas. In fact, the first Spaniard to explore what is now the United States was the friar Manos de Niza, who journeyed to the Americas in 1539. Soon churches and schools, orphanages and missions sprang up. It was a beginning built on the vision of the chosen forerunner, the "Christ-bearer." The door of the Gospel had been opened to a whole "new world." America went on to become the center for the spread of the Gospel to all the world. One hundred years after his death, God raised up a poor but committed remnant to settle the shores of North America, and that they would carry with them the seeds of a lasting liberty and a world-changing constitutional republic. These poor artisans and farmers would not come for gold, but, in their own words, to "bring the Gospel of Christ to the remotest parts of the world, even though they be but stepping stones to others in the performance of so great a work."[3] But the great events of the sixteenth century would have to transpire before these precious actors would be thrust upon the stage.

THE REFORMATION

The central event of the sixteenth century took place on 31 October 1517. On that day, a young priest and professor nailed his 95 theses to the door of Wittenburg Castle. He was protesting the trafficking of indulgences by the infamous Tetzel, a German Dominican monk. Tetzel would excite the masses with a sermon highlighting the torments of purgatory, concluding with his well-known line, "Once the coin into the coffer clings, a soul from purgatory heavenward springs." Martin Luther's denunciation of the corrupt practices of the Church started a revolution he never planned or expected.

Luther was excommunicated; thousands joined him, and Frederick the Wise, one of the most powerful princes in Germany, protected him. The Protestant Reformation swept Europe in the next century and changed the course of history.

69

There were other important figures that preceded the Reformation, like John Wycliffe, as well as John Hus, the Waldensians, and members of other reform movements. But Martin Luther, armed with the power of movable-type printing and the freedom to translate and teach the Bible, brought the fundamental questions of all time to the attention of all Europe: How is man saved? Is he justified by faith in Christ alone, or is obedience to the Church and its ordinances the only door that opens to Heaven?

Luther, reading the book of Romans, was set free by the truth of justification by faith based upon God's grace. His famous words were, "Here I felt as if I were entirely born again and had entered paradise itself through gates that had been flung open."[4]

In the following years, millions of new believers began to join the ranks of the reform. Along with Huldrych Zwingli, John Calvin, and John Knox, they proclaimed "Sola Scriptura"—the Word of God alone was the basis for their faith and practice. They called for the reinstitution of the "crown rights" of King Jesus, declaring that He alone, not the pope or the king, could claim ultimate sovereignty. God alone was sovereign.

In no way were the reformers themselves perfect. They often fought violent verbal battles among themselves. In fact, Luther could be a severe and profane opponent to all who disagreed with him. But Desiderius Erasmus, a Dutch scholar, answered this charge by saying, "Because of the magnitude of the disorders, God gave the age a violent physician."[5]

If there is one religious figure in the formation of modern thought who has surpassed Luther, it is John Calvin (1509–1564). In 1536, this brilliant 27-year-old convert to the faith wrote his *Institutes of the Christian Religion*, which is, after the Bible and Augustine's *City of God*, probably the most influential book of all time. His systematic biblical reasoning provided the foundation for the reformed denominations, which became the dominant influence in Holland, England, Scotland, and America for centuries. Calvin's major emphasis was on the sovereignty of God in heaven and on earth. This teaching brought shivers of fear to the tyrants of Europe. If God was sovereign, then the king was not, and neither was the Church. John Calvin is, by virtue of this doctrine and its implications, the forgotten founder of the American republic.

REFORMER WILLIAM TYNDALE

It is hard for us in our day to comprehend the fact that the Bible has only been available to the common Christian in his own language for four hundred years. Before the printing of Luther's German Bible in 1534 and the Geneva Bible in 1560, laymen for fifteen hundred years had never had a Bible of their own. Most people could not read before the Reformation and the explosion of common literacy. And the Church forbade all but the clergy and readers of Latin to delve into the depths of the Scriptures.

In 1526, a young scholar from England escaped to Germany and then to Belgium to fulfill a commitment made shortly after his conversion. Speaking to a Dublin cleric, William Tyndale had declared:

> If God spare my life, ere many years pass, I will cause a boy that draggeth the plow shall know more of the Scriptures than thou dost.[6]

JOHN CALVIN
Born: 1509
Died: 1564

Claim to fame:

Systematized Protestant thought in his book Institutes of the Christian Religion.

Did you know?

Calvin's followers in France were called Huguenots; his followers in England were called Puritans.

WILLIAM TYNDALE
Born: c.1494
Died: 1536

Claim to fame:

English translator of the New Testament and the Pentateuch.

Did you know?

He condemned the divorce of Henry VIII, drawing the wrath of the king.

Fulfilling his promise in that year, he translated and published the first-ever mechanically printed New Testament in the English language. Six thousand first-edition copies were smuggled back into England and lit a fire that could not be extinguished.

Tyndale moved to Antwerp, hiding as a fugitive from the court of King Henry VIII. In 1536, as he was about to complete his printing of the Old Testament, he was betrayed by a spy and imprisoned in the grim castle of Vulroode, where he continued to write for eighteen months. After a mock trial, he was led out to be strangled and burned at the stake on 6 March 1536. His last words were, "Lord, open the King of England's eyes."

His prayer was answered in an unexpected way. Henry, the pompous tyrant, wanted a Bible of his own after his divorce and excommunication from the Catholic Church. In 1536, while Tyndale was still in prison, Henry licensed Miles Coverdale, William Tyndale's collaborator, to set a Bible in every parish in the land. Unknown to Henry, this was William Tyndale's Bible under another name. This divine-right monarch had placed a time bomb under his throne and every other throne in Europe. Henry may have taken Tyndale's life, but Tyndale had landed a blow for liberty that would reverberate for centuries.

Tyndale was not the last from the British Isles to strike a blow for Christian faith and liberty. Little more than a decade later, another reformer would appear who would revolutionize Scotland, unseating her religious and political institutions with nothing more (or less) than biblical truth.

JOHN KNOX: A FIRE IN THE PULPIT

The march of liberty that would find its full expression in the American experiment had perhaps its greatest impetus from an unlikely northern kingdom, and a former bodyguard named John Knox.

In the 1540s, the burning of Protestant "religious heretics" was still a way of life in Scotland. As the nobility and Cardinal Beaton took their padded seats to watch the burning of reformer George Wishart, little did they know that Wishart's bodyguard and friend, John Knox, would liberate Scotland in another decade.

As the flames rose, Wishart declared to the cardinal, "He who from yonder place beholds me with such pride, shall within a few days lie in the same as ignominiously as he is now seen proudly to rest himself."[7] Sure enough, not long after the execution, the cardinal's enemies broke into his chambers and ran him through.

John Knox became Wishart's successor. He was an improbable leader— born of obscure origins, a defrocked priest, homely, undiplomatic, socially graceless, and full of fire. Though he tried to bring true Christianity to Scotland, he was ill-equipped to face off against a thousand years of Catholic rule.

Before he could even get started, he was captured by the French and placed in a French warship as a galley slave. It is said that while imprisoned, he gazed on his homeland and cried out to God, "Give me Scotland or I die!" Knox was released, but was forced to flee to the continent, where he spent four years strengthening his mind and soul in Geneva,

HENRY VIII
Born: 1491
Died: 1547

Claim to fame:
In breach with Rome over his divorce from Catherine of Aragon, the king, through Parliament's Act of Supremacy, became head of the Church of England.

Did you know?
A number of prominent churchmen and laymen who opposed royal supremacy of the Church of England, including Sir Thomas More, were beheaded at Henry's command.

JOHN KNOX
Born: 1513
Died: 1572

Claim to fame:
The spokesman for the Reformation in Scotland.

Did you know?
After his capture at Saint Andrews Castle, Knox served nineteen months as a slave in the French galleys.

Switzerland, under the teachings of the great Calvin at his school of reformers.

When Knox returned to Scotland in 1558, he was shot at and chased from place to place; but he proclaimed Christ's Lordship and, within two years, had defeated the Roman Church and the godless Queen Mary herself. He had done so largely by preaching and converting the people to the truth, not by the power of the sword, though his followers raised an army to resist the Queen.

Under Knox's influence Scotland became a "people of the Book" and adopted Presbyterian church government. This Christian heritage that brought the government of God back to the people and elders, as opposed to that of the king and the pope, became the major force for the founding of republican government in America a century later. The inscription under Knox's statue in Geneva sums up his life: "One man with God is always a majority."

THE SANQUHAR DECLARATION

The struggle for liberty went on in Scotland until well after the Glorious Revolution of 1688. Between 1638 and 1688, believers went through a trial by fire that tested the faith of all, as Charles I and his son, Charles II, attempted to reimpose the Roman Church upon all of Great Britain, including Scotland. This horrific period of martyrdom was called "the killing time."

A biblical reformation swept through Scotland and the "Covenantors,"—those who stood for the sovereignty of Christ over the king—were slaughtered en masse by order of the English Parliament. Their crime was that they stood for the National Covenant agreed on by most of the people of Scotland in 1638. Charles I and his bishops pledged to exterminate the Scottish believers who stood fast for their faith. Charles said that he pledged to exterminate forever "the new sect sprung up among us from the dunghill, the very dregs of the people. . .whose idol is that accursed paper, the Covenant."[8]

Forty-two years later, after the end of Oliver Cromwell's protectorate, these faithful believers were again enduring GENOCIDE for their faith at the hands of Charles's son. The king's troops were everywhere. Four thousand cavalry were dedicated to finding ministers of the gospel like Richard Cameron, the Lion of the Covenant. Richard, with his brother, Michael, always at his side, would ride out of the hills to preach to the people and then escape into homes of refuge or to a cold marsh to regroup.

On 22 June 1680, Cameron and a band of about twenty ministers and elders rode into the town of Sanquhar. The people gathered by the Town Cross as Michael Cameron clearly and solemnly read what has come to be called the Sanquhar Declaration. He said that he and those with him,

> . . .disown Charles Stuart, who hath been reigning, or rather tyrannizing , as we may say, on the throne of Britain these years bygone, as having any right, title to, or interest in, the said crown of Scotland for Government, as forfeited several years since by his perjury and breach of covenant both to God and His Kirk, and usurpation of His Crown and Royal Prerogatives therein. . .As all we being under the standard

of our Lord Jesus Christ, Captain of Salvation, do declare a war with such a tyrant and usurper, and all the men of his practices, as enemies to our Lord Jesus Christ, and His Cause and Covenants, and against all such as have strengthened him...[9]

These leaders then rode out of town and continued to preach from place to place. A few months later, heavily armed British dragoons found this small band of ministers. Faced with no means of escape and certain annihilation, Richard Cameron mounted his horse and led his fellow believers into the valley of death, declaring:

> Be encouraged, all of you, to fight it out valiantly, for all of you who fall this day I see heaven's gates cast wide open to receive you.[10]

Eight years later, in 1688, the lesser magistrates of Scotland and England threw off the last Stuart monarch and brought William and Mary to the throne of England. They restored religious liberty to the entire commonwealth. This was called the "Glorious Revolution," a turning point in all of history. But how soon we forget that the ensuing liberty which took root in America was built on the sacrifice of the signers of the Sanquhar Declaration.

THE REFORMATION IN FRANCE

The story of the Reformation is one of reformers such as Tyndale and Knox, but it is also the story of entire populations. The history of the Scottish covenantors is one such story; another is that of the French Huguenots.

The great Reformation spread quickly throughout France, which was the richest and most promising nation in Europe in the sixteenth century. By 1560, the minority Huguenots (Calvinist Protestants) were forced to arms by the massacre of their people by the Duke of Guise and his brother, the Cardinal of Lorraine. Admiral Coligny led three million Huguenots against twenty million Catholics in a series of wars to maintain religious freedom.

By 1572, the Huguenots were hoping for peace. Catherine de Medicis was a Machiavellian powermonger who ruled France by controlling her weak son, King Charles IX. She seduced the men of the court for her purposes through a private group of aristocratic courtesans. Catherine and her conspirators knew the Huguenots were too powerful to be crushed in battle. She therefore plotted to destroy the Huguenots through deception by promising religious tolerance, and arranged a marriage between the Huguenot leader, Henry of Navarre, and her daughter, Marguerite, as a cover for that deception. The marriage was to take place on St. Bartholomew's Day in 1572.

Admiral Coligny and the Huguenot leadership were given promises of truce and peace by the king. This was to be a time of joy and the recognition of cultural "pluralism." But on 22 August, one hour past midnight on the last night of feasting after the wedding, the cathedral bells rang and a huge mob of assassins sprung into action, killing the Huguenot leader, Coligny, in his bedroom. His head was sent to the pope as a prize of war. Three thousand Protestant leaders were massacred in the next

---

RICHARD CAMERON
Born: 1648
Died: 1680

Claim to fame:
Renounced allegiance to Charles II in the Sanquhar Declaration.

Did you know?
He was called the "Lion of the Covenant" for his bold defense of Scotland's National Covenant.

CATHERINE DE MEDICIS
Born: 1519
Died: 1589

Claim to fame:
Traditionally implicated in the Saint Bartholomew's Day Massacre of thousands of Protestants.

Did you know?
Before the massacre, she worked for legal toleration for Protestants.

Claim to fame:
First of the Bourbon kings of France.

Did you know?
After the Saint Bartholomew's Day Massacre, the Protestant Henry renounced Protestantism to save his life, but remained a virtual prisoner of the court until 1576. After this time, he brought religious toleration to France through the Edict of Nantes.

PHILIP II
Born: 1527
Died: 1598

Claim to fame:
Spanish king who sent the Armada to invade England in 1588.

Did you know?
Conquered during his reign, the Philippine Islands were named for Philip II.

few days in Paris, and tens of thousands more were cut down all over France in the months that followed.

The war went on for decades, but a fatal blow had been struck to the heart of France. The terrors of the French Revolution and Napoleonic tyranny have their root in this pivotal event. Instead of a reformation, France would experience three hundred years of degeneration as the Huguenots, the majority of the artisans and professionals, fled to England, Holland, and the Carolinas in America. After the St. Bartholomew's Day massacre, Junius Brutus wrote a book that became a classic biblical defense of the right of defensive war against tyranny through lesser magistrates. It was titled *The Defense of Liberty against Tyrants.*

Brutus's *Vindiciae* (Vindication), as it came to be called, along with Calvin's *Institutes* and Samuel Rutherford's *Lex Rex*, became the major biblical apologetic tools for resisting powermongers, up to and including the American War of Independence. In fact, our Declaration of Independence was the capstone of the great resistance declarations in history. Observe that resistance to the tyrannical kings of the sixteenth and seventeenth centuries came from Christians who obeyed a higher sovereign, not from humanists lobbying for freedom and democracy. The price of liberty was too high to be paid by those who served only themselves. The Declaration of Independence shows man's propensity to suffer under wrongs:

> All experience hath shown that mankind are more disposed to suffer, while evils are sufferable, than to right themselves by abolishing the forms to which they are accustomed.

But the reformers, deeply committed to the sovereignty of God, the fact of the sin nature of man, and the priesthood of all believers, would not lie down as serfs before a king or pope and deny their faith. The result was a 150-year trial of faith. The Dutch are a good example of the early and often bloody price that was paid for the liberty we are now enjoying.

THE DUTCH STAND FOR RELIGIOUS LIBERTY

The name Netherlands (lowlands) reminds us that part of the lands now known as Holland and Belgium are below sea level. The hearty people of this region literally reclaimed their land from the ocean through the continual building of dikes. They also endured other hardships, including religious persecution, and much of the liberty that we now enjoy can be traced to their willingness to fight for God's truth and light the torch of biblical liberty. The light of the liberating Gospel swept through this land in 1523 with the Lutherans, followed soon after by an even greater reformation by the Calvinists.

For almost one hundred years (1523–1609), three million Dutchmen endured slaughter and persecution at the hands of Charles V and his son, Philip II, of Spain, as these monarchs vowed to kill all who would not come back to the "mother church."

In June 1574, General Valdez and an army of 25,000 Spaniards besieged the walled city of Leiden. For four months the city held out. Philip II offered them a pardon if they would only lay down their Bibles and come back to the papal system. The Dutch sent him a letter saying, "As long as there is a man left, we will fight for our liberty and our religion."

William the Silent, their elected leader and general, could not raise an army large enough to face the Spanish in the open field. His small force consisted of the Sea Beggars, Dutch seamen and soldiers who were known as the fiercest warriors of their day. Outnumbered five to one, they had only one course of action: destroy the dikes, thereby flooding their own land. The water served as a defense against their besiegers, and would also allow their own supply ships to reach the city when winter storms from the north would shift the location of the seas.

By the end of September, the Dutch had reached an impasse: the people were starving by the thousands, and the winter gales from the north had yet to begin, leaving their ships aground some two miles from Leiden. Peter Van der Werff was Leiden's burgomaster, or magistrate. As he stood in front of the cathedral, the starving masses began to murmur, "Give up the city." Van der Werff answered:

> Would you have me surrender? I have taken my oath to hold the city. May God give me strength to keep it! Here, take my sword; plunge it into my body; divide my flesh to appease your hunger, if you will; but, God helping me, I never will surrender.[11]

The people, encouraged by his words, went to the ramparts and answered the taunting Spanish army:

> You call us rateaters. We are; but so long as you can hear a dog bark inside of the walls, you may know that the city holds out. We will eat our left arms, and fight with our right. When we can stand no longer, we will set fire to the city, and perish in the flames, rather than give up our liberties.[12]

Finally, on 1 October 1574, the great north wind—God's wind—blew a hurricane straight into the lowlands. The ships were lifted and sailed almost to the gates of Leiden. But the great Spanish army still stood between the ships and the starving people. That night, without warning, a huge crash was heard. A fourth of the city walls collapsed. Fear spread throughout the city: the Spanish would surely finish them off now.

But, no! Like the walls of Jericho in reverse, the crumbling city walls frightened the Spanish, who thought the sound was an attack by the Sea Beggars. Instead of walking into the city, they fled all the way back to Spain.

Thirty-four years later, this providentially preserved city and its people were the hosts of a small band of English SEPARATISTS known as the Pilgrims. From the Dutch, these future settlers of New England learned the art of self-government, free enterprise, and the biblical foundations for republican government.

Tens of thousands of the hearty Dutch believers emigrated to America in the seventeenth, eighteenth, and nineteenth centuries, bringing with them their love for liberty under God, civil liberty, and spiritual liberty for all.

LONDON IN THE EARLY SEVENTEENTH CENTURY

The general perception of English life in the early seventeenth century is one of refinement and civility, like a scene out of a Shakespearean

---

WILLIAM THE SILENT (OF ORANGE)
Born: 1533
Died: 1584

Claim to fame:
He was the principal founder of Dutch independence.

Did you know?
In 1583 he married Louise de Coligny, the daughter of the French Huguenot leader Admiral Coligny, who was murdered in the Saint Bartholomew's Day Massacre of 1572.

play. A trip to London during the reign of King James I or his predecessor, Queen Elizabeth I, would immediately change that opinion. Life in the largest city in the world at the time (about 300,000 inhabitants) was, as one philosopher of the day would put it, "nasty, brutish, and short."

Indeed, for one-tenth of London's population in 1603, life was to be very short indeed. In the summer of that year, the plague that would ravage the city for nearly half a century struck thirty thousand people dead. James I, on his way to London to be crowned King of England, was halted outside the city—so bad was the affliction.

Nor was life especially cheerful for those who survived. The city was notoriously unsanitary. In addition to the rats that spread the plague (transmitted by flea bites), human excrement was poured from windows and balconies into the streets, where it either flowed in streams or remained and putrefied.

The citizens of London were largely an ungodly people. Drunkenness was a way of life for a great number of both the peasant class and the aristocracy, and brothels kept a busy trade at all hours. As a result, the spread of syphilis produced a population heavily spotted with dementia, a condition that crossed every class boundary.

Neither was there any safe haven from criminal violence. On the street, in the shops of merchants, and even at home, life and property were in danger from roving bands of robbers who would sometimes pillage entire neighborhoods, even in the light of day.

Dozens of executions occurred daily, although the truly corrupt could often escape imprisonment and death by offering a timely bribe. A common lunch-hour's entertainment might have been the drawing and quartering of some heretical Protestant, guilty of proclaiming the Lordship of Christ in a TRACT.

Was the established Church idle while those around it destroyed their bodies and souls in sin and vice? No, but it might have been better for everyone if it had. The Church capitalized on the corruption of the people, operating a lottery to take advantage of the lust for gambling that so possessed the people that one observer declared in 1586 that "there were in London more gambling houses to honor the devil than churches to serve the living God." Church leaders such as the Dean of York took further advantage of the people by making loans with interest rates ranging from 50 to 100 percent.

Out of this ground of chaos grew a seed of hope. In 1603, the same year that James, the quintessential god-king, ascended the throne, a small Bible study group was begun in the basement of William Brewster's home in Scrooby. This group would grow from a mere bud to a tree in full bloom, though it would only begin to blossom after it had been persecuted and expelled to Holland. It then crossed the ocean to the distant shores of America, and there, off the coast of Cape Cod, in what would come to be known as Plymouth Bay, American religious and civil liberty began.

CD-ROM ANALYSES

• In *Columbus and the Age of Discovery*, we learn of the deeply religious nature of Christopher Columbus and his vision to spread Christianity to other lands. Historians often fail to emphasize that the Christian missionary vision has been the major driving force behind world exploration and the development of the Third World. The student should be aware that the doubtful theory of evolution is briefly taught at the beginning of the CD-ROM.

• In *The Thirty Years' War*, the presentation makes the tenor of war come alive through poetry and song. It does not deal with the internal causes of the war.

• *Discovering World History* makes great use of the medium, including a wide array of instructional materials. In addition, it is a valuable overview of world history, showing in parallel chronology the development of cultures on every continent. With the history chapters of the *Christian Home Learning Guides* as a companion, this CD-ROM will provide a wealth of knowledge, and can stand alone as well as any classroom history text. The absence of a Christian worldview only shows occasionally, as when the authors make reference to the theories of social and biological Darwinism, or when humanism is said to maintain a Christian worldview.

• *History through Art: The Middle Ages*

This CD-ROM focuses on the symbolic art and rugged, primitive life of the period. The student should focus also on the great progress of this age (A.D. 500–1500). The barbarian tribes were converted, modern nations formed, the Magna Carta and English Common Law developed, and great art and literature were produced. It was Christianity that brought about these triumphs.

• *History through Art: The Renaissance*

The art of the Renaissance reflected a combination of the Christian appreciation for human potential and the newly rekindled false hope in the centrality of men in all things—a hope borrowed from the ancients. The CD-ROM presents the fact that much of Renaissance art was religious in nature and reflected a biblical view of God, man, and man's purpose on earth. The parent should be aware that some of the art portrays nudity. With young children, selective viewing may be best.

REVIEW QUESTIONS

1. Did most people in Europe experience the Italian Renaissance?

2. How would you describe the people's attitude toward organized religion in 1500?

3. What was Christopher Columbus's fundamental purpose for discovering the New World?

4. Who nailed his 95 theses to the door of Wittenburg Castle on 31 October 1517, and began the Reformation?

5. Who was strangled and burned on 6 March 1536 for translating the Bible into English?

6. Who brought the Reformation and biblically reasoned government to Scotland in 1558?

7. Name two nations where believers made strong stands for liberty during the Reformation.

RELATED SCRIPTURE

Exodus 14:13

Deuteronomy 7:9

Psalm 119:89–96

Amos Ch. 4

Luke 4:18–19

Romans Chs. 1–8

Ephesians Ch. 1

Deuteronomy 8

Psalm 77:11–12

1 Timothy 6:15

Hebrews Ch. 12

2 Peter 3:2

Revelation 1:5

SUGGESTED READING

Kay Brigham, *Christopher Columbus* (Barcelona: Clie, 1990).

Christopher Columbus, Trans. Kay Brigham, *Book of Prophecies* (Barcelona: Clie, 1991).

John Eidsmoe, *Columbus & Cortez, Conquerors for Christ* (Green Forest, AR: New Leaf, 1992).

J. H. Merle D'Aubigne, *The History of the Reformation of the Sixteenth Century* (Grand Rapids, MI: Baker, 1976).

Jock Purves, *Fair Sunshine* (Carlisle, PA: Banner of Truth Trust, 1990).

Otto Scott, *The Great Christian Revolution* (Windsor, NY: The Reformer Library, 1995).

Material covered in the American Expression of Liberty chapter can be found in the following Zane Publishing Home Library titles:

Elementary U.S. History: Exploring and Colonizing
Elementary U.S. History: Becoming a Nation
Elementary U.S. History: Expanding Our Nation
Elementary U.S. History: Staying One Nation
U.S. History: U.S. Government (1783–1865)
U.S. History: U.S. Government (1866–1977)
Prentice Hall: Discovering American History
American Literature: A Literary History: Common Sense—The Last of the
    Mohicans
History through Art: Native American and Colonial Art

ACT FOUR:
THE AMERICAN EXPRESSION
OF LIBERTY

Thus out of small beginnings greater things have been produced by His hand that made all things of nothing, and gives being to all things that are; and, as one small candle may light a thousand, so the light here kindled hath shown unto many, yea in some sort to our whole nation; let the glorious name of Jehovah have all the praise.

–PILGRIM GOVERNOR WILLIAM BRADFORD

THE MOTTO OF THE SCROOBY congregation was "Reform ourselves without tarrying for any." The members believed that the church should be separate from government control and under Christ's lordship only, a belief that gave rise to their name: Separatists. They simply wanted to live in peace, obeying the teachings of the Scriptures. But the new king, James I, would not tolerate religious liberty. Some Separatists were maimed or burned at the stake. In 1607, the men of the Scrooby congregation were imprisoned for eight months.

> They were not pale plaster saints, hollow and bloodless. They were men—and women, too—of courage and conviction, strong and positive in their attitudes, prepared to sacrifice much for their principles, even their very lives.[1]

The Pilgrims, as they came to be called, escaped from England and much persecution in 1608. For twelve years they lived in relative peace in Holland within the walled city of Leiden, where thirty-four years earlier the Dutch had taken their heroic stand against the Spanish invaders.

But as time passed, John Robinson, the Pilgrims' faithful minister since the early years in Scrooby, and his congregation began to realize the need to emigrate. As foreigners, they could hardly find work in Holland, although they wanted to be successful so that others would join them and place their faith in Christ's redemption. Their children were being corrupted by the increasing moral laxity of Dutch life. And, the Spanish were planning a new offensive to wipe out all religious dissent. There also was a fourth reason, as William Bradford recorded, for wanting to emigrate. He wrote:

> Last, and not least, they cherished a great hope and inward zeal of laying good foundations, or at least of making some way towards it, for the propagation and advance of the gospel of the kingdom of Christ in the remote parts of the world. . .[2]

In 1620, the Pilgrims were able to obtain a charter to the "northern parts of Virginia." This charter was granted by James I, who had despised and hounded them for seventeen years. Yet, as providence would have it, he unwittingly set the stage of liberty for God's unsung heroes.

Most of the congregation, including the pastor, John Robinson, had to remain behind. The king feared the potential effect of Robinson's influence in distant America and would not permit him to go. However, the

See the appendix for
The Mayflower Compact
The Rights of the Colonists
The Rules of Civility
The Westminster Shorter Catechism

congregation sent thirty-eight of their number, including their most trusted leaders—William Brewster, William Bradford, and John Carver—to pioneer the desolate wilderness of North America.

Departing from Plymouth, England, in August 1620, with 102 passengers aboard the *Mayflower*, they endured a terrifying sixty-six-day voyage across the Atlantic. They arrived in America in November, far north of their intended charter. Fearing mutiny since they were out of the territory of the king's charter, all of the men gathered in the captain's cabin on 11 November 1620 and signed a covenant with each other to form their new government to glorify God and to advance the Christian faith.

The Mayflower Compact is America's first great constitutional document, and it is a fine example of the covenantal, or compact, theory of government, which is echoed in all of America's colonial charters and founding documents:

> In ye name of God, Amen. We whose names are underwritten, the loyall subjects of our dread soveraigne Lord, King James, by ye grace of God, of Great Britaine, France & Ireland King, defender of ye faith, &c., haveing undertaken, for ye glorie of God, and advancemente of ye Christian faith, and honour of our king & countrie, a voyage to plant ye first colonie in ye Northerne parts of Virginia, doe by these presents solemnly & mutually in ye presence of God, and of one another, covenant & combine our selves togeather into a civill body politick, for our better ordering & preservation & furtherance of ye ends aforesaid; and by vertue hearof to enacte, constitute, and frame such just & equall lawes, ordinances, acts, constitution & offices, from time to time, as shall be thought most meete & convenient for ye generall good of ye Colonie, unto which we promise all due submission and obedience. In witness wherof we have hereunder subscribed our names at Cap-Codd ye 11. Of November in ye year of ye raigne of our soveraigne lord, King James, of England, France, & Ireland ye eighteenth, and by Scotland ye fiftie fourth. Ano:Dom. 1620.

It should be mentioned that the Jamestown colony had already led the way in stating similar goals in its charter for the Virginia colony in 1606, declaring that they had come to America to propagate the "Christian Religion to such people as yet live in Darkness and miserable Ignorance of the true knowledge and worship of God." The desire to reach the lost world with the Gospel and to fulfill the Lord's great commission (Matthew 28:18–20) was an impelling force behind the settling of America from Christopher Columbus to the blazing of the Oregon Trail by Marcus and Narcissa Whitman.

If, by God's grace, the men of Jamestown had not been successful in maintaining their colony, the Pilgrims probably would have never followed them to America. These Jamestown settlers, after twelve years of trial and turmoil, met in July 1619 in the first church built in the colonies to start America's first representative assembly, called the House of Burgesses. These Virginians would hone their governing skills for 150 years, until the 1770s, when the founding generation of Virginia patriots would turn the world upside down.

THE PROVIDENTIAL LANDING AT CAPE COD

The landing of the Pilgrims at Cape Cod was an important providential event, for they were bound for Virginia. But the *Mayflower* was blown hundreds of miles off course and ended up at Cape Cod instead. Because their patent did not include this territory, they consulted with the captain of the *Mayflower* and "resolved to stand for the southward…to find some place about Hudson's River for their habitation." But God did not allow them to do so. They soon encountered "dangerous shoals and roaring breakers" and were forced to return to Cape Cod. From there they began their scouting expeditions to find a place to settle, finally discovering what is now Plymouth. Had they arrived a few years earlier they would have been greeted by the fiercest tribe in the region, the Pawtuxet; but in 1617, the tribe had been wiped out by a plague. It was perhaps the only place where they could have survived.

This leads to another major providential event in the lives of the Pilgrims. There was *one* survivor of the Pawtuxet tribe, and how he survived shows the Hand of God in history. This Indian, Squanto, was kidnapped in 1605 by Captain George Weymouth and taken to England. He learned English and, in 1614, returned to New England with Captain John Smith. Though Smith wanted to return him to his people, this was not God's timing. Shortly after Smith left for England, Squanto was again kidnapped, this time by Captain Thomas Hunt, who lured Squanto and twenty-four other Indians on board his ship. According to William Bradford, Hunt intended to sell the Indians into slavery in Spain. "But he [Squanto] got away for England and was entertained by a merchant in London, and employed to Newfoundland and other parts, and lastly brought hither into these parts by Captain Dermer."[3] Thomas Dermer was on a voyage of discovery to the New England coast in 1618 and probably intended to use Squanto as an interpreter with the Indians, but Squanto apparently jumped ship and headed home—only to find that all of his tribe had been wiped out by the plague. After searching in vain for survivors, he attached himself to the neighboring Wampanoag tribe. Fluent in English, he was led of God to offer his friendship and help to the Pilgrims when he learned of their presence at Plymouth. He joined with them thereafter and was converted to Christianity. Bradford said that Squanto "was a special instrument of God for their good beyond expectation."[4] Without Squanto's help, they might not have survived, for he showed them how to plant corn, fertilizing it with fish. He also acted as their guide and, most importantly, was their interpreter in their dealings with the Wampanoag chief, Massasoit, in the crucial early days when it was vitally important to the Pilgrims to establish friendly relations with their Indian neighbors. With Squanto's aid as interpreter, a peace treaty was agreed upon, which treated both Indians and Pilgrims justly under the law. Through the hand of God, the Pilgrims did not share the fate of other English colonies in the New World, which were wiped out by hostile Indians.

The Pilgrims lost 47 of the 102 settlers in the first four months in the New World due to disease and cold. Many of the women did not survive because they gave their covering and food to their children.

SQUANTO
Born: ?
Died: 1622

Claim to fame:
Acted as interpreter in concluding a 50-year treaty between the Pilgrim settlers and the Indian chief, Massasoit.

Did you know?
Squanto spoke En glish because he had been captured and taken to England twice before the Pilgrims arrived.

After two years of near starvation under the rule of the merchant adventurers who had helped to finance their venture, Governor William Bradford led them to abandon the contracts that mandated communal farming and labor, and go to free enterprise on their own land. Their productivity increased geometrically as a result.

Bradford's words concerning this economic policy are especially revealing in light of the "enlightened" socialism of our day:

> The failure of this experiment of communal service, which was tried for several years, and by good and honest men proves the emptiness of the theory of Plato and other ancients, applauded by some of latter times,—that the taking away of private property, and the possession of it in community, by a commonwealth, would make a state happy and flourishing; as if they were wiser than God. For in this instance, community of property (so far as it went) was found to breed much confusion and discontent, and retard much employment which would have been to the general benefit and comfort.[5]

During the summer of 1623, a severe drought destroyed their crops. Furthermore, they had no water reserves. The Pilgrims declared a day of fasting and prayer to confess their sins and pray for rain. On that very day, Bradford recorded that:

> For all the morning, and greatest part of the day, it was clear weather and very hot, and no cloud or any sign of rain to be seen; yet toward evening it began to overcast, and shortly after to rain with such sweet and gentle showers as gave them cause of rejoicing and blessing God. It came without either wind or thunder or any violence, and by degrees in that abundance as that the earth was thoroughly wet and soaked therewith. Which did so apparently revive and quicken the decayed corn and other fruits, as was wonderful to see, and made the Indians astonished to behold…. For which mercy, in time convenient, they also set apart a day of thanksgiving.[6]

This was the real foundation for America's Thanksgiving tradition, which has survived almost four hundred years. Bradford recorded that from that day, they never again experienced famine or drought.

THE LEAVEN OF LIBERTY

Because of the Pilgrim success, other believers were encouraged to come to New England. In 1628, John Endicott led a group of Puritans to settle Salem. Governor Bradford sent the Pilgrim physician, Deacon Fuller, to help the people of Salem, as they were dying from an epidemic. Fuller labored among the sick, and in the evening defended the Pilgrim theology of congregational rule against the accepted Puritan theology that still clung to the notion of a state church—the Church of England. By 1630, when the great Puritan exodus began and one thousand Puritans embarked for New England, the Puritans in America had adopted congregational church government.

The Puritans had not been trained in the philosophy of liberty of conscience that pervaded the Pilgrims. It took them several generations to develop a balance of spiritual and governmental liberty under law. Historian Edward Eggleston noted:

JOHN ENDICOTT
Born: 1588
Died: 1665

Claim to fame:
Led the first group of Puritan colonists to Massachusetts Bay.

Did you know?
He was the first governor of the colony at Salem.

The church discipline and the form of government in Massachusetts borrowed much from Plymouth, but the mildness and semi-toleration—the 'toleration of tolerable opinions'—which Robinson had impressed on the Pilgrims was not so easily communicated to their new neighbors who had been trained in another school.[7]

The gradual transformation of the New England colonies into self-governing entities changed the course of history because it freed the Church in New England from the top-down bureaucracy of the Church of England. It also set the stage for the development of free churches and a free government that would be the wonder of the world.

THE MOSES OF A NEW EXODUS

On 23 March 1630, some one thousand Puritans embarked for New England on four well-provisioned ships. In the years that followed, tens of thousands of Puritans were forced to migrate to escape the persecution by Charles I and his archbishop, William Laud. Arranging the 1630 expedition had been an enormous burden, but in John Winthrop, the New England Company had found a man who was fully equal to the task. "He was a man of remarkable strength and beauty of character," wrote historian John Fiske. "When his life shall have been adequately written…he will be recognized as one of the very noblest figures in American history."

> From early on he had that same power of winning confidence and commanding respect for which Washington was so remarkable; and when he was selected as the Moses of this great Puritan exodus, there was a wide-spread feeling that extraordinary results were likely to come of such an enterprise.[8]

The son of a prosperous lawyer from Suffolk, Winthrop had followed his father's footsteps into a career in law. He gave up a lucrative position as attorney in the Court of Wards in order to emigrate to New England. He was to substantially deplete his estate in Suffolk in order to help sustain the Bay Colony during its early years.

While at sea aboard the flagship *Arbella*, this thoughtful, self-sacrificing Christian leader wrote an important paper known today as "A Model of Christian Charity," which he shared with his fellow Puritans. It was an eloquent statement of their motives and their goals for the new colony. First and foremost, Winthrop wished them to remember *who* they were. "We are a company, professing ourselves fellow members of Christ knit together by this bond of love," he told them. And what was their purpose? He wrote that the work they had was to seek a place to live together "under a due form of government, both civill and ecclesiastical." But theirs was not to be a mere legal agreement. As with the Mayflower Compact, their relationship to God and to each other was described in covenantal terms:

> Thus stands the cause between God and us, we are entered into Covenant with Him for this Worke…Now if the Lord shall please to bear us, and bring us in peace to the place we desire, then hath he verified this Covenant and sealed our Commission…

With a clear vision of their place in history, Winthrop prayed that God

JOHN WINTHROP
Born: 1588
Died: 1649

Claim to fame:
Founded the settlement that became known as Boston.

Did you know?
Winthrop's journal is one of the most valuable of American historical sources.

...shall make us a praise and glory, that men shall say of succeeding plantations: the Lord make it like that of New England for we must consider we shall be as a city upon a hill, the eyes of all people are on us; so that if we shall deal falsely with our God in this work we have undertaken and so cause Him to withdraw His present help from us, we shall be made a story and a by-word throughout the world.[9]

What a reminder to twentieth-century American Christians of our duty, and what a solemn warning! Are not the eyes of the world, as well as the eyes of God, focused upon America today, critically evaluating how well we are living out the principles of our founding covenants?

THE CONNECTICUT PROTOTYPE OF CONSTITUTIONAL GOVERNMENT

Before we leave this discussion of New England's development, we should mention one more spiritual leader who led the way to liberty. His name was Rev. Thomas Hooker, and his story shows the basis of the American Constitution.

The Reverend Thomas Hooker was a learned man who, like so many other Puritans, had been educated at Cambridge University, and had become one of England's most eloquent supporters of scriptural Christianity. Unfortunately, he was so eloquent that he attracted the attention of William Laud, the archbishop of Canterbury. Learning that Laud was planning to arrest him, Rev. Hooker escaped to Holland in 1630. Here he lived for three years until he felt that the Lord was calling him to New England.

Rev. Hooker soon came to a disagreement with the ELITIST view of government of John Winthrop, who believed that the leaders of the colony should lead for life, unless guilty of some serious misdeed. Hooker also felt that in political decisions in the town, those who were not members of the Church should be able to vote.

But Governor Winthrop and the Boston Puritans were adamant. So, in June 1636, Rev. Hooker and his congregation—some one hundred people—left the Massachusetts Bay Colony to settle in the Connecticut Valley. They were followed by the congregations of Dorchester and Watertown. By May 1637, some eight hundred people had moved from the Boston area to populate Windsor, Wethersfield, and Hartford. The Bay Colony had lost not just a few individuals, but virtually three whole towns in this dispute over self-government.

These Connecticut towns consented to be governed by a board of commissioners from Massachusetts for one year, but then they assembled together and elected their own representatives in the General Court held in Hartford in 1638. For many years, historians did not know the critical role Thomas Hooker played in producing the new government and its landmark constitution. It was not until the middle of the nineteenth century, when a little volume was found in Windsor, that the world knew of Hooker's involvement. In this volume, in which someone had transcribed notes in cipher on the sermons and lectures given by Rev. Hooker and other ministers, was discovered a digest of the remarkable, statesmanlike sermon Hooker gave before the General Court on 31 May 1638.

THOMAS HOOKER
Born: 1586
Died: 1647

Claim to fame:
Founder of Hartford, Connecticut.

Did you know?
His Fundamental Orders became the basis for Connecticut's state constitution.

Taking Deuteronomy 1:13 as his text, he asked the people to "Take you wise men and understanding...and I will make them rulers over you." He then told them that "the foundation of authority is laid...in the free consent of the people" and that "the choice of the public magistrates belongs unto the people by God's own allowance"—that they who have the power to appoint officers and magistrates have the right also "to set the bounds and limitations of the power and place unto which they call them."[10]

The various points Rev. Hooker enumerated in his sermon formed the basis of the Fundamental Orders of Connecticut, which were adopted as the Constitution of Connecticut by the freemen of the three towns assembled in Hartford on 14 January 1639.

In the Fundamental Orders of Connecticut, we have a document that is far ahead of its time in recognizing the origin of all civil government as derived from God and "the agreement of the whole body of the governed." Here the American covenant, begun by the Mayflower Compact, developed into a full-fledged body of laws.

> It was the first written constitution known to history, that created a government, and it marked the beginnings of American democracy, of which Thomas Hooker deserves more than any man to be called the father.[11]

Not only is this so, but to historian Fiske, the government of the United States is "in lineal descent more nearly related to that of Connecticut than to any of the other thirteen colonies."

> The most noteworthy features of the Connecticut republic was that it was a federation of independent towns and that all attributes of sovereignty not expressly granted to the General Court remained, as of original right, in the towns. . .[12]

Here, in the Fundamental Orders, is a microcosm of the federal constitution to come.

Significantly, the Fundamental Orders did not require church membership in order to vote or hold most offices (an exception was the governor, who was to be a member of "some approved congregation"). This was a distinct departure from the Puritan view of civil government as an ecclesiocracy which, in practice, meant rule of the state by a specific Christian denomination with its specific interpretation of Scripture. But it was in no way an attempt to secularize the state or separate it from biblical law. On the contrary, the document reflected the sincere biblical consensus of the people. It acknowledged that wherever a people are gathered together, the Word of God requires them to set up "an orderly and decent government established according to God." Thus did they "enter into combination and confederation together to maintain and preserve the liberty and purity of the gospel of our Lord Jesus Christ."

Providentially, this little federal republic grew until "it became the strongest political structure on the continent, as was illustrated in the remarkable military energy and the unshaken financial credit of Connecticut during the Revolutionary War." It was Connecticut, too, that broke the deadlock at the Constitutional Convention of 1787 with its compromise by which it was decided that the states would be represented equally in the Senate, but on the basis of population in the House of Representatives.

What great steps forward in the art of Christian self-government were taken as the result of one New England minister's vision sustained by Divine Providence! In the century that followed, Christians of all three forms of church polity (government) would emigrate to America. In 1787, the strengths of each of the forms were incorporated into the U. S. Constitution. The Episcopal form, which emphasized hierarchical rule, was paralleled in the executive branch. The Presbyterian form of elder rule was manifest in the election of senators and the appointment of judges. The congregational form, which emphasized congregational participation, was mirrored in the election of the House of Representatives.

AMERICA: A LINK, NOT THE KINGDOM

Before proceeding with the eventful history of the American experience, we pause to reflect on the providence of God in the formation of the United States of America.

When all of history is seen as the unveiling of God's purpose within time and space, America's Christian history and the liberty that it produced can be viewed in a much more strategic light. Seen in the context of God's greater plan for the whole world, America can be placed in its proper perspective as a link on the chain, a vessel for God's use, but not the pinnacle of history. America is not the final expression of the kingdom of God, but it has been the highest expression of Christian culture the world has known to date, which makes its study extremely important.

It is not our intention to portray Americans as God's chosen people or nation, as some modern religious cults have suggested. Nor are we trying to suggest America has a "manifest destiny," or that it is destined to rule because of some inherent greatness. The idea of a manifest destiny grew up in the nineteenth century as a secularization of the original Pilgrim covenant and Puritan hope. God's purpose for America can be clearly seen in history through the covenants of our people and divine intervention in events.

That purpose is molded by the hand of the Creator and it is to His glory if we as a nation have been used to spread His Gospel. Our forefathers understood that our commission was to spread the message of Christ to the world and build a biblically based civilization; they also understood that if they denied their commission, God would surely judge them and their culture. America's current condition is evidence of that judgment.

PROVIDENTIAL TURNING POINTS

Yet these disclaimers should not make us any less appreciative of the divine goodness and far-reaching power that has attended our rise as a nation. In fact, it is the obvious providence that should cause the student of American history to bow in humble adoration before the Creator and Author of liberty. For the believer in providence, it is obvious that a divine design orchestrated America's development—from the location of the continent with three thousand miles of ocean to the east and six thousand to the west; to the timing of its discovery just as the Bible was being unleashed into the hands of the individual for the first time in history; to the specific, unlikely settlers, the Pilgrims, who laid the seedbed of liberty and Christian character; to the many acts of divine providence that again and again saved the land from desolation.

George Washington was a firm believer in divine providence. In the French and Indian Wars, he was saved from hostile fire in which all the officers in the field were either killed or wounded except him. He wrote to his brother:

> By the miraculous care of Providence, that protected me beyond all human expectations; I had four bullets through my coat, and two horses shot under me, and yet escaped unhurt.[13]

In his Thanksgiving Proclamation of 3 October 1789, he said:

> It is the duty of all nations to acknowledge the providence of almighty God, to obey His will, to be grateful for His benefits, and humbly to implore His protection and favor.[14]

The centrality of the doctrine of providence is also enshrined in our political documents. The Fundamental Orders of Connecticut begin with this statement concerning God's power and providence, and then move on to enumerate the state's Constitution:

> For as much as it has pleased the almighty God by the wise disposition of His divine providence so to order and dispose of things. . .

The Declaration of Independence concludes with a similar testimony: "With a firm reliance on the protection of divine Providence."

CROMWELL'S REVOLUTION LEADS TO EXODUS

In London in 1629, James I was dead and his son, Charles I, ruled an increasingly Calvinistic people with unbridled tyranny. More subdued than his father but more systematically arrogant, Charles closed Parliament "permanently" for eleven years, ruled by divine right, and persecuted and tortured all who stood against his religious and civil heresy. Christians were killed or imprisoned for merely speaking of predestination in public or questioning the king's compromised prayer book.

On 30 January 1637, three prisoners were brought to the pillory. Before a huge crowd the sheriff heated the branding iron red hot and stamped it into their foreheads, then slit their nostrils and chopped off their ears. Rev. Bastwick's wife pulled a stool up to the pillory and kissed her husband and gently laid his shredded ears upon her handkerchief.

The people never forgot that day. Three years later the Parliament was finally called again to raise money because Charles was broke. Instead, Parliament raised an army, and from 1642 to 1646 England endured the bloody English Civil War between the Loyalists (Charles's supporters) and the Parliamentary Party, which came under the leadership of the courageous, godly Oliver Cromwell. Cromwell shaped his army by recruiting men of prayer (with the best horses) who feared God more than they feared the king's dragoons. Before the great battle at Marston Moor, Cromwell's men prayed all night. They came off their knees in the morning and routed the king's troops. On 12 June 1645, the last great battle was fought. The king was soon captured and on 30 June 1649, after a trial for treason against the people, Charles I was beheaded.

But the war and the elevation of Cromwell to "Protector of England" could not bring lasting liberty to England—yet. The people's hearts still turned back to slavish submission to a king. The nation was divided in theology (Arminianism vs. Calvinism) and in character. A decade later, in 1660, Charles II assumed the throne at the people's request. Like his father, he fiercely persecuted the church in England and Scotland.

Lasting liberty is only possible for a people well-trained in Christian self-government who hold a strong biblical commitment to the Lordship of Christ. James Madison said it well:

> To suppose that any form of government will secure liberty and happiness without virtue in the people, is a CHIMERICAL idea. . .we do not depend on or put confidence in our rulers, but in the people who are to choose them.[15]

Although Cromwell's republic was short-lived, the impact of the first English experiment with liberty upon the American colonies was tremendous. Within a decade after Charles II restored the monarchy of England, Jamestown grew from nine thousand to forty thousand settlers. New England saw a similar flood of immigrants, most of whom were Christian Puritans, who would not compromise their faith under the tyranny of Charles.

God truly took the "wrath of men to praise Him" and used the restoration of monarchy in England to bring the flower of the old world to lay a holy seedbed in the new.

"NEW ENGLAND STOOD STILL AND SAW THE SALVATION OF GOD"

The following story illustrates an event that saved the biblically founded remnant that provided the foundation of our republic.

The most miraculous sea battle of the eighteenth century has been hidden from nearly all Americans and their children. It is not found in textbooks, in libraries, or spoken of in public school history classes. Why? Because in our secular society, any outbreak of the supernatural power of God is censored and must be hidden or erased, even if it means omitting a nation-changing event of immense proportion.

Here is that story, which was preserved for us through the faithful preaching and writings of Rev. Thomas Prince, Rev. Jonathan French, and Rev. George Whitefield, to name a few.

Wherever the French conquered, they allowed only the Roman Catholic religion to be practiced, and the New Englanders greatly feared them. The Stuart monarchs in England were sympathetic to France's Catholic monarch, but when a firmly Protestant king, William of Orange, ascended the English throne, the French began to attack the English colonists in America with great savagery. In 1745, the New England forces, with the aid of a British squadron, captured Louisbourg in Nova Scotia. Here God used the weather to the advantage of the New Englanders. "The

English appear to have enlisted Heaven in their interest," wrote one of the town's residents later. "So long as the expedition lasted they had the most beautiful weather in the world." No storms, no unfavorable winds, and no fog, which was most surprising for the area. After the capture of Louisbourg, the French sent half of their navy, under the command of the Duc d'Anville, "to lay waste the whole seacoast from Nova Scotia to Georgia."[16]

The Rev. Thomas Prince, pastor of the South Church in Boston, later preached a sermon of Thanksgiving for God's protecting hand when New England was "a long while wholly ignorant of their designs against us. . . ."[17] Even when rumors reached them, they were not greatly worried because they understood that the British fleet would prevent the French from leaving the shores of France. But, unknown to the colonists, the French eluded Admiral Martin's squadron and slipped out to sea. But, as Rev. Prince observed, "While we knew nothing of Danger, God beheld it, and was working Salvation for us. And when we had none to help in America, He even prevented our Friends in Europe from coming to succour us; that we might see our Salvation was His Work alone, and that the Glory belongs entirely to Him."[18]

Having eluded the British, the proud French fleet "of about 70 sail" put to sea on 20 June 1746. As the vessels crossed the Atlantic heading for Halifax, they were delayed at first in a prolonged calm, and then they encountered storms in which several ships were disabled by lightning. Pestilence broke out. Then the entire fleet was scattered to the four winds by tremendous storms. By these means, "they were. . .so dispersed in the midst of the Ocean that by Aug. 26, they had left but twelve Ships of the Line and forty-one others. . ."[19] On 2 September, as they were nearing the dangerous shoals off the Isle of Sables, they encountered another violent storm and lost several more vessels.

When the Duc d'Anville's ship finally reached Halifax, a lonely, isolated area, he fully expected to rendezvous with other French ships sent from the West Indies to meet him. The West Indies squadron had indeed been there, but discouraged by the long delay of d'Anville's fleet, had given up and left!

During all this, what had the New England colonists been doing? Another New England pastor, Rev. Jonathan French, wrote that as soon as the French vessels were sighted off the coast, the people were "filled with consternation. The streets filled with men, marching for the defense of the sea ports, and the distresses of women and children, trembling for the event, made. . .deep impressions upon the minds of those who remember these scenes. But never did the religion, for which the country was settled, appear more important, nor prayer more prevalent, than on this occasion. A prayer-hearing God, stretched forth the arm of His power, and destroyed that mighty Armament, in a manner almost as extraordinary as the drowning of Pharaoh and his host in the Red Sea."[20]

What happened was this: Shortly after his arrival at Halifax, the Duc d'Anville was so appalled at the loss of the major part of his fleet "and finding his few Ships so shattered, so many Men dead, so many sickly, and no more of his Fleet come in; he sunk into discouragement, and Sept. 15 died; but in such a Condition. . .it was generally tho't he poisoned himself, and was buried without Ceremony."[21] More ships finally limped into port, but many of the men on board were ill and their food supplies were quickly running out. The commander who took d'Anville's place committed suicide by falling on his sword only days after their arrival. The third in command ordered the men ashore to recruit French and Indians so that an attack on Annapolis could proceed. But before they could leave Halifax, approximately three thousand men died of a pestilence. Finally, the fleet's new commander, La Jonquiere, set sail on 13 October 1746, intending to attack Annapolis. He was probably unaware of the fact that on 6 October, the New England colonies had set 16 October as a day of fasting and prayer for their deliverance.

Rev. French described the events that followed: "On this great emergency, and day of darkness and doubtful expectation, the 16th of October was observed as a DAY OF FASTING AND PRAYER throughout the Province. And, wonderful to relate, that very night God sent upon them a more dreadful storm than either of the former, and completed their destruction. Some overset, some foundered, and a remnant only of this miserable fleet returned to France to carry the news. Thus NEW ENGLAND STOOD STILL, AND SAW THE SALVATION OF GOD."[22] (cf., Exodus 14:13)

BIBLICAL ROOTS OF LIBERTY

Returning to our discussion of the foundations of liberty from 1517 to 1776, let us briefly survey the elements discussed to this point. First, we explained that the roots of America's admittedly fine institutions did not lie in the humanistic revival of the Renaissance or the Enlightenment or in pagan antiquity. Instead we saw that the foundations of our institutions were laid in biblical principles and a biblically trained and uniquely prepared people. We saw that the doctrines of the great reformers had a liberating effect on individuals and upon civil liberty, free enterprise, and morality wherever the Bible was individually read and obeyed. The suffering of persecuted Christians who dared to resist tyranny was detailed. We showed how the Huguenot, Dutch, Scottish, and English experience prepared the way for Americans, and their descendants, to build a new nation against all odds.

We observed the providence of God in the settling of early America and in the development of a biblically based covenantal-compact theory of government, and we gave illustrations of God's providence that attended the founding era.

Now, as we analyze the eighteenth century, we will see a Christianity that has become complacent.

THE GREAT AWAKENING

As the eighteenth century dawned, the grandchildren of our forefathers had grown cold toward God. England, too, had lost the fire of the Reformation and wallowed in greed, immorality, and stock speculations. In 1720, a great stock crash ushered in an empire-wide depression that devastated the English colonies in America as well.

In 1741, nine-tenths of the world's population was groveling to subsist on the land, in sweatshops, or as slaves. The world's standard of living and life expectancy had not changed much in four thousand years. Half of all children died within a few months of birth.

Medicine was an undeveloped science, a far-fetched, fantastic affair of animal remedies. In Europe especially, few could read; and witchcraft and superstition ruled life, seasons, and the ever-present reality of death. Politically, the idea that government exists for the good of the people was a rare and novel heresy. Even in the colonies, where the wellspring of republican government had been planted with Pilgrim blood, most colonists had left the faith of their forefathers. Most New Englanders were more concerned with fighting Indians and increasing their land holdings than they were with building God's kingdom.

But in the summer of 1741, new conversation began to fill the taverns of the Connecticut Valley with a mighty wind of change. The God of history was moving among His people. George Whitefield, the famous preacher, had just swept across the country the preceding autumn. Suddenly, churches were filled, not just with bodies, but with hungry souls.

On 8 July 1741, in the little village of Enfield, a group of ministers and many curiosity seekers from all over Connecticut were descending upon the church of Jonathan Edwards for his afternoon lecture. Edwards, over six feet tall with a high forehead and long narrow face, ascended the pulpit with his customary white wig and black gown. He began with a text from Deuteronomy: "Their foot shall slide in due time…"

Going directly to the point, Mr. Edwards made hot application to his audience, knowing that many of his own congregation were lost:

> You have nothing to stand upon, nor anything to take hold of; there is nothing between you and hell but the air…. The God that holds you over the pit of hell, much as one holds a spider, or some loathsome insect over the fire, is dreadfully provoked; you are ten thousand times more abominable in his eyes than the most hateful venomous serpent is in ours…this is the dismal case of every soul in this congregation now hearing this discourse, that has not been born again…. And it would be no wonder if some persons, that now sit here in some seat in this meeting house, in health, quiet and secure, should be there before tomorrow's morning.[23]

Like a forest smitten by a hurricane, many in the congregation fell to their knees and on their faces, crying out to God. The ministers descended from the stage and began to console the repentant.

The Great Awakening, which laid the moral foundation for the War of Independence, began in that little village. It turned the world upside down for forty years, and its impact still shapes us today. The above sermon, titled "Sinners in the Hands of an Angry God", has become the best-known religious oration in our history.

The Great Awakening was no short-term tent revival. It swept from Massachusetts to Georgia over a thirty-year period. Hundreds of young ministers, such as William Tennant and Samuel Davies, began to proclaim the Gospel. But George Whitefield, an English evangelist, brought the colonies together under the banner of Jesus Christ like no other could. He preached over 18,000 sermons in America from 1737 to 1770, to crowds of up to 20,000 people.

JONATHAN EDWARDS
Born: October 5, 1703
Died: March 22, 1758

Claim to fame:

A leader of the Great Awakening and author of the sermon, later published, "Sinners in the Hands of an Angry God."

Did you know?

Because he was unbending in a controversy over tests for church membership, his congregation in Northampton dismissed him in 1750.

There is no doubt that the pastors in the colonies in the eighteenth century were the most powerful intellectual and political, as well as spiritual, influence on the lives of the people. Attorney John Whitehead explained:

> In colonial America. . .the sermon delivered by the local minister was the basic, and many times only, form of communication for the colonists.[24]

"The New England Sermon," wrote Yale professor and historian Harry S. Stout, "had a topical range and social influence. . .so powerful in shaping cultural values, meanings and a sense of corporate purpose that even television pales by comparison." Stout continued to say, "The average weekly churchgoer in New England [and there were far more churchgoers than church members] listened to something like seven thousand sermons in a lifetime, totaling somewhere around fifteen thousand hours of concentrated listening."[25]

Imagine being immersed in the intelligent exposition of God's power and plan for every area of personal and national life. Just think: Instead of an establishment media interpreting life and events for them, they had George Whitefield, Jonathan Edwards, and hundreds of other men of the Word explaining God's providential hand in political, social, and religious issues of their day. Carl Bridenbaugh explained that on the eve of the Revolutionary War, "who can deny that the very core of existence was their relation to God?" This reality was chiefly due to the "Black Regiment," as the New England clergy were called because of their black robes. Not just in the north, but throughout the colonies, pastors from different denominations were steeped in a deep sense of history and a knowledge of the great treatises on the biblical rights of resistance from the Reformation. They reinforced the call for liberty that came from Puritan patriots like Samuel Adams. In 1774, Adams's Committees of Correspondence warned the colonists:

> If England can do this [the blockade] to Boston, she can do this to any of us. George III has become a tyrant. We have no King...no King but King Jesus.[26]

By the spring of 1775, the central issue of the sovereignty of God over the sovereignty of the king had reached the final impasse. On 20 March of that year, Christian patriot Patrick Henry laid down the gauntlet before the Virginia assembly in Richmond:

> Three millions of people, armed in the holy cause of liberty...are invincible.... We shall not fight alone. A just God presides over the destinies of nations.... Is life so dear, or peace so sweet, as to be purchased at the price of chains and slavery? Forbid it, Almighty God!— I know not what course other may take; but as for me, give me liberty or give me death.[27]

LEXINGTON AND CONCORD

On 18 April 1775, General Gage, the military governor sent out from England to subdue the rebellious colony of Massachusetts, secretly planned a raid on the patriots' ammunition stores at Concord. He also

PATRICK HENRY
Born: *May 29, 1736*
Died: *June 6, 1799*

Claim to fame:
Fiery, patriotic orator and four-time governor of Virginia.

Did you know?
He said, "Give me liberty, or give me death!"

hoped to arrest Samuel Adams and John Hancock, who were rumored to be in nearby Lexington. Providentially, patriot Dr. Joseph Warren got wind of the plot and sent Paul Revere, Samuel Prescott, and William Dawes through the countryside that night sounding the alarm. Revere arrived at the home of Rev. Jonas Clark, where Adams and Hancock were staying, just in time to warn them to make their escape.

Rev. Clark was one of New England's great patriot pastors. For years, he had been preaching on the basic biblical principles undergirding righteous government: that the people's rights to their life, liberty, and property came from God; that the people had the right to form their governments by sacred covenant before God. Many of the public documents that express the dissatisfaction of Lexingtonians with their English king were written by his hand.

On 19 April 1775, the British detachment of soldiers arrived at Lexington Green to find the town's militia assembled and ready to defend their community. The British officer ordered the militia to disperse. According to Rev. Clark, who saw all that happened that day from his church on the Green, the British began to fire on the militia even as it was dispersing. Only then did the men of Lexington return the enemy's fire. Eight of the colonists were killed.

This conduct is in character with their pastor's teaching that only a defensive war could be just. The Battle of Lexington, brief as it was, gave the patriots at Concord the time they needed to collect their arms and ammunition and hide them carefully, as well as to muster their militia. These arms were their property, obtained to ensure their means of defense and not for the taking by the British for use against them. They would die first! Here, too, at Concord, patriots were not the first to fire. Historian Richard Frothingham related that the British posted a guard of one hundred men at the Old North Bridge.

About ten o'clock, as a body of militia were approaching this bridge, the guard fired upon them, when more citizens were killed and wounded.

The minutemen defended themselves well. They forced the British into a disorderly retreat. By the time the British reached Charlestown, they were on the run and only narrowly missed being defeated by seven hundred militia bearing down on them just as they reached the shelter of the British fleet. On that day, the British lost 273 men, the American militia, 93. If the Lexington farmers had not made their stand—thus buying time for Concord—and if Revere had not reached Hancock and Adams in time to warn them, many more American lives might have been lost; in short, if Providence had not intervened several times, the day would have been a total disaster for the Americans.

One thing the people of Lexington probably did not realize was that on that very day, the colony of Connecticut held a day of prayer and fasting for all the colonies. When Governor Trumbull proclaimed 19 April 1775 as the date, he little dreamed what momentous events would be taking place at Lexington. His proclamation asked:

> ...that God would graciously pour out His Holy Spirit on us to bring us to a thorough Repentance and effectual Reformation that our iniquities may not be our ruin: that He would restore, preserve and secure the Liberties of this and all the other British American colonies, and

SAMUEL ADAMS
Born: 1722
Died: 1803

Claim to fame:
Leader in agitation that led to the Boston Tea Party (1773).

Did you know?
He was the second cousin of John Adams, who would become the second president of the United States.

PAUL REVERE
Born: January 1, 1735
Died: May 10, 1818

Claim to fame:
He made the famous midnight ride of April 1775 through parts of Massachusetts warning of the approach of British troops.

Did you know?
Revere designed and engraved the first official seal of the thirteen colonies, as well as the Massachusetts state seal.

make the Land a mountain of Holiness, and Habitation of Righteousness forever.[28]

God answered this prayer, and a nation was born.

CD-ROM ANALYSES

Elementary U.S. History

Becoming a Nation engagingly portrays the events that led to America's founding and early development. It also gives insight to family life during the colonial era. The CD-ROM, however, does not give emphasis to the religious basis for the colonists' resistance to English tyranny, nor the religious principles upon which our nation was built.

The widening panorama of American history is the well-documented subject of *Expanding Our Nation.* Families may benefit from a discussion of how frontier families managed to overcome the difficulties of isolation and privation that were an inescapable part of their daily lives. A distinction, however, must be made between orthodox Christianity and the Mormon religion. As this distinction is not made clearly in the presentation, parents should be aware of this historical reference and explain these differences to students.

Prentice Hall

The computer-skilled student will spend hours exploring the features of *Discovering American History.* This CD-ROM allows the student to delve beyond the immediate text to learn about whatever interests him or her, demonstrating the flexibility of multimedia and the comparative rigidity of standard texts. Furthermore, it is unique among history texts in that it acknowledges the basic importance of Christianity in the development of the United States as a nation. Look for chances to coordinate the *Christian Home Learning Guides* chapters on American history with this excellent, highly interactive CD-ROM.

REVIEW QUESTIONS

1. Give four reasons why the Pilgrims came to America.

2. Which successful English settlement came before the Pilgrims?

3. Describe the settlers who arrived in 1628 and 1630 to settle just north of the Pilgrims.

4. What event inspired the Pilgrims to declare a day of thanksgiving?

5. Who was the man who led the development of the Connecticut Constitution in 1639?

6. What great spiritual event of the 1740s laid the foundation for the War of Independence?

7. Who were the people called the "Black Regiment" by the British during the War of Independence?

8. Where and when was the first battle of the War of Independence fought?

RELATED SCRIPTURE

Exodus 14:13
Deuteronomy 7:9
Deuteronomy 8
Psalm 77:11–12
Psalm 119:89–96
Amos Ch. 4
Luke 4:18–19

Romans Chs. 1–8
Ephesians Ch. 1
1 Timothy 6:15
Hebrews Ch. 12
2 Peter 3:2
Revelation 1:5

SUGGESTED READING

Mark A. Belilies and Stephen K. McDowell, *America's Providential History* (Charlottesville, VA: Providence Foundation, 1992).

William Bradford, *Of Plymouth Plantation 1620–1647* (New York: Modern Library, 1981).

Charles C. Coffin, *Sweet Land of Liberty* (Gainesville, FL: Maranatha).

Marshall Foster and Mary-Elaine Swanson, *The American Covenant.* (Thousand Oaks, CA: Mayflower Institute, 1992).

Peter Marshall and David Manuel, *The Light and the Glory for Children* (Grand Rapids, MI: Revell, 1992).

———. *The Light and the Glory.* (Grand Rapids, MI: Revell, 1992).

———. *From Sea to Shining Sea.* (Grand Rapids, MI: Revell).

Material covered in the Birth of a Nation chapter can be found in the following Zane Publishing Home Library titles:

Elementary U.S. History: Exploring and Colonizing
Elementary U.S. History: Becoming a Nation
Elementary U.S. History: Expanding Our Nation
Elementary U.S. History: Staying One Nation
U.S. History: U.S. Foreign Policy (1788–1933)
U.S. History: U.S. Foreign Policy (1933-1963)
U.S. History: U.S. Government (1783–1865)
U.S. History: U.S. Government (1866–1977)
World History: European History: The French Revolution
Prentice Hall: Discovering American History
American Literature: A Literary History: Common Sense—The Last of the
    Mohicans
History through Art: Native American and Colonial Art

ACT FIVE:
THE BIRTH OF A NATION

He who shall introduce into public affairs the principles of primitive Christianity will change the face of the world.

          —BENJAMIN FRANKLIN

ALL OF THE PATRIOTS KNEW that a great cosmic drama was unfolding on the American shores. But none had a greater sense of America's destiny in God's plan than George Washington. On 29 August 1788, Washington wrote:

> A greater drama is now being acted on this theatre than has heretofore been brought on the American stage, or any other in the World.[1]

The American War of Independence gave birth to a great nation with the capstone of an unprecedented constitution. But with the major revisionism that has dominated historical academia during the last eighty years, the legitimate foundations of our republic have been obscured.

The reasons for this are obvious. Modern humanists, the major force in today's cultural centers, do not want to admit that biblical Christianity was the central intellectual and inspirational source for the founding of our republic. They would much rather tie the revolution to the French PHILOSOPHES of the eighteenth century and to the ANARCHISTIC, anti-Christian French Revolution of 1789.

We mention this historical distortion because it has had a culturally detrimental effect upon many present-day believers, who find themselves apologizing for America's past. Many Christians, having been taught that our founders were intellectually drunk with the philosophy of the Enlightenment, have unknowingly given away part of the great history of God's liberating power for nations as well as individuals. As Christian families, we must be aware of the major distinctions between the American Revolution (1776) and the French Revolution (1789) because the last two centuries have been an ongoing battle between the two philosophies that spawned these two events.

THE AMERICAN REVOLUTION VS. THE FRENCH REVOLUTION

We documented in the last chapter that the colonial pastors laid the biblical foundations for limited, constitutional, representative government. We also saw how they echoed the biblical reasoning of their persecuted European forebears during the Reformation concerning the foundations of resistance against tyranny. We saw that it was Christian people, not humanistic Enlightenment thinkers, who laid their lives down

See the appendix for
The Declaration of Independence
*The Fundamental Orders
    of Connecticut*
The Northwest Ordinance of 1787
The Rights of the Colonists
The U.S. Constitution
Washington's Farewell Address

for spiritual and civil liberty by the tens of thousands in Germany, Scotland, Holland, France, and England.

There are five major differences between the two revolutions that must be understood. First, the American Revolution was grounded in the biblical foundations of limited, constitutional, representative government that had been taught for 150 years by colonial pastors. The French Revolution, on the other hand, followed illegal and purely rebellious ideals built on the false philosophy of Rousseau and his innocent savage, and the atheism and anarchy of Voltaire.

Secondly, the American Revolution was defensive, fought to defend the patriots' wives, children, and property against the tyranny of George III, who was himself the rebel against the laws of England. The French Revolution was offensive and brutal from the beginning. Tens of thousands of French citizens—the king, royalty, clergy, and commoners—lost their heads to the guillotine in a rebellion against all authority.

Thirdly, the American war had fixed, limited objectives, and was fought against invaders. The French war was bound only by the arbitrary will of the conspirators, who eliminated the changing list of people and groups who tried to stop them.

Fourthly, the American Revolution, because it appealed to a much more Christian populace and used legal means, found limited resistance among the people. The French Revolution, on the other hand, could not bring voluntary union to the people, and had to force its way through brutality and intimidation, just like all modern, unbiblical revolts.

A fifth major difference between the American and French experience was that the French revolutionaries were anti-church and anti-God. They pillaged thousands of churches and killed hundreds of clergy. The American experience was the opposite. The churches supported the war effort and were only destroyed when the British seized a town.

THE CHRISTIAN RIGHTS OF RESISTANCE

Eighteenth-century Christians in America were much more biblically literate than their twentieth-century counterparts. They reluctantly declared their independence, as stated in the Declaration of Independence, after decades of biblical sermons, prayer, constitutional debate, redress of grievances, and endurance of hardship. The 98 percent Protestant population rested upon hundreds of years of biblical legal theory as they made their decision. Law professor Gary Amos said:

> Jefferson's Declaration was a masterpiece of law, government, and rights. He tied together with few words hundreds of years of English political theory. The long shadows of the Magna Carta, the common law, Catholic and Calvinist resistance theories, the English Bill of Rights, and the Petition of Right are cast within its lines.[2]

The three major Christian resistance documents of the Reformation were the *Vindiciae*, written by Brutus in 1574 (French Huguenots), Samuel Rutherford's *Lex Rex*, written in 1638 (Scottish Covenantors), and the Declaration of Independence, written in 1776 (American patriots).

The six principles that follow summarize the biblical reasoning of all these documents; they explain why believers have a right to stand against tyranny, and how they must do so in an orderly and biblical manner. These principles are ingrained in our form of government in the Declaration of Independence, and are still needed today to check the very real threat of renewed pagan tyranny.

First, the reformers agreed that all rulers or civil magistrates are bound by the law of God and by God's specific limitations and purposes for civil government (Psalm 2, Romans 13:1–4). If a government representative commits a crime he must be punished like all other citizens. Scripture gives the people assembled (or represented) the right to punish evil (Genesis 4). Once the principle of equality before the law is lost, all accountability for leaders is gone. Note that the Declaration of Independence says: "We hold these truths to be self-evident, that all men are created equal, that they are endowed, by their Creator with certain unalienable rights, that among these are life, liberty, and the pursuit of happiness."

Secondly, all political leaders are in covenant with God and with the people. This is called the compact theory of government, which comes straight from the Bible (2 Samuel 5:1–3). This principle is totally antithetical to all pagan or classical governmental philosophy. This theory is not open-ended but conditional. Just like all of God's other created institutions, our civil leadership is in a relationship with limits and is bound to serve the people and God. For example, a father cannot abuse his children or his wife and expect to avoid being withdrawn from the home. A church elder can be removed from leadership in the church through church discipline if he breaks his agreements with the people. In like manner, a ruler or government that breaks fundamental promises to the people and God through a material breach of contract can be forcibly removed. Note that the Declaration of Independence says: "That to secure these rights, Governments are instituted among Men, deriving their just powers from the consent of the governed."

Thirdly, one act of tyranny is not enough to overthrow a ruler. There must be protracted DESPOTIC acts and wicked rule before a leader is deposed. Patience, forbearance, suffering under the yoke, and honoring the king are all character traits of godly reformers, and all are commanded in Scripture (Romans 13, I Peter 2:13). Every peaceful means of redressing grievances must be exhausted before defensive physical resistance is begun. Note that the Declaration of Independence says: "Prudence, indeed, will dictate, that Governments long established should not be changed for light and transient causes; and accordingly all experience hath shewn, that mankind are more disposed to suffer, while evils are sufferable, than to right themselves by abolishing the forms to which they are accustomed."

Fourthly, the people must never act as individuals or a mob venting personal vengeance against their government. The French

Revolution of 1789 was a rebellion of mobs and unbelievers overthrowing all authority in the government, church, and family. Almost all of our founders roundly condemned this rebellion and the anarchistic enlightenment philosophy that spawned it. God is a God of order and law, not of theft and murder in the name of DEMOCRACY. Note that the Declaration of Independence says: "But when a long train of abuses and usurpations, pursuing invariably the same object, evinces a design to reduce them under absolute despotism, it is their right, it is their duty, to throw off such government, and to provide new guards for their future security."

Fifthly, the ruler (government, or president) can be replaced if he becomes a tyrant who is bent on ruining the people. But the people must act through representatives, or lower magistrates, who are willing to interpose themselves between the tyrant or tyrannical laws and the people. This is called the doctrine of interposition. The Declaration of Independence was a classic example of interposition in action: each of the signers knew that their lives were on the line for the people. Note that the Declaration of Independence says: "The history of the present King of Great Britain is a history of repeated injuries and usurpations, all having in direct object the establishment of an absolute Tyranny over these States."

A final principle of resistance is that a formal public declaration must be proclaimed detailing the ruler's offenses. The Declaration of Independence named thirty-three specific offenses of King George III. Only when there is no option but to "Conquer or Die" (as George Washington told his troops) can we justify forcibly deposing a tyrannical civil magistrate or king. Note that the entire Declaration of Independence is a formal declaration of biblical resistance. It closes with these words: "And for the support of this Declaration, with a firm reliance on the protection of divine Providence, we mutually pledge to each other our Lives, our Fortunes, and our sacred Honor."

John Quincy Adams, our sixth president and the son of our second president, John Adams, said:

> Why is it that next to the birthday of the Savior of the World your most joyous and most venerated festival returns on this day? Is it not that in the chain of human events, the birthday of the nation is indissolubly linked with the birthday of the Savior?.... That it laid the cornerstone of human government upon the first precepts of Christianity...[3]

He knew what the Old World humanists of Europe knew—that American independence as defined in the Declaration of Independence was a conservative, Christian counterrevolution, one linked "indissolubly" with our Savior and one that is dependent upon His divine providence for its application.

There is a growing need for renewed study of this fundamental charter, or covenant, of our nation. The Zane CD-ROM curriculum has wisely included the Declaration of Independence and the U.S. Constitution on

JOHN QUINCY ADAMS
Born: July 11, 1767
Died: February 23, 1848

Claim to fame:
Sixth president of the United States.

Did you know?
He was the only president to serve in Congress following his presidency.

its CD-ROMs. We recommend that the student read the Declaration of Independence at this time.

The central importance of the Declaration of Independence in our governmental structure must be reinstated in our day. The detailed framework of the Constitution has little or no meaning without it.

Political scientist Daniel J. Elazar, director of the Center for the Study of Federalism, Temple University, Philadelphia, and associated with Bar Ilan University, Israel, wrote that:

> Just as the heart of the covenant of ancient Israel consists of two parts, the Decalogue or Ten Commandments with its electrifying statement of fundamental principles and the Book of the Covenant with its more detailed framework of the basic laws of the Israelite Commonwealth, so too does that of the American covenant consist of two basic documents serving the same—the Declaration of Independence and the Constitution.[4]

DIVINE PROVIDENCE
IN THE REVOLUTIONARY WAR

To understand how a group of independently minded colonies could come together and defeat the most powerful empire in the world in an eight-year war (1775–1783), we must shift our focus from Philadelphia to New York. At the same time that the Continental Congress was signing the Declaration of Independence on 2 July 1776, General Howe was landing thousands of troops in New York, preparing to make quick work of George Washington's army.

On 27 August 1776, Washington and his army of fourteen thousand men were attacked and surrounded on Long Island by General William Howe and his thirty thousand British and German troops. All seemed lost for the patriot cause. General Howe could have finished the annihilation of the patriot army that day. Instead, he stopped to eat cake and drink wine at 3 p.m., putting off the final assault until morning. Washington, in the meantime, began a desperate, bold strategy. He collected rowboats and sloops from the fishermen of Gloucester and Marblehead and set out to evacuate his troops by night. Surely some of the one hundred or so British ships anchored in New York Bay would have seen thousands of men crossing in front of them. But, as historian John Fiske wrote: "The Americans had been remarkably favored by the sudden rise of a fog which covered the East River. . . . "[5] The Americans miraculously escaped annihilation. Mark the first meeting of the man of faith and the man of the flesh.

In the coming months, like the children of Israel running before the horses of Pharaoh, America's mostly untrained, volunteer army was to be tested by fire. Washington's men escaped north along the Hudson River and were often without food or provisions. A smallpox epidemic decimated the army. "The small pox. . .had been so long kept from their doors, that there was scarce a man among them, who was not more afraid of an attack from this kind of pestilence, than the fury of the sword: but no caution could prevent the rapidity of the contagion; it pervaded the whole army; and proved fatal to most of the new raised troops."[6]

On 6 October, Howe went on a full offensive again. He sailed up the

Hudson, taking out the key fort of Washington, where 2,800 Americans surrendered. The colonists were stripped and force-marched back to New York to be imprisoned in old ships like the *Jersey*. They were left there to starve or die of smallpox or exposure. Only a few hundred survived the ordeal. The saga of British cruelty was gaining momentum.

The British marched into New Jersey and appeared ready to devour Philadelphia. The Congress left and took up residence in Baltimore. The British had 33,000 soldiers, 12 ships of the line, 22 frigates, and hundreds of transport ships. The Americans by late autumn had only 3,100 men-at - arms remaining—1,500 of whom were leaving the army on 31 December because their enlistments were up—and no ships.

CHARACTER COUNTS

At this point we see the interposing hand of Providence. All Howe had to do was send Cornwallis and his army across the Delaware River in December, force Washington to fight, and the war would have been over. But his character betrayed him.

Howe liked his mistress, wine, and the good life back in New York. He encouraged his troops by his own words and deeds to rape, and to pillage and burn the villages taken on the Jersey campaign. He settled in for the winter with his troops thinly dispersed.

Mercy Otis Warren, historian of the Revolution wrote:

> . . .every favorable impression was erased, and every idea of submission annihilated, by the indiscriminate ravages of the Hessian and British soldiery in their route through the Jersies. The elegant houses of some of their own most devoted partisans were burnt: their wives and daughters pursued and ravished in the woods to which they had fled for shelter. Many unfortunate fathers, in the stupor of grief, beheld the misery of their female connections, without being able to relieve them, and heard the shrieks of infant innocence, subjected to the brutal lust of British grenadiers, or Hessian Yaughers.[7]

Pagan barbarity became the byword of the British and German soldiers. In a book of general orders belonging to Colonel Rhal, found after the action at Trenton, it was recorded that:

> His excellency the commander in chief orders, that all Americans found in arms, not having an officer with them, shall be immediately hanged.[8]

To compound their sin, the British were paying the German soldiers by the head for the number of Americans killed. By taking these actions, they not only broke the code of conduct written by England herself, but they united an entire nation against them.

While he plundered the colonists, General Howe obviously did not heed the biblical admonition:

> Do not lie in wait, O wicked man, against the dwelling of the righteous; do not plunder his resting place. For a righteous man may fall seven times and rise again, but the wicked shall fall by calamity.[9]

CHRISTMAS DAY: SNOW, HAIL, AND VICTORY

By Christmas Eve, Washington had few options. Like the righteous of Proverbs 24, his troops had fallen at least seven times in the fall of 1776. He was about to lose one half of the small army that shivered with him on the west bank of the Delaware because their enlistments were up in a few days. Most of his men and the majority of colonists still had resolve, but they had lost hope that England could ever be defeated.

Washington decided on one final offensive. He had his beleaguered troops ferried across the half-frozen Delaware on Christmas night. Just before they boarded the boats, Washington had *The American Crisis*, by Thomas Paine, the now-famous pamphleteer (and author of *Common Sense*), read to his men:

> These are the times that try men's souls: The summer soldier and the sunshine patriot will, in this crisis, shrink from the service of his country; but he that stands it now, deserves the love and thanks of man and woman. Tyranny, like hell, is not easily conquered; yet we have this consolation with us, that the harder the conflict, the more glorious the triumph. What we obtain too cheap, we esteem too lightly: 'Tis dearness only that gives everything its value. Heaven knows how to set proper price upon its goods; and it would be strange indeed, if so celestial an article as freedom should not be highly rated. Britain, with an army to enforce her tyranny, has declared that she has a right [not only to tax, but] 'to bind us in all cases whatsoever,' and if being bound in that manner is not slavery, then is there not such a thing as slavery upon earth. Even the expression is impious, for so unlimited a power can belong only to God.

Washington landed near Trenton in a blinding snow and hailstorm that served as a cover for his crossing and approach. His men surprised a detachment of twelve hundred HESSIANS. Colonel Rhal and his men had been partying and drinking with a pompous, false sense of security late into the night. When Washington attacked in early morning, almost all were captured and Rhal was mortally wounded. Before 8 a.m., Washington had re-crossed the river with more than one thousand prisoners, and only five casualties of his own. As was his custom, he did not mistreat his prisoners.

He immediately crossed the river again, avoiding the massive British counterattack, and surprised the British at Princeton. He won another victory, riding his horse between the lines and miraculously remaining unscathed as both armies volleyed. His troops rallied for a final charge and won.

These victories changed the course of history. His men re-enlisted, France began to support the cause, and hope in the providence of God reinvigorated the colonists.

MADE STRONG IN WEAKNESS

The years that followed were hard for the patriot cause: Washington's army had little support from the colonial governments, had few supplies, and faced some of the finest soldiers in the world.

THOMAS PAINE
Born: January 29, 1737
Died: June 8, 1809

Claim to fame:
Wrote the revolutionary pamphlets Common Sense *and* The American Crisis.

Did you know?
He was imprisoned in France for a year during the Reign of Terror, at which time he wrote his famous deistic, antibiblical work The Age of Reason, *which alienated many people. On his deathbed, he recanted all his attacks on Christianity.*

But God's providence continually sustained them. A great victory was won on 17 October 1777, when British General Burgoyne and six thousand of his troops surrendered at Saratoga. Providentially, the orders for General Howe to come to Burgoyne's aid had never been signed by Lord Worth, who had in haste taken leave for a vacation. The result of this stunning victory was that the French entered the war to help win American liberty.

In the winter of 1777–78, the Continental army had to make quarters in a frozen valley outside of Philadelphia called Valley Forge. Thousands were dying of disease and cold, while others were deserting. General Washington, as was his frequent practice, would retreat into the woods for private devotion and prayer.

Washington was staying at the home of Isaac Potts, who was a Quaker and a Tory (against the patriot cause). Mr. Potts was converted to see God's hand upon this new nation when he found the general praying in the woods behind his home. The Quaker returned after this encounter and told his wife why he believed God was for the patriot cause. He said:

> I have this day seen what I never expected. Thee knows that I always thought that the sword and the gospel were utterly inconsistent; and that no man could be a soldier and a Christian at the same time. But George Washington has this day convinced me of my mistake. If George Washington be not a man of God, I am greatly deceived, and still more shall I be deceived if God does not, through him, work out a great salvation for America.[10]

The Americans came out of Valley Forge a renewed fighting force. They soon effected a stalemate in the north, and the British, hoping to break the colonial unity of the new nation, moved south, where many British loyalists lived. But here they met their final Waterloo after several more frustrating defeats at the hands of providence.

Real world-changers are not defeated by circumstances, but overcome them. Our patriot forefathers were such men and their example can be a great lesson for us on the way of success—even in the worst of times.

On 1 January 1781, things looked bleak for the patriot cause. The Pennsylvania line troops had revolted over short enlistments and lack of pay: The Continental paper money had collapsed and was "not worth a Continental." The army had to live off the land and barter for its needs. Washington, who took no salary for his efforts, did not even have sufficient funds to entertain foreign dignitaries when soliciting their help. This war with one of the great world powers had gone on for a full six years, and at the beginning of 1781, it was the worst of times.

But events, directed by providence, would bring the American cause from defeat to victory at Yorktown, Virginia, on 19 October 1781.

On 17 January 1781, the Americans, led by Daniel Morgan, defeated Colonel Tarleton's entire detachment at the battle of Cowpens. Lord Cornwallis, leading the large British army in the south, was infuriated by this defeat. Destroying his heavy baggage, he headed for the Catawba River to cut off the retreat of the small American army.

Cornwallis reached the Catawba River just two hours after General Morgan had crossed. Confident of victory, the British general decided to wait

LORD CORNWALLIS
Born: *December 31, 1738*
Died: *October 5, 1805*

Claim to fame:
Surrendered to Washington at Yorktown (1781), the last important campaign of the American Revolution.

Did you know?
He brought about a series of legal and administrative reforms, called the Cornwallis Code, in British India.

until morning to cross. But during the night a storm filled the river, detaining his troops. Twice more in the next ten days Cornwallis nearly overtook the American army. On 3 February, he reached the Yadkin River in North Carolina, just as the Americans were landing on the eastern banks. But, before he could cross, a sudden flood cut off the British troops again! On the thirteenth, the Americans reached the Dan River that would lead them into friendly Virginia territory. They crossed, and a few hours later, when Cornwallis arrived, rising waters once again prevented him from reaching the American army. Even Sir Henry Clinton, the commander-in-chief of British forces in North America and Lord Cornwallis's superior, acknowledged that Divine Providence had intervened. He wrote:

> ...here the royal army was again stopped by a sudden rise of the waters, which had only just fallen (almost miraculously) to let the enemy over, who could not else have eluded Lord Cornwallis' grasp, so close was he upon their rear.[11]

The significance of the battle of Cowpens and the safe retreat of the patriots that followed was that the small American army in the south was saved by God's providence so that it could harass General Cornwallis and drive him to the sea, which set the stage for the final defeat of the British at Yorktown in October 1781.

The above providential account is but one of many events that converged like parts of a well-laid cosmic plan to defeat the British. For example:

> If General Washington had not decided to leave New York and march to Yorktown when he did, Cornwallis would have been reinforced.

> If Robert Morris, the generous and capable merchant, had not used extraordinary means to raise money to pay Washington's troops, they would have gone home rather than to Yorktown.

> If France had not sent a fleet from the West Indies (unknown to Washington), which arrived just in time to defeat the British fleet sent to relieve General Cornwallis at Yorktown, Cornwallis could have escaped. In this sea battle, the French fleet, under Admiral De Grasse, soundly defeated the British, cutting off all sea routes.

> If a sudden tornado-like storm had not stopped General Cornwallis in his last-minute attempt to cross the York River and escape to New York on 16 October 1781, the war would have dragged on.

After the British surrender at Yorktown, General Washington acknowledged the many providential events of the war. He declared the day after the surrender to be a day of thanksgiving, and his troops were directed to attend religious services. On 15 November 1781, Washington wrote to the president of Congress:

> I take a particular pleasure in acknowledging that the interposing hand of Heaven, in the various instances of our extensive preparations for this operation, has been most conspicuous and remarkable.[12]

ROBERT MORRIS
Born: *January 31, 1734*
Died: *May 7, 1806*

Claim to fame:
Known as the financier of the American Revolution.

Did you know?
He raised the funds that made it possible for General George Washington to move his army from New York to Yorktown, where Lord Cornwallis was forced to surrender (1781).

After the American patriots had defeated the British and signed the Treaty of Paris on 3 September 1783, the daunting task of maintaining national unity loomed before them. The next six years were difficult. The fledgling country lived under the Articles of Confederation from 1781 to 1789. The weak confederation of states led to many problems. A postwar economic depression was compounded by the printing of a valueless Continental currency. In foreign affairs, the nation was in chaos as each state was setting different TARIFFS and negotiating separate treaties with foreign powers.

THE AMERICAN NAPOLEON?

In 1783, a group of George Washington's generals gathered at Washington's headquarters in Newburgh, New York, to force the government to pay their back wages and pensions. Some of those in attendance wanted more. They called for Washington to become the new king or dictator of the United States.

Washington heard of their meeting and walked in uninvited. He spoke kindly to the men, but rejected any elevation of himself as a military ruler. As he began to speak, he took out his glasses and put them on. "Gentlemen," he said, "you will permit me to put on my spectacles, for I have grown not only gray, but almost blind in the service of my country."[13]

Tears filled the eyes of the men as Washington called for them to be patient and to not forsake the ideals of liberty they had fought so hard to attain. Washington's Christian character once again surfaced. There would be no American Napoleon.

THE CONSTITUTION: DEISTIC OR CHRISTIAN?

The Convention that took place at Independence Hall in Philadelphia on 14 May 1787, would go on to produce a new constitution to replace the Articles of Confederation. In the room that summer were fifty-five delegates, the greatest assembly of political thinkers of the age. Over half of the men had fought in the war; they were not theorists only.

What were the fundamental principles that guided these great minds? Were the men themselves DEISTS, as many in our day teach, or were they orthodox Christians? Historian M. E. Bradford said of the fifty-five signers of the Constitution that all but three were

> orthodox members of one of the established Christian communions: approximately twenty-nine Anglicans, sixteen to eighteen Calvinists, two Methodists, two Lutherans, two Roman Catholics, one lapsed Quaker and sometime-Anglican, and one open Deist — Dr. Franklin, who attended every kind of Christian worship, called for public prayer, and contributed to all denominations.[14]

Not only was the vast majority of the delegates Christians, but the evidence is overwhelming that American political life was still under the influence of the Protestant Reformation. Most of the people still saw life and society through the eyes of their forebears.

John Calvin and Martin Luther in their century had reestablished the

Bible, not the state or the church, as the standard for all of life. Their battle cries were "Sola Scriptura" and "Restore the Crown rights of King Jesus." Faith in God's earthly as well as heavenly lordship led the Protestant reformers to stand against the tyranny of the "divine right" tyrants who claimed immunity from judgment or indictment because they were "sovereigns." When Calvin, Luther, and John Knox proclaimed the sovereignty of God, even over the king, entire nations rose up in a decade to challenge the political doctrines of tyrants who had suppressed the people of Europe for a millennium.

Leopold von Ranke, the famous German historian, said, "John Calvin is the virtual founder of America." George Bancroft, America's leading nineteenth-century historian, simply called Calvin "the father of America." The world's foremost Reformation scholar, Merle d'Aubigne, said:

> Calvin was the founder of the greatest republics. The Pilgrims who left their country in the reign of James I, and landing on the barren soil of New England, founded populous and mighty colonies, were his sons, his direct and legitimate sons: and that American nation which we have seen growing so rapidly boasts as its father the humble Reformer on the shore of Lake Leman.[15]

Calvin shaped our republic because he unleashed a biblical theology, a biblical world and life view, if you will, which unveiled man's nature as hopelessly sinful and redeemable only by God's sovereign grace. His teaching also emphasized that all men, including the king, were accountable to obey God. But all of Calvin's systematic theology, whether the priesthood of all believers or the covenantal nature of God's government, rested on the bedrock of God's sovereignty. Once God's church reestablished its faith in the one true Sovereign, the tyrants' days were numbered. Millions of saints died as forerunners of our liberty and constitution, as they rekindled their faith in the inevitability of the victory of their King Jesus.

Three million Dutchmen died rather than bend their knees to Philip of Spain and his heresy. More than a million Huguenots died rather than compromise their faith. Most of the godly ministers of Scotland died martyrs' deaths in the mid-seventeenth century, but their brave optimism was founded in their view of God. As the Scottish reformer James Guthrie cried just before being hung and beheaded, "The Covenants, the Covenants shall yet be Scotland's revival."

Rather than bow to their earthly sovereign, our Pilgrim fathers bowed their whole lives to their true Sovereign. William Bradford recorded their stand:

> They shook off this yoke of antichristian bondage, and as the Lord's free people, joined themselves by a covenant of the Lord into a church estate in the fellowship of the gospel, to walk in all His ways, made known unto them, according to their best endeavours, whatsoever it should cost them, the Lord assisting them.[16]

Each of the colonies that followed in the footsteps of the Jamestown settlement and the Pilgrims of New England established God as the ultimate Sovereign in each of their colonial charters. The Fundamental Orders of Connecticut of 1638, composed by Rev. Thomas Hooker, became the foundation for America's Constitution. The Orders began by acknowledging God's throne rights without hesitation: "For as much as it has pleased the Almighty God by the wise disposition of His divine providence so to order and dispose of things. . . ."

This emphasis upon God's sovereignty extended right up to the founders' generation. Dr. Loraine Boettner, a modern theologian, recorded that "about two-thirds of the colonial population had been trained in the school of Calvin." Bancroft recorded that in 1776, America was 98 percent Protestant and 66 percent Calvinist. Our Declaration of Independence, which is our covenant charter as a nation, ends with the covenantal seal to the parties involved (God and our people) stating, "With firm reliance upon divine Providence, we pledge our Lives, our Fortunes, and our sacred Honor."

THE CONVENTION

The Constitutional Convention began 25 May 1787. By June it was a hopelessly divided group, especially between the delegates of the smaller and larger states. Facing deadlock, Benjamin Franklin, not known for his orthodox Christian sentiments but always a friend of Christianity, rose to speak in this moment of crisis when the convention seemed doomed. Here is an excerpt from his powerful address:

> In the beginning of the Contest with G. Britain, when we were sensible of danger, we had daily prayer in this room for Divine protection. Our prayers, Sir, were heard, & they were graciously answered. All of us who were engaged in the struggle must have observed frequent instances of a superintending Providence in our favor.
>
> To that kind Providence we owe this happy opportunity of consulting in peace on the means of establishing our future national felicity. And have we now forgotten that powerful Friend? Or do we imagine we no longer need His assistance?
>
> I have lived, Sir, a long time, and the longer I live, the more convincing proofs I see of this truth—that God Governs in the affairs of men. And if a sparrow cannot fall to the ground without His notice, is it probable that an empire can rise without His assistance?[17]

Franklin's words and his call for prayer and religious services brought the delegates together. Soon afterward Roger Sherman, a dedicated Christian delegate from Connecticut, offered the Connecticut Compromise. His plan was adapted, which balanced the power between the small and the large states. The majority of the delegates went on to sign the Constitution. They adjourned on 17 September and began the real battle to have the states ratify the new government.

The Federalists (those for the Constitution) and the Anti-Federalists (those who opposed it) debated the merits of the Constitution. Many men, including George Mason and Patrick Henry, felt that the new national covenant would usurp too much power from the states. They demanded a Bill of Rights be added to further ensure that the people would not lose their fundamental rights. Even then they feared that men of lesser caliber than the founding generation would abuse the delegated powers and distort the Constitution. They were right to fear.

Although the Federalists prevailed, a Bill of Rights (the first ten amendments to the Constitution) were added as soon as the First Congress convened in 1789.

THREE CHRISTIAN PILLARS
OF THE CONSTITUTION

The Christian character of America's constitutional republic is not based upon the perfection of the founders or whether they were all sincere Christians. It is grounded in the biblically based structure of the U.S. Constitution and that of the Declaration of Independence.

I. The Principle of Representation

The principle of representation embodied in our Constitution was unique in history. It derived its inspiration from representative church governments, in which members chose representatives (elders) to lead the people, based upon their character (1 Timothy 3). The authors of the Constitution also saw the principle of representation in the history of Israel, as Moses was exhorted to choose representatives to localize the burden of leadership (Exodus 18:13–21).

The founders rejected the direct democracy and simplistic EGALITARI-ANISM of Jean-Jacques Rousseau, the French Revolution, and the Greek city-states. James Madison, our fourth president, warned of the dangers of democracy:

> Democracies have ever been spectacles of turbulence and contention; have ever been found incomparable with personal security or the rights of property; and have in general been as short in their lives as they have been violent in their deaths. Theoretic politicians, who have patronized this species of government, have erroneously supposed that by reducing mankind to a perfect equality in their political rights, they would at the same time be perfectly equalized and assimilated in their possessions, their opinions, and their passions.[18]

Our founders instead chose a constitutional republic, which is a nation of laws rather than of men, in which delegated power is invested in elected representatives. They shunned the idea of a democracy in which citizens exercise direct sovereignty in person or through voting on all matters of state.

Our founders also knew that representative government, a government of the people ruling through their representatives, would fail if the people themselves were not wise and virtuous. Samuel Adams, of the Massachusetts delegation, summarized the great determining factor concerning the success or failure of a republic:

> He therefore is the truest friend to the liberty of his country who tries most to promote its virtue, and who, so far as his power and influence extend, will not suffer a man to be chosen into any office of power and trust who is not a wise and virtuous man. . . . The sum of all is, if we would most truly enjoy this gift of Heaven, let us become a virtuous people. . .[19]

Adams and our other founders knew that only Christianity could provide the transformed people who would elect godly leaders who would maintain liberty.

JAMES MADISON
Born: *March 16, 1751*
Died: *June 28, 1836*

Claim to fame:
Fourth president of the United States; "The Father of the Constitution."

Did you know?
James Madison's wife, Dolley Madison, is still remembered for her great hospitality while First Lady.

II. Principle of the Separation of Powers

Because our founders firmly held to the doctrine of the sin nature of man, they knew, as Lord Acton succinctly stated, that "power corrupts and absolute power corrupts absolutely."[20] Thomas Jefferson said it well: "The functionaries of every government have propensities to command at will the liberty and property of their constituents."[21]

The framers of the Constitution knew that in all governments there are three sorts of power: legislative, executive, and judicial. God's model for this truth is seen in Isaiah 33:22: "For the Lord is our judge; the Lord is our lawgiver; the Lord is our King." The founders trusted God to carry out all three functions of government as He ruled the world by divine providence, but they separated the three powers as it related to man's role in government.

The Constitution is basically a legal framework of limited powers and negative prohibitions, which was designed to

1. keep the powers of government separate with specifically delineated powers;

2. provide a system of checks and balances so that one branch of government would not overstep its authority;

3. reserve all non-delegated authority for the states and for the people (the Tenth Amendment states that "the powers not delegated to the United States by the Constitution are reserved to the states respectively or to the people.").

The founders knew that this delicate system of limited jurisdiction and accountability would succeed only if the people themselves were self-governing according to God's law. James Madison wrote after the Constitution was completed:

> We have staked the whole future of American civilization, not upon the power of government, far from it. We have staked the future of all of our political institutions upon the capacity of mankind for self-government; upon the capacity of each and all of us to govern ourselves, to sustain ourselves according to the Ten Commandments of God.[22]

III. A Dual Form of Government

Throughout the ages, mankind had struggled with the problem of maintaining unity and yet allowing for individual liberty and diversity. The usual solution, even to this day, is a top-down tyranny. The other alternative, unlimited freedom of individuals, always deteriorates into anarchy and then tyranny again. The French Revolution is a good example of this: in their search for freedom, the people threw off the restraints of the Church and God's law. The result was the murderous beheading of thousands, followed by the despotism of Napoleon Bonaparte.

Historian John Fiske described our dual form of government, and accorded James Madison the credit for being the first

> to entertain distinctly the noble conception of two kinds of government operating at one and the same time upon the same individuals, harmonious with each other, but each supreme in its own sphere.[23]

In this unique form of government, the national government would have limited sovereignty in its sphere and the state governments would have the same limited sovereignty in their delegated spheres of authority. We will discuss in the next chapter how this delicate balance of unity and freedom has been destroyed and a unitary, all-powerful national government put in its place.

PASSING ON THE HOLY CAUSE OF LIBERTY

Every student of American history should have the privilege of knowing and understanding the peculiar providence that was experienced in this nation's birth. The divine sense of mission of which we speak was carried over here on the *Mayflower* in 1620. William Bradford recorded this prophetic faith 150 years before the nation was born. He said:

> Thus out of small beginnings greater things have been produced by His hand that made all things of nothing, and gives being to all things that are; and, as one small candle may light a thousand, so the light here kindled hath shone unto many, yea in some sort to our whole nation; let the glorious name of Jehovah have all the praise.[24]

Five generations later, George Washington, upon learning of the ratification of the Constitution, would share his deepest thoughts concerning the birth of the new nation with his friend, General Benjamin Lincoln, in a letter dated 30 June 1788:

> No Country upon Earth ever had it more in its power to attain these blessings.... Much to be regretted indeed would it be, were we to neglect the means and depart from the road which Providence has pointed us to, so plainly; I cannot believe it will ever come to pass. The Great Governor of the Universe has led us too long and too far...to forsake us in the midst of it.... We may, now and then, get bewildered; but I hope and trust that there is good sense and virtue enough left to recover the right path.[25]

CD-ROM ANALYSES

Elementary U.S. History

Staying One Nation is a successful retelling of the story of a very difficult period in America's history. It presents the concerns and motivations of all the involved parties. At certain points, however, the narration may induce a feeling of excessive regret for past wrongs in which today's students have no part. Encourage them that many of the injustices of this tragic era have been rectified, and that none is so great that God cannot effect His will in the situation.

Few historical periods make for such exciting narratives as the age of discovery. *Exploring and Colonizing* touches on some important events in Christian history that the student will find covered more thoroughly in the European Foundations of Liberty chapter and in the suggested reading. The religious influence in early American history is a broad subject discussed in the American Expression of Liberty chapter.

Prentice Hall

The computer-skilled student will spend hours exploring the features of *Discovering American History.* This CD-ROM allows the student to delve beyond the immediate text to learn about whatever interests him or her, demonstrating the flexibility of multimedia and the comparative rigidity of standard texts. Furthermore, it is unique among history texts in that it acknowledges the basic importance of Christianity in the development of the United States as a nation. Look for chances to coordinate the *Christian Home Learning Guides* chapters on American history with this excellent, highly interactive CD-ROM.

REVIEW QUESTIONS

1. To what other event do some people mistakenly link the American War of Independence?

2. Name the five areas of difference between the American and French Revolutions.

3. To what other event is the American War of Independence truly linked, according to John Quincy Adams?

4. What character trait of the British helped the colonists defeat them in the American Revolution?

5. Who has been called the "virtual founder of America"?

6. When the Constitutional Convention was divided, Benjamin Franklin helped to unify it by calling for what?

7. What was added to the Constitution to respond to the criticisms of Anti-Federalists?

8. To what does our constitutional republic owe its Christian nature?

9. What is the difference between a democracy and a representative government? Which does America have?

10. What are the three powers of government, and why did the framers of the Constitution divide them up among three branches?

RELATED SCRIPTURE

Exodus 18:13–21
Deuteronomy 8
1 Samuel 8
2 Samuel 5:1–3
Psalm 2

Proverbs 24:15–16
Romans 13:1–4
1 Timothy 3
1 Peter 2:13

SUGGESTED READING

Gary T. Amos, *Defending the Declaration* (Brentwood, TN: Wolgemuth, 1989).

David Barton, *Original Intent* (Aledo, TX: Wallbuilder, 1996).

Gary DeMar, *God and Government: A Biblical and Historical Study* (3 Vols.) (Atlanta, GA: American Vision, 1982).

John Eidsmoe, *Christianity and the Constitution* (Grand Rapids, MI: Baker, 1987).

M. Stanton Evans, *The Theme is Freedom* (Washington, D.C.: Regnery, 1994).

Alexander Hamilton, James Madison, and John Jay, *The Federalist Papers* (New York: A Mentor Book, 1961).

Charles H. Hyneman and Donald S. Lutz, *American Political Writing During the Founding Era: 1760–1805* (2 Vols.) (Indianapolis, IN: Liberty, 1983).

Ralph Ketcham, ed. *The Anti-Federalists Papers and the Constitutional Convention Debates* (New York: A Mentor Book, 1986).

Tim LaHaye, *Faith of Our Founding Fathers* (Brentwood, TN: Wolgemuth, 1987).

Ellis Sandoz, ed. *Political Sermons of the American Founding Era* (Indianapolis, IN: Liberty, 1990).

Otto J. Scott, *Robespierre: The Voice of Virtue* (New York: Mason, 1974).

John W. Whitehead, *An American Dream* (Westchester, IL: Crossway, 1987).

Material covered in the Christian History of Black America chapter can be found in the following Zane Publishing Home Library titles:

African American History: Leading Black Americans I
African American History: Leading Black Americans II
African American History: The Struggle for Freedom
African American History: The Struggle for Equal Rights
African American History: A Cultural Heritage
Elementary U.S. History: Staying One Nation
U.S. History: The Civil War—Two Views
U.S. History: Reconstruction
Prentice Hall: Discovering American History
American Literature: A Literary History: Little Women—The Call of the Wild
American Literature: A Literary History: The Jungle—The Grapes of Wrath

THE CHRISTIAN HISTORY OF BLACK AMERICA

As you are now free in body, so now seek to be free in soul and spirit, from sin and Satan. The noblest freeman is he whom Christ makes free.
—DANIEL PAYNE,
AFRICAN METHODIST EPISCOPAL BISHOP

LOOK AT THE MODERN BLACK community in America and you will find the Christian church at its center. Follow history back to the struggle for equal rights for black Americans and you will find the church there. It powered the ABOLITIONIST movement and kept hope alive in the slaves' barest shacks. The God of the Bible has ever been the refuge and the strength of African Americans.

Most of the African slaves brought to the Americas had no knowledge of the God of Christianity. They were taught the faith in America, despite the contradictory circumstances in which they learned it.

CHRIST AMONG SLAVES

We are all familiar with the words and sounds of black spirituals such as "Swing Low, Sweet Chariot," "Go Down, Moses," and "Were You There?" These songs remain from a time when men enslaved other men and traded them as property. They are the legacy of the hope black slaves first found in Christianity—of salvation, of freedom on earth, and of eternity. Faith and family were all the slaves had to cling to in the dark days of slavery, and as families were often separated, often only faith remained. Christianity strengthened the slaves' consciousness of injustice and their resolve to be free.

Slaves were, in many cases, kept from such verses as Galatians 3:28,

> There is neither Jew nor Greek, there is neither slave nor free, there is neither male nor female, for you are all one in Jesus Christ.

And Philemon 15–16,

> For perhaps he departed for a while for this purpose, that you might receive him forever, no longer as a slave but more than a slave, as a beloved brother, especially to me but how much more to you, both in the flesh and in the Lord.

Nevertheless, they could not be kept from the spirit of liberty that pervades the Gospel. It is clear that they knew well the story of the Israelites' slavery in Egypt and that they knew that God would emancipate those who followed him. This gave them strength to endure present suffering and a hope that they, too, might some day be free.

The home of this hope was the black church, which began to organize in the late eighteenth century with the founding of the first black Baptist

See the appendix for
The Emancipation Proclamation
Lincoln's Gettysburg Address
Lincoln's Second Inaugural Address

church by George Liele and David George. However, because of the fears many southerners had of slave revolts, the black church was often persecuted, or even prevented from meeting at all. Consequently, many meetings of black Christians were held in secret.

Liele, one of the early church leaders, was given his freedom in order to be able to preach freely. When his former owner's heirs tried unsuccessfully to re-enslave him, he left for Jamaica to avoid further conflict. Here, more than ten years before William Carey pioneered his mission to India and launched the worldwide missions movement, Liele became a missionary, finding even in tribulation an opportunity for Christian service.

Another church founder in Christian history is Richard Allen, who was a founder and the first bishop of the African Methodist Episcopal church. After struggling with the racial discrimination of white churches and denominations, he and leaders of three other northern black churches united to create the first lasting, independent black churches in America.

BLACK AMERICANS AND THE CONSTITUTION

White Christians in early America are often the subject of criticism for their failure in those days to rid America of the evil of slavery. It is a disturbing fact that slavery was an American institution for many years, before and after the drawing up of the Constitution.

As John Quincy Adams testified, many of the founders, including Adams himself, who was known as the "hell-hound of slavery," were strongly opposed to the continuation of that evil after the United States claimed independence from England.

> The inconsistency of the institution of domestic slavery with the principles of the Declaration of Independence was seen and lamented by all the southern patriots of the Revolution. . .No charge of insincerity or hypocrisy can be fairly laid to their charge. Never from their lips was heard one syllable of attempt to justify the institution of slavery. They universally considered it as a reproach fastened upon them by the unnatural step-mother country and they saw that before the principles of the Declaration of Independence, slavery, in common with every other mode of oppression, was destined sooner or later to be banished from the earth.[1]

For the sake of holding the union together, the issue of slavery was poorly handled. While deciding how to determine the population of each state, the delegates to the Constitutional Convention came up against the issue of slavery. In 1776, in their desire to present a united front to the world on the eve of independence, the Continental Congress postponed handling this explosive issue.

Now many voices were raised in favor of abolishing slavery everywhere in the Union. The great political leaders of Virginia—Washington, Madison, and Mason—were all opposed to slavery. But when it was proposed that slaves should be included in computing the population of the states, other voices were raised.

While the northern states opposed including slaves in determining the ratio of representation, the southern states wanted them included. In the end, a compromise was reached providing that three-fifths of the slaves should be counted for purposes of representation in Congress.

Congress then debated the question of controlling interstate and international commerce. Again, the slavery issue arose. Charles Pinckney and John Rutledge of South Carolina spoke in favor of continuing the importation of slaves. At this point, George Mason of Virginia could contain himself no longer. He rose and sternly warned his fellow delegates:

> Every master of slaves is born a petty tyrant. They bring the judgment of heaven upon a country. As nations cannot be rewarded or punished in the next world, they must be in this. By an inevitable chain of causes and effects, Providence punishes national sins by national calamities.[2]

It is truly unfortunate that Mason's timely warning went unheeded by a sufficient number of delegates. Again, this explosive issue was shelved. Congress gained the right to regulate the interstate and foreign commerce that had been causing so much friction between the states, but pro-slavery forces achieved a deplorable victory: they prevented Congress from even considering abolishing the importation of slaves until 1808.

The handling of the slavery issue was unquestionably a tragic blot on the work of the Constitutional Convention, which opened itself to divine direction in so many other ways and accomplished so much of enduring worth. It should serve as a reminder to us of what Madison and John Witherspoon understood so well: the sin nature of man often prevents him from accomplishing all that God would have him do. But God is not mocked. Although it took a disastrous civil war, His Providence achieved the abolition of slavery through blood (600,000 dead) when it could have so easily been achieved by the pen. This episode is also a reminder that God did not bless our Founding Fathers merely because they were brilliant thinkers, but only to the extent that they relied upon Him—and in regard to slavery, they did not. May we learn from their failures and move together as Christians of all races to solve our current racial crisis, not through government coercion, but through Christian love, truth, and sacrifice.

PHILLIS WHEATLEY

Christians are often blamed for historical injustices, and there is some basis for this, as we have seen. But whereas the injustice is usually perpetrated by one who claims the name of Christ but does not submit his life to Him, when there has been a movement to rectify injustice throughout the Western world, there has most often been a true Christian leading the way. Even though she would never live to see the emancipation of her race, Phillis Wheatley was certainly a forerunner of the Christian liberty that would come.

In 1761, at the age of seven, Phillis was bought at a slave auction by John Wheatley of Boston. The Wheatley family loved her dearly and helped educate her rather than merely giving her menial duties. Within five years, she was writing poetry comparable to the finer poets of her day.

Trained as a devout Christian, she wrote most of her poems about her faith. She was freed by her former owners and, as the war approached,

PHILLIS WHEATLEY
Born: c.1753
Died: 1784

Claim to fame:
Considered the first important black writer in the United States.

Did you know?
Even though she was much admired, Wheatley died in poverty.

began to write poems in support of American liberty. She wrote her poems directly to leaders like the Earl of Dartmouth, the secretary to King George, who visited America in 1772. She called on him to release America from the tyranny of England and used her own painful brush with tyrants as a black child snatched from her parents to drive the point home:

> What pangs excruciating must molest,
> What Sorrows labour in my parents' breast?
> Steel'd was that soul and by no misery moved
> That from a father seized his babe beloved:
> Such, such my case. And can I but pray
> Others may never feel tyrannic sway?[3]

Wheatley also wrote a note of encouragement to General George Washington, who wrote her back and invited her to visit his headquarters at Cambridge.

After John Wheatley died, Wheatley married a free black man named John Peters, who broke the young poet both physically and financially. Although she died at the age of thirty-one, Wheatley had in her short lifetime helped inspire the patriot cause and forward the cause of her race. By acknowledging her faith in Christ, she helped set the stage for the world to acknowledge that all men and women are created equal.

In the same year that Wheatley died, God converted an English parliamentarian three thousand miles to the east, who then labored continuously for twenty-two years against incredible odds to abolish the slave trade. His name was William Wilberforce. Wilberforce was a strong evangelical Christian and a model Christian statesman. He stood against slavery despite constant derision. On 23 February 1807, Parliament abolished the slave trade forever, and the United States followed suit the next year. God does indeed hear the cries of His people in bondage.

FREEDOM AND EQUALITY

In America, progress was to come later, though it began early, as Dr. Earle E. Cairns documented in *Christianity through the Centuries*:

> As early as 1796 Congregationalists in Rhode Island spoke out against slavery. John Woolman's Journal (1756–1772) describes the efforts of that godly Quaker to persuade others to emancipate their slaves. About 1833 [when slaves in England had already been officially emancipated] Lane Seminary in Cincinnati became the center of an antislavery movement led by a student, Theodore Weld.... The American Anti-Slavery Society was founded in 1833. Inspired by such people as the editor of the *Liberator*, William L. Garrison, poet John G. Whittier, educator Jonathan Blanchard, and by author Harriet Beecher Stowe, the abolitionist movement grew rapidly.[4]

Many Christians from the North and South knew that there had to be an end to slavery. They had been taught by Paul to look on slaves as brothers rather than as near-animals bred by nature to serve their superior white masters; Paul taught that the only Son of God was no respecter of persons, and that in Him there was neither Jew nor Greek. However, American pulpits in the 1850s did not ring with a clear enough sound or

WILLIAM WILBERFORCE
Born: *August 24, 1759*
Died: *July 29, 1833*

Claim to fame:

A leader in the struggle to abolish slavery in British overseas possessions.

Did you know?

He helped found the Proclamation Society, an organization dedicated to the suppression of the publication of obscenity.

offer clear, peaceful solutions. In the absence of strong Christian leadership, economic and regional concerns plunged America into the horrific war between the states.

One hundred years later, the same spirit of Christian brotherhood that inspired the abolitionists was infused throughout the Civil Rights movement. Rev. Martin Luther King Jr., along with his Southern Christian Leadership Conference, was to lead the way in reforming how Christians looked upon each other. Christians of all colors acknowledged that only God was sovereign, and that He died and rose to save mankind without racial distinction.

Churches were indeed the center of the Civil Rights movement as black Christians mobilized to support each other during bus boycotts, marches and rallies, and lunch-counter protests. The demands of the black community for equal rights did not claim government as the basis of that freedom, nor the sympathy of society, nor human nature, but the endowment of the Creator. They understood that government, society, and human nature itself recognized the right to equality and liberty only because it had been placed in man by God Himself. In demanding it, they knew they were demanding nothing less than obedience to His will.

THE HEART OF BLACK AMERICA TODAY

Even today, with the great diversity of viewpoints within the African American community, the black church and family remain the bulwark institutions that sustain the heart and soul of the people.

No minority in America has had the tremendous obstacles to overcome that African American citizens have had to conquer. In all things, though, much of the black community has persevered in their hope in Christ, embodying the idea of Romans 8:35–37:

> Who shall separate us from the love of Christ? Shall tribulation, or persecution, or famine, or nakedness, or peril, or sword?. . . Yet in all these things we are more than conquerors through Him who loved us.

This is the only hope of black Americans today, as it is of all Americans. That hope is the conquering spirit of Christ.

CD-ROM ANALYSES

• In *The Struggle for Freedom* and *A Cultural Heritage* from the *African American History* series, the rhythm and melody of black spirituals are said to be what strengthened the slaves, rather than the spiritual content. The fact that these were a reminder to place one's hope and faith in Christ is of more significance, as is the fact that Christianity was what kept many slaves alive at this time. This is a point that ought to be brought out, and the mention of the spiritual songs is a good place to do it.

• Only passing reference is made to Christianity in the *African American History* CD-ROMs, most of which is at the very beginning of *The Struggle for Equal Rights*, which then continues to overlook the role of Christianity in the Civil Rights movement itself. The opportunity to bring this fact out

MARTIN LUTHER KING JR.
Born: January 15, 1929
Died: April 4, 1968

Claim to fame:
Defined the Civil Rights movement in his famous speech, "I Have A Dream."

Did you know?
Won the Nobel Peace Prize (1964) for his leadership in applying the principles of nonviolent resistance to the struggle for racial equality.

lies in the mention of Martin Luther King Jr. and the Southern Christian Leadership Conference.

• The two-set series on *Leading Black Americans* does not go into any great detail about the Christianity of those it highlights. See our recommended reading list.

• The *Struggle for Equal Rights* CD-ROM concludes with the assertion that blacks today "still suffer from discrimination in employment, housing, education, and health care." The truth of the matter is that what continues to plague society is not the one issue of discrimination and the government programs established to compensate for it, but the prevailing carnality of most of the American people, with racial, economic, and ideological hatred its obvious manifestations.

REVIEW QUESTIONS

1. Black spirituals, first sung by slaves more than one hundred years ago, are still remembered, sung, and cherished by black Americans. Why do you think that is?

2. Why was slavery not abolished by the Constitution?

3. Name two founding pastors of black churches in America.

4. Name two Bible passages that teach racial equality.

RELATED SCRIPTURE

Matthew 7:12
John 4:42
John 8:34–36
Galatians 3:28

Galatians 5:1
The Epistle of Paul to Philemon
1 Timothy 1:10

SUGGESTED READING

Sidney E. Ahlstrom, *A Religious History of the American People* (New Haven: Yale University Press, 1972).

Mark Sidwell, *Free Indeed* (Greenville, SC: Bob Jones University Press, 1995).

Phillis Wheatley, *Poems* (Bedford, MA: Applewood).

Material covered in the Drama of Modern History chapter can be found in the following Zane Publishing Home Library titles:

Elementary U.S. History: Expanding Our Nation
Elementary U.S. History: Staying One Nation
U.S. History: Jacksonian Democracy
U.S. History: U.S. Government (1783–1865)
U.S. History: U.S. Government (1866–1977)
U.S. History: Foreign Policy (1788–1933)
U.S. History: Foreign Policy (1933–1963)
U.S. History: Reconstruction
U.S. History: The American West
U.S. History: The Great Depression
U.S. History: Social Reform Movements
Prentice Hall: Discovering American History
Prentice Hall: Discovering World History
Crime Collection: Encyclopedia of Western Lawmen & Outlaws
World History: European History: The Rise & Fall of the British Empire
World History: European History: The Making of the German Nation
World History: Nineteenth Century: The Napoleonic Era
World History: Nineteenth Century: The Victorian Era
World History: Nineteenth Century: The Ideas of Karl Marx
World History: Twentieth Century: Causes of World War I
World History: Twentieth Century: Causes of World War II
World History: Twentieth Century: The Russian Revolution
World History: Twentieth Century: Twentieth-Century Nationalism
World History: Twentieth Century: My Brother's Keeper

ACT SIX:
THE DRAMA OF MODERN HISTORY

If we abide by the principles taught in the Bible, our country will go on prospering and to prosper; but if we and our posterity neglect its proper instructions and authority, no man can tell how sudden a catastrophe may overwhelm us and bury all our glory in profound obscurity.

–DANIEL WEBSTER

FOR THREE MONTHS GEORGE Washington drafted a formal farewell to his country. He sent drafts to Alexander Hamilton and James Madison, but the ideas expressed at this eventful time are clearly those of the father of our country. Washington published the address on Monday, 15 September 1796, in Claypoole's *American Daily Advertiser*. He said he had an apprehension of danger for his country and wanted to

> offer to your solemn contemplation, and to recommend to your frequent review, some sentiments; which are the result of much reflection, of no inconsiderable observation, and which appear to me all important to the permanency of your felicity as a People.[1]

As we survey the last two centuries of the growth of the United States, reviewing the sentiments of our first leader is revealing. Washington—like Thomas Jefferson, John Adams, Patrick Henry, and all of our faithful founders—was hopeful but very concerned that future generations would forsake the "holy cause of liberty" that had been earned with so much blood sacrifice and providential intervention.

Those who truly study and understand history know the answer to Washington's rhetorical question in his Farewell Address, as he asked,

> Can it be, that Providence has not connected the permanent felicity of a Nation with its virtue? The experience, at least, is recommended by every sentiment which ennobles human nature. Alas! Is it rendered impossible by its vices?[2]

The very future survival of our republic is tied to whether we heed the warnings of God and of His wise servants. We must recover our virtue as a people or surely, as Washington suggested, we shall be destroyed by our vices.

In his Farewell Address to America, Washington warned of the "baneful effects of the Spirit of Party." He feared we would lose our unity of "religion, manners, habits and political principles," and become dominated by political parties and geographical discriminations that would polarize our people in the North and South. His premonition of division materialized half a century later in the disputes and rivalries that led up to and included the Civil War.

Washington went on to praise our constitutional form of government, but warned that we the people must obey the Constitution and only change it "by an explicit and authentic act of the whole people." Contrary

See the appendix for
Lincoln's Gettysburg Address
Lincoln's Second Inaugural Address
The U.S. Constitution
Washington's Farewell Address

GEORGE WASHINGTON
Born: *February 22, 1732*
Died: *December 14, 1799*

Claim to fame:
First president of the United States of America.

Did you know?
He was unanimously chosen as president and unanimously reelected in 1793. He declined to serve a third term.

ALEXANDER HAMILTON
Born: *January 11, 1757*
Died: *July 12, 1804*
(Killed in a duel with Aaron Burr.)

Claim to fame:
First U.S. Secretary of the Treasury.

Did you know?
Hamilton's ideas and plans for the nation's trade and financial systems were controversial, but helped to form American economic policy.

JAMES MADISON

Born: March 16, 1751
Died: June 28, 1836

Claim to fame:

Fourth president of the United States; "The Father of the Constitution."

Did you know?

James Madison's wife, Dolley Madison, is still remembered for her great hospitality while First Lady.

THOMAS JEFFERSON

Born: April 13, 1743
Died: July 4, 1826

Claim to fame:

Wrote the first draft of the Declaration of Independence; third president of the United States.

Did you know?

Jefferson founded the University of Virginia.

JOHN ADAMS

Born: October 30, 1735
Died: July 4, 1826

Claim to fame:

First vice president of the United States; second president of the United States.

Did you know?

John Adams and Thomas Jefferson died on the same day, exactly fifty years after the signing of the Declaration of Independence.

PATRICK HENRY

Born: May 29, 1736
Died: June 6, 1799

Claim to fame:

Fiery, patriotic orator and four-time governor of Virginia.

Did you know?

He said, "Give me liberty, or give me death!"

to his hopes, our Constitution has been undermined and changed without any "authentic act" of the people, but rather through "legal positivism" and "judicial supremacy," which have negated nine hundred years of common law and biblical reasoning.

Washington warned of a breakdown in the separation of powers:

> It is important, likewise, that the habits of thinking in a free country should inspire caution in those entrusted with its administration, to confine themselves within their respective Constitutional spheres; avoiding in the exercise of the Powers of one department to encroach upon another. The spirit of encroachment tends to consolidate the powers of all the departments in one, and thus to create whatever the form of government, a real despotism. A just estimate of that love of power, and proneness to abuse it, which predominates in the human heart is sufficient to satisfy us of the truth of this opinion.[3]

Sadly, a survey of the last two centuries reveals that our constitutional separations of power have been blurred and a unitary government has subjugated the states and turned much of the populace into dependents upon national LARGESSE.

Washington, with incredible foresight, urged the American people to fight against the "insidious wiles of foreign influence" and treaties with European powers who would entangle us in their wars. His words were heeded until the twentieth century, when we fought two wars in Europe, and now have a standing army that spans the globe, often under international United Nations control.

Washington, in his final public words before he died three years later at his beloved Mount Vernon, laid out the means of maintaining our nation:

> Of all the dispositions and habits which lead to political prosperity, Religion and morality are indispensable supports. In vain would that man claim the tribute of Patriotism, who should labour to subvert these great Pillars of human happiness, these firmest props of the duties of Men and citizens. The mere Politician, equally with the pious man ought to respect and to cherish them. A volume could not trace all their connections with private and public felicity. Let it simply be asked where is the security for property, for reputation, for life, if the sense of religious obligation desert the oaths, which are the instruments of investigation in Courts of Justice? And let us with caution indulge the supposition, that morality can be maintained without religion. Whatever may be conceded to the influence of refined education on minds of peculiar structure, reason and experience both forbid us to expect that national morality can prevail in exclusion of religious principle.
>
> 'Tis substantially true, that virtue or morality is a necessary spring of popular government. The rule indeed extends with more or less force to every species of free Government. Who that is a sincere friend to it, can look with indifference upon attempts to shake the foundation of the fabric?
>
> Promote then as an object of primary importance, Institutions for the general diffusion of knowledge. In proportion as the structure of a government gives force to public opinion, it is essential that public opinion should be enlightened.[4]

Washington saw two hundred years ago that the constitutional republic that our founders were leaving to their posterity could only be preserved through the "indispensable supports" of religion and morality. He also said that the promotion of education must be of primary importance if we are to maintain an "enlightened public opinion." Note that the promotion of education was for the purpose of teaching virtue and morality, which he made clear cannot be maintained without religion.

We shall see how education has been promoted in America over the last two centuries and how it has been torn from its biblical foundations and used "to shake the foundation of the fabric" of our civilization.

Such insights from Washington should remind us of the scriptural warning in Deuteronomy 8 to God's people when they have been blessed by His grace:

> When you have eaten and are full, then you shall bless the Lord your God for the land which He has given you.
> Beware that you do not forget the Lord your God by not keeping His commandments, His judgements, and His statutes which I command you today...then you say in your heart, 'My power and the might of my hand have gained me this wealth.'

The following analysis of the development of America's institutions and those of its European counterparts is a vivid lesson in the unyielding truth of Scripture and the wisdom of our founding leader.

THE DECLINE OF MODERN THEOLOGY

The rise and decline of America must ultimately be traced to the theology of the American people. Theology is pivotal when analyzing a nation's history because a people's theology (study of God) determines their view of man, which determines their view of government, the sanctity of life, and so on.

For example, Hinduism, which is the dominant religion of India, teaches pantheism (God is in all things) and reincarnation. This results in great poverty because animals are seen as sacred. Under Hindu rule, the practice of "sati," requiring Hindu women to throw themselves on their husband's funeral pyre to be cremated alive, was common. Not until the English brought Christianity to India did the government outlaw sati and make progress toward equal rights for the "untouchable" lower classes. In fact, the first act of social reform through legislation in Hinduism was the outlawing of sati by Lord William Bentinck.[5]

As we have documented in previous chapters, orthodox Christianity, meaning Christianity that holds to the historic creeds of the faith, was the dominant theology of early America. In 1776, 98 percent of Americans were Protestant Christians, with about 1.6 percent Catholics and 0.4 percent of the Jewish faith.

The theology of America was taught from one generation to the next by godly parents through daily devotions; by homeschooling (which was the most common choice); by a well-trained clergy schooled at one of many fine colleges such as Harvard, Yale, Princeton, and William and Mary; and by the schools which had a Christian foundation for all of learning.

By the end of the American Revolution, however, that foundation was already eroding. Economic dislocation, pioneering without pastors or churches on the frontier, and pure worldliness were taking their toll.

In 1798, the General Assembly of the Presbyterian Church sent out a pastoral letter that was read in every pulpit in the land:

> We perceive, with pain and fearful apprehension, a general dereliction of religious principle and practice among our fellow-citizens, a visible and prevailing impiety and contempt for the laws and institutes of religion, and an abounding infidelity which in many instances tends to Atheism itself....
>
> The profligacy and corruption of the public morals have advanced with a progress proportionate to our declension in religion. Profaneness, pride, luxury, injustice, intemperance, lewdness, and every species of debauchery and loose indulgence greatly abound....
>
> The eternal God has a controversy with this nation.[6]

In 1785, the First Episcopal Church in Boston had become the first Unitarian church in America. UNITARIANISM, a deceptively mild version of English Deism, which denied the deity of Christ while maintaining His other teachings, swept like a wildfire through the educated of New England. At the same time, the Enlightenment philosophy of the French skeptics made its way to our shores, especially after the French Revolution in 1789.

This growing HERESY did not go unchallenged. In 1795, Timothy Dwight became president of Yale. He was one of the great-grandsons of Jonathan Edwards, the father of the Great Awakening. He exposed the evils of Deism, the Enlightenment, and materialism. A revival began, and one-half of the students at Yale were converted. Other colleges, such as the College of New Jersey, Amherst, and Dartmouth, experienced similar awakenings. The Second Great Awakening was stirred by this movement of young students. Samuel Mills and four of his friends at Williams College began an association devoted to prayer for the evangelization of Asia. By 1810, their group had helped to found the foreign missions movement in America.

With the opening of the American frontier and the immigration of millions of Europeans to the United States, the nineteenth century became a mixed story for Christianity. On the one hand, millions were brought to Jesus Christ, but on the other, the knowledge of the basic doctrines of the faith that had changed the world in the Reformation and brought about America's free institutions was greatly diminished. In the Second Great Awakening, many of the preachers were untrained circuit riders who were weak in doctrine but strong in emotion. Experience began to overshadow truth rather than truth bringing forth experience. Many Christians mistakenly focused exclusively upon their spiritual relationship to God and neglected the cultural institutions that were built through godly reasoning and sacrifice. This weakness would render Christians vulnerable to foreign philosophies, and ultimately, most societal institutions were surrendered to humanists who took advantage of this vulnerability.

For example, a failure to grasp the doctrine of Divine Providence—i.e., God's constant superintendence and control of all He has created—led many Americans to accept Deism. Deism is the belief that God is an absentee landlord who wound the clock of history and let it run without His interference. In other words, man is free to be his own god. This places in question the very sovereignty of God. If God is not sovereign, then the state or the will of the people or a cult leader can declare sovereignty and find willing listeners.

The scriptural doctrine of the total depravity of human nature was also an accepted axiom of the eighteenth century. If one believes and understands this biblical truth, then it directs his view of all things. He knows that there is an absolute need for the saving grace of God in Jesus Christ since man, because of his universal sin nature in Adam, can never save or change himself. This doctrine leads people to limit the power of their representatives and, as Jefferson said, "bind them down with the chains of the Constitution."

If, on the other hand, a person believes that human beings are basically good, or perfectible through environmental conditioning as did the French philosophers of the Enlightenment, then there is no need for salvation. Also, if a people believe that man is naturally good, then there is no need to impose institutional restraints on the power of rulers. Laws can be lax and socialism can be implemented so that work and wealth can be shared equally and overseen by the beneficent state.

As you study Zane's CD-ROMs on the development of the United States, observe how Americans have placed increasing trust in the government, schools, and international organizations such as the United Nations.

Another fundamental Christian doctrine is that of the Trinity. The truth that God is one but that there are three personalities in the Godhead—all co-equal and yet unique—is fundamental to Christianity. The Unitarians, who derived their heresy of denying the Trinity from Laelius and Faustus Socinas, who started the movement back in 1560, became a powerful force in the doctrinally weak nineteenth and twentieth centuries. Socinianism, as it was called, became Unitarianism during the eighteenth century in England. In 1779, the English Parliament amended the Toleration Act and allowed non-Trinitarians to stay in the Church. Within a few years, the first Unitarian church was established in Boston. Its deistic philosophy swept like a plague across New England, and by 1805, the Unitarians captured the governing board of Harvard College, never to relinquish it to Christians again, with disastrous consequences.

Unitarianism led to TRANSCENDENTALISM (nature worship, by such writers as Ralph Waldo Emerson). Its warped theology aided in the establishment of the first statewide public school system in Massachusetts—by Horace Mann (a Unitarian)—with an educational philosophy which was devoid of a biblical foundation. It also opened the door to new "Christian" cults, Darwinism, and liberal theology. With the opening of the twentieth century, most of the mainline churches in America found themselves far from the historic biblical faith, denying the inerrancy of the Bible and questioning the deity of Christ. The mutated Socinas family dynasty from three centuries earlier had precipitated the fall.

Most of the major non-Trinitarian sects known today had their beginnings in frontier America and its weak doctrinal teaching. These sects all denied the Trinity, and many other cults followed in their wake. America

HORACE MANN
Born: May 4, 1796
Died: August 2, 1859

Claim to fame:
The "Father of American Public Education."

Did you know?
Visited Europe in 1843 and brought back ideas for mass education.

has the dubious distinction of being the cult capital of the world. This opened the door for other false religions to gain strongholds in the minds of millions of Americans in the twentieth century.

If Jesus Christ is not God, the second person of the Trinity, then the Scriptures are not true. Therefore, a search must be made for a new theory of the origin of the universe: enter the evolution myth and Charles Darwin's *On the Origin of Species*, published in 1859.

The complete history of the influence of theology and the Church upon America cannot be told here. Other fundamental Christian doctrines had great influence in shaping American life. Doctrines like the law of God, the covenants of God, the limited power of civil government, and the Puritan work ethic shaped America to the extent that they were applied and understood by believers. If that theology is strong and true, then the institutions thrive. If it is warped, then the institutions mutate and degenerate rapidly.

THE SINS OF THE CHURCH

Thus far we have analyzed the positive impact of biblical theology on the development of America and the negative impact of its demise. In the following pages, we will see how the truths of Christianity gave birth to American education, free enterprise, social welfare, and legal systems.

Before we proceed, let us address the stereotype of Christianity invented by modern secularism. Its loaded question is: "Do you really want to begin another series of holy crusades, witch hunts, Indian massacres, and slave trading?" This tactic of stereotyping Christians or Christianity as the cause of bigotry and intolerance is inaccurate but effective, especially in dealing with Christians who do not know the truth of their inherited history.

Succumbing to this well-worn method of Marxists and pluralists, entire segments of the Church have been immobilized. Confronted with these unfounded accusations, most Christians turn tail and run, apologizing for their faith as they go.

Instead of running, Christians must stand and answer their accusers with the facts of history and the truths of biblical teaching. A vital first step is differentiating between Christendom and Christianity. Christendom is a geographic term describing a region in which Christianity has been the predominant historical faith. Millions of citizens in such regions do not live out Christian truth through faith in Christ. True Christianity is an individual relationship with God through Christ that will bring a change of heart and action.

Contrary to the assertions of the secularist, Christianity has not been the historical cause of societal ills. Instead, the cause has been sinful deeds provoked by the degenerate nature of man, and the failure of many Christians to live out their faith. The absence and the neglect of Christianity—not its practice—have initiated and allowed to continue the sins of Western civilization. True Christianity brings real liberty. Jesus said, "If you abide in My word, you are My disciples indeed; and you shall know the truth, and the truth shall set you free."[7]

CONFESSING GREAT SIN

Christians must refuse to accept this false guilt thrown at them by the enemies of God through deception and historical revisionism. At the same time, we must confess and repent of some great wrongs that were committed on our watch. The true sins of Christianity are the ones that humanistic historians do not want to expose, for the great sin of Christianity in America has been its failure to confront and expose HUMANISM. We have already seen how humanism overtook theology in America in the nineteenth century through weak doctrinal teaching. In the following pages we shall see the fruit borne by the tree that has been corrupted.

The history of nineteenth- and twentieth-century America may truly be seen as the history of the sins of the Church, for as the true Church retreated from the cultural scene, it abandoned its vital role in society. This vacancy was filled by government, by secular intellectuals, and by the whims of the people. The task of this generation of students is to prepare themselves to resume their God-given roles within a society that is in desperate need of the light of the Gospel.

EDUCATION—IN SEARCH OF ITS ROOTS

Contrary to much popular teaching, the American emphasis on universal education did not come from ancient Greek or Enlightenment philosophers. It came directly from the Protestant Reformation. The biblical doctrine of the "priesthood of all believers" teaches that all Christian men and women are capable of approaching God in Christ through His written Word. Luther said that every plowboy should be able to read and interpret the Scripture for himself, since he was accountable for his own soul. The early colonists took this admonition to heart. John Eidsmoe, citing Pierre Samuel du Pont de Nemours, had this to say of their success:

> He concluded: 'Most young Americans...can read, write, and cipher. Not more than four in a thousand are unable to write legibly—even neatly.' He compared the low rate of literacy throughout the world to the relatively high literacy rate in the United States, England, Holland, and the Protestant Cantons of Switzerland. He attributed the difference to the fact that 'in those countries the Bible is read; it is considered a duty to read it to the children; and in that form of religion the sermons and liturgies in the language of the people tend to increase and formulate ideas of responsibility.' He went on to say that for the most part, education in America was accomplished in the home through reading Bibles and newspapers.[8]

Dr. Benjamin Rush, famous signer of the Declaration of Independence, said concerning education:

> In contemplating the political institutions of the United States, I lament that we waste so much time and money in punishing crimes, and take so little pains to prevent them. We profess to be republicans [believers in a republic] and yet we neglect the only means of establishing and perpetuating our republican forms of government; that is,

131

the universal education of our youth in the principles of Christianity by means of the Bible.[9]

The Bible was the fundamental textbook for most of the nineteenth century. From Noah Webster, whose *Blue-Backed Speller* taught a nation to read for eighty years, to the McGuffey readers that taught biblical and moral stories to American children into the twentieth century, Christian education was synonymous with becoming civilized. As Noah Webster said:

> In my view, the Christian religion is the most important and one of the first things in which all children, under a free government, ought to be instructed.... No truth is more evident to my mind than that the Christian religion must be the basis of any government intended to secure the rights and privileges of a free people.

EDUCATIONAL NEUTRALITY— THE IMPOSSIBLE DREAM

Horace Mann, a former congressman and Unitarian, is called the "Father of American Public Education." In 1838, he became the secretary of the Massachusetts Board of Education. During the following years, Mann promoted a philosophy of education that was opposed to that of the founding generation.

Mann supported taxation for state schools, which undermined parental control and was detrimental to private schools. He, and those who followed him, de-emphasized the biblical doctrine of salvation as the basis of character development, replacing it with the optimistic, humanistic view of the perfectibility of man through education and environment. He encouraged group thinking and study rather than independent thinking and creativity. He also standardized teacher training, textbooks, and accreditation, beginning the transition away from the principles of the Christian philosophy of education taught by the great founder of America's educational system, Noah Webster.

As the twentieth century dawned, John Dewey, with his progressive method of education derived partially from his exposure to the Russian educational system, carried on the march toward secularism. By 1935, a man-centered curriculum had become the dominant influence in most fields of scholarship in this country, with the theories of biological, social, and legal evolution the cornerstone of the educational establishment. Today, the vast majority of public schools and colleges are steeped in non-Christian RELATIVISM with no absolute values. Most textbooks ignore the contemporary relevance of our Christian roots. According to a study conducted by Paul Vitz for the U. S. Department of Education:

> Those responsible for these books appear to have a deep-seated fear of any form of active contemporary Christianity, especially serious, committed Protestantism...not one of forty books totaling ten thousand pages had one text reference to a primary religious activity occurring in representative contemporary American life.[10]

As Christian families forge a new millennium, we can learn much from the study of the history of education in America. No nation on earth has the legacy of godly education that we enjoy in America. But we must confess, without rationalization, that entire generations of our youth have suffered from the failure of a dream of education without God's Word as its foundation. We must be able to offer the biblical alternative to secular indoctrination. This includes Christian school or homeschool alternatives for families regardless of their economic status, and in-depth comparative worldview training for parents and students who choose to stay in the public schools. The Christian Home Learning Guides are intended to help accomplish that purpose.

SOCIAL WELFARE—
THE EARLY AMERICAN MODEL

When Benjamin Franklin visited London in 1766, he saw in the streets of that great city the fruit of a new law that had been passed called the British Welfare Act, which provided public assistance to the poor. He said:

> There is no country in the world in which the poor are more idle, dissolute, drunken and insolent. The day you passed that act you took away from before their eyes the greatest of all inducements to industry, frugality and sobriety, by giving them a dependence on somewhat else than a careful accumulation during youth and health for support in age and sickness.... Repeal that law and you will soon see a change in their manners. St. Monday and St. Tuesday will cease to be holidays.[11]

Franklin was expressing a typical early American dismay of government largesse that was then beginning in Europe. In contrast, a European visiting America in the 1830s was astonished by the effects of successful Christian charity operating without government controls. D. Griffiths Jr. recorded that "during the whole two years of my residence in America, I saw but one beggar."[12]

In the nineteenth century, Christians started orphanages, urban missions, the YMCA (in 1844) and the YWCA (in 1855) to meet the physical and spiritual needs of the poor in cities. Hundreds of charities were founded and are still the bulwark of support for the truly needy. The Salvation Army, founded in 1887 by William Booth, is probably the best-known organization.

With the unleashing of the evolution myth in the 1860s, faith in "Jehovah Jira," the God Who provides, diminished greatly. Social Darwinism soon made its way into the American consciousness, with its premise that man is merely an evolved animal to be fed and clothed, not an eternal soul in need of salvation.

In the twentieth century, the American people progressively began to give over the responsibilities of the family and church to the civil government, including the biblical mandate to care for the widows and orphans, which, according to the Apostle James, defined "pure and undefiled religion" in action (James 1:27). Beginning with the New Deal under President Franklin D. Roosevelt, and the Great Society under President Lyndon B. Johnson, the poor in America were treated by the government as though they were a permanent underclass.

Christian scholars like Dr. Marvin Olasky are helping to turn the tide of opinion concerning the future of the welfare state. Instead of giving

BENJAMIN FRANKLIN
Born: *January 17, 1706*
Died: *April 17, 1790*

Claim to fame:
Patriot, ambassador, writer, postmaster, inventor.

Did you know?
He invented the Franklin stove, bifocal glasses, and the lightning rod.

WILLIAM BOOTH
Born: *April 10, 1829*
Died: *August 20, 1912*

Claim to fame:
Founder of the Salvation Army.

Did you know?
He was a traveling Methodist minister before founding the Salvation Army.

up on America's future, he reminds us of the past success of Judeo-Christian charity.

Christian students must be constantly encouraged to appreciate the poverty-transforming power of the gospel of Jesus Christ. No government in history has solved the poverty problem, but Jesus Christ, through His power working in His people, has lifted mankind from material and spiritual poverty. J. C. Ryle, writing in the nineteenth century, brilliantly stated the power of Christ to transform people and cultures:

> The veriest infidel cannot deny the effect that [Christianity] produced on mankind. The world before and the world after the introduction of Christianity were as different worlds as light and darkness, night and day. It was Christianity that starved idolatry, and emptied the heathen temples,—that stopped gladiatorial combats, elevated the position of women, raised the whole tone of morality, and improved the condition of children and the poor. These are facts which we may safely challenge all the enemies of revealed religion to gainsay.[13]

CHRISTIAN FREE ENTERPRISE

Biblical Christianity played the pivotal role in the development of free enterprise, the Scientific Revolution, and the Industrial Revolution. Many economists and historians in our day teach that the Industrial Revolution and the development of American enterprise was the product of a combination of greed, abundant natural resources, and luck. Others, like the humanist historian Charles Beard, in his thesis titled *The Economic Interpretation of the Constitution*, teach that America's productivity can be traced to the silk-stocking aristocrats who wrote the Constitution to cushion their fortunes and save their property. Beard and his wife have written more than thirty volumes of history in the last half of the twentieth century, revising or ignoring America's Christian history.

Why have we enjoyed such abundance in the West, and especially in America, while so many Asian and African countries have struggled simply to stave off starvation? Proverbs 23:7 gives us the answer: "As a man thinketh in his heart, so is he." In North Africa, where the fatalism of Islam has destroyed human initiative, the people survive on $100–$200 a year. Islam teaches that whatever is, Allah has fated. So what motivation is there for self-improvement? Stagnation is the result.

Some of the nations of Asia, including Japan, South Korea, and Taiwan, are just now escaping the poverty of several millennia because they are adopting the economic principles of the West. In doing so, many are rejecting the reasoning of eastern religions like BUDDHISM. Buddhism teaches that life is irreparably evil, and man must seek to rid himself of all desires, including the desire for self-improvement. Others are beginning to question the teachings of Hinduism, which sees life as an illusion. It is only the worldview taught in Scripture that provides the foundation for long-term economic progress. In the Bible, we are made accountable to the cultural mandate given to Adam in Genesis to govern the earth.

THE ECONOMICS TEXTBOOK

The development of what we now call free enterprise, or the capitalist system of economics, can be traced to the unleashing of the Bible into the hands of the people in their own languages in the sixteenth and seventeenth centuries. John Chamberlain wrote in *The Pools of Capitalism* that, "Christianity tends to create a capitalistic mode of life whenever siege conditions do not prevail." America was blessed because it had freedom from European wars and "siege conditions" to apply the principles of the Reformation, especially those economic principles taught by John Calvin.

These biblical principles of economics were brought to America by the Puritans and have become known as the Puritan, or Protestant, work ethic. These principles are not part of the economics curriculum at American universities, but they were the driving force behind the explosion of prosperity in Protestant lands. Historian Richard Dunn wrote:

> Was it mere coincidence that the most dynamic businessmen were to be found in Protestant Holland and the most vigorous industrial growth in Protestant England, both states heavily tinctured with Calvinism? Why were the Huguenots so prominent in the business community of Catholic France? Or Protestant Brandenburg-Prussia under the Calvinist Great Elector almost the only seventeenth-century German state to exhibit increasing prosperity?[14]

As the student of America's heritage peruses Zane's CD-ROMs and the Christian Home Learning Guides, these fundamental, unchanging principles are the best tools for understanding America's economic history. These principles, derived from Scripture, are actually character traits that are to be developed by parental instruction and role modeling.

Firstly, the stewardship of private property is a basic foundation of the Puritan work ethic. The sanctity of property in pagan countries was nonexistent. But Judaism and Christianity brought to the world two great engines of prosperity. The first was a sanction to place possessions in private hands and within families. The Ten Commandments specifically forbids stealing personal property or coveting another's possessions. The second great truth that unleashes incredible productivity every day is the biblical mandate of stewardship. We are stewards for God to invest, replenish, and superintend all that He has entrusted to us. Knowing that we are to give account at the end of time (1 Corinthians 3:12–14), we Christians are inspired to "work as unto the Lord," who will reward our stewardship.

A second principle of the Christian ethic was that of the nobility of work. Contrary to the pagan view of work, which sees it as a curse, the early Americans saw work from a biblical perspective. Work is a blessing because:

Work is God's will (Genesis 3:17–19)

Work builds His kingdom (I Corinthians 10:31)

Work keeps us from idleness and sin (Proverbs 6)

Work's reward is from the Lord; it is much more than a paycheck (Galatians 6:9)

Families who capture the biblical joy of work in our generation can excel and succeed if they (1) work six days and rest on the seventh, (2)

135

work as a family unit to build the family inheritance and not just as autonomous individuals (this family unit can include members of the church family as well as blood relatives), and (3) work not only for money but for excellence and for the Lord.

A third important part of the Christian work ethic is the biblical emphasis on Divine calling. Historian Perry Miller pointed out that the Puritans changed the "aristocratic" dominance of Europe and its class system by viewing all honest work as honorable, as a "holy calling." God does not only call those who are in full-time ministry; all are called to work, and all honest work should be regarded as a Divine appointment. The Puritans did not look down upon menial labor, as did the French DILETTANTES, but disapproved of those who were indolent as "unclean beasts," regardless of wealth. This is the reason that the French aristocracy never gained a foothold in America. They were condemned as lazy because they refused to work for God or man.

A fourth element is the TITHE and offerings. This is the basis of God's welfare system, which meets the physical and spiritual needs of others. There is no doubt that one of the foremost acts of obedience of each family unit is the paying of tithes and offerings to God. We are told in I Corinthians 16:2 that each week, each of us should analyze our profit and lay aside some of it for God's work.

Tithing in early America was a way of life for most believers. The tithe supported not only private schools and churches, but also the first 150 universities in our nation, as well as the poor, hospitals, and all social charitable necessities.

Many Christians have lost God's vision for the tithe. It is not only a command of God that keeps our minds focused upon His ownership of all we are and have, but it is also God's alternative to confiscatory government, and it meets the real charitable needs of society with greater efficiency.

Honesty is the fifth biblical economic principle. In early America, and even today in rural communities, personal accountability and the need for a good reputation demanded that justice and honesty be fundamental character qualities.

As these qualities lost importance in the modern world, "quick and dirty" business became the rule of the day. Coercion and tyranny have supplanted the "word-is-my-bond handshake," which was the standard when the Ten Commandments were the rule of life.

In contrast to this collapse of character, honest covenant keepers can witness with their lives and gain the respect of millions looking for integrity. And they will gain the respect and emulating admiration of their children as they battle for the next century, and pass on a godly inheritance.

A sixth principle of the Christian work ethic is the concept of savings and investment. The Reformation taught Christians that saving was a scriptural command, and, as a result, capital for investment was made available. The Industrial Revolution and American prosperity were funded by the Christian saving ethic. One of the tragic results of our "consumption" society is that debt is the inevitable result, and debt always leads to bondage. "The borrower is the servant to the lender"(Proverbs 22:7). If families do not forgo consumption and save for their own future, they will almost certainly turn to government to meet their needs in a crisis (e.g., Franklin Roosevelt's New Deal). R. E. McMaster Jr., in *No Time for Slaves*, stated that "only 3% of the American people are financially self-sufficient now in a bare bones sense."

A seventh aspect of the Christian ethic of work is creativity. Man is the only being created in God's image. We can be recreatively creative, under His direction. Sin mars our creativity and guilt destroys the freedom of the mind to think God's thoughts after Him. But history proves that whenever there is spiritual renewal and forgiveness there is an explosion of creative activity.

Many of the creative activities we see today may seem to be dependent upon technology. George Gilder, in his book, *Microcosm*, said:

> Broadly considered, the computer is the most important product of the quantum era. By exploring this central machine of the age, however, we discover not the centrality of machines and things but the primacy of human thought and creativity.[15]

Contrary to many who are predicting an age of robots and runaway technology, God's redeemed man, created in His image, is a creative force far greater than the machines he produces.

We do not live in a world with shrinking resources. God's resources are limitless. It is only our lack of faith and perspective that conceals the quantum leap in creativity under God that may await us.

Today, on average, there are more than 650 Americans to every ten square miles of the United States. The American farmer, only 3 percent of the American population, feeds the entire nation and 20 percent of the rest of the world. Why? Because of the Bible and its view of man. The "new man in Christ" desires to understand and replenish God's earth in the biblical pattern. The Reformation sparked science, discovery, great music and art, and inventions that revolutionized the world. Most of the great scientists of history have been creationists and believers. The forgiveness of Christ and a knowledge of His Word unleashed a godly creativity and entrepreneurship that is unparalleled in history. It is not the state or socialism that has produced or will produce prosperity in the future. Gilder said:

> This good news for individuals and entrepreneurs, however, is bad news for socialism. The state can dig iron or pump oil, mobilize manpower and manipulate currencies, tax and spend. The state can expropriate the means of production. But when it does, it will find mostly sand. For the men of production, the entrepreneurs, run for the daylight of liberty. One way or another, most of the time, the entrepreneurs take their money with them or send it on ahead. But always they take their minds, and knowledge is their crucial power.[16]

The twenty-first century lies before us, and we must believe God for the ability to be "recreatively creative" under Him. The essence of wealth is not in physical things, but in ideas that are invisible. We will be able to rise above economic turbulence and cultural malaise to create real wealth that can cover the world with the blessing and the gospel of Jesus Christ.

The eighth principle of the Christian work ethic is optimism. "All things work together for good for those who love God and are called according to His purpose" (Romans 8:28). Only those who see with "the mind of Christ" can, without naivete, look forward to the challenges of the future. Gilder pointed to the reasons why Christianity and its innate optimism is the cornerstone of risk capitalism and the age of discovery:

> Faith in man, faith in the future, faith in the rising returns of giving, faith in the mutual benefits of trade, faith in the providence of God are all essential to successful capitalism.[17]

We do not have to tie our hope or optimism to market trends or Washington, D.C.'s ability to pull us out of our economic quagmire. We, as Christians, are building long-term for our children's children, and the kingdom of the sovereign God. Knowing that God controls history, and our futures, we can risk and can confidently build an inheritance and financial dynasty as good stewards for the King of Kings.

FROM GOD'S LAW TO THE LAW OF THE JUNGLE

Throughout this chapter, a recurring theme appears in the background of the American experience. That theme was expressed eloquently by the great grandson of John Winthrop, who came to America on the *Arbella* in 1630. Robert Winthrop said:

> All societies of men must be governed in some way or other. The less they may have of stringent State Government, the more they must have of individual self-government. The less they rely on public law or physical force, the more they must rely on private moral restraint.
>
> Men, in a word, must necessarily be controlled either by a power within them, or by a power without them; either by the word of God, or by the strong arm of man; either by the Bible or by the bayonet.
>
> It may do for other countries, and other governments to talk about the State supporting religion. Here, under our own free institutions, it is Religion which must support the State.[18]

All of our colonial charters taught the preeminence of God and His Word. Our Declaration of Independence was our national covenant to resist tyrannical power and preserve the inalienable rights of man with "firm reliance upon the protection of Divine Providence." Our Constitution specifically defined the "enumerated" and limited powers of the national government, reserving all other powers "to the respective states and the people."

In his Farewell Address, George Washington expressed the concern that the leaders of our nation "confine themselves within their respective Constitutional spheres." He knew what would happen if "the sense of religious obligation desert[ed] the oaths." Washington knew the tyrannical fire of government released from moral constraint. He said, "Government is not reason, it is not eloquence—it is force. Like fire, it is a dangerous servant and a fearful master."

What Washington feared came true in the 1870s in American law. Until the middle of the nineteenth century, most legal training was done in law offices through apprenticeships. Under the Christian leadership of United States Supreme Court Justice Joseph Story (1829–1845), Harvard College developed a strong legal education department, for which it became well-respected. Justice Story held to the unchanging biblical view of law and justice. But in 1869, Charles William Eliot became president of Harvard. As a committed enemy of the God of the Bible and a firm believer in Charles Darwin's new theory of evolution, he set out to revolutionize American education, especially in the field of law.

In 1870, he hired Christopher Columbus Langdell, and soon thereafter appointed him dean of the Law School. Langdell shared Eliot's radical view that nine hundred years of Christian legal theory had to be jettisoned.

When Langdell came to Harvard, William Blackstone's *Commentaries on the Laws of England,* first published in the 1760s, was the standard textbook for teaching law. Blackstone taught that the Creator established certain unchanging laws, which he called the will of the Maker, or the "Law of Nature." But he also believed that man, because his reason as well as his nature was fallen, needed God to reveal His divine law in the Scripture. He taught that no law was valid that contradicted God's revealed law.

Law professor Herb Titus summarized Blackstone's teaching:

> Not only did Blackstone believe that God dictated the law governing man, he identified God as the God of the Bible and God's law as that which is contained in the Bible. Could man have discovered these laws by studying legal cases and reasoning? Blackstone did not believe so. God, after man's fall, 'in compassion to the frailty, the imperfection, and the blindness of human reason,' was pleased to enable man 'to discover and enforce' His laws 'by an immediate and direct revelation':
>
> The doctrines thus delivered we call the revealed or divine law, and they are to be found only in the Holy Scriptures.
>
> Human reason, corrupted by sin, is an inadequate mechanism for understanding and implementing Divine law. Blackstone warned that we are not, therefore, 'to conclude that knowledge of these truths was attainable by reason, in its present corrupted state; since we find that, until they were revealed, they were hid from the wisdom of ages.'[19]

Christopher Langdell broke with the religious foundations of law and postulated that legal cases were "original sources" of legal doctrines and principles. He believed that judges, through their rulings, simply create law over time. There was no need for God's revealed law, and no real need for a fixed Constitution.

As Darwinists, Eliot and Langdell believed that all life gradually evolved; there was no creation. Applying this theory to law, they taught that laws were simply evolving mores of an animal that change over time. Influential lawyers like Oliver Wendell Holmes Jr. and Louis P. Brandeis soon became vocal supporters of this theory, which by 1920 had become standard teaching in most law schools. Case law had become the god of legal theory. It was not long before the secular judges of the twentieth century would break the barriers of the separation of powers and begin to dictate and write the law of the land, not just interpret the original intent of the Constitution.

Earlier, we noted that Christians allowed a Unitarian-dominated board to sweep into Harvard College in 1805, never again to relinquish its control. By the 1870s, Harvard was primed with ample classical paganism, and Christians were withdrawn from the world. Harvard College led a legal revolution that has changed the world.

After 1947, the Supreme Court applied a new doctrine that was never in the Constitution. The fictional "wall of separation between church and state," a phrase that they derived from a private letter of Thomas Jefferson to a group of Baptists in Danbury, Connecticut, in 1802, became a justification for the immoral decisions of the next thirty years. First, organized prayer and Bible reading were removed from public schools in 1962 and 1963. Without the influence of the Church, the court was deprived of its conscience, and so in 1973, abortion was legalized. Finally, in 1980, the court ruled that the Ten Commandments, the foundation of Western civilization and law, could not be posted in public schools, even at private expense. The result of this has been devastating. As Chief Justice Charles Evans Hughes said, "The Constitution is what the judges say it is." The entire court system has become what the former Dean of Cornell Law School, William Forrester, calls "the Legiscourt":

> We have failed to see that the Supreme Court has evolved into a new institution—one that is even more unique and unprecedented than commonly supposed. Indeed, the institution can no longer be described with accuracy as a court, in the customary sense. Unlike a court, its primary function is not judicial but legislative. It is a governing body in the sense that it makes the basic policy decisions of the nation, selects among the competing values of our society, and administers and executes the directions it chooses in political, social, and ethical matters. It has become the major societal agency for reform.[20]

Thomas Jefferson was against allowing the judges the right to judge the legality of laws in other branches of government. He foresaw the danger of judicial supremacy when he wrote:

> To consider the judges as the ultimate arbiters of all constitutional questions [is] a very dangerous doctrine indeed, and one which would place us under the despotism of an oligarchy.[21]

We are experiencing that tyrannical OLIGARCHY today. The original intent of the founders, nine hundred years of common law tradition, and four thousand years of biblical law tradition, have all been discarded in this century by a few judges who enjoy lifelong tenure.

What can be done to restore constitutional sanity to our nation? We must first know what is in our Constitution. We must become informed. We, as Christians, also must once again become students of God's law, which was the foundation for the Constitution. We can then elect godly leaders who will appoint judges who share a biblical legal philosophy.

The Zane CD-ROMs have the entire Constitution in its reference section for your study. If a citizen studies and knows the Constitution, he knows that Congress has the right to limit the APPELLATE jurisdiction of the Supreme Court. Article III, Section 2.2 of the Constitution states:

> The Supreme Court shall have appellate jurisdiction in all cases arising under the Constitution or the federal laws and treaties, as to both law and fact, with such exceptions and under such regulations as the Congress shall make.

If Congress exercised the power granted to it in this article, it could limit the power of an immoral court to overturn the laws the people have passed. Another way to control an out-of-control court is to impeach judges who politicize their trust and abuse their power.

Judge Robert Bork suggested in his informative book *Slouching Towards Gomorrah* that

> …the only practical way of reining in the Supreme Court is a constitutional amendment making its rulings subject to democratic review. As matters now stand, the Court's assumption of complete governing power is intolerable, and yet, absent a constitutional amendment, we have no way of refusing to tolerate it.[22]

We should not be discouraged by the daunting task of restoring our legal institutions. Jesus Christ gave us the commission to disciple the nations in Matthew 28, and through his Word and the Holy Spirit we can obtain the wisdom and power to "build the old waste places" (Isaiah 58:12).

20TH-CENTURY SURVEY:
THE DAWN OF THE 20TH CENTURY (1900–1925)

In 1900, Christians should have been poised to expand God's kingdom in America. The foundations of liberty had been laid by the faith, blood, and labors of our founders. We were just coming out of the greatest missionary century in history, with America leading the way. And the major institutions and laws of our land still mirrored the biblical nation of a century before, with the added advantage of prosperity sparked by Christian free enterprise.

But behind the soothing facade of the Victorian era and its family values, dangerous theological heresy—including cults, the evolutionary theory, Marxist ideology, and Freudian psychology—was capturing the minds of the new generation, especially those in the universities.

Christianity, which had essential unity of belief a century earlier, was deeply divided. Many of the mainline denominations became progressively more liberal, denying the deity of Christ and the inerrancy of Scripture, mainly due to German higher criticism in seminaries. At the same time, millions of evangelical, Bible-believing Christians left the old denominations and withdrew to start their own schools and churches. In their desire to hold on to the faith, many of these believers withdrew from involvement in social, political, or cultural issues. This left society open to the dominance of humanist thought, even though committed humanists numbered less than 3 percent of the population.

The institutional collapse of Christian influence culminated in 1929, when J. Gresham Machen, the last great orthodox theologian at an Ivy League school, withdrew to start Westminster Seminary, and Princeton Seminary fell to liberal theological heresy. The enemies of God now controlled the chairs of learning and the minds of the coming generations.

The Scopes trial in 1925, which dealt with the teaching of evolution to schoolchildren, was devastating to the Christian cause. The media portrayed Christians as intellectual escapists. In this trial, evolutionary science (non-scientific as it was) captured the minds of Americans, while Christians were perceived by many as holding on to a fairy tale.

Prohibition (1920–1933) was the last great experiment in Christian activism in the first quarter of the century. Energy was wasted in a futile attempt to stop alcohol consumption through a constitutional amendment. In the meantime, humanists were busy rewriting school textbooks, preparing for government service, and moving into Hollywood and New York to influence the entertainment industry.

THE SECOND QUARTER (1925–1950)

The second quarter of the twentieth century was dominated by the Great Depression and World War II. Both of these tragedies should have caused Americans to turn to God and experience a great spiritual awakening such as happened in the Great Awakening (1739–1750) and the Civil War Awakening (1857–1865). But instead, what our founders most feared happened: Americans made a conscious choice to turn from dependence upon God to dependence upon government. The American welfare state was born in the 1930s. The Church did not stand against the dangers of statist power and we, its grandchildren, are now paying the price.

THE THIRD QUARTER (1950–1975)

The third quarter of this century was the greatest institutional revolution in history. Most cultural pillars were divided of their Christian roots. Most families, while still nominally Christian, moved to the suburbs for the good life, and had no stomach to carry on a cultural war for the sovereignty of God. Christianity was reduced to a personal, private matter, while public policy was secularized. By 1975 and the end of the war in Vietnam, the '60s revolution had succeeded in breaking down most authority. The only values that were highly esteemed in this generation, according to Francis Schaeffer, were personal peace and affluence.

In the midst of this disintegration of our society, an evangelistic explosion led by Billy Graham, Bill Bright, and the charismatic "Jesus Movement" began pointing millions back to Jesus. Young believers began to grow, reading Christian cultural philosophers like Francis Schaeffer, and questioning the religious escapism of the past seventy-five years. Hope was born.

THE FOURTH QUARTER (1975–2000)

At this writing, the final chapter of this century is yet to be completed, but the pattern is clear: the American Church, as a whole, by withdrawing from active leadership in our culture, gave secularists control of our major institutions for most of the twentieth century. These optimistic humanists have failed in all their tinkering and brought us to the brink of cultural chaos. Their experiments with our schools have failed, their statist bureaucracy is intrusive and headed for bankruptcy, and their moral relativism has left America plagued with violence, illegitimacy, drugs, and pornography. *Zane's History through Art: The Twentieth Century* CD-ROM correctly analyzes the end of the twentieth century where it quotes "The Hollow Men" by T.S. Eliot:

> We are the hollow men
> We are the stuffed men
> Learning together
> Headpiece filled with sorrow, Alas!
> Our dried voices, when
> We whisper together
> Are quiet and meaningless
> As wind in a dry grass
> Shape without form, shade without colour
> Paralyzed force, gesture without motion
> This is the way the world ends
> This is the way the world ends
> Not with a bang but a whimper–

The secular Camelot that seemed destined to rule the world, with "progress" as its most important product, is proving to be a charade. The mainstream intellectuals and media pundits of the Western world have proved themselves poor guides to the future. These self-proclaimed "experts" have led millions from Darwin, through Marx, to Freud, often ending in despair.

Historian Paul Johnson analyzes many of these twentieth-century thinkers in his important book *Intellectuals*:

> It is just about two hundred years since the secular intellectuals began to replace the old clerisy [clergy] as the guides and mentors of mankind.... I detect today a certain public skepticism when intellectuals stand up to preach to us, a growing tendency among ordinary people to dispute the right of academics, writers, and philosophers, eminent thought they may be, to tell us how to behave and conduct our affairs. The belief seems to be spreading that intellectuals are no wiser as mentors, or worthy as exemplars, than the witch doctors or priests of old. I share that skepticism. A dozen people picked at random on the street are at least as likely to offer sensible views on moral and political matters as a cross-section of the intelligensia.[23]

Here lies our hope. Faith in the humanist's idealized man is dying. People are seeing through the "New Deal," the "Great Society," and "the bridge to the twenty-first century." They know America's greatness taps into a much greater source than political slogans. Millions of parents and students are rediscovering the covenants of our forebears. They are learning the truths about God's world and His rules for living in it. As parents train a new generation in the unchanging biblical principles of life, these young leaders of the future can rise up and offer real hope to restore the "holy cause of liberty."

Building upon our inheritance, which requires knowing our true history, we can be a "city upon a hill" for the twenty-first century, becoming an example to other nations, rather than a reproach.

John Winthrop had such a vision when he landed in Boston in 1630:

> We shall find that the God of Israel is among us, when ten of us
> shall be able to resist a thousand of our enemies, when He shall make

us a praise and glory, that men of succeeding plantations shall say, 'The Lord make it like that of New England.'

For we must Consider that we shall be as a City upon a Hill, the eyes of all people are upon us.[24]

CD-ROM ANALYSES

U.S. History

• *U. S. Government* (2 CD-ROMs): Factually, these CD-ROMs are very good, and a thorough familiarity with their material is a good foundation for understanding the Christian view of American government. Of special interest is the detailed history of the growth of power in the federal government, and the internal power struggles that have resulted from it. It would be hard to communicate this more effectively than these CD-ROMs do.

One thing parents should be aware of is the conclusion to the second CD-ROM, *U.S. Government* (1866–1977), in which the question is put forth whether the Constitution has any validity in the modern world. This is a fair question, given the changes and challenges the Constitution has faced in its two hundred years as the law of the land. The CD-ROM, however, does not answer the question. Parents can help their children to understand why the Constitution is, and will always be, a relevant document.

• *U. S. Foreign Policy* (2 CD-ROMS): Following the history of America's international involvements, students can see the development of the role America has chosen for herself among the powers of the world, and the consequences of her actions. The conclusion describes the interdependence of nations, though if one has been attentive to the presentation, it is apparent that the state of affairs is more one of worldwide dependence upon America in times of crisis.

• *Jacksonian Democracy*: Here the student will find a complete history of the growth of government power under the Jackson and Van Buren administrations, and of the failure of government to accomplish the purposes it claimed to be pursuing when it was granted that power.

• *Reconstruction*: A good basic history of a time in America's history that few understand and fewer still agree upon. The CD-ROM's only flaw is that at one point it makes it seem as though anything that is benevolent should be constitutional. The federal government, as we have pointed out in this chapter, is not a benefactor, nor is it a charitable organization.

• *The Great Depression*: An introduction to the background, events, and effects of this disastrous period. At points it reflects the subtle infiltration of socialist ideas into our culture that we have chronicled above, as in its suggestion that the uneven distribution of wealth is somehow unjust.

• *Social Reform Movements*: There is so much good news about this CD-ROM that we will begin with the bad news and get it out of the way. The author attributes the Declaration of Independence to Enlightenment ideas. This should not pose a problem for parents, as this book contains ample evidence that the opposite is true.

The CD-ROM triumphs in pointing out the Christian roots of most real social reform, in contrast to the uncaring attitude that is shown to be the result of social Darwinism. It portrays the lapse of social concern in the Church with accuracy, and illuminates the differences between private and public (government) charity.

• *The American West*: This CD-ROM does a good job of demythologizing the "Wild West," showing that there was more work than gunfighting for cowboys.

World History

• *The Napoleonic Era*: This CD-ROM presents a balanced view of Napoleon's conquest. It shows the good ideals he claimed to be pursuing and the evils he performed in their pursuit. Students will be able to see how and why the ends do not justify the means.

• *The Victorian Era*: For the most part, this is an excellent CD-ROM with accurate historical information. It lacks the Christian worldview that would make it complete, and shows some tendencies to the inescapable socialism of today's thought.

• *Causes of World War I* and *Causes of World War II*: The facts of these wars are sad and sometimes upsetting, but important for the student to know. The CD-ROMs are effective in communicating not only the facts, but the sense of drama that pervades these two great wars. There are many lessons to be learned from great tragedies such as these. The great danger of all-powerful centralized governments is clear in these histories.

In the first CD-ROM, the imperialism of most European powers at the turn of the century is attributed to Christianity and to the Industrial Revolution. Parents will want to point out that neither Christianity nor the work ethic it instills caused imperialism. Imperialism was the result of national greed and pride, not Christianity.

Some of the images in these presentations may be upsetting.

• *The Russian Revolution*: From a Christian perspective, there is little to admire in the violence and chaos that are intrinsic to communism. This CD-ROM very simply sets forth the information without any specific worldview taking an upper hand in interpreting it. Be sure that students know which worldview to use.

• *The Making of the German Nation*: A CD-ROM that is very nearly perfect. All that remains for the Christian student is to observe that the German people never trusted God, only government. The one flaw in the CD-ROM is a slight accommodation of communism.

• *The Rise and Fall of the British Empire*: Another historically accurate CD-ROM, which succeeds in covering the long history of the far-reaching British Empire. Noteworthy is the attention given to British missionary efforts in India, highlighting one of the historical successes of Christianity. However, the abolition of slavery in England is attributed to economic forces rather than to Christian convictions, and God is left entirely out of its references to the Declaration of Independence.

• *The Ideas of Karl Marx:* Parents may be surprised, but this is quite a good CD-ROM. It is more or less objective about his ideas without passing judgment either for or against them. For Christian students to understand this enemy of the faith is important, and so this is a useful resource. The fatal flaw of Marx's ideology is his atheism; from there, everything goes downhill. The CD-ROM does make an attempt at a positive ending, but the real nature of Marx's ideas is very clear.

• *Twentieth-Century Nationalism:* Of all the history CD-ROMs, this presentation is most reflective of the spirit of socialism. It does succeed in showing the failure of the European empire-builders, but its tendency is to view history as the struggle between economic classes rather than as the unfolding plan of God. This departure from the typical fair-mindedness of the Zane CD-ROMs is unfortunate, but students armed with a knowledge of history and a Christian worldview can engage this ideology without fear.

• *My Brother's Keeper:* This unique CD-ROM, which explores historical events through paintings, is best suited to older students. It examines the many aspects of the terrible tragedy of the holocaust. It is odd that the idea expressed in the title—my brother's keeper—is brought in at the end, almost as an afterthought, but in that position it serves as a positive conclusion to a description of events that may seem at times overwhelmingly negative.

• *Discovering World History* makes great use of the medium, including a wide array of instructional materials. In addition, it is a valuable overview of world history, showing in parallel chronology the development of cultures on every continent. With the history chapters of the *Christian Home Learning Guides* as a companion, this CD-ROM will provide a wealth of knowledge, and can stand alone as well as any classroom history text. The absence of a Christian worldview only shows occasionally, as when the authors make reference to the theories of social and biological Darwinism, or when humanism is said to maintain a Christian worldview.

REVIEW QUESTIONS

1. What two things did George Washington say bring about political prosperity?

2. Why is theology central to the study of history?

3. What Christian doctrine does Unitarianism deny?

4. Name some of the results of Unitarian heresies.

5. Of what great sin is the Church guilty? Of what sin is it innocent?

6. What book was the basis of education in early America?

7. Which two men were largely responsible for secularizing public education?

8. How did America care for its poor before government welfare programs?

9. What are the eight principles of Christian free enterprise?

10. What are two forms of restraint, according to Robert Winthrop?

11. What did Charles Langdell consider to be the original source for legal principles?

RELATED SCRIPTURE

Genesis 1:26–28	Isaiah 10:33; 58:12
Deuteronomy 8	Malachi 3:8
Psalm 112:1–3	John 8:31–32
Proverbs 6:6–11; 10:4; 10:16; 16:11; 22:7; 23:7; 29:4	Acts 6:3
1 Corinthians 16:2	Romans 8:28
Galatians 6:9	Hebrews 11:1
Ephesians 2:10	1 John 5:4–5

SUGGESTED READING

Jim Nelson Black, *When Nations Die* (Wheaton, IL: Nelson, 1994).

Robert H. Bork, *Slouching Towards Gomorrah* (New York: Harper, 1996).

James Dale Davidson and Lord William Rees-Mogg, *The Great Reckoning* (New York: Summit, 1991).

M. Stanton Evans, *The Theme Is Freedom* (Washington, DC: Regnery, 1994).

Os Guinness, *The American Hour* (New York: Free Press, 1993).

Paul Johnson, *Intellectuals* (New York: Harper, 1988).

David L. McKenna, *The Coming Great Awakening* (Downers Grove, IL: InterVarsity, 1990).

Catherine Millard, *The Rewriting of America's History* (Camp Hill, PA: Horizon, 1991).

Marvin Olasky, *The Tragedy of American Compassion* (Wheaton, IL: Crossway, 1992).

Francis A. Schaeffer, *How Should We Then Live?* (Wheaton, IL: Crossway, 1976).

Material covered in the Crime: Its Causes and Its Cures chapter can be found in the following Zane Publishing Home Library titles:

Crime Collection: World Encyclopedia of Assassination
Crime Collection: World Encyclopedia of Con Artists & Confidence Games
Crime Collection: World Encyclopedia of 20th Century Murder
Crime Collection: World Encyclopedia of Organized Crime
Crime Collection: Encyclopedia of Criminal Language
Crime Collection: Encyclopedia of Western Lawmen & Outlaws
Crime Collection: Encyclopedia of the JFK Assassination

CRIME: ITS CAUSES
AND ITS CURES

Men, in a word, must necessarily be controlled either by a power within them, or by a power without them; either by the word of God, or by the strong arm of man, either by the Bible, or by the bayonet.
— ROBERT C. WINTHROP

CRIME HAS BECOME A MAJOR epidemic in America, and its portrayal has become a popular pastime. Film producers clear hundreds of millions of dollars playing off the crime fever, and criminals often think of themselves as celebrities rather than as rebels against God's law.

In 1994 alone, U. S. residents aged twelve and older committed 42.1 million crimes (U.S. Department of Justice statistics). The United States now ranks with Russia and South Africa as the crime capitals of the world.

Our forefathers came out of Europe in the seventeenth century in search of a new land of liberty, a land where they would not be subject to the forfeiture of their land or their political and religious liberties to the government. They wanted a place where their children could not compromise with the existing amoral culture of Europe. They wanted to live under God's law, to fear Him rather than be under the organized crime of the king, the bishops, or the highwaymen (gangs). They understood that God's law was the standard of all good societies and the means of crime prevention. They came to America not seeking to escape law and live autonomously (as anti-law ANARCHISTS), but seeking to be self-governed under God.

James Madison stated it well when he said,

> We have staked the whole future of American civilization, not upon the power of government, far from it. We have staked the future of all our political institutions upon the capacity of mankind for self-government; upon the capacity of each and all of us to govern ourselves, to control ourselves, to sustain ourselves according to the Ten Commandments of God.[1]

The crime rate in early America was very low. Alexis de Tocqueville, the French historian and social philosopher, toured America in 1831. He wrote that American cities did not even need a police force, whereas in Paris the GENDARMES would run the beggars through with bayonets as they clamored to steal bread.

De Tocqueville wrote of the reasons for America's civility and blessing:

> In the United States the influence of religion is not confined to the manners, but it extends to the intelligence of the people...
> Christianity, therefore, reigns without obstacle, by universal consent; the consequence is, as I have before observed, that every principle of the moral world is fixed and determinate....

ALEXIS DE TOCQUEVILLE
Born: *July 29, 1805*
Died: *April 16, 1859*

Claim to fame:
French political scientist and writer.

Did you know?
He belonged to an aristocratic French family.

I sought for the key to the greatness and genius of America in her harbors...; in her fertile fields and boundless forests; in her rich mines and vast world commerce; in her public school system and institutions of learning. I sought for it in her democratic Congress and in her matchless Constitution.

Not until I went into the churches of America and heard her pulpits aflame with righteousness did I understand the secret of her genius and power.

America is great because America is good, and if America ever ceases to be good, America will cease to be great.[2]

Note that this foreigner comprehended the real strength of our republic, which was true Christianity that trusted God for the power to be good.

TWENTIETH-CENTURY AMERICA

Increasingly, America in our century has drunk deeply from the HUMANIST philosophy of social Darwinism. Under this theory, man and his sinful nature are not the problem. Man is just a social animal, adapting to his environment, with no fixed laws governing his behavior and no holy God to answer to on Judgment Day.

What has been the result of this philosophy? We have seen a geometric explosion in the commission of violent crimes, which increased 560 percent from 1960 to 1990, while the population only increased 41 percent.[3] Concerning the recent drop in crime rates, Judge Robert Bork cited the Council on Crime report as saying that "Recent drops in serious crime are but the lull before the coming crime storm." Bork went on to say, "That is because the population of young males in the age groups that commit violent crime is about to increase rapidly, producing more violence than we know at present."[4]

While crime was spiraling upward in the last three decades, the "great society" programs expanded, and social spending at all levels of government increased more than five times to $787 billion per year.[5] Government has not solved the problem. In fact, it can be argued that by giving over the problem to "Big Brother," especially one who does not reason biblically, the people have opened up a PANDORA's box. Zane's *World Encyclopedia of Organized Crime* CD-ROM shows that crime syndicates have penetrated government at all levels. What is to keep the government itself from becoming criminal, like that of the Soviet Union, China, or King George in the days of our Founders? Is there an answer to crime that does not require the people to give their liberties away to the government in exchange for protection, like feudal VASSALS?

CHRISTIANITY ADDRESSES THE CRIME PROBLEM

As Christian parents and students, we, of course, do not study crime simply out of a morbid curiosity. We are called by our Lord to be peacemakers (Matthew 5:9). What solutions can we offer to the world for the crime epidemic that is engulfing our society?

Before we can offer answers, we must first properly offer the biblical analysis of our dilemma. The root of crime is not environment, poverty, or poor education. Environmental determinists believe that a bad environment is the cause of crime. With this assumption, criminals can all be reformed by placing them in a better environment. But Adam and Eve were in the perfect environment and still chose to sin. The Bible does not allow us to blame our environment for our crimes. Jesus said it definitively:

> What comes out of a man, that defiles a man. For from within, out of the heart of a man, proceed evil thoughts, adulteries, fornications, murders, thefts, covetousness, wickedness, deceit, licentiousness, an evil eye, blasphemy, pride, foolishness. All these evil things come from within and defile a man.[6]

Nor is poverty at the root of our crime problem. America's crime rate is many times higher than that of the poor nations of the world like India, China, and many African countries. Relative poverty in a materialistic/godless culture is a contributing factor to crime, but not the cause.

Is lack of education the cause of crime? Many social scientists and educators would answer this question in the affirmative. They believe that a child is simply *tabula rasa*—a blank slate, much like an unprogrammed computer ready to be activated with the right software. Horace Mann, the founder of public education in America, believed this fallacious assumption.

> Let the Common School be expanded to its capabilities, let it be worked with the efficiency of which it is susceptible, and nine-tenths of the crimes in the penal code would become obsolete. . .[7]

The twentieth century has proved Mann's theory to be preposterous. In 1933, Germany was among the most educated nations in the world, yet Hitler led it into the most violent war in history, killing millions of innocent victims. More recently, the United States has outspent the world on education, and yet it remains one of the most violent cultures in history.

The Bible clearly teaches, and Western civilization has concurred for 1,700 years, that the human heart and its propensity to sin is the root cause of crime. At the age of thirty-four, Augustine of Hippo came face to face with his own internal crime problem, his own warring lusts. He read Romans 13:13–14:

> Let us walk properly, as in the day, not in reveling and drunkenness, not in licentiousness and lewdness, not in strife and envy. But put on the Lord Jesus Christ, and make no provision for the flesh, to fulfill its lusts.

These words so humbled Augustine before God that he immediately trusted Christ and went from death to life. He was empowered by God to give up his lawless lifestyle and went on to become perhaps the greatest Christian philosopher of all time. When we come to grips with the reality of indwelling sin, as Augustine did, then we can realistically apply biblical solutions to the crime problem. But what are these solutions?

First, we must reach out to a dying world and offer it the good news that Christ died for sinners and criminals; that He can change their hearts, forgive their sins, and give them a new spirit to live for Him and for others.

The best drug rehabilitation programs in America are run by Christians who lead addicts and criminals to faith in Jesus Christ. Chuck Colson,

HORACE MANN
Born: *May 4, 1796*
Died: *August 2, 1859*

Claim to fame:
The "Father of American Public Education."

Did you know?
Visited Europe in 1843 and brought back ideas for mass education.

AUGUSTINE OF HIPPO
Born: *November 13, 354*
Died: *August 28, 430*

Claim to fame:
Saint; wrote The City of God *and* Confessions.

Did you know?
His father was a pagan and his mother was a Christian.

151

the former White House staffer who went to jail during Watergate in the '70s, was converted and has since led tens of thousands of his fellow prisoners to Jesus through his Prison Fellowship ministry. Most of these men and women who are truly saved do not go back to a life of crime. Colson and thousands of other believers have dedicated themselves to teaching the ultimate rehabilitation: the transforming power of Christ.

Secondly, we must offer help to the needy children, families, and homeless in our society. Most of the truly needy are victims of the crime wave. The bulk of this charity (love) must come from churches, synagogues, private charities, and individual families.

Up until the Depression, almost all social welfare was the responsibility of the extended family and of the church, synagogue, or charitable mission. Now, with government programs in place, many have drawn back from their role of "loving their neighbor as themselves."

In his benchmark book *The Tragedy of American Compassion*, Marvin Olasky documented the real compassion that stirred the hearts of early Americans like the Pilgrim fathers, the colonists, and the Americans in cities during the nineteenth-century period of heavy immigration. He conclusively debunked the myth of social Darwinism and called for Christian families to pour out their love in practical ways to the truly needy.

Governor William Bradford, chronicler of the Pilgrim saga, described how the Pilgrims cared for one another when they first landed at Plymouth in 1620. He said that half of their number died in the first four months, and that for a long period only "6. or 7. sound persons" could still move about. Those people

> in most times of distress. . .spared no pains night nor day, but with abundance of toyle and hazard of their owne health, fetched them woode, made them fires, drest them meat, made their breads, washed their lothsome cloaths, cloathed and uncloathed them; in a word, did all ye homly and necessarie offices for them.[8]

Real love for people in real need can stop crime before it begins. This ounce of prevention would be worth a ton of cure.

Thirdly, there must be a restoration of the proper role of civil government under God. Romans 13 defines that role clearly:

> Let every soul be subject to the governing authorities. For there is no authority except from God, and the authorities that exist are appointed by God. Therefore whoever resists the authority resists the ordinance of God, and those who resist will bring judgment on themselves. For rulers are not a terror to good works, but to evil. Do you want to be unafraid of the authority? Do what is good, and you will have praise from the same. For he is God's minister to you for good. But if you do evil, be afraid, for he does not bear the sword in vain; for he is God's minister, an avenger to execute wrath on him who practices evil.

The Bible clearly teaches that civil government is a divinely ordained institution commissioned to punish evildoers and protect the godly so that they can raise their families and build God's kingdom. When civil government properly administers justice using the biblical principles as contained in the Magna Carta, English Common Law, and the U. S. Constitution, then it is doing its job well.

Law professor John Eidsmoe pointed out that "as government officials keep the criminal element under restraint, the safety and freedom of law-abiding citizens is preserved. This also facilitates the spread of the Gospel."[9] There are at least four major benefits of a biblically based prosecution and punishment of criminals:

1. **Justice.** We say it is an injustice when a person commits a crime and gets away with it; crime demands punishment. Rulers are a "terror to those who do evil" (Romans 13:3). Every crime is paid for by someone. In a biblically based society, the criminal pays for his crime, either through restitution, with his life, or with his property. In an ungodly culture, the innocent and the victims pay for crime through trauma, loss of property, death, and taxes, which pay for prisons, and through increasing government tyranny.

Judge Robert Bork wrote that if we do not bring justice back quickly, we as a people will lose our freedom:

> When physical safety becomes a major problem even for the middle classes, we must necessarily become a heavily policed, authoritarian society, a society in which the middle classes live in gated and walled communities and make their places of work hardened targets.[10]

2. **Deterrent.** The knowledge that criminals are severely punished will deter others from breaking the law. The purpose of punishment is that all "shall hear, and fear" (Deuteronomy 13:11, 17:13, 21:21). Swift punishment is essential for the punishment to be a deterrent, for otherwise the connection between the crime and the punishment is lost (Ecclesiastes 8:11).

3. **Restitution.** This is the major punishment set forth in the Bible. Other biblical forms of punishment include (1) capital punishment, (2) forfeiture of property (fines), (3) involuntary servitude, and (4) corporal punishment. Note that the cornerstone of American justice, the prison system, is not mentioned in the Bible. Chuck Colson, perhaps the foremost Christian authority on prisons, says that our system is an abject failure, and needs to be replaced with rehabilitation and restitution, which builds character and repays the victim.[11]

4. **Prevention of Private Vengeance.** "If society does not take action against criminals, the victim or his relatives will. In fact in some early systems of judgment such as the Viking law, once the court found the defendant guilty, it was up to the victim's relatives to carry out the sentence."[12] The result of this system was civil war and much bloodshed. We are headed back to private vengeance because our courts no longer bring swift justice to evildoers. We must elect biblically trained legal minds to be our judges.

At the same time we are asking civil authorities to carry out their biblical mandate to punish crime, the government itself must be kept in check through the election of godly leaders. Because it has the power of the sword, civil government is a potential danger to become the perpetrator of crime itself. The history of pagan nations, which we surveyed in this book, proves that the caesar, emperor, or tribal chieftain usually breaks his vows to the people and impoverishes the innocent while protecting the guilty. Tyrants, misusing their God-given authority to punish evildoers, usually become co-conspirators in the crimes they are commissioned to punish. Thomas Jefferson said, "The functionaries of every government have propensities to command at will the liberty and property of their constituents."[13] Our founders knew that only a virtuous people demanding virtuous leaders could perpetuate a free republic.

Fourthly, godly families must reestablish their authority in the home and their influence on their children. It appears at times that our whole society, especially the state and the media, is at war with the family. It is within the family that the war on crime is won or lost. Parents must once again become teachers of the moral law (Deuteronomy 6:4–10). Proverbs 22:6 says, "Train up a child in the way he should go, and when he is old he will not depart from it."

Noah Webster, the founder of American education and author of the original Webster Dictionary said:

> The education of youth is an employment of more consequence than making laws and preaching the gospel, because it lays the foundation on which both law and gospel rest for success.[14]

One of the great benefits of studying with the Zane CD-ROM titles is that they stimulate independent study and inquiry. As Christians we are called to "disciple the nations," teaching them all that our Lord has commanded (Matthew 28:18–20). We are commanded to bring God's Word to bear on every area of life. This includes crime and punishment. There are answers and great hope if we are willing to learn the truth and live it out. By God's grace, the church can be "called the Repairer of the breach, the Restorer of streets to dwell in."[15]

Daniel Webster called Americans back to their roots on 22 November 1820 at the bicentennial celebration of the landing of the pilgrims at Plymouth Rock:

> Finally, let us not forget the religious character of our origin. Our fathers were brought hither by their high veneration for the Christian religion. They journeyed by its light, and labored in its hope. They sought to incorporate its principles with the elements of their society, and to diffuse its influence through all their institutions, civil, political, or literary.
>
> Let us cherish these sentiments, and extend this influence still more widely; in full conviction that that is the happiest society which partakes in the highest degree of the mild and peaceful spirit of Christianity.[16]

True Christianity, restored first in our homes and churches, then in the streets, will restore to America the "peaceful spirit of Christianity."

CD-ROM ANALYSES

• The *World Encyclopedia of Organized Crime* CD-ROM traces the historical

---

NOAH WEBSTER

Born: October 16, 1758
Died: May 28, 1843

Claim to fame:

Compiled An American Dictionary of the English Language.

Did you know?

He was the pioneer of American copyright laws.

DANIEL WEBSTER

Born: January 18, 1782
Died: October 24, 1852

Claim to fame:

American orator and statesman.

Did you know?

He was the hero of Stephen Vincent Benet's short story "The Devil and Daniel Webster."

roots and international scope of organized crime. It also touches upon the unspoken reality that organized crime is playing a major role in the political and economic destinies of the modern world. This survey illustrates the biblical reality that mankind tends toward corruption without the restraint of a strong Biblical faith.

As Christian parents, we must give our children hope that evil, even international crime families, will not long prosper. We should teach our children not to fear powermongers and conspirators in our day, but to fear God. As Isaiah 8:12–13 says,

> Do not call conspiracy all this that people will call conspiracy; neither be in fear of what they fear, nor in dread. The Lord of Hosts—regard him as holy and honor His holy name, and let Him be your fear, and let Him be your dread.

• The *World Encyclopedia of 20th Century Murder* graphically portrays the most violent century in history. Some of the descriptions are very explicit, and caution should be used with small children. But the CD-ROM ends with an analysis that places a major responsibility upon the media and television for ever-more violent false portrayal of what life is really like. It also points to the decline of values and strong families as reasons for our increasingly violent culture.

• The *Encyclopedia of the JFK Assassination* CD-ROM is an excellent, balanced analysis of this pivotal event in American history. The CD-ROM encourages two very positive solutions. We are encouraged to know history by going back to the original sources and being independent thinkers, not to be taken in by media manipulation. We also are encouraged to examine the actions of those in office, holding them accountable, which is our responsibility as American citizens.

• In the *Encyclopedia of Western Lawmen & Outlaws*, the ups and downs of law and order in the American West of the nineteenth century is examined. Christian parents should also emphasize the fact that lawlessness was not the determining factor of western development. The missionaries began the great adventure, and Christian families completed the settlement of the West, bringing with them lawfulness, morality, family values, churches, and schools.

REVIEW QUESTIONS

1. What did Madison say was the basis for the future success of American government?

2. To what did Alexis de Tocqueville attribute the greatness that he saw in America?

3. What does social Darwinism consider to be the source of crime?

4. What does the Bible consider to be the source of all crime?

5. According to Romans 13, what is the purpose for civil government?

6. Name four biblical solutions to crime.

7. How can the government itself be prevented from becoming criminal?

RELATED SCRIPTURE

Genesis 9:1–4

Exodus 21:23–25

Deuteronomy 6:4–10

Deuteronomy 13:11

Ecclesiastes 8:11

Isaiah 8:12–13

Mark 7:20–23

Matthew 5—the Sermon on the Mount

Matthew 28:18–20

Proverbs 22:6

Romans 13:1–4,13–14

SUGGESTED READING

William J. Bennett, ed. *The Index of Leading Cultural Indicators.*

Robert H. Bork, *Slouching Towards Gomorrah* (New York: Harper, 1996).

John Eidsmoe, *God and Caesar* (Westchester, IL: Crossway, 1984).

Marvin Olasky, *The Tragedy of American Compassion* (Wheaton, IL: Crossway, 1992).

PART THREE

Academic Disciplines That Manifest God's Principles

Material covered in the Worldview Expression in Art chapter can be found in the following Zane Publishing Home Library titles:

History through Art: Ancient Greece
History through Art: Ancient Rome
History through Art: The Middle Ages
History through Art: The Renaissance
History through Art: The Baroque
History through Art: The Enlightenment
History through Art: Romanticism
History through Art: The Pre-Modern Era
History through Art: The Twentieth Century
History through Art: Native American and Colonial Art
History through Art: Great Works of Art Explained, Part I
History through Art: Great Works of Art Explained, Part II
Art & Music: The Medieval Era
Art & Music: The Renaissance
Art & Music: The Baroque
Art & Music: The Eighteenth Century
Art & Music: Romanticism
Art & Music: Impressionism
Art & Music: The Twentieth Century
Art & Music: Surrealism

WORLDVIEW EXPRESSION IN ART

. . .the Lord has called by name Bezaleel. . .and He has filled him with the Spirit of God, in wisdom and understanding, in knowledge and all manner of workmanship, to design artistic works, to work in gold and silver and bronze, in cutting jewels for setting in carving wood, and to work in all manner of artistic workmanship.

—EXODUS 35:30–33

THE TRADITIONAL CHRISTIAN APPROACH to art is based on the aesthetics of the greatest Christian thinker of the ancient world, Augustine of Hippo. Aesthetics, simply stated, is the study of what we enjoy and why we enjoy it. For Augustine, to enjoy something was to find it beautiful; therefore, a thing that was aesthetically perfect would be perfectly beautiful. Augustine saw the greatest expression of AESTHETIC beauty in God's created order:

> Beauty of form has been added to the whole of this material world, even in its lowest parts[1]. . . It was you then, O Lord, who made them, you who are beautiful, for they are beautiful; you who are good, for they are good; you who are, for they too are.[2]

Human beings, created in God's image, imitate this first creative act in their own creations, whether they create art, literature, a new invention, or a scientific law. Humans cannot bring anything into existence that has not already been created by God, but they can highlight certain aspects of creation in unique ways. In doing so, they reflect the creative genius of God; they are being "recreatively creative." Individual creations are good in the same way that all of creation is good: by reflecting God-created aesthetic qualities.

> . . .Scripture tells us seven times that you [God] saw that what you had made was good, and when you looked for the eighth time and saw the whole of your creation, we are told that you found it not only good but very good, for you saw all at once as one whole. Each separate work was good, but when they were all seen as one, they were not merely good: they were very good.
>
> The same can be said of every material thing which has beauty. For a thing which consists of several parts, each beautiful in itself, is far more beautiful than the individual parts which, properly combined and arranged, compose the whole, even though each part, taken separately, is itself a thing of beauty.[3]

The definition of art is "the dispositions or manifestations of things by human skill, to answer the purposes intended." We are called of God to arrange the elements of this world to manifest His glory and beauty. That is the challenge to the artist. In this sense all art is religious art, for God Himself, the infinite, is the source of all beauty. Art is to be the finite expression of God's infinite beauty.

Art, then, the creations of one's hands, is not just an amusement for the cultured. It serves an eternal purpose. Author Cynthia Maus put it well:

> Art is the interpretation of the great eternal realities of life, and as soon as the artist tries to embody the greatest feelings and aspirations of the human soul, he gets on Biblical ground, for there is no great interest or aspiration of man which the Bible has not treated. It is for this reason that great artists have dealt so largely with Biblical themes. Painting and the Bible could not be kept separate. They are congenial companions, because they have one common characteristic: both deal, not with the immediate and material, but with the eternal and spiritual. The function of art is to embody the universal and the eternal.[4]

The ultimate expression of beauty was the incarnation of God in Jesus Christ. He has provided the underlying themes for the greatest art in the world. As the God-man, all the treasures of wisdom and knowledge reside in Him. He answered, once and for all, the great philosophic and artistic dilemma of the ages. He brought the eternal to the temporal, and in doing so brought unity out of the diversity of the particulars of life.

Plato struggled with the problem of bringing unity out of disjointed particulars. He realized that without a universal absolute, all of life is chaos, and particular people, events, works of art have no meaning. Leonardo da Vinci understood this problem. He was not only a great artist and scientist, but also a phenomenal mathematician. He died in despair, knowing that all mathematical calculations, without a universal absolute, lead only to man as a machine with no moral compass.

Instead of finding harmony in an understanding of the relation of every particular to the ultimate truth of God, men search for meaning in particulars, finding each of them hollow, and abandoning each for another. This phenomenon can be observed in art. The historical tendency of art has been like a pendulum swinging from the emotional to the intellectual. But this observation, though accurate, reflects a deeper tension in the human soul.

God does not call man to pendular extremes between form and freedom, or between our intellect and emotions. He calls mankind to liberty within the bounds of the laws of His universe. To the extent that cultures have lived within this balance, they have created art that manifests the reality of life and that, therefore, glorifies God in the artistic experience. Throughout human history, most cultures have run from God's created order. Philosophy, art, and music are important BELLWETHERS of man's spiritual condition. For instance, the artist often manifests the prevailing worldview, before a society begins to manifest its dangerous outcomes.

As Christians, we need to perceive the artistic temperatures of our time and of times past in order to, first of all, understand our generation and be able to give a defense for the hope that is in us. The Apostle Paul demonstrated this cultural awareness when he observed Athenian temples, quoted Athenian poets, and used the Athenians' statue to the "unknown god" to point to Christ.

Furthermore, we must comprehend the meaning and purpose of art so that we can reestablish the arts to glorify the Creator. Our children will not stop being influenced by modern art forms, music, drama, or movies if we simply withdraw them from some exposure to the worst manifestations of their popular expressions.

In his book *The Abolition of Man*, C. S. Lewis called us to "irrigate" our children's sentiments and aesthetic tendencies through quality aesthetic education:

> For every one pupil who needs to be guarded from a weak excess of sensibility there are three who need to be awakened from the slumber of cold vulgarity. The task of the modern educator is not to cut down jungles but to irrigate deserts. The right defense against false sentiments is to inculcate just sentiments. By starving the sensibility of our pupils we only make them easier prey to the propagandist when he comes. For famished nature will be avenged and a hard heart is no infallible protection against a soft head.[5]

CLASSICAL GREEK ART

The ancient Greeks were the world's first self-conscious humanists. They placed great emphasis upon man's potential, his power, and his mind. "Mind over matter" is an expression in a Greek manner of thought. This positive emphasis on human significance led to great advances in the fields of art and architecture. The Greek influence on Western thought and art is significant even to our day.

The idealistic Greek view of life also distorted their perception of reality. This distortion was reflected in their art. In the sculpture of the Discus Thrower, the nude man is perfect, without blemish or even strain in his face as he tosses the discus. The Greeks eventually had to come to grips with the other side of life—cruelty, wars, tyranny, death, and, ultimately, the need for salvation. The sin nature of man and his need for a savior were made clear to the idealistic Greeks over the centuries. Wars, famines, the destruction of Athens, plagues, political tyranny and intrigue, and philosophies without ultimate answers all prepared Greek civilization and art to face reality. From the flat, emotionless figures of the sixth century B.C., to the perfectly proportioned men in the classical period, to the panicked emotionalism of the fourth century, Greek art and architecture displayed to the world mankind's potential. At the same time, we can see in Greek culture the depravity men and society face without faith in the true God.

The psalmist gives the balance between too highly and too lowly esteeming the value of man. Psalm 139:14 says that man is fearfully and wonderfully made. But Psalm 144:3–4 tells us "But what is man that you [God] take notice of him? Man is vanity and a breath; his days are as a shadow that passes away." So the psalmist, in Psalm 146, goes on to admonish us to "put not your trust in. . .man in whom there is no help."

Throughout our study of art, the balanced biblical ground of reality is a plumb line and a hope for every age. For example, the Romans, who absorbed the Greek culture as it died, tried to imitate the art of Greece. The Romans were more utilitarian than the Greeks and less idealistic, building coliseums for pleasure and aqueducts for water distribution. Their art as well as their architecture reflected the reality and cruelty of life. The Romans, like the Greeks, were searching for balance. They tended toward the materialism of their day and away from spiritual reality.

The art of antiquity gives us insight into the people of the time. We can appreciate their works of art for their inherent beauty without making idols of their accomplishments. Most of the great early Christian thinkers, such as Ambrose, Jerome, and Augustine, appreciated and integrated classical artistic learning into the superior Christian curriculum that came to prevail in Europe. We can do the same without compromising our faith with pagan misconceptions.

THE MIDDLE AGES

The Middle Ages is often misunderstood as an artistically backwards age. In reality, it was an age of change that came to be known as the age of faith. It should be remembered that this period began with the overthrow of the Roman Empire by a series of fierce barbarian tribes who came to dominate Europe and Asia. It took several centuries for Christianity to permeate and convert these pagan tribes. Christian art began in the catacombs in Rome where Christians hid from Roman authorities. More than four thousand inscriptions, mosaics, and frescoes have been discovered in these underground tombs where more than 500,000 Christians were buried.

By the sixth century, medieval art began to thrive as the Church became the major patron of the arts. Until the Reformation, most people were illiterate. The depictions of biblical scenes in frescoes, mosaics, and stained glass windows in churches were called the "people's Bible," and were often the only source of God's truth for commoners. This need produced memorable images that depicted Christ in His divinity and power. Medieval art was intentionally symbolic, not realistic. The art was almost exclusively religious in theme, and was meant to teach a lesson rather than mimic reality.

Religious art in the Middle Ages faced some serious problems. Because many people were illiterate and still lived in a state of semi-paganism, there was a tendency to worship the art or sculpture as an icon rather than see it as a help in worship or as beautiful art. Miracles were attributed to many of these images, and these images became the objects of prayer. Eventually, replicas of icons were sold by the clergy to provide spiritual favor for the purchaser and money for the church coffers. This heresy of idolatry was exposed in the Reformation with its emphasis on the Word of God as the only source of doctrine and practice.

By the eleventh century, the barbarians had been converted throughout Europe. In this age of faith, Christianity was central to life. The great cathedrals began to be built in the eleventh century and for four hundred years the building continued. Some of the most important art of history is enshrined in these cathedrals, their sculpture, and their stained-glass windows. Many artisans would spend their entire lives building these works of art to glorify God. The Cathedral of Chartres was built without the patronage of the Roman Church and paid for by the people themselves. Cathedrals were more than great works of art and architecture; they were the centers of medieval culture and life.

In the late Middle Ages, Christian painters like Giotto, Jan van Eyck, and Fra Angelico brought the transition to the Renaissance painters. Each of these artists exhibited their love for God through their choice of biblical subject matter. Giotto (1266–1337), the most famous painter of the late Middle Ages and early Italian Renaissance, broke free from the unrealistic, symbolic BYZANTINE art of Florence. Medieval art had been stiff and flat, without any sense of depth. Giotto painted people and nature as real, attempting, without mastering, the technique of perspective. Van Eyck (1395–1441) was the first great painter of landscapes. In his masterpiece *Adoration of the Lamb*, people of all classes—the rich and poor—are coming to Christ. Christ is authentically portrayed as the living Lamb of God. In the background is a beautiful, realistic landscape.

Sadly, it was about this time that humanism moved in and began to take over the Renaissance. By the fifteenth century, the developing Renaissance could have either followed Giotto and Van Eyck in the pursuit of biblical art, or the humanism of classical antiquity. It took the latter course and resurrected the humanism that has endured to our day.

THE RENAISSANCE

The Renaissance marked a golden age of artistic expression. Most early Renaissance art was church-related and concerned religious themes. But as the movement turned more completely toward the philosophies of the ancient Greeks and Romans, it naturally became more humanistic.

During this period, artists and thinkers, like the clergy and merchant class, were throwing off the restraints of biblical reasoning and struggling to find meaning in a world with no absolutes. The rich merchants of Venice, Florence, and Rome also became artistic patrons, sanctioning secular art works as well as religious.

Two great artists struggled with the humanism of this period, with different outcomes. Michelangelo (1475–1564) was one of the greatest artists in all of history. His love for God gave great inspiration to his work, although a mixture of humanism is apparent in much of his work as well. In Michelangelo's great room in the Academy in Florence are his statues of men "tearing themselves out of the rock." They clearly say that man will be independent of nature and creation, that man will tear himself out of the rock and be AUTONOMOUS. His eighteen-foot marble statue of David is magnificent. But his idealized form, confident look, even his oversized hands, speak of humanistic man, powerful man. Michelangelo's work in the Sistine Chapel depicts the story of Creation, the Flood, and Old Testament prophets who revealed the redemption of man. But within this breathtaking biblical fresco are included pagan prophetesses—the infiltration of humanistic thought. In his later works, such as his *Pietas*, such a humanistic influence is not apparent. His Christianity became more personal in his later life, due to the influence of Christian leaders known as the Waldensians.

Leonardo da Vinci (1452–1519), the archetype of the Renaissance man, was a painter, sculptor, architect, poet, musician, inventor, and engineer. Da Vinci was a humanistic man consistently through his life, but he struggled with the eternal problem of bringing unity out of diversity. Da Vinci the mathematician and artist beautifully manipulated the particulars of man's life, following the philosophy of Aristotle and his emphasis on

MICHELANGELO
Born: 1475
Died: 1564

Claim to fame:
Great Italian painter and sculptor who painted the ceilings of Rome's Sistine Chapel.

Did you know?
He was one of the architects of Saint Peter's Church in Vatican City, the principal and largest church of the Christian world.

LEONARDO DA VINCI
Born: 1452
Died: May 2, 1519

Claim to fame:
One of the greatest artists and thinkers of the Renaissance.

Did you know?
He painted the Mona Lisa *and* The Last Supper.

man's centrality. But without a comprehensive biblical worldview, in which God gives meaning to finite man, da Vinci faced the problems of modern man's attempt at Aristotelian autonomy from God's creation. He died a frustrated and unfulfilled genius. Giovanni Gentile, a great Italian philosopher, said that da Vinci died in despondency because he could not give up hope of uniting the particulars and the universal.

The accomplishments of Renaissance artists transformed the artistic perspective on man's place in the universe. Their emphasis on man as the center of the world's drama acknowledged God's high plan for man, even though it was often idolized. It was left to Reformation artists, however, to most clearly capture the balanced perspective of man's purpose in a fallen but beautiful creation.

THE REFORMATION

The art of northern Europe, where the Reformation took hold, was greatly affected by its renewed view of God and man. Contrary to the puritanical censors that they are made out to be by some secular historians, the reformers actually lifted the arts to some of its greatest heights in painting, music, and literature.

Lucas Cranach was one of Martin Luther's good friends and the godfather of his children. His paintings drew together the spiritual life, mystically portrayed in the medieval period, with the earthiness of the physical world. Life was a blending of these two spheres, not a pendular alternation between asceticism and hedonism.

The Reformation artists did not have ecclesiastical funding for their projects like the painters of the Renaissance. The Dutch artists gained some support from the wealthy Dutch merchants of the time, especially for portraiture painting. However, great Christian artists like Rembrandt did not paint biblical themes merely for commissions. Rembrandt painted out of a sincere Christian faith and a love for scripture. He illustrated almost every chapter and theme of the Bible. He did 150 paintings, 70 etchings, and 575 drawings on biblical themes.

Before 1643, the young Rembrandt practiced the more flamboyant baroque style of the time. As he matured, he became a master at bringing out the spiritual heart, personal pain, and depth of spirit of those he painted. Rembrandt truly was the creator of a new style of painting, unique and classically beautiful. Francis Schaeffer pointed to the fact that Rembrandt exhibited a balanced biblical view of life. He neither downplayed nature nor exalted it. He expressed the hearts of those he painted, portraying them as created in God's image and important, but at the same time fatally flawed and often cruel. In his *Raising of the Cross*, Rembrandt painted himself raising the cross during the crucifixion of Christ.

One innovation of Reformation artists was to portray ordinary families, as in Rembrandt's *Family Group*— farmers, soldiers, merchants, and politicians in real life settings. These seemingly secular artistic drawings were actually a reaffirmation of the holy calling of all people, regardless of position, to carry out their vocations as ministers of God. This contradicted the medieval teaching that a completely committed spiritual life was only found in celibacy, as in the monastery or clergy. This was Calvin's

REMBRANDT

Born: *July 15, 1606*
Died: *October 4, 1669*

Claim to fame:
Premier Dutch artist of the seventeenth century.

Did you know?
He became famous for his dramatic use of light and shadow.

priesthood of the believer put to canvas, and it lifted the common people, setting the stage for the political and religious liberty of the eighteenth century.

THE ENLIGHTENMENT AND ROMANTICISM

The Enlightenment was the intellectual reaction of many of those who rebelled against God's rule in the eighteenth century. To them, man was autonomous, and all problems could be solved by human reason alone. Jean-Jacques Rousseau is the best known of the French "philosophes," many of whom were deists. Deism teaches that God created the world and then left it alone to run by mechanistic natural principles, without interfering.

In line with this philosophy, the art of the Enlightenment period was scientifically orderly and subdued as opposed to the wild exuberance of the baroque period. But later in the eighteenth century, even Rousseau himself realized that man could not reason his way to a better world. Many Europeans then turned on reason and sought an escape, not from reality, but from rationality.

The world of nineteenth-century art was filled with emotion, violence, and passion. Whereas Enlightenment thinkers and artists stressed the ordered, reasoned universe from a deistic perspective, many romantics laid emphasis on God's presence in all things, especially nature. In the extreme, some romantics became pantheists, such as the American writers Emerson, Thoreau, and Whitman. The ideal for the romantic period was not ordering the world or freeing mankind, but personal fulfillment and expression.

Romantic art can be appreciated by Christians who understand the beauty of God's nature. Albert Birstadt, for example, in his *Hudson River School* landscape, portrays the awesome living reality of God's creation with such power that it draws the viewer into an attitude of worship.

By the late nineteenth century, the romantic ideal was breaking down. Man's significance in a hostile world was coming into question with Darwin's theory of evolution. This materialistic view of life, which saw man as simply the product of time and chance, has influenced art into our day.

IMPRESSIONISM

In the mid to late nineteenth century, another artistic trend added beauty and an interesting perspective to the artistic world. Impressionism, a movement led by such painters as Claude Monet and Pierre-Auguste Renoir, painted beautiful soft "impressions" of life as seen by the viewer with all sharp images removed. The impressionist painted only what he saw. Eventually, as in the paintings of the leading impressionists after 1885, what they saw became more indiscernible and less realistic. The influence of impressionism declined, but this development set the stage for the modern art revolution of the twentieth century.

MODERN ART

The twentieth century brought an era of art that vividly portrayed introspective, analytical, and lonely Western culture. Artists such as Pablo

CLAUDE MONET
Born: *November 14, 1840*
Died: *December 5, 1926*

Claim to fame:
French artist who perfected the style known as Impressionism.

Did you know?
Built a water-lily pond that inspired his last paintings.

165

Picasso created paintings that dissected the human experience and figure from the artist's perspective, not the viewer's. Picasso was a talented artist who used the method of fragmentation to communicate his own reality. His figures, though sometimes grotesque, made sense to him. His paintings reflected fragmented people and reality, making a complete break with the Renaissance and Reformation view of man as created in God's image and as beautiful.

Later modern artists took the NIHILISTIC philosophy of Nietzsche and Sartre to its chaotic conclusion. They realized that if God is dead, as Nietzsche declared, then life is meaningless. By the time Marcel Duchamp painted *Nude Descending a Staircase*, No. 2 in 1912, the human had completely disappeared from the picture, and was reduced to abstract blocks of color. With no absolute standard other than individual taste, the blasphemous pornography of Robert Mapplethorpe can be considered as much a work of art as Raphael's *School of Athens*.

CONCLUSION

Modern man, like his art, is in a quandary. He cannot live in the world he has created around himself. Picasso broke out of his cubism when he painted his children and two wives in a traditional manner. Man instinctively knows that he is made for a higher aesthetic purpose.

Franky Schaeffer highlighted our modern artistic dilemma:

> One cannot listen only to *musique concrète*, punk rock, or atonal noise: Bach is played now more than ever. Jackson Pollack and deKooning must at some point be relieved by the eye's pleasure in the natural forms of Gothic architecture, the light in a Vermeer, and the feeling for weight, mass, and power in the work of Michelangelo. The hopelessness of Beckett's trashcan characters must at some point be exchanged for the joy of the lovers in "A Midsummer Night's Dream."
>
> *In other words, the proud secular humanist cannot live in the world he has created and remain sane without drawing on the Judeo-Christian artistic heritage.* This alone should make him rethink his position. Why the need for music, artworks, literature, and other cultural artifacts that in terms of his own philosophical position are absurd? If he is right, why does he still need these things? Because, whoever the humanist believes man to be, man is who he is: a being created in God's image. His longing for beauty, resolution, order, and transformation cannot simply be canceled by philosophical fiat![6]

The unbelieving world is philosophically inconsistent. It continues the admiration of Michelangelo, Rembrandt, Bach, and Handel, but then denies the God who inspired them to create. Christian students in this generation have a responsibility to point out the hypocrisy of our secular culture in not recognizing the positive influence of Christianity upon the arts.

The visual arts have great importance within God's plan for His world. Five chapters of Exodus are devoted solely to describing the artistic works of Bezaleel, who was called of God to be an artist. We have a great opportunity, and a challenge, to raise up students with such gifts to create works of art for "glory and beauty."

PABLO PICASSO
Born: *October 25, 1881*
Died: *April 8, 1973*

Claim to fame:
Spanish painter known for his use of Cubism.

Did you know?
Created decors for Diaghilev's Ballets Russes.

CD-ROM ANALYSES

History through Art

• *The Baroque*

This CD-ROM presentation vividly portrays the art and music of the baroque era. However, the distinction is not made clear between the baroque style of the Catholic south and the Reformation art of Rembrandt and others from Holland.

• *Native American and Colonial Art*

This CD-ROM thoughtfully portrays the American Indians' art and the integral role it played in their everyday life. It is obvious that God has placed a love of aesthetics in the hearts of all peoples in all parts of the world.

Concerning colonial artists, the CD-ROM concentrates upon those key figures who developed American painting. The Christian student may want to study Benjamin West, who earns a brief mention on the CD-ROM, and who is known as the father of American painting. After training in Europe, West, a devout Christian, became a prominent artist in London, where he trained most of the next generation of American artists, including Charles Wilson Peale, Rembrandt Peale, John Copley, Gilbert Stuart, and John Trumbull.

Note that the individual is very important to the colonists, and that, therefore, the people desire to have their portraits painted for posterity. Contrast this concept of Christian individuality with the Indian monism discussed on the CD-ROM, which sees no more significance for man than for a tree, since we are all part of god and one with nature.

• *The Enlightenment*

The content of this CD-ROM provides a wealth of information on the art and philosophy of the Enlightenment. It also ends realistically, portraying the age as ending in dismay and revolution. One distinction that is not made clear in this presentation is the divergence of ideas between the Enlightenment and the American War of Independence. Enlightenment thinking led to Napoleon, while Christian thinking led to constitutional liberty.

• *Romanticism*

This presentation of the romantic period gives an excellent survey of the art and philosophy of the time. It clearly portrays the pendulum swing from form to freedom and from reason to emotion that characterized the late eighteenth century. It is interesting to note that the early American art of the colonial era was not deeply influenced by this trend, probably because America had a much more serious commitment to the biblical balance of unity and diversity and was not enthralled with the deistic and revolutionary tendencies of the Old World.

• *The Pre-Modern Era*

This CD-ROM intelligently details the leading artists, especially in America, who shaped the foundation for our modern art forms. The presentation accurately records the influence of Charles Darwin, Karl Marx, and others in compromising the foundations of Western civilization and its art. The CD-ROM ends with the statement that the vision, ideals, and pastoral escapes of past ages were gone, ruined by technology and a world devoid of standards. In this artistic environment, it makes sense that the CD-ROM ends with the declaration "there is no escape."

• *The Twentieth Century*

Like *The Pre-Modern Era*, this CD-ROM very accurately depicts the chaos left after Western culture abandoned its Christian principles. Modern art, as is pointed out, is a mirror to the state of man in this century; it is a chronicle of the decline of society. Christian students should not allow themselves to be disheartened by the bleak view taken by most of the artists whose works appear to communicate no hope for the future. Christianity is the hope that Western culture has forgotten or rejected, and in it the Christian finds strength to resist the anxiety of the modern world.

REVIEW QUESTIONS

1. What is the greatest expression of beauty, according to Augustine?

2. According to Cynthia Maus, what do the Bible and painting have in common?

3. Why does C. S. Lewis think aesthetic education is important?

4. During different periods, Greek art was distorted in different ways. What were they?

5. Where did Christian art first appear?

6. What architectural works stand today as monuments of Christian art?

7. Describe the effects of humanism in the art and lives of Michelangelo and Leonardo da Vinci.

8. How did Rembrandt express his love for the Bible through his art?

9. What innovation of Reformation art was an artistic expression of the doctrine of the priesthood of the believer?

10. What two movements followed the Reformation and were philosophical rebellions against God's laws?

11. What is the relationship between Impressionism and Abstractism?

12. What is the dilemma of modern art and modern man?

RELATED SCRIPTURE

Genesis 1:31
Exodus 35:30–36:2
Psalms 118:8–9;139:14; 144:3–4
Romans 1:17–19

1 Corinthians 10:31
Colossians 2:8
Revelation 1:5

SUGGESTED READING

Kenneth A. Myers, *All God's Children and Blue Suede Shoes: Christians and Popular Culture* (Westchester, IL: Crossway, 1989).

Leland Ryken, *Culture in Christian Perspective* (Portland, OR: Multnomah, 1986).

Dorothy L. Sayers, *The Mind of the Maker* (San Francisco: Harper, 1941).

Francis Schaeffer, *Escape from Reason* (Chicago, IL: Inter-Varsity Press, 1968).

——————. *How Should We Then Live?* (New Jersey: Revell, 1976).

Franky Schaeffer, *Addicted to Mediocrity* (Westchester, IL: Crossway, 1981).

Gene Edward Veith Jr., *State of the Arts* (Wheaton, IL: Crossway, 1991).

WORLDVIEW EXPRESSION
IN ART

Material covered in the Worldview Expression in Literature chapter can be found in the following Zane Publishing Home Library titles:

American Literature: A Literary History: Common Sense—The Last of the Mohicans

American Literature: A Literary History: Little Women—The Call of the Wild

American Literature: A Literary History: The Jungle—The Grapes of Wrath

American Literature: A Literary History: Catch-22—The Color Purple

American Literature: Time, Life, & Works: Nathaniel Hawthorne

American Literature: Time, Life, & Works: Henry David Thoreau

American Literature: Time, Life, & Works: Walt Whitman

American Literature: Time, Life, & Works: Ernest Hemingway

European Literature: A Literary History: Beowulf—Hamlet

European Literature: A Literary History: Paradise Lost—Ivanhoe

European Literature: A Literary History: Lyrical Ballads—Silas Marner

European Literature: A Literary History: The War of the Worlds—Brave New World

European Literature: Time, Life, & Works: Geoffrey Chaucer

European Literature: Time, Life, & Works: William Wordsworth

European Literature: Time, Life, & Works: Charles Dickens

European Literature: Time, Life, & Works: Thomas Hardy

European Literature: Time, Life, & Works: William Shakespeare

European Literature: Shakespeare's London

European Literature: Shakespeare's Theater

European Literature: Strange Case of Dr. Jekyll and Mr. Hyde

Literature As Art: Understanding Drama

Literature As Art: Understanding Poetry

Literature As Art: Understanding Short Fiction

Literature As Art: Understanding Biographies

European Literature: The Ancient World—The Renaissance

European Literature: The Enlightenment—The Twentieth Century

World Literature: Women in Literature: Heroines, Sirens, Shrews

World Literature: Women in Literature: Novelists, Playwrights, Poets

The Writing Series: Treasure Island: *Sensory/Descriptive Writing*

N.C. Wyeth Illustrated Classics: Kidnapped: *Imaginative/Narrative Writing*

N.C. Wyeth Illustrated Classics: The Yearling: *Practical/Informative Writing*

N.C. Wyeth Illustrated Classics: Robinson Crusoe: *Analytical/Expository Writing*

World Literature: The Writing Series: Short Story Writing

World Literature: The Writing Series: From the Classics—Great Themes

WORLDVIEW EXPRESSION
IN LITERATURE

*Take out of all secular literature the truth that had its birth in the gospel of
Jesus, and you have made a wound in the literature of the nations from which
the lifeblood will speedily ebb away.*

–JOSEPH NELSON GREENE

DESPITE THE EXPANDING ARRAY of entertainments that are available today—
television, films, concerts, sports, video games, and the Internet—millions
continue to enjoy a centuries-old pastime: reading. Spy thrillers, mysteries,
romances, and other formula novels sell billions of copies yearly. In a day
when television and computers were expected to eliminate the market
for books, reading for recreation is actually on the rise.

The student who reads well and enjoys reading has an advantage that
will benefit him throughout his life. It is important for the student to
develop the habit of reading, and it is equally important that the student
read good books. Thankfully, these are not in short supply, but discern-
ment in choosing what to read is important. The best books are usually
those that have been both popular for many years and important in influencing the course of literature as it has developed. *A Tale of Two Cities,* for
example, is of more lasting importance, and, therefore, probably better
than the latest thriller on the best-seller lists.

As we study the literature that has endured throughout the centuries,
we can see that the Christian worldview is more liberating than many
of its present-day critics would like to admit. Many of the greatest writers in history have written on Christian themes or from a Christian perspective. Furthermore, we can perceive in the writings of those who
participate more in man's rebellion than in his redemption the ultimate
failure of humanistic worldviews. It is true, as Gene Edward Veith makes
clear, that

> Surveying the literature of these times also demonstrates the strength
> and wholeness of the Christian perspective. Each new movement
> attacks Christianity for a different reason. Each seizes upon some one
> truth (which Christians might agree with) and tries to build a whole
> view of life around it to the exclusion of the more complex reality
> described by Scripture.[1]

THE VALUE OF READING

Literature is important to students first of all because it is a form of
entertainment that demands participation and requires mental activity,
training the mind to think with more organization. Veith says of the activity of reading,

> The pleasures of reading are, for the most part, good for us. We might

171

even say that the reason we enjoy a book is that it is doing something good for us. We can benefit not only from a book's themes and ideas; we can benefit from the very pleasures that impel us to keep turning the pages.[2]

What is the benefit of reading? Simply put, it is mental exercise. Unlike television and films, reading demands the participation of the viewer in understanding the worldview that is implicit in every work of literature. Recognizing and evaluating the worldviews that are expressed or depicted in a work is an automatic activity that occurs for every reader. There are few other pastimes that can make such claims. Many entertainments allow participants to remain mentally static, and certainly few, if any, demand the mental vigor and exertion needed to read the ideas Shakespeare, Dickens, or Dante.

In fact, literature stands out from the other arts as the one most directly connected to ideas. Visual arts work in images, musical arts through sounds to express ideas. Only literary art begins with ideas and expresses itself through ideas. It is this direct contact with the ideas of generations of authors that constitutes the rich body of knowledge that is available to students and casual readers at every level of education.

Finally, great literature is about truth. A Christian reader must be prepared to evaluate the ideas present in a poem, play, or novel and make a judgment about their truth in light of his own worldview. A work of literature is an expression of a worldview, and a Christian must be ready to understand and critique the view that such a work presents.

Often, major periods of literary creation reflect a single dominant worldview. As we begin a brief survey of literature, we will be looking for the worldview or worldviews that characterize an age.

THE ROLE OF THE BIBLE

The Bible is not only the infallible source of Christian doctrine. It is acknowledged to be the monument of Western literature. It contains examples of various literary styles—historical narrative, poetry, and epistolary essay, to name a few—and is increasingly recognized for its value as a work of pure literature. In fact, in many school districts, the Bible has reentered the public classroom as a work of literature, and will again be able to influence young lives through the reading and study of God's Word. Zane Publishing includes the King James version of the Bible on all its titles.

Indeed, the study of literature is nearly impossible to conduct with out a working knowledge of the Bible. It is the most influential work of literature ever produced. Authors who love God and authors who hate God alike show in their writings the influences of scripture. We are considered to be living in a post-Christian age, but the literature of this age still bears the stamp of Christian doctrine and of the Bible.

THE AGE OF FAITH

Although every age has authors who acknowledge their indebtedness to the Bible for literary inspiration, none is more unified in doing so than the years of the Middle Ages. For many reasons this period has been called an age of faith. The culture had been infused with the doctrines of Christianity, and with the strong cultural and political influence of the Church, the presence of this Christian influence was very stable and permanent. The writings of the time reflect the Christian worldview, then taken for granted, that the universe was the creation of a sovereign God whose will would be done in all things.

This period is often depicted as a bleak time, when humanity was constantly struggling for survival. It is difficult to understand how, under such oppressive conditions, creative literature could flourish as it did in the Middle Ages. In truth, while the Middle Ages were marked with devastating plagues, religious wars, and superstition, life for many was stable enough to permit significant writing.

The great contribution of the early Middle Ages was the beginnings of modern drama. Veith remarks that while classical drama predated this second beginning by centuries,

> When Rome fell, drama disappeared, and no one really missed it. Drama had to be re-invented. Just as Greek drama grew out of religious rituals, modern drama grew out of Christian worship.[3]

Through dramatizations of Bible stories, the largely illiterate masses could learn about the important events of Christian history. As drama developed and began to concern itself with non-religious affairs, it retained the imprint of its origins.

Though in much of culture the age of faith ended with the growth of the humanistic Renaissance, in much of literature the influence of Christianity remained strong. The greatest dramatist of Elizabethan England, and probably the greatest author in history, William Shakespeare, drew extensively from the Bible and from centuries of religious tradition in writing his unmatched plays. His plays are not devotional works, but neither are they immune to the spirit of the age. Nevertheless, whereas Renaissance Europe tended to deify man, Shakespeare shows him in strength *and* weakness, understanding rather than glorifying him. A biblical worldview undergirds his thinking and Christian allusions are to be found throughout his writings. Though there is very little biographical information about Shakespeare, perhaps the only testimony to his beliefs can be found in his last will and testament, in which he said:

> I commend my soul into the hands of God my Creator, hoping and assuredly believing through the only merits of Jesus Christ my Saviour, to be made partaker of life everlasting; and my body to the earth, whereof it is made.[4]

The age of faith continued during the Renaissance because of the influence of Reformation ideas on many of Europe's best minds. Classical aestheticism produced many artists and more libertines, but only a few truly great writers. On the other hand, Christian writers at the end of the age of faith included such great writers as John Milton, George Herbert, and John Donne.

THE AGE OF MAN

The humanistic Renaissance did not supplant the place of faith in literature primarily because it was a movement of many pleasures but few

JOHN MILTON
Born: *December 9, 1608*
Died: *November 8, 1674*

Claim to fame:
English poet best known for his epic poem Paradise Lost.

Did you know?
Was blind when he wrote Paradise Lost.

JOHN DONNE
Born: *1572*
Died: *March 31, 1631*

Claim to fame:
English poet known for his intelligence, wit, and religious devotion.

Did you know?
Wrote "A Valediction: Forbidding Mourning," "Hymn to God the Father," and the sonnet to death, "Death be not proud."

ideas. As we have discussed, since literature is concerned with ideas, the humanism of the Renaissance had little effect on it. However, a movement that was to redefine much of literature for centuries followed the Renaissance, borrowing its humanism but also adding an emphasis on ideas.

The Enlightenment, as this movement was called, placed its greatest emphasis on the rational faculties of man. It took its inspiration from the Scientific Revolution of the early eighteenth century, of which the poet Alexander Pope wrote:

> Nature and Nature's Laws lay hid in night:
> God said, Let NEWTON be: And all was Light!

In such an age, we should expect to see an approach to writing that is more rigid and formal than that of prior literature. And, in fact, there is a distinct contrast between the long, complicated sentences of Shakespeare and Milton and the brief, terse writing of Pope and Dryden. Much of Enlightenment literature is contained in essays by writers such as Francis Bacon and John Locke, and this period saw the birth of what has since become the prevalent mode of literary expression: the novel.

All these developments centered on a view of man and of the universe that, in its scientific pose, ignored their supernatural aspects. Although it has lost most of its influence on literature, this worldview can still be found today in many schools of thought. Enlightenment literature, despite its inclination to ignore the significant spiritual aspect of human existence, brought some very important ideas to the forefront of social consciousness. Foremost among these is the dignity and uniqueness of man as a rational being, a capacity that reflects God's nature and that is intended by God for use to His glory. Enlightenment rationalism also recognized the ultimate equality of all men before God, though it was not the rationalists but the Christians who practiced this idea of equality.

In reaction to the Enlightenment emphasis on order and regularity were a group of poets who influenced each other as well as much of the literature of the last three centuries. The Romantic movement, best known for the poets Wordsworth, Coleridge, Byron, Shelley, and Keats, responded with a philosophy of man and nature that emphasized their spirituality. Of particular interest to the romantic mind was the human capacity for creativity, which Christians understand to be part of God's nature reflected in His creation, but which the romantics enshrined without a religious context. This eventually amounted to the virtual deification of man, and occasionally even showed a tendency to pantheism. Later, the American transcendentalists would draw from these romantics to create a real pantheism, such as that expressed by the poet Walt Whitman.

The older romantics, Wordsworth and Coleridge, lived to old age, and eventually turned to a more conservative philosophy and orthodox Christianity. Because of this, they were often scorned by the younger generation of romantics, all of whom died early, tragic deaths.

This humanistic age was not without its Christian influence. The ideas from which both romantics and enlightenment rationalists drew were in essence Christian ideas. Man and nature, created by God, are good things, though sin has corrupted both. The romantics' error lay in emphasizing the ideas over the Christian worldview in which context they make sense.

Furthermore, there were authors who maintained a Christian perspective while understanding and participating in the important events and the spirit of the day. This was the time of the political writings of the founders of the United States, the devotional poetry of Gerard Manley Hopkins and Henry Wadsworth Longfellow, and the novels of Charles Dickens.

The influence of rationalism and romanticism was dominant in literature until the end the nineteenth century, when they were supplanted, not by a specific movement, but by what must be called an "un-movement"—that is, a shift in thought that cannot be unified into a single movement. It has been called deconstruction, post-modernism, MULTICULTURALISM, and pluralism, but what it amounts to is a chorus of voices all competing to drown each other out.

THE AGE OF CHAOS

The literature of the late nineteenth and twentieth centuries is the product of what critic Harold Bloom has called "the chaotic age." The rise of the chaos of modern times is attributed to the further decline of religious influence in Western thought, brought about largely by Charles Darwin's theory of biological evolution. The growing acceptance of Darwin's theory forced Victorian society to reevaluate its idea of man as important within the scope of creation. Without a creator, man became insignificant within a vast universe, and his life became meaningless. This is the beginning point of our chaotic age, which, lacking a comprehensive Christian worldview, pursues meaning in trivia.

The literature of the age of chaos may be said to have begun with the NATURALISTIC writing of Joseph Conrad, Jack London, and others. These authors no longer thought of nature as the benevolent force that the romantics thought it was, nor did they think of it in the predictable terms of the rationalistic mindset. They demonstrated no faith in man's ability to either control or harmonize with nature. Instead, man is depicted as being infinitesimally small within an uncaring environment in which he may live or die, with little consequence in either case. Subsequent authors have emphases on things other than nature, but the essential meaninglessness of human existence remains as a fundamental theme to most modern and contemporary writing. Authors from Franz Kafka to Jean-Paul Sartre to Ernest Hemingway have narrated, in various ways, the absurdity of existence without God.

It should not be surprising, in what we are told is a "post-Christian" era, to find that people consider life to be fundamentally meaningless and hopeless, as it certainly is without the hope of salvation. In depicting life this way, authors refute the false hopes of lost generations. While such bleak nihilism is far from the whole story for those who are in Christ, it is all the story that many people know. The task of the Christian author, as well as of the Christian society at large, is to point out the hope that is in Christ. Many Christians have done so, including T. S. Eliot, C. S. Lewis, and Flannery O'Connor.

CONCLUSION

Some consider the study of literature to be an impractical project, since

HENRY WADSWORTH LONGFELLOW
Born: *February 27, 1807*
Died: *March 24, 1882*

Claim to fame:

American poet, known for the rhythm of his works who, unlike many writers of his time, kept quiet about most religious and social issues.

Did you know?

Wrote The Song of Hiawatha, The Courtship of Miles Standish, *and* "Paul Revere's Ride."

JACK LONDON
Born: *January 12, 1876*
Died: *November 22, 1916*

Claim to fame:

American naturalist, novelist and short-story writer, known for his vivid scenes of nature, animals, and action.

Did you know?

Wrote The Call of the Wild, The Sea Wolf, *and* White Fang. *He wrote openly about alcoholism, a disease that plagued him until his tragic suicide at age forty.*

ERNEST HEMINGWAY
Born: *July 21, 1899*
Died: *July 2, 1961*

Claim to fame:

One of American's greatest writers. His works frequently dealt with characters who faced danger with courage. An existentialist known as the spokesman for "the lost generation," who were disillusioned by World War I.

Did you know?

Wrote For Whom the Bell Tolls, The Old Man and the Sea, A Farewell to Arms, *and* The Sun Also Rises, *among others.*

Born: *September 26, 1888*
Died: *January 4, 1965*

Claim to fame:

Great Christian poet, winner of the Nobel Prize for Literature. Wrote The Wasteland *, "The Love Song of J. Alfred Prufrock," and* Murder in the Cathedral.

Did you know?

Born in Saint Louis, Missouri, but became a British citizen. Proponent of Anglo-Catholicism.

they do not see that it has any connection to the real world. Nevertheless, the function of literature within God's universe is not to allow Christians to escape the reality of their evil world. Neither is it to allow the lost to escape from a world which, without God, is meaningless. At a very basic level, literature involves the reader with the real world. Professor Roger Lundin illustrates the relationship of what we read to everyday existence:

> One of the ways we can deepen our understanding of our world and actions is through a careful reading of books from the past. . . "In life," writes Alasdair MacIntyre, "we are always under certain constraints. We enter upon a stage which we did not design and we find ourselves part of an action that was not our making." To learn how to act in our present scene and to make sense of the stage we find ourselves upon, we explore earlier scenes of our play as they have been recorded, in part, in the significant books that have come down to us from the past.[5]

The relationship between the reader and the book is reciprocal. The reader brings his experiences and views to the book, affecting how he understands it. The book brings the author's words to the reader, which, depending upon the quality of the book, may enhance or degrade the reader's perspective on life. Reading is, therefore, a worldview-shaping activity. It is not escape, but involvement. Veith says,

> Serious literary art tends to be honest; as such, it often confronts realities—the search for love, the ugliness of evil, the futility of life without God, the mysterious splendors of ordinary life—that Christians can recognize as part of the human condition and what God has ordained in the created order.[6]

The books a person reads do not go back on the shelf when he has finished them. They go with him, influencing his worldview, or his understanding of other worldviews. Books concern the ideas that have the power to affect the reader, and, through the reader, the world.

CD-ROM ANALYSES

• *European Literature: A Literary History*

This four-CD-ROM survey of European literature is not only good, it is nearly flawless. It has clearly been written from a secularist's perspective, but the attention of a Christian parent will adjust this sufficiently for this series to be used often as a thorough study of the English language since that language came into being. It is unfortunate that so little can be said about such a good series of CD-ROMs other than that it comes highly recommended.

• *European Literature: Time, Life, & Works*

These four CD-ROMs concern Geoffrey Chaucer, William Wordsworth, Charles Dickens, and Thomas Hardy. Like the *Literary History* CD-ROMs, they are practically perfect; however, there is a secular perspective expressed that should be corrected through parental attendance. These, too, come highly recommended.

• *European Literature: Shakespeare's London/Shakespeare's Theater*

Following in the tradition set by the other British literature series, these two CD-ROMs about the world of William Shakespeare are both enthralling and virtually without flaws. They are a good bridge between the student and the sometimes difficult-to-understand plays of the greatest author in the English language.

• *American Literature: A Literary History*

This four-CD-ROM series on American literature is fast-paced and covers most significant authors. As an introductory survey of more than three centuries of American literature, this series is ideal. Of concern to Christian parents are two statements that need correction from a Christian worldview. On the first CD-ROM, *Common Sense—The Last of the Mohicans*, a statement is made that diminishes the significance and the effect of the Great Awakening. Parents will want to address this, as well as the too-positive take on American transcendentalism in *Little Women—The Call of the Wild*. On the whole, this series is strongly recommended.

• *American Literature: Time, Life, & Works*

The first CD-ROM in this set studies Nathaniel Hawthorne. It is very well done. However, an important fact to observe about the *Time, Life, & Works* series is that of the four authors selected, two are transcendentalists: Henry David Thoreau and Walt Whitman. Of these two writers, only one, Walt Whitman, is considered to be a major American author. On behalf of the Henry David Thoreau and Walt Whitman CD-ROMs, it must be said that while the transcendental philosophy opposes orthodox Christianity, the writers are allowed to speak for themselves without any strong editorial endorsement. The Christian student is therefore free to refute the humanism and pantheism of the two authors for himself. [For help in addressing humanism, refer to the *Preparing the Christian Student for College* chapter.] Understanding the *Ernest Hemingway* CD-ROM is similarly simple. As discussed in this chapter, most modern literature is about the meaninglessness of life without absolutes. This is made abundantly clear on the CD-ROM. Responding to the hopelessness of society with the hope of Jesus should be encouraged as the student reviews this author's works.

• *World Literature: European Literature*

These two CD-ROMs give a general overview of the currents of world literature from the ancient epics to recent developments in novels and dramatic literature. The first CD-ROM attributes the Reformation to the Renaissance, a connection that has been often alleged but never substantiated. For the history of these dramatically different epochs of history, refer to the history chapters of this book. The second CD-ROM rightly notes the effect that the ideas of Charles Darwin, Karl Marx, and Sigmund Freud have had on modern literature, particularly on the European continent. Because of this, parents will want to observe closely the modern portion of this CD-ROM.

• *Literature As Art*

Each of the four CD-ROMs in this series discusses a different genre of literature, and how to understand it, by examining its historical development, with specific examples of the genre. The *Understanding Poetry* and *Understanding Short Fiction* CD-ROMs are valuable and even-handed in their approach to the topic. In the case of *Understanding Drama*, however, the matter is not so simple. Modern drama, such as it is, tends to be extremely, self-consciously activistic. Most of the causes on behalf of which it acts are in opposition to a Christian idea of life and morality. Parents should review this CD-ROM before students in order to be prepared to contradict the many assertions of modern drama, all of which seem to drive at a single point: the world today is more confusing than it used to be. The Christian sees that the world is no different than it was yesterday; the problem is that many people (and a surprising number of them are modern dramatists) are willfully confusing themselves rather than turning to Christ.

REVIEW QUESTIONS

1. In what way is literature beneficial?

2. What must a Christian reader be able to do with the books he reads?

3. What is the most influential work of literature ever produced?

4. What historical and literary period most clearly shows the influence of Christianity? What literary form was reborn in this period?

5. What inspired the Enlightenment and how was this reflected in Enlightenment literature?

6. Describe the Romantic response to the Enlightenment's emphasis on rationality.

7. What is the theme of much of modern literature?

8. What should the Christian author do to respond to bleak modernism?

RELATED SCRIPTURE

Genesis 1:28; 8:21
Jeremiah 23:16–32
John 17:14–18
Ephesians 5:3–6

Hebrews 5:14
2 Timothy 3:16
2 Peter 1:16–21

SUGGESTED READING

Susan V. Gallagher and Roger Lundin, *Literature Through the Eyes of Faith* (San Francisco: Harper, 1989).

Peter J. Leithart, *Brightest Invention of Heaven: A Christian Guide to Six Shakespearean Plays* (Moscow, ID: Canon Press, 1996).

Rosalie June Slater, *A Family Program for Reading Aloud* (San Francisco: Foundation for American Christian Education, 1991).

Gene Edward Veith Jr., *Reading Between the Lines* (Wheaton, IL: Crossway, 1990).

Material covered in the Faith and Music chapter can be found in the following Zane Publishing Home Library titles:

Art & Music: The Medieval Era
Art & Music: The Renaissance
Art & Music: The Baroque
Art & Music: The Eighteenth Century
Art & Music: Romanticism
Art & Music: Impressionism
Art & Music: The Twentieth Century
Art & Music: Surrealism
History of Music: Through the Classical Period
History of Music: Romanticism to Contemporary
History of Music: The Art of Listening
History of Music: Music and Culture
History of Music: American Folk Music
History of Music: History of Jazz
Elementary Music: Bach, Schumann, Rakhmaninov
Elementary Music: Handel, Chopin, Debussy
Elementary Music: Mozart, Mendelssohn, Dvorak
Elementary Music: Beethoven, Grieg, Hanson
Elementary Music: Haydn, Tchaikovsky, Ravel
Elementary Music: Schubert, Brahms, Strauss
Elementary Music: Appreciating the Orchestra
Elementary Music: Instruments of the Symphony Orchestra

FAITH AND MUSIC

Music is a gift of God. Next after theology, I give music the highest place and the greatest honor.

—Martin Luther

There had never been a musical moment like this. Thousands of wild fans stormed the theater doors. Millions of Americans gathered in living rooms to watch—the British invasion had begun! Four boys from Liverpool, England, were rewriting the books on musical popularity.

Other acts had created crazes before. Jerry Lee Lewis had been famous with hits like "Great Balls of Fire"; Bill Haley and the Comets would "Rock Around the Clock"; and the king of all acts, Elvis Presley, had topped the charts for years. In fact, Elvis Presley sold so many records in the 1950s that he remains even today the best-selling artist in the history of popular music. But no one had anticipated the shock wave of the Beatles. When they performed on the *Ed Sullivan Show*, the results were spectacular. Newspapers and periodicals began referring to a British invasion of new music, complete with new sounds and new looks. For the rest of the decade, the Beatles dominated popular music, with occasional competition from The Beach Boys and later, The Rolling Stones. The Beatles' album, "Sergeant Pepper's Lonely Hearts Club Band" shifted popular music into directions it has not entirely left even today.

What do these musical changes mean and what are the sources of music and celebration? In Western civilization, music has for generations been an expression of thanksgiving and worship toward God. The Book of Psalms in the Old Testament is actually a song book. Most of its contents were originally written to be sung. It has the flow and cadence of poetry and naturally rises to music. Here are some examples.

Psalm 30:4 says "Sing to the Lord, you saints of his; praise his holy name."

Psalm 33:1–3 urges you to "Sing joyfully to the Lord, you righteous; it is fitting for the upright to praise him. Praise the Lord with the harp; make music to him on the ten-stringed lyre. Sing to him a new song; play skillfully, and shout for joy."

Psalm 40:3 is a reminder that "He put a new song in my mouth, a hymn of praise to our God. Many will see and fear and put their trust in the Lord."

Psalm 150:1–6 concludes the entire book by shouting "Praise the Lord. Praise God in his sanctuary; praise him in his mighty heavens. Praise him for his acts of power; praise him for his surpassing greatness. Praise him with the sounding of the trumpet, praise him with the harp and lyre, praise him with tambourine and dancing, praise him with the strings and flute, praise him with the clash of cymbals, praise him with resounding cymbals. Let everything that has breath praise the Lord. Praise the Lord."

THE GIFT OF GOD

Music by its nature is a gift of God and should always be uplifting, positive, and instructive. Music, when it is in a form that helps people, contains the following elements:

1. Order

Music should reaffirm a sense of organized peace. It should bring a sense of balance to the listener. Music as given by God brings a feeling of cohesion or togetherness. This is reflected in many traditional music forms by a balance of regulation and beat—upbeat is followed by downbeat and so on. Everything is in balance and gives a sense of stability.

2. Peace

Much Christian music creates a climate of inner calm. It quiets the soul and gives assurance of God's care, comfort and protection. This form of music is a reminder of scripturally based security. It conveys ideas found in great Christian hymns such as "How Firm A Foundation":

> How firm a foundation, ye saints of the Lord, Is laid for your faith in his excellent Word!
> What more can he say than to you he hath said, To you who for refuge to Jesus have fled?
> Fear not, I am with thee; O be not dismayed, For I am thy God, and will still give thee aid;
> I'll strengthen thee, help thee, and cause thee to stand,
> Upheld by my righteous, omnipotent hand.
> When thro' fiery trials thy pathway shall lie, My grace, all sufficient, shall be thy supply; The flame shall not hurt thee; I only design,
> Thy dross to consume, and thy gold to refine.
> The soul that on Jesus hath leaned for repose.
> I will not, I will not desert to his foes; That soul, though all hell should endeavor to shake, I'll never, no, never, no, never forsake!

Note how this is based on such important scriptural statements as Isaiah 46:4: "Even to your old age and gray hairs I am he, I am he who will sustain you. I have made you and I will carry you; I will sustain you and I will rescue you." And also from Isaiah 43:2–3: "When you pass through the waters, I will be with you; and when you pass through the rivers, they will not sweep over you. When you walk through the fire, you will not be burned; the flames will not set you ablaze. For I am the Lord, your God, the Holy One of Israel, your Savior; I give Egypt for your ransom, Cush and Sebain your stead."

3. Instruction

Christian music is a door through which godly, biblical information is introduced into the mind and heart. Think of the great hymn, "Holy, Holy, Holy"—the song is filled with biblical images of the greatness of

God. When you learn to sing this song you learn important information on who God really is—information that will change your life:

> Holy, holy, holy! Lord God Almighty! Early in the morning our song
>   shall rise to thee;
> Holy, holy, holy, merciful and mighty! God in three Persons, blessed
>   Trinity!
> Holy, holy, holy! all the saints adore thee,
> Casting down their golden crowns around the glassy sea;
> Cherubim and seraphim falling down before thee,
> Who wert, and art, and evermore shalt be.
> Holy, holy, holy! tho the darkness hide thee,
> Tho the eye of sinful man thy glory may not see;
> Only thou art holy; there is none beside thee, Perfect in pow'r, in love,
>   and purity.
> Holy, holy, holy! Lord God Almighty!
> All thy works shall praise thy name, in earth, and sky, and sea;
> Holy, holy, holy; merciful and mighty! God in three Persons blessed
>   Trinity!

4. Relaxation

This is different from peace and calm because in relaxation you are brought down from a high state of tension, stress, and anxiety. It is a musical transition away from upper levels of intensity.

5. Thankfulness

It is hard to be depressed when you are expressing gratitude to God. In thankful music you learn to replace your negative worries and self-focus with thankfulness to God for His love and purpose in your life. Positive Christian "gratitude" music will lift you out of your down time and push you upward to appreciation for God's care for your life.

6. Excitement and Praise to God

This is music that thrills you as it pulls praise and joy from your heart. Many modern Christian songs are exciting expressions of praise; songs such as "O Lord, Our Lord, How Majestic Is Your Name," "This is the Day the Lord Has Made," and "The Church Triumphant."

7. Worship

These are songs that make you happy to be in God's presence—songs that teach you to love God, not for what you can get out of Him but because He is your God and loves you so much.

GREAT CHRISTIAN COMPOSERS

Many of the great composers wrote for the glory of God. The Christian nature of their compositions and the Christian commitment of their lives reflected their desire to glorify God. Patrick Kavanaugh, in his book, *The Spiritual Lives of Great Composers*, examined the lives of these musical geniuses and identified the Christian content of their works. Handel's *Messiah*, Mendelssohn's *Ave Maria*, and Haydn's *The Creation* are all examples of attempts by men to honor God and his world.

GEORGE FRIDERIC HANDEL

Born: February 23, 1685
Died: April 20, 1759

Claim to fame:

Composed Messiah.

Did you know?

He is buried in Westminster Abbey.

George Frideric Handel (1685–1759) was born in Germany and raised as a Lutheran. When he was eight or nine years of age, a local duke heard him play an organ postlude following a worship service. The duke was so impressed that Handel's father was then encouraged to provide formal music education for the boy. By the time Handel had turned twelve, he had written his first composition and had become unusually proficient at the organ. Later in life, he mastered the clavichord, the oboe, and the violin. In 1702, he entered the University of Halle to study law but soon dropped out of legal studies to devote himself entirely to music. He became a violinist and composer at Hamburg Opera Theater and then traveled to Italy from 1706–1710. His first religious oratorio was *The Resurrection*, composed while visiting Rome.

In 1712, Handel moved to England where he lived for the rest of his life. Handel surprisingly received much opposition from the institutional leadership of the Church of England. They attacked him for what Kavanaugh called "his notorious practice of writing biblical dramas, such as *Esther and Israel* to be performed in secular theaters." He achieved very little musical and financial success and decided to retire from public performance at the age of fifty-six.

Then something dramatic happened. A friend, Charles Jennings, gave Handel a libretto based on the life of Christ taken entirely from the Bible. He also received a commission from a charity in Dublin, Ireland, to compose a work for a benefit performance. Handel then decided to compose the work based on the life of Christ and perform it on behalf of the Dublin charity. He started composing on 22 August 1741 in his home on Brook Street in London. He became utterly captivated by his project. He completed Part I in six days and Part II in nine more days. In another six days he completed Part III. The orchestration was completed in two more days. He wrote 260 pages of musical manuscript in just twenty-four days. Sir Newman Flower, one of Handel's biographers, wrote, "Considering the immensity of the work and the short time involved, it will remain perhaps forever the greatest feat in the whole history of musical composition." Handel called the completed work, *Messiah.*

He premiered *Messiah* on 13 April 1742 as a benefit for the Dublin charity, raising 400 pounds sterling. A year later he staged it in London with the king of England in attendance. As Kavanaugh writes, "As the first notes of the triumphant 'Hallelujah Chorus' rang out, the King rose. Following royal protocol, the entire audience stood too, initiating a tradition which has lasted for more than two centuries."

Following this performance, success was assured for Handel and he remained popular until his death. Handel was known as a committed Christian. He told a friend that, while writing "Hallelujah Chorus," his experience had been so profound that it made him sob with joy and worship toward God, and even quoted a New Testament verse on his process of composition: "Whether I was in the body or out of my body when I wrote it, I know not." His morals were above reproach in a very immoral era and it was said "he would often be seen on his knees expressing by his looks and gesticulations the utmost fervor of devotions."

Handel would frequently speak of his great pleasure in setting the Word of God to music and once commented to his brother-in-law on the death of his mother, "It pleased the Almighty that to Whose great holy will I submit myself with Christian submission."

A few days before he died, he told a friend that he hoped he would die on Good Friday because he wanted to die "in the hopes of meeting his good God and sweet Lord and Savior on the day of his resurrection." He actually lived until the morning of Good Saturday and died on 14 April 1759. A good friend of his, James Smyth, wrote, "He died as he lived—a good Christian, with a true sense of his duty to God and to man, and in perfect charity with all the world." He was buried in Westminster Abbey and a statue erected there shows him holding the manuscript for the solo that opens Part III of *Messiah*, with the words carved in stone "I know that my Redeemer liveth."

JOHANN SEBASTIAN BACH

Of Johann Sebastian Bach (1685–1750), Kavanaugh writes, "Throughout history, Bach has been acclaimed as The Christian Composer, almost a kind of "patron saint" for church musicians. All around the world he is recognized as one of the greatest composers who has ever lived." He wrote an incredible amount of music, well known for its diversity. For example, he wrote chorales, cantatas, masses, oratorios, passions, concerti, and solo works for almost every instrument known in his day.

Bach was born in Eisenach, Germany, and was orphaned at the age of nine. He began musical training shortly after that and showed outstanding ability as a vocalist and demonstrated unusual ability to play the organ, violin, and many other instruments. Bach spent his entire life in Germany and worked mostly as a church musician. He loved the life and works of Martin Luther and once quoted Luther's statement on music that "music's only purpose should be for the glory of God and the recreation of the human spirit." He would often initial his musical manuscript pages with special marks, such as *JJ* (*Jesu Juva*—"help me Jesus") or *INJ* (*In Nomine Jesu*—"in the name of Jesus"). At a manuscript's end, Bach would usually initial *SDG* (*Soli Deo Gloria*—"to God alone the glory").

One biographer is quoted as saying of Bach, "The focus of his emotional life was undoubtedly in religion and in the service of religion through music." He had a happy marriage and a large family. He once wrote a son of his who was having financial difficulty, "What can I do or say more? My warnings having failed and my loving care and help having proved unavailing. I can only bear my cross in patience and commend my undutiful boy to God's mercy, never doubting that He will hear my sorrow stricken prayer and in His good time bring my son to understand that the path of conversion leads to Him."

He once dedicated a book, "To God alone the praise be given for what's herein written," and would often inscribe, "In the name of Jesus" on his works. He invoked great emotion in his music, ingeniously using the notes to create an emotional response that would reflect the teaching of Scripture in the story he had put to music. For example, Kavanaugh writes, "Another memorable scene is found in his colossal Mass in B Minor.

JOHANN SEBASTIAN BACH
Born: *March 21, 1685*
Died: *July 28, 1750*

Claim to fame:
Considered the very best of the baroque composers.

Did you know?
He had twenty children.

Toward the end of the dramatic 'Crucifixus' movement, the voices and instruments quietly sink into their lowest registers as the body of Jesus is musically lowered into the tomb. This is immediately followed by an explosion of blazing glory in the 'Et Resurrexit,' an effect composers have copied for centuries."

He studied the Bible all his adult life and at his death had a personal library containing eighty-three books, all of them on Christian spiritual subjects, including two different editions of *The Works of Martin Luther*. One of his favorite passages in the Bible was II Chronicles 5:13, which reads, "The trumpeters and singers joined in unison, as with one voice, to give praise and thanks to the Lord. Accompanied by trumpets, cymbals and other instruments, they raised their voices in praise to the Lord and sang: He is good; his love endures forever. Then the temple of the Lord was filled with a cloud."

Bach once wrote, "where there is devotional music, God is always at hand with his gracious presence." By the age of sixty-five he was completely blind, and he died relatively unknown in 1750; his grave, unmarked. His last work was a chorale titled "Before Thy Throne I Come." It wasn't until much later that he was rediscovered and recognized as one of the great masters of all time.

FRANZ JOSEPH HAYDN

JOSEPH HAYDN
Born: March 31, 1732
Died: May 31, 1809

Claim to fame:

Helped to establish musical trends of his time.

Did you know?

He composed 104 symphonies, 54 piano sonatas, and 76 quartets, among other works.

Franz Joseph Haydn (1732–1809) was one of the most famous composers in history. Born of poor parents in Rohrau, Austria, Haydn's musical talent was recognized early and he began formal musical training at the age of six. At the age of eight, he became a choirboy in Vienna and for nine years sang in the famous Saint Stephen's Cathedral of Vienna. He often expressed gratitude to his parents for "bringing him up in the fear of God." He considered the Roman Catholic priesthood but decided that God had instead called him to music. He wrote, "I know that God has favored me and recognize it thankfully. I also believe I have done my duty and have been of use to the world through my works. Let others do the same."

In 1761 Haydn was hired by Prince Paul Esterhazy. He moved to the prince's country estate and for the next thirty years wrote and performed compositions for the Esterhazy family and friends. He completed 104 symphonies, 76 string quartets, a number of masses, oratorios, operas, concerti, and dozens of chamber works. Often he would struggle in writing his music and once wrote, "I prayed to God—not like a miserable sinner in despair—but calmly and slowly. In this I felt that an infinite God would surely have mercy on his finite creature, pardoning dust for being dust. These thoughts cheered me up. I experienced assured joy so confident that as I wished to express the words of the prayer, I could not express my joy that gave vent to my happy spirit and wrote above the miserere allegro." His music was normally so happy and uplifting that he was at times criticized for his cheerfulness. Haydn's reply was "since God has given me a cheerful heart, He will forgive me for serving Him cheerfully." He wrote once that his goal in writing music was to "depict divinity through love and goodness."

At the age of sixty-six, he wrote his great work *The Creation*, saying he had written it to inspire "the adoration and worship of the Creator" and to put the listener "in a frame of mind where he is most susceptible to the kindness and omnipotence of the Creator." Haydn later wrote after completing this great work, "never was I so devout as when I composed *The Creation*." He further wrote, "When I was working on *The Creation* I felt so divinely impregnated with the divine certainty that before sitting down to the piano I would quietly and confidently pray to God to grant me the talent that was needed to praise Him worthily."

He died in Vienna. The last performance he attended was his own work, *The Creation*, on 27 March 1808. When the music had finished and the audience was applauding him vigorously, Haydn turned to the audience and said, "Not for me—from there above comes everything."

WOLFGANG AMADEUS MOZART

Wolfgang Amadeus Mozart (1756–1791) was born in Salzburg, Austria, and was playing piano by the age of three. He began formal musical training at four and began composing simple music at the age of five. At six he was performing on concert tours throughout Europe. He composed a number of works—symphonies, operas, chamber music, concerti, and masses, often working out the details in his mind and only later transferring the notes to paper. Energetic and continually composing, he was generous and supportive to other composers.

But what of his spiritual life? He was often happy, sanguine, and carefree. He loved games and dances and he was generous, positive, and well loved by many friends. One friend, Frederich Kerst, wrote, "Mozart was of a deeply religious nature. Mozart stood toward God in a relationship of a child full of trust for his father."

He once wrote his father, "Papa must not worry for God is ever before my eyes. I realize his omnipotence and I fear His anger; but I also recognize His love, compassion and tenderness towards His creatures. He will never forsake His own. If it is according to His will, so let it be according to mine. Thus all will be well and I must needs be happy and contented." Mozart further wrote, "I cannot possibly live like the majority of our young men [in reference to their morality]. In the first place I have too much religion. In the second, too much love for my fellow men and too great a sense of honor."

He once canceled a tour with two other musicians who were very immoral, writing "friends who have no religion are not stable."

Two of his most famous works, Mass in C Major and *Davidde Penitente*, were the compositional results of personal vows he had made to serve God. He had a very happy marriage. His wife, Constance, and he were musically compatible and wonderfully in love. He was concerned to praise God and also aware of the spiritual lives of other people. He once wrote "It will greatly assist such happiness as I may have to hear that my dear Father and my dear sister have submitted wholly to the will of God, with resignation and fortitude, and have put their whole confidence in Him in the firm assurance that He orders all things for the best."

He once wrote a prayer for the success of a new symphony: "I prayed to God for His mercy that all might go well for his greater glory."

WOLFGANG AMADEUS MOZART
Born: *January 27, 1756*
Died: *December 5, 1791*

Claim to fame:
A gifted prodigy, a composer whose music still thrills audiences today.

Did you know?
He began to compose at the age of five.

Toward the end of his life he wrote, "I never lie down in my bed without reflecting that perhaps I, young as I am, may not live to see another day yet none of all who know me can say that I am socially melancholy or morose. For this blessing I daily thank my Creator and wish it from my heart for all my fellow men."

He died young at the age of thirty-five on 5 December 1791.

LUDWIG VAN BEETHOVEN

LUDWIG VAN BEETHOVEN
Born: December 16, 1770
Died: March 26, 1827

Claim to fame:

Helped to achieve new eminence for composers and musicians.

Did you know?

He became almost completely deaf by age thirty-nine.

Ludwig van Beethoven (1770–1827) is considered by many scholars to be the greatest composer of all time. He was born in Germany and moved to Vienna as a young man. He was always unusual in dress and somewhat rough in behavior. He remained a bachelor all his life, although he had proposed to several women who did not consider him proper material for a husband. The greatest tragedy of his life was, of course, his deafness, which nearly drove him to suicide. He once said in a letter to his brothers in 1802 that deafness meant "he must live as an exile." But he did write much of his music to the glory of God. Beethoven once wrote, "Almighty God, you look down to my innermost soul. You see into my heart and You know that it is filled with love for humanity and a desire to do good." His deafness increased and became total until his death. On his deathbed he told his brother "of his great readiness" to make peace with God.

Beethoven was born and baptized into a Roman Catholic family and sent to a Catholic school, but his principal instructor and mentor, Christian Gottlob Neese, was a Protestant. He did seem to have a searching for God in his heart. He considered his relationship to God deeply personal and wrote, "Therefore calmly will I submit myself to all inconsistency and will place all my confidence in your eternal goodness, O God. My soul to rejoice in thee, immutable being, be my Rock, my Light, forever my Trust." He wrote many prayers in his diary, such as "In whatsoever matter it be, let me turn to Thee and become fruitful in good works."

He wrote a friend in 1810, "I must live by myself. I know, however, that God is nearer to me than others. I go without fear to Him. I have constantly recognized and understood Him." To his friend, Grand Duke Rudolph, Beethoven wrote, "Nothing higher exists than to approach God more than other people and from that to extend His glory among humanity."

He read the Bible in French and Latin all his life and had regular prayers, at least late in life, every morning and evening. In his library, he had many positive Christian books that were a great influence on him, such as *The Imitation of Christ*, by Thomas a Kempis. One of the great Christian masterpieces of all time was written by Beethoven, "Christ In the Mount of Olive," and he wrote a number of other songs that gave great thanksgiving and worship to God. Beethoven is difficult to understand, but his music, nonetheless, was composed for the glory of God.

FRANZ PETER SCHUBERT

Franz Peter Schubert (1797–1828) was born in Vienna, Austria, and never received a full, formal musical education. He was extravagantly talented and in 1808 became a chorister in a court chapel at the age of eleven. Schubert wrote a popular song, "The Erl-King," but foolishly sold the rights to the classic for a small amount of money and did not receive the financial benefit of his genius. His great hero was Beethoven, and he began to write orchestrals and other works. He remained in financial difficulty for much of his life, but began to turn to God and ask for God's help. His close friend, Anselm Huttenbrenner, wrote, "Schubert had a devout nature and believed firmly in God and in the immortality of the soul. His religious sense is also clearly expressed in many of his songs. At the time he was in want, he in no way lost courage. And if, at times, he had more than he needed, he willingly shared it with others who appealed to him for alms."

Schubert's father was a particularly powerful spiritual influence in his life. Once in a letter to another son after Schubert's death, the father wrote, "seek comfort in God and bear any affliction that may fall on us according to God's wise dispensation with resolute submission to his holy will. And what befalls us shall convince us of God's wisdom and goodness, and give us tranquillity. Therefore, take courage and trust implicitly in God. He will give you strength that you may not succumb and will grant you a glad future by his blessing."

Schubert would often thank God for his talents. In 1825 he wrote his family, describing the response to a new work he had composed: "It grips every soul and turns it to devotion." He further wrote that the audience "wondered greatly at my piety. . . I think this is due to the fact that I have never forced devotion in myself and never composed hymns or prayers of that kind unless it overcomes me unawares but then it is usually the right and true devotion."

Schubert's music had an intense, spiritual element. One of his biographers, Peggy Woodford, writes that his music indicates "an intense spiritual life" and his writings "imply that he was a deeply religious man." One musical historian, Carl Abram further wrote, "Certainly it is impossible to doubt the heartfelt piety and God-fearing humility which shines through even the most extended and turbulent of all the masses, namely the E-Flat Major. Only a truly religious spirit could prompt Schubert to have the chorus cry out utterly alone as though from the wilderness of despair at the beginning of the *Gloria*. Only an inner longing for divine help and release could have sustained the brooding and melancholy Schubert over the last years (the mass was composed in the last six months before his death)." Although raised Catholic, Schubert wrote music for Protestant denominations as well, and produced great works that are loved and performed today.

Schubert died of typhus at the age of thirty-one.

FELIX MENDELSSOHN

Felix Mendelssohn (1809–1847) was born to a Jewish family that converted to Christianity; he later joined the Lutheran Church. He considered Bach's work "the greatest Christian music in the world" and loved the Christian composition *Saint Matthew Passion*.

His wife, Cecile, was the daughter of a French Reformed pastor and was

FRANZ PETER SCHUBERT
Born: January 31, 1797
Died: November 19, 1828

Claim to fame:
Developed the German lied, or art song.

Did you know?
He composed his first symphony at age thirteen.

FELIX MENDELSSOHN
Born: February 3, 1809
Died: November 4, 1847

Claim to fame:
Widely respected German composer.

Did you know?
Mendelssohn's music for Shakespeare's A Midsummer Night's Dream *includes "The Wedding March."*

a committed Christian known as a woman of prayer. Kavanaugh writes, "For Mendelssohn, the Bible served as the cornerstone for daily life as well as the inspiration for much of his work. When he set passages of scripture to music, he was painstakingly precise about the wording. According to a friend who knew him well, he felt that all faith must be based on holy writ.'"

In one of his letters, Mendelssohn wrote, "Pray to God that He may create in us a clean heart and renew a right spirit." To a nephew he wrote, "Nothing is attained without the fulfillment of one fervent wish—May God be with you. This prayer comprises consolation and strength, and also cheerfulness in days to come."

His *Ave Maria* is famous throughout the world today, and his other compositions are consistently performed wherever great music is honored and appreciated. He fell at the age of thirty-eight, rupturing a blood vessel in his head, and never recovered.

CD-ROM ANALYSES

• The *Art & Music* series is one of the strongest in the entire curriculum. *The Medieval Era, The Renaissance, The Baroque, The Eighteenth Century, Romanticism, Impressionism, The Twentieth Century,* and *Surrealism* are all effectively dealt with, with representative samples. A vital element of education is to develop an awareness of the contributions made by art and music through the centuries. It is important to remember that you need not agree with every depiction or representation in the program, but rather it is important to be acquainted with them for the purpose of general knowledge. This series' particular strength is in the individual works of art and music that are presented.

• The *Elementary Music* series examines the lives of eighteen of the world's greatest composers, with excerpts from their most memorable works.
Instruments of the Symphony Orchestra, though it is part of the Elementary Music Series, is probably too complex for younger students. For older students, however, it is a very complete beginning course in music appreciation. The knowledge of the different instruments in the orchestra adds greatly to enjoyment and understanding of orchestral works. Also, if a student plays an instrument, he or she will benefit from understanding its role in a larger instrumental ensemble.
Appreciating the Orchestra is an ideal introduction for even very young children. The story of Peter and the Wolf captures their attention while they are exposed to numerous orchestral instruments being played both alone and in various combinations. This CD-ROM may very well become a favorite reward for a student who has diligently studied the material on other academic subjects.

REVIEW QUESTIONS

1. Which book in the Bible is actually a song book?

2. When music is in a form that helps people, it contains seven elements.

What are they?

3. Which composer wrote *Messiah?*

4. Which composer lived at Prince Paul Esterhazy's country estate?

5. Which composer was deaf, but used this to enhance his spiritual life?

6. Which composer never received formal musical training but was extravagantly talented, of which he was thankful to God?

SUGGESTED READING

Patrick Kavanaugh, *The Spiritual Lives of Great Composers.*

Material covered in the Faith and Science chapter can be found in the following Zane Publishing Home Library titles:

Survey of the Animal Kingdom: Sponges, Anemones, Corals, and Flatworms
Survey of the Animal Kingdom: Molluscs, Segmented Worms, and Minor Phyla
Survey of the Animal Kingdom: Insects—Springtails through Wasps and Bees
Survey of the Animal Kingdom: Noninsect Arthropods and Echinoderms
Survey of the Animal Kingdom: Urochordates and Craniata through Fish
Survey of the Animal Kingdom: Amphibians and Reptiles
Survey of the Animal Kingdom: Birds—Ostriches through Guinea Fowl
Survey of the Animal Kingdom: Birds—Cranes through Passerines
Survey of the Animal Kingdom: Mammals—Echidna through Whales
Survey of the Animal Kingdom: Mammals—Canids through Sheep
Biological Sciences: The Five Kingdoms of Life
Biological Sciences: Cell Biology I
Biological Sciences: Cell Biology II
Biological Sciences: Biochemistry I
Biological Sciences: Biochemistry II
Biological Sciences: Genetics
Biological Sciences: Heredity
Biological Sciences: Evolution
Biological Sciences: Biomes I
Biological Sciences: Biomes II
Biological Sciences: Ecosystems
Biological Sciences: Botany
Biological Sciences: Plant Anatomy
Biological Sciences: Introduction to Vertebrates
Elementary Science: Animals
Elementary Science: Plants
Elementary Science: The Human Body
Elementary Science: The Earth
Elementary Science: The Solar System
Junior Science: Plants & Animals
Junior Science: The Oceans
Junior Science: Introducing Oceanography
Junior Science: The Amazing Coral Reef
Junior Science: Life Science Patterns
Junior Science: The Universe
Earth Science: The Earth
Earth Science: Ecology I
Earth Science: Ecology II
Earth Science: Earth's Natural Resources
Earth Science: Understanding Weather and Climate

FAITH AND SCIENCE

Atheism is so senseless. When I look at the solar system, I see the earth at the right distance from the sun to receive the proper amounts of heat and light. This did not happen by chance.

–SIR ISAAC NEWTON,
THE FOUNDER OF MODERN SCIENCE

IN THE 1930s, UNIVERSAL STUDIOS dazzled moviegoers with a presentation of Mary Shelley's famous novel, *Frankenstein.* In one dramatic scene, Dr. Frankenstein, after raising the dead form of his creation into the heavens, brings the body back after it is struck by lightening. Moviegoers watched with utter fascination as the hand of the creature began to twitch and Dr. Frankenstein screamed, "It's alive! It's alive!"

In novels and movies such as *Frankenstein,* the arena of science is a tantalizing signpost into the possibilities of human life. Science has made available inventions that have greatly eased the demands of life; it has brought about discoveries that have benefited us all. In the late nineteenth century in England, following the Industrial Revolution, science was credited with arousing a new optimism in people. Because of the advances in technology and machinery, the idea that the basic problems of human life could be solved scientifically was popular in intellectual circles all over the world. Today, of course, we know that science itself is not the solution to the deepest needs of the human heart. Only God Himself can provide the security, the comfort, and the reality that the human soul needs. It cannot heal the human heart or bring forgiveness from God. The Bible teaches that Jesus Christ is the fulfillment of all of human creation, including that which is scientifically discovered. Colossians 1:15–17 says, "He is the image of the invisible God, the firstborn over all creation. For by him [Jesus Christ] all things were created; things in heaven and on earth, visible and invisible, whether thrones or powers or rulers or authorities; all things were created by him and for him. He is before all things, and in him all things hold together."

On the basis of this biblical presentation, it is obvious that all of creation, scientifically understood and otherwise, finds its source in Jesus Christ. In order to understand the created world, one must understand the God who made it.

CHRISTIAN SCIENTISTS

Many scientists have traditionally honored God as they have been humbled by His creation. Sir Isaac Newton (1642–1727), the English physicist and mathematician, is rightly considered one of the greatest scientists of all time. He is not only known for his idea of universal gravi-

SIR ISAAC NEWTON
Born: January 4, 1643
Died: March 31, 1727

Claim to fame:

Considered the founder of the Scientific Revolution of the seventeenth century.

Did you know?

He invented calculus.

tation and his invention of a reflecting telescope, but he is also well known for his commitment to Jesus Christ. In addition to his great works of science, he left behind a remarkable manuscript on the prophecies of Daniel in the Old Testament and a history of creation. It is obvious that he believed that God had made this amazing world, for he wrote in his greatest work, *Principia Mathematica,*

> This most beautiful system of sun, planets and comets could only proceed from the counsel and dominion of an intelligent and powerful being. This being governs all things not as the soul of the world but as Lord of All.

He also wrote that

> . . .the motions which the planets now have could not spring from any natural cause done but were impressed by an intelligent agent. The universe was rightly designed a temple of God. This being governs all things as Lord over all. If all the great books of the world were given life and brought together in convention, the moment the Bible entered, the other books would fall on their faces as the gods of Philistia fell when the Ark of God was brought into their presence in the Temple of Dagon.

Newton spent much of his life studying the Bible and was known to the people of his day as a great Christian thinker.

There have been other great scientific thinkers who have held such a belief. Johannes Kepler (1571–1630), the German astronomer who discovered the laws of planetary motion, said,

> We may behold how God, like a master builder, has laid the foundation of the world according to Lord and law. I give thee thanks, Lord and Creator, for thou hast given me joy through thy creation.

Galileo Galilei (1564–1642), the Italian mathematician and astronomer who was denounced for advocating the Copernican system and attempting to show scriptural confirmation of it, said,

> A hundred passages of Holy Scripture teach us that the glory and greatness of Almighty God are marvelously displayed in all His works and divinely read in the open Book of the heavens.

Robert Boyle (1627–1691), the British physicist and chemist who is considered the father of modern chemistry, received Christ as his Savior when he was thirteen years old. His father, the Earl of Cork, was a committed Christian who taught his son the Bible. Boyle is known for his work in optics (the study of light), acoustics (the study of sound), and for Boyle's law, which describes the behavior of gases under pressure. He was a student of the Bible all his life and would continually praise God for what he observed in creation. His belief was that his life was a life not only dedicated to studying science, but to turning men and women to Jesus Christ and encouraging them in their study of the Bible.

Modern scientists also have stated a great belief in God the Creator. Wernher von Braun, considered to be the father of modern rocket science, was generally thought to be the most capable astronautical engineer in the world. Von Braun, who was instrumental in developing NASA's space program and who was in charge of the development of the Saturn V rockets

---

GALILEO

Born: *February 15, 1564*
Died: *January 8, 1642*

Claim to fame:

Helped to prove Copernicus's theory that the earth revolved around the sun and was not at the center of the universe.

Did you know?

He was persecuted by the Church for his theories, and he was forced to recant.

ROBERT BOYLE

Born: *January 25, 1627*
Died: *December 30, 1691*

Claim to fame:

Famed Christian chemist who studied the properties of gases.

Did you know?

He invented the vacuum pump.

WERNHER VON BRAUN

Born: *March 23, 1912*
Died: *June 16, 1977*

Claim to fame:

American rocket scientist and engineer.

Did you know?

He was president of the National Space Institute from 1975 to 1977.

used in Apollo flights, wrote:

> One cannot be exposed to the law and order of the universe without concluding that there must be a divine intent behind it all. The creator is revealed through His creation.

EVOLUTION VS. CREATION

Science, unfortunately, has often become a weapon in the hands of those who oppose God. In an effort to discredit the Bible, some people use so-called scientific evidence. This is nowhere more apparent than in the theory of evolution

When Charles Darwin published *On the Origin of Species*, he never anticipated the earth-shattering effects of his research. Out of his observations and ideas grew the theory of the spontaneous generation of life and its evolution to advanced forms.

Most public schoolchildren are taught this theory as a fact. Is this proper or fair? Our answer is no—it is neither proper nor fair to make claims for this theory of evolution when the theory cannot logically support itself.

The idea of evolution commonly taught is the "mechanistic" or "mechanical" (non-directed) theory of evolution. This teaches that life began accidentally in some ancient sea, possibly by the accidental combining of chemical elements; that life unexplainably developed and diversified into the awesome complexity and variety of life now on earth.

This is, of course, a great oversimplification of this idea, but in essence, the "accidental" and "mechanical" elements are essential to its understanding.

Actual evidence for this theory of human life is embarrassingly limited. There are, for example, honest questions concerning fossils. When Lucy, the fossil remains of a creature found in Africa, was discovered, it seemed to support Darwin's theory of evolution. It was touted as the "missing link" between humans and apes. However, Lucy is in skeletal structure neither ape nor human. And though she is considered staggeringly old—millions of years—her age is truly guesswork. Even the famous Carbon 14 test, which measures the remains of carbon in an object, is unreliable.

Nothing about Lucy supports the conclusions of evolution that have been made about her. There is so little actually known about her that her position as a "missing link" is impossible to prove. And her fossil record is actually a problem for evolutionists. It is widely held that the existence of fossil remains of extinct species implies evolution, but is this necessarily so? No! Many experts believe that there was a great catastrophe at some point in history that created the extinction of these species, and that the existence today of such fossil remains is evidence of that great disaster and not of evolution.

The great French naturalist Georges Cuvier rejected the theory of evolution and instead believed in catastrophism. He believed that the geological record showed a pattern of catastrophic events involving mass extinctions, which were followed by periods of creation in which new forms of life appeared without any trace of evolutionary development.

Darwin himself posed a question in writing on this problem when he asked "Why if species have descended from other species by insensibly fine

CHARLES DARWIN
Born: February 12, 1809
Died: April 19, 1882

Claim to fame:
Documented the theory of evolution in On the Origin of Species.

Did you know?
He conducted research on the HMS Beagle.

195

gradations, do we not everywhere see innumerable transitional forms? Why is not all nature in confusion instead of the species being as we see them well defined." This problem troubled even Darwin's loyal supporter, T.H. Huxley, who "warned Darwin repeatedly in private that a theory consistent with the evidence would have to allow for some big jumps." This means that the fossil record itself of mass extinctions followed by the creation of new species goes against the theory of evolution rather than supporting it.

According to Steven J. Gould of Harvard University, "the history of most fossil species includes two features particularly inconsistent with gradualism" Those two features of gradualism, which is the idea that evolution happens gradually over many, many millions of years, are:

1. Stasis

Stasis means to stay in the same state and not change. Most species exhibit no change during their time on earth. They appear in the fossil record looking pretty much the same as when they disappear. Morphological change, that is change in body form, is usually limited and directionless.

2. Set in Appearance

This means that a species appears all at once and fully formed. Thus, there is no evidence for evolution when these fossils are discovered, for they are fully formed.

Paleontologist Steven Stanley, in writing on fossils found from the early age of mammals in the Big Horned Basin in Wyoming, said that "the fossil record does not convincingly document a single transition from one species to another." He further wrote,

> Let us suppose that we wish hypothetically to form a bat or a whale by a process of gradual transformation of established species. If an average chrono species [a segment of fossil lineage where there is so little observable change that it has remained a single species] lasts nearly a million years, or even longer, and we have at our disposal only ten million years, then we have only 10 or 15 chrono species to align end to end to form a continuous lineage connecting our primitive little mammal with a bat or a whale. This is clearly preposterous. Chrono species by definition grate into each other, and each one encompasses very little change. A chain of ten or fifteen of these might move us from one small rodentlike form to a slightly different rodentlike form, perhaps representing a new genus, but not to a bat or a whale.

What all of this says is that the greatest fossil experts in the world are forced to conclude that evolution, as taught in public school and as currently understood by millions of people, does not have a basis in paleontological research.

So what was it that caused the destruction of these species that created the fossils that we now find? The idea of a catastrophe or a worldwide disaster is gaining ground among scientific thinkers, although it is a controversial subject among geologists and paleontologists. Some scientists theorize that dinosaurs and other species were destroyed by a great meteor striking the earth. Others speak of the ice age destroying many of these animals. It is equally plausible that it could have been the great

196

flood. Genesis 6:4 says, "The nephilim were on the earth in those days." That translates as "there were giants in the earth in those days." Could there have been what we term prehistoric animals that were destroyed in the flood? The Bible says in verse 7 of Genesis that

> So the Lord said 'I will wipe mankind whom I have created from the face of the earth, men and animals and creatures that move along the ground and birds of the air, for I am grieved that I have made them.'

It is certainly possible that the catastrophe of which many scientists speak could have been the great flood of Noah, which dramatically changed the human and animal population of the planet.

PROBLEMS WITH THE EVOLUTION THEORY

There are further serious problems with the idea of mechanical evolution. One is the problem of complexity, which is often called the "watch argument."

If you take all the component parts of a well-assembled wristwatch and toss them high in the air, what are the odds of every piece landing together fully reassembled as a functioning watch? If you're smiling at the absurdity of this possibility, you have a good idea of the core of the watch argument. If the reappearance of the watch is for all practical purposes impossible, how much more difficult is it to believe that all life forms on this planet are accidentally generated and mechanically developed?

Life is so fascinatingly complicated, so unbelievably complex, that it is decidedly difficult to believe that life as we know it in all of its vast variety could possibly be accidentally produced. If the theory of evolution is true, how then does one explain the complexity of the human eye?

What is remarkable about the eye is that it is so complex and so unusually formed, yet works with such perfection in its appointed purpose. That in itself is a statement of creation—not of accidental or mechanical evolution. The eye is a living example of the hand of God in human creation. How could something so remarkable have been accidentally produced?

Consider just how complex the eye is. It is really a form of camera. It has an adjustable opening to admit light, a lens that focuses light waves to form an image, and a sensitive film within the eye on which the image is recorded. The cornea is transparent, which helps in bending light rays as they enter the eye. The retina is made up of ten very thin layers of cells that line the inside of the eye. The iris and regulates the light coming in; it closes the opening to a tiny whole in bright light and expands in dim light. The lens bends the waves of light so that they come to a focus on the retina.

The human eye is proof not of an accidental evolution but a demonstration of the hand of God in making you and every organ in your complex body.

Another problem with the theory of evolution concerns basic physics. The second law of thermodynamics states that systems left to themselves tend to run down, to deteriorate, to go from complexity to simpler and simpler forms. This is an absolute law of physics that contradicts the very concept of evolution itself, which maintains that organisms move from the simple to the complex.

Do you see how these problems are connected? The complexity of human beings and a basic law of physics both point to the guiding hand of a Creator God.

PHILOSOPHICAL DARWINISM

Philosophical Darwinism is a worldview based on the belief that evolution is a solid fact and is not theory at all. It is known for its refusal to consider other positions because the question is considered settled. It explains all of life in terms of evolution, with its premise of the "survival of the fittest."

To further explain this, let's put crime within the context of this belief. The Bible teaches us that we are made in the image of God: "So God created man in his own image, in the image of God he created him; male and female he created them." (Genesis 1:27 *NIV*) Because of this, men and women are morally accountable for their actions. Because God's creation is so uniquely valuable and because we are morally accountable, when one man kills another in cold blood he is held accountable by giving up his life for the crime of killing another human being. Capital punishment is a correct biblical view that reinforces the moral nature of the human race and the precious importance of each individual. It is a form of punishment instituted by God for our benefit and protection

Yet, in the twentieth century, as a result of Philosophical Darwinism, people are often considered victims of their environment, their childhood, their society. They therefore need not punishment but help and rehabilitation. They need help to "evolve" in a particular direction. What Philosophical Darwinism does is replace a God-created view of the world with the idea that all of life is human-centered. It gives men and women the option to live their lives without a personal Creator God to whom they are ultimately accountable.

There is within each of us a principle of sin—a rebellion toward God. This began with Adam and Eve in the Garden of Eden and has been passed to every generation since. The appeal of Philosophical Darwinism, of the idea of accidental mechanical evolution is simple: It appeals to the in-built sinfulness of man and his rebellion against God's authority.

A THEORY LOSING SUPPORT

There are a number of men and women, scientifically trained and educated, who do not believe that the theory of evolution is valid. One is Professor Philip Johnson, a graduate of Harvard University and the University of Chicago, who was a law clerk for Chief Justice Earl Warren. He has taught law for more than twenty years at the University of California at Berkeley. He took up the study of Darwinism because he concluded that the books defending the theory were unconvincing. Writing from a legal and scientific standpoint, he gave the other side of the argument. In his book *Darwin on Trial*, Professor Johnson stated that scientists from all over the world are defecting from the belief in the evolution theory and are now shying away from the Academy of Science, which is critical of Bible-based creation science. The Academy accuses those who believe the Bible and believe in creation of using the teaching of creation as a way to avoid what they consider the truth of evolution. Professor Johnson stated that there are many scientists who disagree strongly with the Academy's position that evolution is not something that has been scientifically proved; they contend that if one talks in terms of scientific proof and scientific method, then one must discount the theory of evolution.

Colin Patterson, the senior paleontologist at the British Natural History Museum and the author of that museum's general text on evolution, gave a lecture in 1981 at the American Museum of Natural History in which he said:

> Can you tell me anything you know about evolution—any one thing that is true? I tried that question on the geology staff at the Field Museum of Natural History and the only answer I got was silence. I tried it on the members of the Evolutionary Morphology Seminar at the University of Chicago, a very prestigious body of evolutionists, and all I got there was silence for a long time and eventually one person said, 'I do know one thing—it ought not to be taught in high school.'

The following quotes are from others who disagree with Darwin's theory:

> No one in all human history has ever observed one species evolve into a more complex and better adapted species by NATURAL SELECTION or any other mechanism. No one has seen evidence of any mechanism that would make evolution work. In the fossil record of the past, with billions of fossils preserved in the earth's crust, no one has ever found any fossils showing incipient or transitional structures leading to the evolution of more complex species.[1]

> We are now about 120 years after Darwin and the knowledge of the fossil record has been greatly expanded. We now have a quarter of a million fossil species but the situation hasn't changed much. The record of evolution is still surprisingly jerky and, ironically, we have even fewer examples of evolutionary transition than we did in Darwin's time.[2]

> Every advance in fundamental physics seems to uncover yet another facet of order. The very success of the scientific method depends upon the fact that the physical world operates according to rational principles which can therefore be discerned through rational inquiry. Logically, the universe does not have to operate this way. We could conceive of a cosmos where chaos reigns. In the place of the orderly and regimented behavior of matter and energy one would have arbitrary and haphazard activity. Stable structures like atoms or people or stars could not exist. The real world is not this way. It is ordered and complex. Is that not in itself an astonishing fact at which to marvel?[3]

> Since MACROEVOLUTION requires increasing complexity through natural processes, the organism's information content must increase. But since natural processes cannot increase the information content of a system such as a reproductive cell, macroevolution cannot occur.[4]

> Apart from artificial language used in computers and human language itself, the genetic code, or the language of life as it has been

called, is without any analogue in the physical universe. Like cilia and like so many of the characteristics found in living things on earth, the genetic code is not led up to gradually through a sequence of transitional forms.[5]

When all relevant lines of evidence are taken into account, and the problems squarely faced, I think we must conclude that life owes its inception to a source outside of nature.[6]

Since science has not the vaguest idea how life originated on earth. . . it would be honest to admit this to students, the agencies funding research, and the public. Leaders in science. . .should stop polarizing the minds of students and younger creative scientists with statements for which faith is the only evidence.[7]

If evolution happened, the fossil record should show continuous and gradual changes from the bottom to the top layers and between all forms of life. Actually, many gaps and discontinuities appear throughout the fossil record. Many fossil links are missing among numerous plants, between single-cell forms of life and invertebrates, invertebrates and vertebrates, fish and amphibians, amphibians and reptiles, reptiles and mammals, reptiles and birds, and between primates and other animals. The fossil record has been studied so thoroughly that it is safe to conclude that they are real; they will never be filled. The hypothetical evolutionary tree has no branches.[8]

If by evolution we mean macroevolution, then it can be said with the utmost rigor that the doctrine is totally bereft of scientific sanction. . .there exists today not a shred of bona fide evidence in support of the thesis that macroevolutionary transformations have ever occured.[9]

[Darwin's] general theory, that all life on earth had originated and evolved by a gradual accumulation of fortuitous MUTATIONS, is still, as it was in Darwin's time, a highly speculative HYPOTHESIS without direct factual support and very far from that self-evident AXIOM some of its more aggressive advocates would have us believe.[10]

The more I study science, the more I am impressed with the thought that this world and universe have a definite design—and a design suggests a designer. It may be possible to have design without a designer, a picture without an artist, but my mind is unable to conceive of such a situation.[11]

I remember well the time when the thought of the eye made me cold all over, but I have got over this stage of the complaint, and now small trifling particulars of structure often make me very uncomfortable. The sight of a feather in a peacock's tail, whenever I gaze at it, makes me sick![12]

[There] has never been a case established where a living organism was observed to change into a basically different organism with different structures. No observed mutation has ever been demonstrated to be more beneficial to the overall population out in nature.[13]

While breeding experiments and the domestication of animals had revealed that many species were capable of a considerable degree of change, they also revealed distinct limits in nearly every case beyond which no further change could ever be produced. Here then was a very well established fact, known for centuries, which seemed to run counter to [Darwin's] whole case, threatening not only his special theory—that one species could evolve into another—but also the plausibility of the EXTRAPOLATION from micro to macroevolution, which, as we have seen, was largely based on an appeal to the remarkable degree of change achieved by artificial selection in a relatively short time. If this change was always strictly limited, then the validity of the extrapolation was obviously seriously threatened.[14]

The extreme rarity of transitional forms in the fossil record persists as the trade secret of PALEONTOLOGY. The evolutionary trees that adorn our textbooks have data only at the tips and nodes of their branches; the rest is inference, however reasonable, not the evidence of fossils. . . . We fancy ourselves as the only true students of life's history, yet to preserve our favored account of evolution by natural selection we view our data as so bad that we never see the very process we profess to study.[15]

As far as the individual defining characteristics are concerned, one could continue citing almost ad infinitum complex defining characteristics of particular classes or organisms which are without analogy or precedent in any other part of the living kingdom and are not led up to in any way through a series of transitional structures. Such a list would include structures as diverse as the vertebral column of vertebrates, the jumping apparatus of the click beetle, . . .the wing of a bat, . . .the neck of the giraffe, . . .the male reproductive organs of the dragonfly, and so on until one had practically named every significant characteristic of every living thing on earth.[16]

I have come to the conclusion that Darwinism is not a testable scientific theory, but a METAPHYSICAL research programme—a possible framework for testable scientific theories.[17]

Harvard Professor Steven J. Gould in 1980 published a paper in a scientific journal where he predicted the emergence of "a new and general theory of evolution" to replace the old theory. Gould said that the theory of evolution as taught "as a general proposition is effectively dead despite its persistence as textbook orthodoxy." This means that the rebellion among scientists on this theory is prominent and well known within scientific circles.

CONCLUSION

The problem with evolutionary thinking today is not so much that of factuality and scientific research, but the problem rather is one of what again is called Philosophical Darwinism. It is the desire of men and women who have often rejected God in His biblical authority to manufacture a system of thought that will conveniently leave God out. That is why so many men and women have so quickly embraced this unproved theory. It caters to the sinful nature of the human race, which is in fundamental rebellion against God.

We have examined a number of difficulties with Darwinian thought and mechanical evolution. It is your responsibility, now, to make a decision. We encourage all of you to use the Zane CD-ROM program to gain a working knowledge of scientific research. With Zane's information, you will develop an understanding of scientific knowledge. You will survey the animal kingdom; you will learn how scientific knowledge is organized; you will develop an awareness of biological, cellular development; and you will learn the most important theories of physics, astronomy, and biology. However, you must remember that everything taught in the biological and physical science sections of Zane's CD-ROMs can be and should be understood through a creation framework—the realization that this incredible planet, with all of its unbelievable complexity, has been produced by an intelligent, personal, loving God, and that the most awesome fact about this is that this is a God you can know personally through Jesus Christ, His Son, who died for you on the cross and rose in power from the dead. And, you should remember that God is God, and He is the one who has made this beautiful and amazing creation. He is the one who has created the planets and the stars. He is the one who originated the laws by which the universe operates. He is the one who is the Lord of creation.

CD-ROM ANALYSES

• The Science CD-ROMs are worthy of study but do have an evolutionary bias that is addressed in this chapter. The rest of the material is factual, dealing with aspects of the physical sciences and animal kingdom that your students need to know.

REVIEW QUESTIONS

1. All creation, scientifically understood and otherwise, finds its source in whom?

2. Which scientist left behind a remarkable manuscript on the prophecies of Daniel in the Old Testament and a history of creation?

3. Can the theory of evolution logically support itself?

4. Charles Darwin posed this question: "Why, if species have descended from other species by insensibly fine gradations, do we not everywhere see innumerable transitional forms?" What did he mean by this question?

5. The second law of thermodynamics states that systems left to themselves tend to run down and go from complex to simpler and simpler forms. How does this contradict the theory of evolution?

6. Philosophical Darwinism, based on the unproved theory of evolution, gives men and women the option to live their lives without a personal Creator God to whom they are ultimately accountable. List some areas where this thinking has created some major problems.

SUGGESTED READING

W. R. Bird, *The Origin of Species Revisited, 2 Vols.* (New York: Philosophical

Library, 1989).

Charles Darwin, *On the Origin of Species.*

Michael Denton, *Evolution: A Theory in Crisis* (Bethesda, MD: Adler and Adler, 1986).

Philip Johnson, *Darwin on Trial.*

Norman Macbeth, *Darwin Retire: An Appeal to Reason* (Boston: The Harvard Common Press, 1971).

Josh McDowell, *Evidence That Demands A Verdict.*

Henry Morris, *The Long War Against God* (Grand Rapids, MI: Baker, 1990).

Luther D. Sutherland, *Darwin's Enigma* (Santee, CA: Master Book, 1988).

Charles B. Thaxton, Walter L. Bradley, and Roger L. Olsen, *The Mystery of Life's Origin* (New York: Philosophical Library, 1984).

Material covered in the Myths & Legends chapter can be found in the following Zane Publishing Home Library titles:

Elementary Literature: Greek Mythology I
Elementary Literature: Greek Mythology II
Elementary Literature: The Voyages of Ulysses and Aeneas
Elementary Literature: African, Arabic, Celtic, and Norse Mythologies
European Literature: The Ancient World—The Renaissance
History through Art: Ancient Greece
History through Art: Ancient Rome

MYTHS & LEGENDS

Mythology: A system of fables or fabulous opinions and doctrines respecting the deities which heathen nations have supposed to preside over the world or to influence the affairs of it.

–NOAH WEBSTER,
ORIGINAL 1828 DICTIONARY

MYTHS AND LEGENDS ARE NOT just a thing of the past; they surround us daily. The Disney Corporation makes its livelihood from its animated movies, which resurrect old legends and update them. Much of the Hollywood motion picture industry is concerned with creating characters that it believes have the potential to become modern legends—the next Ferris Bueller or Dirty Harry. Both screen stars and the characters they create have become a part of modern mythologies, influencing the way we think of ourselves and of the world in much the same way the myths of the ancients influenced them.

Christian families using Zane's CD-ROM titles and this book can and should be able to see beyond the surface-level story of myths to their more subtle religious side. Teaching children to discern the futile attempt at salvation without Christ that these myths represent is an important part of teaching children to stand firm in the face of religious opposition. Also, exposure to ancient myths is useful in understanding the literature of the nineteenth and early twentieth centuries, on which the mythological literature of classical Greece and Rome was a strong influence.

Paul wrote to the Corinthians that "the preaching of the cross is to them that perish, foolishness; but unto us who are being saved, it is the power of God."[1] In another sense, the myths of ancient cultures seem foolish to us, but were to them the basis of religious belief and moral behavior. The difference is that the Gospel is the revealed Word of God, whereas the myths of ancient cultures were stories created by the minds of men.

MYTHS IN CHRISTIAN PERSPECTIVE

Should Christian parents be wary of teaching their children about these myths? Not wary, perhaps, but certainly aware. Aware, first, that these are, after all, religious texts, and not just amusing tales. Aware that they and the religions they supported were the cause of great immorality and cruelty. Aware, also, that Christian missionaries encountered and overcame these false teachings with the truth of salvation through Christ.

Some of the myths and legends in Zane's CD-ROM library are stories written more for entertainment than for religious purposes. Stories like the *Odyssey,* the *Aeneid,* the legends of King Arthur, and others do not have any religious function. Though gods sometimes appear in them, they

KING ARTHUR

Legendary medieval king

Claim to fame:

Mythical king of Britain; founder of the Round Table.

Did you know?

According to legend, he pulled a sword from a stone, proving himself to be the rightful king.

appear as characters rather than as objects of worship. These stories are called legends.

Those with a more religious purpose are called myths. Students should not have any difficulty finding the Christian approach to these, since the gap between understanding them and actually believing them is great. Even the youngest children know better than to believe that the sun is the chariot of Apollo riding across the sky.

The study of the myths of ancient cultures is an opportunity to teach the student the difference between Christianity and other religions. Myths are often described as

> entertaining stories with a serious purpose. . . . A myth's serious purpose is either to explain the nature of the universe or to instruct members of the community in the attitudes and behavior necessary to function successfully in that particular culture. . . . Myths reflect human nature, with its needs and desires, hopes and fears. . . . Myths reveal cultural responses to the ever-important questions: Who am I? How should I lead my life? Thus, they reveal the different ways in which human beings respond to the issues that unite them.[2]

Christianity, on the other hand, is God's revelation of Himself to man.

Some myths do contain a grain of truth, as in the practically universal creation and flood myths, but for the most part they are part of a larger system of false religious belief. In most creation myths, for instance, one of the first creations of the "Supreme Being" is several less-than-supreme beings, who are designated "gods" despite their shortcomings, and who fight among themselves for power. None of these man-made religions can compare to God's revealed plan of salvation through Christ.

The world's attitude towards ancient mythologies tends to run to extremes. While we understand that these myths are false, the world sometimes concludes that all religions are myth-based, and therefore all are false. This is the position of the extreme of materialism, whether it be advocated by a MARXIST or a DARWINIST or some other ATHEIST. These people often believe that the only reliable truth comes from science. From this point of view, religion is not only false, since it does not base itself on science, but foolish as well, since it is concerned with completely unscientific things.

On the other extreme is the popular doctrine of PLURALISM, often called "multiculturalism." In this view, there is no such thing as "Truth," only "truths." In other words, in the sense of "Truth," everything is false; nothing is absolutely true. In the sense of "truths," everything is true; *all things are subjectively true—Christianity, HINDUISM, MORMONISM, ANIMISM, DRUIDISM, and so on.* All roads lead to heaven. All are true all at once.

Christian belief, however, requires a different perspective on truth, and consequently the Christian perspective on myths will be different from that of the SECULARIST. The Christian will not be unwilling to study myths, as the MATERIALIST would, because the Christian believes that some things are true and some false, and is able to discern between the two. Nor is the Christian equivocal about what is "True." Myths are false, and are useful only as a literary and ESTHETIC reference and as a case study in the false religions of ancient cultures. The Christian perspective on myths and legends, as on most things, must be different than secular worldviews. It is vital for students to have this Christian perspective, because just as our contemporary entertainment culture surrounds us with the myths of the past, it also creates new myths. From television shows and movies, and mystical New Age religions, new myths are constantly being created and offered to young and old alike. To be able to judge these for what they are is essential to the life of a Christian in today's world.

IS CHRISTIANITY A MYTH?

There are many in our day who would like to categorize Christianity as a myth. Without intelligent investigation of the facts, they presuppose that all religions are the same—faith-based, anti-scientific leaps into the void.

As Christians, we do not need to cower intellectually before New Age pseudo-scientists or evolutionists who cling to an unproved creation theory like the Viking warriors of old, who believed a cow licked the ice of the Arctic and released the first man into existence.

Christianity is a historical faith, not a mythological creation of man. It is founded on the historic reality of its biblical chronology, miracles, and especially upon the bodily resurrection of Jesus Christ from the dead. Unlike the Marxist or New Age prophets, we do not need court historians or a biased media to bolster Christianity under intense scrutiny. In fact, as the history and science sections of this book document, the truth of Christianity and its Bible will withstand any honest investigation.

Many notable skeptics have taken up the challenge of attempting to prove Christianity to be a myth. Here are two of the more famous doubters.

Lew Wallace, a nineteenth-century lawyer, general, and the author of *Ben-Hur*, was convinced that the stories of Jesus' deity were myth, or untrue. He began to study for the writing of *Ben-Hur*, a work initially conceived to present Christ as a mere man. Using his training as a lawyer, Wallace vowed to study "such elemental themes as God and life hereafter and Jesus Christ and His divinity." While studying the Bible and the historical evidence for Christ's claims, he became a firm believer, and went on to write *Ben-Hur*, one of the classics of history, to present Jesus Christ as the divine Savior.[3] He said, "After six years given to the impartial investigation of Christianity, as to its truth or falsity, I have come to the deliberate conclusion that Jesus Christ was the Messiah of the Jews, the Saviour of the world, and my personal Saviour."[4]

C. S. Lewis, the brilliant Oxford professor, was one of the great authors and scholars of the twentieth century. He was a skeptic and reviler of Christianity until the age of thirty-five. He was brought to Christ in 1933 and spent the next thirty years as the premier intellectual defender of the Christian faith. In his brilliant defense of Christianity, *Mere Christianity*, Lewis makes this statement:

> A man who was merely a man and said the sort of things Jesus said would not be a great moral teacher. He would either be a lunatic— on a level with the man who says he is a poached egg—or else he would be the Devil of Hell. You must make your choice. Either this man was, and is, the Son of God: or else a madman or something worse. You can shut Him up for a fool, you can spit at Him and kill

---

LEW WALLACE
Born: *April 10, 1827*
Died: *February 15, 1905*

Claim to fame:
Wrote the historical novel Ben-Hur.

Did you know?
He held the rank of major general in the Union Army during the Civil War.

C.S. LEWIS
(CLIVE STAPLES LEWIS)
Born: *November 29, 1898*
Died: *November 22, 1963*

Claim to fame:
The Chronicles of Narnia, *a series of seven fantasy books for children, written between 1950 and 1956.*

Did you know?
Lewis was one of the first science fiction writers. His first science fiction novel, Out of the Silent Planet, *was published in 1938, a time when the genre was hardly known.*

Him as a demon; or you can fall at His feet and call Him Lord and God. But let us not come with any patronizing nonsense about His being a great human teacher. He has not left that open to us.[5]

Christian students need not fear intellectual investigation into their faith. The truth is that Jesus Christ rose from the dead and reigns with God the Father on high. His name is not to be found among the ranks of imaginary gods—Jupiter, Zeus, Odin, or Osiris—who never existed at all.

CD-ROM ANALYSES

• The four CD-ROMs of the *Elementary Literature: Myths & Legends* series are well done, covering the basics of world mythology, and covering Greek mythology extensively.

• The African myths section in *African, Arabic, Celtic, and Norse Mythologies* shows an inclination, however moderate, to the false worldviews of materialism and pluralism.

• The description of the "Underworld" in *African, Arabic, Celtic, and Norse Mythologies* is rather different than the Heaven and Hell of Christianity. This could be turned into a very interesting discussion for older students.

• As the CD-ROMs point out, the object of the hero legend in almost every culture is to inspire character. Some of these legends could still be useful in this way, and the fact that most of the heroes are flawed opens up yet more discussion possibilities.

REVIEW QUESTIONS

1. A myth is a story about religious ideas. A legend usually has a single human hero and is more for entertainment. Which of the stories on the CD-ROMs are myths and which are legends?

2. Why do people write myths?

3. What are some of the similarities among myths of different cultures?

4. How is Christianity not based on myths and legends?

RELATED SCRIPTURE

Romans 1:18–23   2 Peter 1:16
1 Corinthians 10:20   2 Timothy 4:4
Colossians 2:8–9

SUGGESTED READING

1001 Arabian Nights [Note: Parents might want to find an expurgated version as the stories are sometimes a bit racy.]

Thomas Bullfinch, *Bullfinch's Mythology.*

Stephen R. Lawhead, *The Pendragon Cycle*, Vols. 1–3.

Sir Thomas Malory, *Le Morte D'Arthur.*

Donna Rosenberg, *World Mythology: An Anthology of Great Myths and Epics*, 2nd ed.

PART FOUR

Christian Leaders

LEADERS IN CHRISTIAN HISTORY

It was wonderful to see the change soon made in the manner of our inhabitants. From being thoughtless or indifferent about religion, it seemed as if all the world were growing religious, so that one could not walk thro' the town in an evening without hearing psalms sung in different families of every street.

–BENJAMIN FRANKLIN
WRITING ON THE EFFECT
OF GEORGE WHITEFIELD'S PREACHING

THE STUDY OF HISTORY is necessary. In this academic area you learn the lessons that protect the future for you and your family. It is an opportunity to gain insight to the lives of men and women who have influenced politics, science, education, art, music, literature, and spiritual life. The leaders mentioned on Zane's CD-ROMs—presidents, military dictators, generals—are historical figures of great importance. But what can be more important than the influence of Jesus Christ one man or woman can bring to their generation? One example today of such a monumental figure is Billy Graham, a man respected throughout the world for his integrity of life and the clarity of his communications about Jesus Christ.

There have been other individuals such as Graham in the last two and one-half centuries who have had great influence on their generations for Jesus Christ. We are now going to examine the lives of some of those individuals and their roles in shaping world history.

JOHN WESLEY

History books frequently mention the importance of John Wesley (1703–1791), one of the truly great figures of world history. Thomas Carlyle, in his great work, *French Revolution*, theorized that England had not experienced such a society-wrenching revolution because of the great spiritual awakening led in part by John Wesley. In his early life, his father, an Anglican pastor, and his mother fled their home when the house caught fire. During the blaze, the shocked parents realized that five-year-old John remained behind. Rescuers then rushed into the building and brought him out, as he said later, "plucked as a brand from the fire." Wesley believed all his life that this incident revealed God's special purpose for him even from his childhood. During Wesley's childhood, England was thought by many contemporary scholars to be in the midst of sin and degradation. The historian J. Wesley Brady described Wesley's childhood generation as one of "stark skepticism that gripped the lives of the leaders of religion and government; the church prelates were blind guides; the court life was unchaste and indecent, the sinful social life fostered horrible conditions for children; universal gambling and such unchristian practices as slavery; unspeakable prison conditions; political bribery and corruption; ghastly drunkenness and vicious sensuality were the accepted order."

211

Wesley was the fifteenth of nineteen children born to Samuel Wesley and his wife, Susanna. Wesley went into the Anglican priesthood as a young man, having been educated at Oxford University, and then volunteered to serve a term as a missionary to the Indians in the American colony that is now the state of Georgia. Wesley, during this era, had an intense internal struggle. He wrote in his journal on 24 January 1738: "I went to America to convert the Indians but oh, who shall convert me? Who? Who is He that shall deliver me from this evil heart?"

Wesley, convinced he was a failure, encountered a group of Moravian missionaries led by Peter Bohler while on a sailing vessel. He began to seek the reality of a relationship with Jesus Christ as a result of the spiritual influence of Bohler and his friends. A violent storm had terrified everyone on board except the Moravians. Wesley, amazed at their calm and courage, asked the secret of their strength. Bohler told Wesley it was a personal relationship with Jesus Christ. When the voyage ended, Wesley urgently began to seek this relationship with Jesus Christ. What happened next is well known. Wesley recorded in his *Journal* on 24 May 1738, "In the evening I went very unwillingly to a Society in Aldersgate Street where one was reading Luther's *Preface to the Epistle of Romans*. About a quarter before nine while he was describing the change which God works in the heart through faith in Christ, I felt my heart strangely warmed. I felt I did trust in Christ, Christ alone for salvation, and an assurance was given me that He had taken away my sins, even mine, and saved me from the law of sin and death."

Eighteen days later, on the grounds of the University of Oxford, he preached his first sermon titled "By Grace Are Ye Saved Through Faith." The religious establishment of his day was outraged at Wesley's bold and clear preaching, and forced him out of their churches. He began speaking in fields, public halls, streets, graveyards—anywhere he could. He wrote, "I look on the world as my parish." He once preached from his father's tombstone to the largest crowd ever assembled in that region of England. A spiritual movement erupted that lasted eight days, with people coming by the thousands to hear Wesley speak. Everywhere he went thousands of people crowded in to hear this man speak about Jesus Christ.

Wesley, not a big man at slightly over five feet tall, was a giant for God in his nation. Up until his death at the age of 88, he preached 42,000 messages and wrote 200 books urging men and women to come to Christ. The revival movement that God sparked through Wesley's ministry is now known as the Methodist revival movement. Out of it was born the Methodist Church, which today is known as the United Methodist Church. It was a denomination born in the fires of spiritual awakening. God used John Wesley to generate a movement that astounded the known world and stopped England's slide into corruption and moral filth. John Wesley was a great leader, a great man of God, whom you need to study further. If you want to know more about John Wesley, there is an excellent biography written by John Pollock, the official biographer of Billy Graham. There also is a small book on John Wesley by Basil Miller that is a good introduction to his life and influence.

One of John Wesley's brothers, Charles, is well known as one of history's great Christian songwriters. He wrote thousands of hymns, such as "O, for a Thousand Tongues to Sing" and "Hark! The Herald Angels Sing." Charles Wesley was an important partner for his brother John because Charles took popular ballads from bars and saloons and then wrote Christian words for them, creating an excitement for Christian music that had not existed for centuries. "O, for a Thousand Tongues to Sing" is one such hymn based on a barroom ballad that Charles transformed into one of the great Christian songs of modern history: "O, for a thousand tongues to sing, my great redeemers praise. The glories of my God and King, the triumphs of his grace."

GEORGE WHITEFIELD

Another critically important leader during this era was George Whitefield (1714–1770), thought by many scholars to be the spark of the Methodist revival movement while John Wesley was developing and organizing it. Whitefield is considered one of the greatest public communicators of the gospel in history. A man of tremendous dramatic talent, David Garrick, the most famous English actor of his generation, said that Whitefield was the greatest natural stage actor he had ever seen in his professional life.

George Whitefield worked with John Wesley to move England back to God. He came to Christ just prior to enrolling at Oxford University, where he became a friend of the Wesleys, and was ordained to the ministry 20 June 1736. The crowds he attracted were even greater than Wesley's. At twenty-two years of age, he had crowds in London that were so "vast it was necessary to place constables to preserve the peace." His crowds reached the tens of thousands, and everywhere he went the response was phenomenal. A sampling of Whitefield's audiences: Mooreheads in 1739, 30,000; Philadelphia, in the New World, 12,000; Boston, 22,000. On and on and on—these numbers demonstrate the incredible power and influence of this godly man. Benjamin Franklin heard George Whitefield speak in Philadelphia. Franklin was notoriously opposed to giving money to Christian causes. He was very frugal with his income and often refused to participate in efforts to raise money for the growing Christian movement in the colonies. But when George Whitefield finished preaching, Franklin emptied his pockets and fled, telling a friend he had no power to resist such an incredible man. He and Whitefield then became friends and would speak frequently of the need for Franklin to come to know Jesus Christ as his Savior.

Whitefield crossed the Atlantic on numerous occasions; he was the first great international evangelist of modern times. On 30 September 1770, at fifty-five years of age, George Whitefield—who had preached for 34 years, crossed the Atlantic 13 times, and delivered more than 18,000 sermons—died and was buried at Newburyport, Massachusetts.

JONATHAN EDWARDS

Jonathan Edwards (1703–1758) is considered by many scholars to be the greatest intellect America has ever produced. He is well known to students all over the world for a sermon he delivered at Enfield, Connecticut, on

18 July 1741. The name of the sermon is "Sinners in the Hands of an Angry God." The results were phenomenal. He read the manuscript quietly, without emotion, as men and women began to melt before God and cry for His mercy. Here is a section of Edwards's world-famous sermon:

> His wrath towards you burns like fire. He looks upon you as worthy of nothing else but to be cast into the fire. He is of purer eyes than to bear to have you in his sight. You are ten thousand times more abominable in His eyes than the most hateful, venomous serpent is in ours. You have offended Him infinitely more than ever a stubborn rebel did his prince, and yet it is nothing but His hand that holds you from falling into the fire every moment. Consider the fearful danger you are in. It is a great furnace of wrath, a wide and bottomless pit, full of the fire of wrath that you are held over, and the hand of that God whose wrath is provoked and incensed as much against you as against any of the dammed in hell. You hang by a slender thread with the flames of divine wrath flashing about it and ready any minute to singe it and burn it to sunder. And you have no interest in any mediator and nothing to lay hold of to save yourself; nothing to keep off the flames of wrath; nothing of your own; nothing that you have done; nothing that you can do to induce God to spare you one moment.

Hundreds responded. Thousands were affected. The Great Awakening, the preeminent revival of the eighteenth century, blazed through the colonies and transformed hundreds of thousands of men and women as they came to Jesus Christ. This sermon is sometimes presented as an example of the harsh, unloving, "fire and brimstone" preaching common of that era, but it should also be noted that Jonathan Edwards was a man, not only of great intellectual power, but immense compassion and love for people. His congregation was intensely loyal to this quiet, bookish man, who only cared about their eternal destiny. He was a man of great sensitivity, of tremendous tenderness toward the members of his congregation, and the people responded immensely to his love. His wife often said it was difficult being married to such a man because he gave so wholeheartedly to the members of his congregation.

It is important to note that this message is biblically accurate—the Bible does teach the reality of hell that exists for all those who do not know Jesus Christ as their Lord and Savior. But the Bible also teaches, as Jonathan Edwards would emphasize, the great love of God in trying to reach every man and woman with the message of Jesus Christ and the love of God for them through Jesus' death on the cross. Jonathan Edwards's sermon is not an example of harsh uncaring, unloving, hard-heartedness. It is an accurate warning of the future of those men and women who die without Jesus Christ as their Lord and Savior. It is actually an expression of love, a statement of compassion, a wonderful sermon that points people to the truth. Remember what Jesus says in the New Testament: "You shall know the truth and the truth shall make you free." That truth is not any truth—it is the truth about the Lord, Jesus Christ. Jesus spoke more about hell than any man in the Bible, and He was the most compassionate man who ever lived. Jesus loves us enough to tell us the truth, and that is exactly what Jonathan Edwards is doing in this remarkable sermon in July 1741.

The wave of revival that broke out dwarfed anything that had previously happened in American history. A movement of God swept the colonies and brought tens of thousands of men and women to Jesus Christ.

You should know more about Jonathan Edwards and his remarkable life. Edwards was an incisive intellect, born 5 October 1703—the same year that John Wesley was born—in East Windsor, Connecticut. He studied Latin at the age of six and read Latin, Greek, and Hebrew when he went to college at the age of thirteen. At seventeen, he graduated from Yale. Although he died prematurely of smallpox, he had already phenomenally influenced the colonies. At his death, he was the president of the College of New Jersey, which became Princeton University. Margaret Drew has written an excellent study of Jonathan Edwards called *Marriage to a Difficult Man*. It is a study of the home life of Jonathan Edwards and his wife as they reared their children in the knowledge of the Bible and in love for Jesus Christ. It is remarkable insight into a remarkable man.

CHARLES G. FINNEY

Another spiritual influence to his generation was one of the great evangelists of the nineteenth century, Charles G. Finney (1792–1875), an unusual figure who was never trained as a minister and never went to theological school. He was an attorney of vicious ambition who was to become one of the great Christian leaders of all time. This angry, selfish, ambitious lawyer came to Jesus Christ due to the influence of his partner in his law firm on 10 October 1821. Finney was so dramatically converted that one of his biographers writes, "Finney went up and down the village street like a merchant, like a salesman searching for customers, conversing with any with whom he might meet. The slain of the Lord fell like people machine gunned in the village streets, pious frauds, young Unitarians, smart allecks, booze makers, the unsaved scoffers—it made no difference who they were. A few words spoken to an individual would stick in his heart like an arrow."

Finney himself said of that first day of witnessing, "I believe the spirit of God made a lasting impression upon every one of them [the people I spoke with]. I cannot remember one with whom I spoke who was not converted."

Finney was a man who transferred the intensity of his law practice to winning men and women to Jesus Christ. The first public meeting Finney held to present Jesus Christ was in Evansmill, New York. One person said, "The whole town buzzed with profanity against him. They talked of tarring and feathering him, riding him on a rail." But Finney's preaching was so fearless, so powerful, so clear and so effective, that a tremendous spiritual awakening erupted. He called it "an avalanche of revival power."

In New York state, he preached at Utica, Rome, Auburn, Troy, Rochester, and New York City. He traveled to Wilmington, Delaware; Philadelphia, Pennsylvania; Boston, Massachusetts; and Great Britain. All over the world, wherever Finney went, incredible results occurred. Finney was a logical, effective speaker. He invented what is known as public altar response, perfected by such leaders today as Billy Graham. This is the procedure of calling people forward to pray publicly and acknowledge their need for Jesus Christ. This, of course, is now a common element in modern Protestant evangelism.

Finney's most famous book is his *Lectures on Revivals of Religion*. If you want to know the heart of this great man of God, study this book. It will take you time to master its principles, but its insights are powerful.

A small book by Basil Miller on Charles Finney is an excellent introduction to his life and influence. Finney became president of Oberlin College in Ohio and was a strong, aggressive leader against slavery—one of the first national voices to speak out consistently against slavery in the United States. He supported the North vigorously in the Civil War. Finney also championed the right of women to vote.

DWIGHT LYMAN MOODY

The greatest American Christian leader of the nineteenth century was Dwight Lyman Moody (1837–1899). The Mount Everest of Christian influence of his time, Moody had no theological training or religious education. In addition, his academic education was extremely limited, and all his life he was embarrassed by this lack of formal training and the resultant difficulty he had in expressing himself properly. But there is no question about his remarkable influence.

He came to Jesus Christ as a young man working for his uncle in a shoe store in Boston, Massachusetts. His Sunday school teacher came to speak to him and to present Jesus Christ to the young Moody. Moody's sole ambition in life was to become outrageously wealthy. Everything changed when he came to Christ in the back of the shoe store. He was so uneducated that the church to which he applied for membership refused him for months because they didn't think he understood enough of the Bible to become a member. In fact, he was only educated through the eighth grade.

Moody was short, stout, and weighed nearly three hundred pounds. When he spoke, he was unpolished and as one contemporary said, "His words rushed from his bearded face like a torrent, often 230 per minute, short, staccato sentences, imperfect pronunciation." One man said that he was so uneducated but so powerful that he was "an evangelist sent from God for no man could have done the ministry he accomplished except God was with him."

For forty years, Moody presented the Christian gospel to more than fifty million people. Remember, this was in an age before radio, television, and motion pictures. He presented the Christian message to people in live audiences. It's one of the great stories in Christian world history. He was extremely close to his family and he was financially honest. No scandal ever endangered his ministry. His son, William R. Moody, after his father's death, wrote, "Father lived solely for the glory of God and for the spread of the gospel of Jesus Christ."

Moody founded great educational institutions such as the Chicago (now Moody) Bible Institute. He also founded the Northfield Seminary for girls and the Mount Hermon School for boys, both in Northfield, Massachusetts. In 1971, the two schools merged and became the Northfield Mount Hermon School.

Moody is well-known today for having pioneered the invasion of the Christian gospel into secular settings. He would take Jesus Christ anywhere and everywhere. During the great World's Fair in Chicago in the early 1890s, Moody was everywhere, organizing the first modern movement of evangelism in a secular setting.

He always had a great love for children. When he moved to Chicago shortly after coming to know Jesus Christ as his Lord and Savior, he organized a Sunday school for orphaned boys. Those boys loved him for life. Moody always had for people a heart that never failed, until his physical heart failed in 1899.

John Pollock has written a wonderful introduction to the life of Moody. Basil Miller has also written an introduction to the life of Moody for children.

JOHN R. MOTT

John R. Mott (1865–1955) was well-known to the intellectual and spiritual establishments of his generation. Mott was well-acquainted with the political leadership of his day. He was influential in the World's Student Christian Federation, which he founded in 1895. This movement sent students from the best colleges and universities in America all over the world to present Jesus Christ. It's one of the most exciting Christian action stories in modern history. Mott served in President Wilson's Mexican Campaign and the Elihu Root Mission to Russia. He chaired the United War Work Campaign, which raised $200 million in 1918, an incredible sum of money for the time. He received honorary doctorates from several universities and honors from religious leaders. In 1946 he shared the Nobel Peace Prize. Here is a remarkable individual who also was a committed Christian.

An effective biographical study of Mott is *John R. Mott, A Biography* by C. Howard Hopkins, a detailed 700-page book that gives fascinating information on the Christian movements of the early twentieth century.

CHARLES SPURGEON

Charles Spurgeon (1834–1892) was the greatest English pastor and Christian influence of his day. He came to Jesus Christ at sixteen years of age on 15 December 1850. At the age of seventeen, he was already pastor of a small Baptist church in Waterbeach, England. Two years later, at age nineteen, he was called to pastor the New Park Street Chapel in London, one of the great Protestant churches of the nation. The church had fallen on hard times. When Spurgeon arrived, it had an auditorium with a seating capacity of 1,200 and an average attendance of 100. The church, in deep depression, hoped young Spurgeon could turn the negative situation around. For the next 38 years, Spurgeon more than fulfilled that hope. He preached so powerfully and people came in such phenomenal numbers that finally the congregation had to build a new church, the Metropolitan Tabernacle, that seated more than 5,000 and had standing room for another thousand. For the rest of his ministry, Spurgeon filled the church and the standing area twice every Sunday, for a total of 12,000 people every Sunday for 38 years. At twenty-two years of age he was the best-known preacher in the world. His sermons went literally around the globe. Queen Victoria would often come in secret and listen to this amazing

Christian leader. Spurgeon was a man of fearless commitment to Christ and total dedication to the Bible as the Word of God. Charles Spurgeon—the great pastor of England of the nineteenth century—is a man you should know more about.

BILLY SUNDAY

Billy Sunday, a controversial man who was once a professional baseball player, was born in 1863 and died in 1935. William Ashley Sunday, better known as Billy, was a human dynamo on stage. After getting drunk one weekend following a baseball game in Chicago, Sunday accepted an invitation from a Salvation Army street team to attend a meeting at the Pacific Garden Mission. To his great shock, he was totally captivated by the message and surrendered his life to Jesus Christ. As a professional baseball player, he was making $500 a month, which was a large sum for that time, with a promise of many years of playing time because of his blazing speed on the bases. He was never a great hitter, but he was considered one of the great base runners of his generation. He gave up his baseball contract for an $83.33 monthly salary with the YMCA. He then became an associate of evangelist J. Wilbur Chapman in 1896. He entered full-time Christian evangelism himself at the age of thirty-four.

His crusades over the next several years saw more than one million people come forward to give their lives to Jesus Christ. He was known even by the journalistic standards of that day as a sensationalist. An example of his preaching, which is blistering, is as follows:

> I'm no spiritual masseur or osteopath. I'm a surgeon and I cut deep. They tell me a revival is only temporary. Well, so is a bath but it does you good. It won't save your soul if your wife is a Christian. You've got to be something more than a brother-in-law to the church. They say to me "Bill, you rub the fur the wrong way." I don't. Let the cats turn around.

His colorful language is also expressed in sermon titles: "Some Nuts for Skeptics to Crack"; "Chickens Come Home to Roost"; "Hotcakes Off the Griddle"; and "The Devil's Boomerang". Sunday was the first evangelist to organize his campaigns into technically competent crusades. No one had ever done it on a grander, bigger scale before. Temporary tabernacles, called Sunday Tabernacles, would be built in the cities where he would speak to accommodate at least 20,000 people per location.

Late in life, Sunday did become less effective and may have possibly stayed on the evangelism trail for too long, but his influence was phenomenal in his heyday and millions came to Jesus Christ because of his energetic presentation of the gospel. He died at the age of seventy-two and is remembered to this day as a great influence for Jesus Christ.

BILLY GRAHAM

Later in the twentieth century, something occurred as the result of an amazing sequence of events. You already know the story of the young Sunday school teacher who went to a shoe shop in Boston, Massachusetts, to introduce young Dwight L. Moody to Jesus Christ. What you may not know, as Paul Harvey says, is "The rest of the story." Dwight L. Moody became a world figure, presenting Jesus Christ to the world. Moody had a profound influence on a young Presbyterian pastor named J. Wilbur Chapman. Chapman, as a Christian evangelist, took on a young man named Billy Sunday. Sunday at one point conducted a great campaign in Charlotte, North Carolina, where a young dairy farmer was converted. Years later, in an effort to reach his generation for Jesus Christ, that dairy farmer organized a meeting and invited the evangelist Mordecai Ham to speak for a number of nights in an outdoor tent location. During that meeting, a tall, lanky, rebellious sixteen-year-old named William walked to the front to surrender his life to Jesus Christ. This amazing sequence of events connects a young, relatively unknown Sunday school teacher in Boston to the worldwide ministry of Billy Graham. What an incredible sequence of God-ordained circumstances. The schoolteacher led Moody to Christ; Moody influenced J. Wilbur Chapman to go into evangelism; Chapman trained a young baseball player named Billy Sunday; Sunday went to North Carolina where a young dairy farmer named Graham was converted; Graham grew up and organized a meeting in that same place and invited Mordecai Ham to present the message of Jesus Christ; the dairy farmer's young son Billy came to Jesus Christ and would soon become the greatest evangelist of modern times.

This is a remarkable example of how God guides human history to produce the results that He wants.

Billy Graham has not always been popular. There was a time when Graham was seriously opposed because of his methodology. Graham was considered too modern by some Christian leaders. It was thought that he risked the purity of the Christian message by his efforts to take it into secular locations. But Graham has been a part of a tradition going back to John Wesley, when men of God would go to where people were to introduce them to Jesus Christ.

John Pollock has also done a masterful work on the life of Billy Graham. Pollock is the great Christian biographer of our generation, and his work on Billy Graham should be read and studied by every Christian family.

Graham, as a young man, went first to Bob Jones University where he was asked to leave because he was not considered serious enough for that institution. Old Bob Jones, as Graham left, uttered a now famous quote: "Young man, if you leave this school, you'll never amount to anything."

Graham then went to the Florida Bible Institute in Tampa, Florida, where, late one night in prayer on a golf course, he surrendered his life to present the message of Jesus Christ all over the world.

He then went to Wheaton College in Illinois where he studied anthropology and met the daughter of a medical missionary named Ruth Bell. At first, Ruth did not have any interest in Graham, preferring to return to the mission where her medical physician father and her mother had faithfully worked in China to lead men and women to Christ. Graham persuaded Ruth to marry him. He then became the pastor of a small Baptist church on the outskirts of Chicago. He started a radio program called "Songs in the Night." After a number of broadcasts, he enlisted the help of a singer named George Beverly Shea. Young Graham, in excitement for his future ministry, decided that he would build that church.

But then another call came to his life. The world was challenged by war and Billy Graham decided to enlist in the military. He would have left his preaching ministry and entered the war except for a case of adult mumps which devastated him for months. After that experience, he became involved in a new organization called Youth For Christ International, becoming their first paid staff speaker. He would speak to huge rallies under a banner that read "Youth For Christ—anchored to the Rock but geared for the times." Graham then formed an evangelistic team. He met a young man named Cliff Barrows and asked him to do the music. Graham was going from town to town, doing well in some areas and not so well in others. He went to Altoona, Pennsylvania, had a disastrous meeting, and nearly quit evangelism. Another great crisis in his life occurred in California when another young evangelist said to him, "Billy, people don't believe the Bible any more. It's not true. It's full of holes. You're going to commit intellectual suicide if you don't surrender your belief in the Bible." Graham said it was the greatest crisis of his life. Late one night in California he went into the woods to pray. He knelt down and, with tears streaming down his face, he said, "Dear God, I am choosing to believe your Word is true. I will always believe it and I will always preach it. And I'm making that decision today." Graham now believes that decision saved his life and ministry.

Some time after that Graham was invited by a group of Los Angeles businessmen to do a crusade. At this point, Graham was toying with the idea of quitting entirely because he doubted his effectiveness. He went to Los Angeles with his team and history was made. The Los Angeles crusade grew weekly in power and numbers. It was extended once, then again. It was a tremendous expression of modern evangelistic power—of the blessing of God on a sincere young man who honestly presented Jesus Christ. The crowds came from everywhere. William Randolph Hearst Jr., watching the phenomenon develop, became so intrigued that he wrote a two-word order to all of his newspapers nationwide that has now become famous: "Puff Graham." In the vernacular of the news journalism of that day, the meaning was very simple. It meant to promote this young man everywhere his newspapers were sold. When Billy Graham rode the train back east to see his family at the conclusion of that great crusade, he suddenly, astoundingly, was a national figure. He wrote that as he rode in the train watching the scenery blur past, he realized that God alone had opened this remarkable door of opportunity.

In the early 1950s, Graham's organization developed and became more sophisticated. He still received criticism for his modern methods and use of technology. But more and more he was respected for his integrity. One of the great changing points in his ministry came in a crusade in Atlanta when the *Atlanta Journal & Constitution* published a picture of Graham smiling at the crowd, and a picture next to it of people walking out of the arena with bags of money. He determined he would never again be associated with even the appearance of the abuse of money. It is important to know that no abuse ever occurred in that crusade; the newspaper had misrepresented the story, but the image was negative nonetheless. Graham then determined to be the first evangelist in history to operate on the basis of salary determined by a Board of Directors. Graham has been scandal-free all these years. He is a tremendous example of committed Christian ministry in evangelism.

Billy Graham has grown in stature over the years to become a world figure. Well into his seventies, he still does crusade evangelism. Billy Graham—the great evangelist of the twentieth century.

OTHER IMPORTANT CHRISTIAN LEADERS

There are a number of present-day Christian leaders of great influence who are important in the presentation of Jesus Christ to the world. Here are some examples:

> Jerry Falwell and the Moral Majority movement in the 1980s, which has helped move our country back toward God.
>
> Pat Robertson and his pioneering work on Christian television.
>
> Charles Stanley, the great pastor/teacher of our generation.
>
> James Kennedy, an effective Christian thinker at Coral Ridge Presbyterian Church in Fort Lauderdale, Florida.
>
> James Dobson of *Focus On the Family*, a man who is not a minister but a Ph.D. psychologist who has been of immense importance in influencing his generation for Jesus Christ and returning America to an understanding of conservative, traditional, and biblically based beliefs of marriage and family.

These are outstanding leaders who are an influence for Jesus Christ in their generation. Great godly movements, such as Promise Keepers, are sweeping America because godly biblical guidance is so urgently needed. It is important for you to understand Christian history in conjunction with general world history. You need to understand why Theodore Roosevelt was the pivotal presidential figure of modern times. You need to understand why Woodrow Wilson was one of our great foreign policy presidents. You need to know why Franklin Roosevelt and Ronald Reagan are giants in presidential politics for the twentieth century. You need to understand the influence of Alexander Graham Bell, Thomas Edison, Eli Whitney, and other leaders of invention. You need to know great composers from Handel to Bach to Beethoven to Stravinsky. You need to understand those who exhibit great influence in art. You need to understand world literature and world events. You need to understand world leaders. But most importantly, you need to understand godly men and women who exhibit Christian influence and are moving the world toward an understanding of who Jesus Christ is as Savior and Lord.

In addition to what you've already heard about great Christian leaders and movements such as Promise Keepers, there are other men who are tremendously important, such as Dexter Yager, a Christian businessman who is involved in evangelism on a grand scale during Sunday services following his great business rallies all over the world. He is an example of business thinking in balance with Christian influence. He lovingly and clearly presents Jesus Christ even as he teaches men and women to have financial freedom. Dexter Yager is a great example of the new breed of twentieth-century evangelistic leadership. He is a man, who, like Moody, is not ordained, and like Finney and Sunday, has no theological training. But he is a man of great organizational ability, tremendous business competence, and great financial success who not only teaches people financial principles of achievement, but uses his platform of achievement to present Jesus Christ as well in voluntary separate Sunday services following his great business functions around the world.

History is the great teacher of human life. Without history you fail to learn the right principles that make life work. History is filled with exciting people and the most amazing adventures. You need to know history to know people; and you need to know people to know life. Christian history is the deeper level of all history. In Christian history and Christian biography you discover how God has used men and women in the past and how He can use you right now. Learn history—all history—and you will be educated for life.

REVIEW QUESTIONS

1. Which Wesley was an evangelist and which Wesley was a Christian songwriter?

2. Which leader of the Methodist revival movement is buried under the pulpit of a church in Massachusetts?

3. Who was the author of "Sinners in the Hands of an Angry God" and the spiritual leader of the Great Awakening that blazed through the American colonies?

4. This spiritual leader was never trained as a minister. He was a lawyer before coming to Jesus Christ. Who was he?

5. Whose conversion took place in the back of a shoe store in Boston?

6. What great English pastor had an attentive listener in Queen Victoria?

7. Sunday Tabernacles were built in cities where what evangelist would speak?

8. What did Billy Graham say was the decision that saved his life and ministry?

SUGGESTED READING

Margaret Drew, *Marriage To A Difficult Man.*

Charles G. Finney, *Lectures on Revivals of Religion.*

C. Howard Hopkins, *John R. Mott, A Biography.*

Basil Miller, *Charles G. Finney, A Biography.*

Basil Miller, *Dwight L. Moody, A Biography.*

Basil Miller, *John Wesley, A Biography.*

John Pollock, *Dwight L. Moody, A Biography.*

John Pollock, *John Wesley, A Biography.*

(Note: Basil Miller's books have been written as an introduction for young children.)

PART
FIVE

Preparing
for the
Twenty-first
Century

PREPARING THE CHRISTIAN STUDENT FOR COLLEGE

The philosophy of the school room in one generation will be the philosophy of government in the next.

— ABRAHAM LINCOLN

THE CLASSROOM TODAY, especially at the college level, has become a patchwork of ideologies and worldviews vying for the student's mind and soul. Gone, with rare exceptions, are the days of the university where there was a "unity" of unchanging principles and a "diversity" of subject matter based on the same principles. Today's institutions are multiversities where the plumb line of all truth (the Word of God) is banished and demeaned, and in its place a plethora of diverse academic and pseudo-academic subjects are studied without regard for a unified field of knowledge or a purpose for learning.

To the casual observer, this reality may appear to be the natural extension of academic freedom, and perhaps a "good experience" for students to taste various worldviews. But this freedom is deceptive, for beneath the facade of "freedom of thought" there is an entrenched agenda and a new set of absolutes that have replaced the biblical truth.

The fundamental absolute of the modern multiversity is that there are no absolutes. Dr. Allan Bloom of New York University, in his best-selling book *The Closing of the American Mind*, described the new absolute that has permeated the colleges of America:

> There is one thing a professor can be absolutely certain of: almost every student entering the university believes, or says he believes, that truth is relative.... Openness—and the relativism that makes it the only plausible stance in the face of various claims to truth and various ways of life and kinds of human beings—is the great insight of our times. The true believer is the real danger. The study of history and of culture teaches that all the world was mad in the past; men always thought that they were right, and that led to wars, persecutions, slavery, xenophobia, racism, and chauvinism. The point is not to correct the mistakes and really be right; rather it is not to think you are right at all.[1]

To enforce the new absolute that all is relative, a group of unproven assumptions have become part of the college's "politically correct" doctrine[2] and are enforced with rigor:

Multiculturalism—the belief in the blending of all cultures and the diminution of Western culture to fit into a "world community."

Unisexualism—the view that endorses the elimination of the differences between the sexes, and of the moral differences among sexual lifestyles.

See the appendix for
The Apostle's Creed
The Ten Commandments
The Westminster Shorter Catechism

225

Egalitarianism—the unification of assessments of performance and ability with the goal of bringing everyone to a set standard, always a lower standard.

Relativism—the theory that there are no absolutes that apply to all of life, which is directed specifically at Christianity's claim of knowable truth based on the Word of God.

Underlying these four contemporary ideologies is a philosophy as old as the human race: humanism, the elevation of man to the station of God.

Sending children to college, or even to high school, today is to send them into an intellectual war zone. The battleground of this war is not fair, but has been manipulated to undermine the faith of students, as millions of grieving Christian parents can attest when their now-unbelieving children come home to visit.

We, as Christian families, have gradually absorbed the ideologies of twentieth-century humanism. English historian E. R. Norman highlights the deceptive agenda behind humanistic pluralism: "Pluralism is a word society employs during the transition from one orthodoxy to another."[3]

Such concepts as tolerance, pluralism, and the melting pot of cultures lured much of the Christian community into withdrawing its superior and once-dominant worldview from the public arena. The result of the Christian community's withdrawal from cultural leadership has been that it has often failed to understand the paradigm shift in educational content and philosophy during this century, and has tended to concentrate on courses, majors, sports, and other less important factors.

Christians in the Reformation recognized the war of ideas and launched the world's great universities to teach God's truth. This concern illuminates Martin Luther's strong words concerning the likely outcome of education without the Bible:

> I am much afraid that the schools will prove the gates of hell, unless they diligently labor in explaining the Holy Scriptures and engraving them in the hearts of youth. I advise no one to place his child where the Scriptures do not reign paramount. Every institution in which men are not unceasingly occupied with the Word of God must be corrupt.[4]

There is no neutrality in education. It always has a religious bias. This has been true throughout history, but is especially true in our secular age. If a family believes that higher education will enable a child to better serve God's kingdom, then preparation for the spiritual, intellectual, and moral challenges of today's educational world is paramount. There are many vocations and leadership positions that require a college degree, and constant vigilance must be maintained in order to avoid the shipwreck of faith.

ETERNAL VIGILANCE

In every generation, the numerous false philosophies that are the result of man's rebellion against God are the tools of our adversary, Satan. Families must work to maintain and strengthen the faith of their children against these false teachings. The New Testament Christians refused to dedicate their children to Caesar in the days of Rome, and faced the consequences of their decisions. During the Reformation, believers in England and Scotland refused to allow the king to force his religion upon their children, and suffered greatly. William Bradford detailed the reasons the Pilgrims chose to leave the "libertine" atmosphere of Holland and move their children to train them in the wilderness of America. He explained the rebellion of some of their young who were wandering into "dangerous courses":

> But still more lamentable, and of all sorrows most heavy to be borne, was that of many of the children, influenced by these conditions, and the great licentiousness of the young people of the country, and the many temptations of the city, were led by evil example into dangerous courses, getting the reins off their necks and leaving their parents. Some became soldiers, others embarked upon voyages by sea and others upon worse courses tending to dissoluteness and the danger of their souls, to the great grief of the parents and the dishonour of God. So they saw their posterity would be in danger to degenerate and become corrupt.[5]

Our Pilgrim forebears settled this land with the hope of being free to bring up their children apart from European corruption, but they knew that wherever they traveled the spiritual battle for the minds of their progeny would follow.

PREPARING FOR THE BATTLE

It appears that many parents do an exceptional job of training their children, loving them, and providing financial resources for further education, but still watch with horror as the child returns from college a skeptic or unbeliever. How can a Christian student avoid the pitfall of the destruction of their faith on their way through high school and college, and then to the workplace?

The need to address this crisis with our whole hearts and minds is highlighted by Dr. James Dobson and Gary Bauer:

> Nothing short of a great Civil War of Values rages today throughout North America. Two sides with vastly differing and exclusive worldviews are locked in a bitter conflict that permeates every level of society.... Someday soon, a winner will emerge and the loser will fade from memory. For now, the outcome is very much in doubt.[6]

There are four steps that can be taken to prepare for the onrush of humanism that awaits the student at the modern American university.

STEP ONE: KNOW GOD

The first step in preparing a young person to succeed in building and defending his faith in a hostile world is to train him in a thorough knowledge of God. Counterfeits in currency, gemstones, art, and other valuables are easily detectable to the extent that one is trained to recognize the authentic item. In like manner, counterfeit cults and philosophies have much less effect on the individual who has a thorough knowledge of the one true God as revealed in the Bible.

God has revealed Himself to man in three basic ways.

First, He can be seen in His creation and the outworking of His historic plan. Psalm 19:1–2 says, "The heavens declare the glory of God; and the firmament shows His handiwork. Day unto day utters speech, and night unto night reveals knowledge."

Secondly, God has revealed Himself through His inerrant Word, the Bible. In 2 Peter 1:20–21, we are told, "Knowing this first, that no prophesy of scripture is of any private interpretation, for prophesy never came by the will of man, but holy men of God spoke as they were moved by the Holy Spirit." We are to be nourished on His Word. Matthew 4:4 tells us, "Man does not live by bread alone, but by every word that proceeds out of the mouth of God."

The third way that God reveals Himself to us is through Jesus Christ, who became a man and dwelt among us. We can have a personal relationship with Him if we repent of our sins and accept His gift of forgiveness and eternal life through faith in His finished, substitutionary death.

An intellectual knowledge of God in and of itself does not ensure a relationship with God. A knowledge of the holiness and justice of God as seen in His perfect laws (i.e., the Ten Commandments) should, however, lead all people to repent. Paul says in Timothy, "the law of God is our tutor to lead us to Christ." People need to recognize from the law their inability to reach God's standard, and accept the forgiveness of Jesus Christ, which is offered by His grace to all who believe in Him.

But millions of young people growing up in Christian homes go on into adulthood unrepentant and without the assurance of salvation. This is a sobering reality in light of the fact that most of those who become authentic Christians do so before the age of twenty-five. It would be good to review the message of salvation at this time with your child to be sure that he has been transformed by Jesus Christ from death to life, through faith in His finished work.

In a Christian home, faith in Christ should be the natural result of consistent training in God's Word and the essence of a relationship with Him. Once a person's relationship with God is restored through Christ, He promises to give us the Holy Spirit to guide us into all truth. In John 16:13, Jesus says, "However, when He, the Spirit of truth, has come, He will guide you into all truth." It was a relationship with God and the enlightenment of the Holy Spirit that brought about the greatest expansion of true learning in history during the Reformation and in early America.

STEP TWO: KNOW GOD'S WORD

To maintain a strong spiritual life on the battleground of the campus, a student must have a love for, and knowledge of, the Bible. The Bible is the blueprint for life, and this book gives abundant evidence that wherever biblical truths are believed and obeyed great blessing follows.

Developing a systematic reading program through the Bible requires the development of spiritual discipline over time (Hebrews 5:14). The earlier this habit of reading and studying the Bible is learned, the better for the student. Whenever Christians rediscover the power and wisdom of the

Bible, all of culture is affected for the better, and the inroads of pagan philosophies are closed.

For an enhanced, deeper study of the Bible, a student will greatly benefit from some popular study aids. First, a Bible that has good cross-references should be obtained. These references will direct the reader to other passages that address the topic of a verse. Other helpful study tools include a good topical reference Bible such as the *New Nave's Topical Bible*; a good Bible dictionary such as the *New Bible Dictionary*, which will give background on people, places, and events in the Bible; a complete concordance such as *Strong's Concordance*, which lists every word in the Bible and where it can be found; and a Bible handbook, such as *Unger's Bible Handbook*, which offers brief commentary on all the books of the Bible.

In the appendices to these learning guides, the reader will find several tools for systematically learning about God and His Word. Three of these key landmarks of truth were memorized by most students in colonial America: the Ten Commandments, the Apostle's Creed, and the Westminster Confession of Faith (there are other catechisms for different denominations).

There is tremendous power in memorizing the Word of God and systematic summaries of biblical truth. The psalmist declares, "Your word I have hid in my heart, that I might not sin against you." He goes on to say, "You, through Your commandments make me wiser than my enemies; for they are ever with me. I have more understanding than all my teachers."[7]

STEP THREE: ASSOCIATE WITH GOD'S PEOPLE

The peer group has become the great molder of character in our day. It has always been true that, as Paul says, "bad company corrupts good morals." Especially today, when parents often send students to colleges hundreds of miles away, they are susceptible to incredible peer pressure to conform to the humanistic values that pervade every cultural sphere.

To counter this influence, a good church and campus fellowship is vital for a Christian student in college or high school. The book of Hebrews discourages "forsaking the assembling of yourselves together, as is the practice of some, but exhorting one another, and so much the more as you see the day approaching." It is worth a special trip to the campus for the parents and student to meet with pastors and campus Christian leaders. Parental leadership and oversight is all-important in college. Parents should be aware that they may be advised by the educational establishment to "overcome the protective urge," as the admissions director at the College of William and Mary puts it.[8]

Thomas Sowell warns parents not to withdraw from participation in the decisions of their children, despite the educators' call for autonomy for students.

> Unfortunately, all sorts of activists with their own ideological agendas, including administrators and professors, show little or no regard for students' autonomy or need for respect. Parents who heed the constant drumbeat of advice to get out of the picture are only making it easier for others to get into the picture with their own special agendas.[9]

One way to keep strong ties with students is to keep them home at least the first two years and have them attend a local community college or Christian school. They can also enroll in one of the numerous correspondence degree programs being offered through colleges on the Internet. Such alternatives may give opportunity for work experience and insight into vocational and other major decisions.

STEP FOUR: KNOW GOD'S WORLD

The key to real education is self-discipline and a desire to learn for a greater goal. Christianity supplies a greater goal that much of our culture lacks, and Christians should consequently be constantly on the forefront of learning.

The means of building one's knowledge base is undergoing a drastic change in this decade. Observers of social phenomena are predicting that the future holds a transformed cultural landscape.

> The microchip has set in motion what promises to be the third great revolution of human life, comparable in its sweep to the Agricultural Revolution that set history in motion, and the Gunpowder Revolution that initiated the great surge of human progress at the end of the fifteenth century.[10]

With the invention of the computer, the self-governing individual has access to all the great learning in the world. With this tool, the student can be free from the influences of institutional bias and modern revisionism by handling subject matter without the interference of humanistic interpreters.

This is why Zane's CD-ROMs are an invaluable resource. Students can read, hear about, and see the facts, places, events, people, literature, and art that will be prerequisite learning for the Scholastic Aptitude Test and college success (*Zane Publishing's Complete Multimedia Course for the SAT*). On account of rampant grade inflation, the SAT is becoming increasingly important for college admissions.[11]

Two cautionary notes concerning the acquisition of knowledge: first, all information comes to us with a bias, because all facts are interpreted facts. Education cannot be neutral or values-free education. Every teacher and every book has a specific worldview, and that worldview influences all that is communicated. Therefore, all learning should be filtered by a biblical world and life view, rather than accepted on the authority of a professor or textbook. Second, we should remember that "knowledge puffs up, but love edifies." The pride of intellect in today's humanist society has attempted to turn college degrees into feudal class distinctions. Real knowledge tied to godly wisdom and humility can be acquired with or without college. Most successful entrepreneurs were not college graduates, nor were many of our greatest founding fathers.

THE BATTLE OF WORLDVIEWS

The impartation of an all-encompassing biblical worldview is a high priority for students in their formative years. The psalmist says, "As a man thinks in his heart, so is he." A person's perception of reality, his intellectual and spiritual presuppositions, determines his future actions. One of the great problems of our day is that most Christians have been raised with a split worldview. They have looked to God in times of spiritual crisis, but have imbibed deeply the humanist worldviews, especially in the fields of university study, popular culture, and vocation. The result of refusing Christ the lordship of every institution and discipline has been devastating. John Whitehead surveyed the impact of the Christian retreat from the educational battle to an inner world of what he calls "revivalistic piety":

> During the nineteenth century humanists were thrusting their ideas into education, science, and the arts. Revivalistic piety, however, with its emphasis on the inner self, virtually abandoned these areas.
>
> Unfortunately, the church has been all too willing to use the categories of 'secular' and 'religious,' when no such distinction exists in reality. All things have been created by God. Thus, all things have their origin in God and should be under Christ's lordship. The pietist renunciation thus raises a core issue: the lordship of Christ.
>
> To the true Christian, Christ cannot be Savior and not Lord. Christ is Lord over all areas of life—not merely the spiritual. Indeed, it is incorrect to make a fundamental distinction between spiritual and secular. Christ is Lord of the intellectual life, the business life, the political life.
>
> If Christ is not Lord over the arts and science, then man is. This is humanism in practice. It was difficult for the church to dispute humanistic ideology because the church itself was practicing humanism by separating the spiritual from the totality of life and reality.[12]

There are ultimately only two worldviews, and all people adhere to one or the other. Henry Morris and John Whitcomb explain:

> There are really only two basic philosophies or religions among mankind. The one is oriented primarily with respect to God, the Creator, of Whom and by Whom and for Whom are all things.... The other basic philosophy is oriented primarily with respect to man. This system, appearing in an almost infinite variety of forms, supposes that man is inherently capable of acquiring by his own efforts all he needs in this present life and in any possible life to come.[13]

The first is the biblical worldview. Carl F. H. Henry says, "The Christian belief system, which the Christian knows to be grounded in divine revelation, is relevant to all of life." A Christian worldview, as lived out in the life of a Christian, is a set of fundamental assumptions (the Christian belief system) that become the ground of reality upon which God, man, and the world are understood. The biblical world and life view was almost universally taught before the Civil War and the flood of skepticism that engulfed the educational community after the publication of Darwin's *On the Origin of Species.* Darwin's theory became a good rationale for rewriting first science and geology texts. Then legal theory developed evolving laws for evolving man, in keeping with its adopted social Darwinism. Finally, the social sciences, history, and our heritage of government were refitted to the humanist mold.[14]

The opposing ideology or worldview is the man-created system of rebellion against God's will—often called humanism. It is important to differentiate between humanitarianism, the humanities, and humanism. Francis Schaeffer clarifies these terms:

> *Humanitarianism* is being kind and helpful to people, treating people humanly. The *humanities* are the studies of literature, art, music, etc.—those things which are the products of human creativity. *Humanism* is the placing of man at the center of all things and making him the measure of all things.[15]

The humanism we speak of here is the enemy of biblical revelation. In a real sense, it is the modern Western expression of the original rebellion of Lucifer, when he says in his heart, "I will be like the most high."[16] It is the same tempting rebellion offered to our progenitors, Adam and Eve, in the Garden of Eden, "Your eyes will be opened, and you will be like God, knowing good and evil."[17] In this sense, humanism is representative and inclusive of all ideologies and religions that deny the biblical Creator.

Schaeffer goes on to say concerning humanism's impact on modern western cultures,

> The humanist world view includes many thousands of adherents and today controls the consensus in society, much of the media, much of what is taught in our schools, and much of the arbitrary law being produced by the various departments of government.[18]

From the time of Nimrod, much of the world has remained locked in intellectual, spiritual, and often physical combat against God or His people. All man-centered philosophies and religions are at war with the God of the Bible. Although the ideological enemies of the biblical view of life take on many religious forms (Islam, Buddhism, Hinduism, Secular Humanism), they have but one root.

We should be aware of modern versions of humanist idolatry and be able to "give a defense for the hope that is in us." Otherwise, our students' lives may be overrun by one or more of these worldviews.

NON-CHRISTIAN WORLDVIEWS

The following religions and philosophies are worldviews derived from humanism.

Eastern Mysticism: Eastern mysticism represents such religions as Buddhism and Hinduism. It is monistic. Monism is the belief that all that is, is one; that God is not separate from His creation, but one with it. Therefore, trees are divine, animals can be godlike, and people lose their distinct character as created in God's image. The modern New Age movement is derived from this irrational philosophy. Paul McCartney and John Lennon, who joined with the Maharishi Yogi in 1967, wrote a song that exemplifies the irrationality of Eastern mysticism called "I Am the Walrus." The song begins with the monistic declaration "I am he as you are he as you are me and we are all together." Westernized versions of this philosophy have since inundated our culture. New Age ideas are pandemic at modern colleges. They often hide their Eastern roots and are seemingly optimistic, promising a better world. We must not be deceived. New Age religion is old-fashioned paganism behind a false front, and extremely enticing.

Marxism: Marxism is an ideology formulated by Karl Marx that denies Christianity and considers all religions to be illusions. It is a materialistic worldview that sees man as merely an evolving creature of the state. Marx was deeply influenced by Darwin's theory of evolution. Marx's theory of history, called "dialectical materialism," sees man (the corporate state) progressing from feudalism to capitalism to socialism. Through class warfare, the perfect socialist state was to appear. Contrary to theory, the fruit of Marxist ideology lived out in Russia, China, and elsewhere in the twentieth century has been devastating. Well over one hundred million people have lost their lives in this century under the tyranny of Marxist thinking. Half the world still withers from its effects. Christians must not underestimate the power of Marxist thought, especially on America's college campuses. In spite of its monumental failure worldwide, Marxism has a virtual lock on most liberal arts curricula and a preponderance of professors. According to the *U. S. News & World Report*, there are 10,000 Marxist professors on American campuses. Journalist Georgie Anne Geyer has said that "the percentage of Marxist faculty members can range from an estimated 90% in some Midwestern universities."[19]

Liberation Theology: Liberation theology is a twentieth-century Christian cultic ideology that finds its foundations in Marxism, but sells itself with Christian terminology.

Theologian Emilio Nuñez says,

> Liberation theology teaches that the mission of the church is not, as Jesus said, to "disciple the nations," but to "opt for the cause of the poor, to denounce the injustice of the oppressors, to announce the kingdom of God in order to 'conscientize' and 'politicize' the oppressed, and to participate directly in liberating praxis with a view toward establishing a socialist society that is "more just, free, and human."[20]

Liberation theology is a subtle deception that uses the Marxist logic to justify forced economic equalization by the state, and has attracted millions of Christians. It creates a false guilt for America's success in the face of Third World poverty, and postulates socialism, revolution, and massive government as a solution. The Christian student must be aware of this philosophy, since it has become prevalent, even at many Christian colleges in America.

Secular Humanism: Secular humanism has become the dominant worldview in America in the twentieth century. In the 1961 case of *Torcase v. Watkins*, the Supreme Court declared secular humanism a religion equivalent to other nontheistic religions.

Francis Schaeffer points out the hypocrisy of the government and the courts as they ejected all religious viewpoints from federally-funded classrooms: "Ironically, it is humanist religion which the government and the courts in the United States favor over all others!"[21] The theological foundation of secular humanism is atheism. It is committed to seeing man as an evolved animal setting his own standards. Of all the modern pagan ideologies, secular humanism is the one that sets itself most directly in rebellion against God.

With the failure of humanism's social experiments in the twentieth century and the deaths of tens of millions in two world wars, optimistic secular humanism, the faith that man is evolving naturally upward, has been losing credibility. Millions have turned from the rationalistic, naturalistic religion of secular humanism to the cosmic humanism of the New Age, rather than back to the faith of our fathers.

Cosmic Humanism—the New Age Movement: Cosmic humanism is an ever more prevalent religion, captivating millions in the West. It is an irrational faith that combines classical humanism and Eastern mysticism. It is theologically pantheistic (all is God) and embraces a kind-faced pluralism, calling on all religions and creeds and people to unite in a new world order that will supposedly culminate in a revived environment, the end of all wars, and the ascent of all people to a "higher consciousness."

The New Age movement manifests itself in meditation, channeling (communicating through spirits), and monistic philosophies, among other things. In today's world, there is perhaps no greater danger to the mind and to our culture than ignorance of the openly demonic nature of cosmic humanism. The Apostle Paul said, "But I say that the things which the Gentiles sacrifice they sacrifice to demons and not to God, and I do not want you to have fellowship with demons."[22] Christian students should flee from all forms of New Age thinking and warn their friends of this multifaceted humanism.

There are a myriad of other anti-Christian worldviews. They are all a part of the same fundamental rebellion that tries to ignore, distort, or eliminate the real God. Here is a partial list for further study: existentialism, hedonism, radical feminism, materialism, behaviorism, nihilism, pragmatism, polytheism, naturalism, environmentalism, and libertarianism—just some of the mind-bending philosophies that derail people from the truth.

THE CHRISTIAN WORLDVIEW ANSWERS THEM ALL

The Christian view of life is the only balanced, intelligent perspective that can be adopted. It gives hope to all who are facing the collapse of other worldview systems. Humanism in all its varieties self-destructs, because it is built upon the false assumption that man can reason himself to a better world. Christians have the biblical solutions for a dying world groping in the dark without God.

Charles F. Baker gives an insightful position concerning this truth:

> The Bible avoids all of the extremes and lopsided views of life and the world. Idealistic philosophy denies the existence of matter, holding that only mind is a reality. Materialism holds just the opposite extreme view. The Bible teaches the objective reality of both mind and matter, but points out the ephemeral character of the physical and the abiding character of the spiritual (2 Corinthians 4:18). The pantheist denies the transcendence of God and the deist denies His immanence. The Bible teaches both: God is all in all and God over all (1 Corinthians 15:28; Romans 9:5). Secularism places all of the emphasis upon the present life; fanaticism ignores the present and concerns itself only with the life to come. Buddhism would suppress all human desire; Hedonism would do nothing but fulfill human desire. Manicheanism held that the human body is evil; Hinduism teaches caste; Confucianism ignores God and the future. The Bible, on the other hand, brings all of these extremes into sharp focus and presents a well-rounded, common-sense world view.[23]

It is time for Christians to expose the bankruptcy of these humanistic ideologies at the college level and begin a major counteroffensive concerning the truth.

THE FINAL STEP

If there is one phrase that embodies the atmosphere in today's colleges, it is a pervasive "lack of vision" in today's students. Yet it is this crucial vision, God-directed optimism and creativity, that is needed to spark another great revival. William Bradford began his journey to greatness as the pilgrim pioneer at the age of thirteen in a secret Bible study in a livery stable. At the age of twenty-four, John Calvin wrote *The Institutes of the Christian Religion*, the classic doctrinal thesis, which has shaken the world for nearly five hundred years. George Washington was a colonel in the Virginia militia at twenty-three years of age, and the hero of his countrymen even at that time. These young believers had a vision for their lives, and found their purpose under God.

Perhaps of all the keys to success in college and in choosing a career, none is more vital than having a vision and a purpose for life. The Psalmist says, "Without a vision the people perish." This is where Christian students should be able to lead rather than follow. True biblical optimism can inspire them as they comprehend and believe the words of Jesus, "I have come that they might have life, and have it more abundantly."[24]

The first question of the remarkable 1646 Westminster Confession of Faith is, "What is the purpose of man?" The answer is, "To glorify God and enjoy Him forever." As Christians we know that we are created to serve our Creator and glorify Him (1 Corinthians 10:31). He has a specific purpose for each of us. No one is insignificant in His kingdom and nothing can stop His plan.

Christians have a real advantage as they plan their lives and vocations. We should make sure that our children enter college with great optimism; that, in spite of the obstacles such as the secular humanist dominance of the chairs of learning, they can change their world as they trust in God's providence.

A small army of Christian young people, totally committed to God's will for their lives, can transform the twenty-first century and all our institutions. As students are choosing their vocations, they should know and ponder the fact that the great pinnacles of human achievement have been inspired by God. The *Christian Home Learning Guides* have given ample proof that:

> The greatest universities were and will be founded to learn of and subdue God's world,

> The greatest art, music, literature, and architecture ever created was made to glorify the Creator,

> The greatest civil and religious liberty in the world directly follows wherever the Bible is unleashed and obeyed in society,

> The greatest system of justice over man was engendered from the biblical reasoning of sincere Christians,

> The greatest scientific discoveries are primarily the product of the Christian world and life view of a closed universe with fixed laws,

> The greatest prosperity and system for economic success and freedom, free enterprise, came out of the biblical command to steward God's world, and to be fruitful and multiply.

The Christian student today stands at the apex of opportunity to serve God and man. The humanist institutional experiments of the last two centuries have failed, and people are looking for a relationship with God which gives answers for all of life. Pollster George Barna said,

> The encouraging news is that tens of millions of American adults are seeking a deeper relationship with God. Half of the unchurched adult interviewed (49%) told us that as they think about their future, it would be very desirable to have a close relationship with God. Even among those people who are not born again Christians, three out of five (60%) said having a close relationship with God is something they view as a very desirable element for their future.[25]

MORE THAN CONQUERORS

On 22 July 1620, the Pilgrims left Holland for England, and then for America. Their sacrifice was made in part because they desired an unpolluted, godly education for their children. They left behind their dearly beloved pastor, John Robinson. In Robinson's final letter to them he charged them, as a general on the battlefield. You can smell the powder of the battle as his final words ring out:

> Thus this holy army of saints is marshalled here on earth by these officers, under the conduct of their glorious Emperor, Jesus Christ. Thus it marches in this most heavenly order and gracious array, against all enemies, both bodily and ghostly; peaceable in itself, as Jerusalem, terrible to the enemy as an army with banners, triumphing over their tyranny with patience, their cruelty with meekness, over death itself with dying.

> Thus, through the blood of that spotless Lamb, and that Word of their testimony, they are more than conquerors, bruising the head

of the Serpent; yea, through the power of His Word, they have the power to cast down strongholds, and everything that exalteth itself against God.

The gates of hell, and all the principalities and powers on earth shall not prevail against it.

The deeply felt optimism of this letter is incredible, for we know that Pastor Robinson was sending the flower of his church into a desolate wilderness to face likely death. They landed as combatants in a cosmic struggle for the hearts of men. They initiated a bloodless revolution that has freed more people, both physically and spiritually, than any army in history.

May we, as Christian parents and students, be faithful in the coming century to reach and disciple our world, as our Pilgrim forebears did theirs. Just as they could believe against all odds that God would bring them through to victory, we, too, can believe God to "do exceedingly, abundantly, more than we can ask or think."

REVIEW QUESTIONS

1. What philosophy is the basis for modern pluralism?

2. What did Martin Luther think should be the central educational text?

3. Explain the four steps to prepare to confront academic humanism.

4. What three religious "landmarks of truth" were memorized in colonial classrooms?

5. What is the danger of parental absence in students' decisions?

6. What prompted Christians to withdraw from society in the nineteenth century?

7. Describe the two fundamental worldviews.

8. Describe the five humanistic worldviews discussed in the chapter. Study one or more of the anti-Christian worldviews mentioned but not discussed.

9. What do today's students often lack, and what can be done to restore it to them?

10. Name six great achievements of the biblical worldview.

RELATED SCRIPTURE

Genesis 3:5
Psalm 19:1–2; 119:11, 98–99
Isaiah 14:12
Matthew 4:4
John 16:13

Romans 9:5
1 Corinthians 10:20, 31; 15:28
2 Corinthians 4:18
Hebrews 5:14
2 Peter 1:20–21

SUGGESTED READING

James Dale Davidson and Lord William Rees-Mogg, *The Great Reckoning* (New York: Summit Books, 1991).

D. James Kennedy, *Truths that Transform* (Old Tappan, NJ: Fleming H. Revell, 1974).

Henry M. Morris and John C. Whitcomb, *The Genesis Flood* (Phillipsburg, NJ: Presbyterian & Reformed Publishing Company, 1995).

David A. Noebel, *Understanding the Times* (Manitou Spring, CO: Summit Press, 1991).

Francis A. Schaeffer, *He Is There and He Is Not Silent* (Wheaton, IL: Tyndale, 1972).

————. *A Christian Manifesto* (Westchester, IL: Crossway, 1981).

Thomas Sowell, *Inside American Education* (New York: Free Press, 1993).

John W. Whitehead, *The Second American Revolution* (Elgin, IL: Cook, 1982).

PART SIX

Conclusion

A MAGNIFICENT OPTIMISM

Do not let us speak of darker days; let us speak rather of sterner days. These are not dark days: these are great days—the greatest days our country has ever lived; and we must all thank God that we have been allowed, each of us according to our stations, to play a part in making these days memorable...

–WINSTON CHURCHILL,
SPEAKING TO ENGLAND IN 1941

THE STABILITY OF CHRISTIAN society has always been based on the family and on the passing of the torch of truth from one generation to the next. One colonial American family illustrates the power of biblical family education over time.

Jonathan Edwards and Sarah Pierrepont were married in 1727. He was the son of a minister, and the only boy of eleven children. The couple had eleven children of their own, which continued a generational blessing that has populated America with godly offspring for centuries.

Jonathan believed in rising before sunrise for prayer. He would then read a chapter of the Bible to his children before the day began. Though he was perhaps the greatest intellect produced in colonial America, he took time out from his writing, pastoring, and mission work among the Indians each day to give one hour of undivided attention to his children. During this time, he would go over their lessons or answer any questions they might have. Jonathan and Sarah's shared priority was to train and prepare their progeny for service to God and man.

In 1900, 173 years after their marriage, a study was made of some 1,400 of their descendants. Their union had produced thirteen college presidents; sixty-five professors; one hundred lawyers. including the dean of an outstanding law school; thirty judges; fifty-six physicians, including the dean of a medical school; eighty holders of public office; three United States senators; three mayors of large American cities; three governors; one comptroller of the United States Treasury; and one vice president of the United States. Members of the family had written 135 books and edited eighteen journals and periodicals. They had entered the ministry in droves, with nearly one hundred of them becoming missionaries overseas.

Likewise, each of us stands at the apex of an unfolding generational drama. We are heirs to the past, and ancestors to the future. Counting our grandparents through our early mentors through our grandchildren, we will mentor, or have been mentored by, people whose lives extend over two hundred years and include parts of four centuries.

From its inception, Christianity has been a religion of ideas and learning. Oxford historian Robin Lane Fox documented that Christianity became the marvel of the world because it was spread by ordinary people who, despite a lack of formal education, were able to explain the mysteries of God more effectively than the educated elite of the pagan world.

Christians became a people of the Book and started schools of learning that civilized a barbarian Europe. The educational legacy left to us by the reformers and our forefathers is unsurpassed. Luther's training spawned the universities of Germany. Calvin's Geneva was an international center of scholarship and the cradle of civil and religious liberty for the world. Knox enlightened and trained a whole generation of Scots, bringing them from tribal passions to a powerful, biblical view of life and government, all within a twenty-year span. These early saints of the reformation fought state tyranny, epidemic illiteracy, and poverty that rival any of our problems today. Our founders carried on this tradition of Christian education, seeing the home as the foundation for its propagation. They left us a great legacy to replicate.

This legacy of educational excellence is a Christian inheritance. Jesus tells us that much is required of him to whom much is given. In our generation, we, as believing families, have the mandate to revive the great tradition of Christian learning. By making full use of this book and the many resources that it references, the Christian family is taking a bold step, reasserting its rightful leadership in the education of its children. Our entire nation will be blessed by the godly, intelligent young believers who will emerge from such homes.

Early Christians exhibited a "magnificent optimism," according to Fox, even in the face of Roman hegemony and persecution.[1] Their optimism was well-rewarded, as the small sect starting with twelve Jewish disciples spread and permeated the Roman empire in two centuries.

We too should be optimistic in our day. Our hope is not built upon the strength of our own resources, but upon the promises of God. As parents we are promised that if we "train up a child in the way he should go…he will not depart from it."[2] The psalmist declares "Blessed is the man who fears the Lord, who delights greatly in His commandments. His descendants will be mighty upon the earth; the generations of the upright will be blessed."[3]

Just as He has given His people hope through His scriptural promises, God has acted through history to spiritually renew whole generations in times of impending crisis and despair. There have been four great awakenings in American history. All have been about fifty years apart, and in each one young people and their visionary faith played a significant role. For example, the first Great Awakening in America had its roots in the Holy Club at Oxford, made up of Christian students like John Wesley and George Whitefield. The Second Great Awakening gained great impetus from the revival at Yale under Timothy Dwight, the grandson of Jonathan Edwards. In 1795, fully one-half of the student body was converted. In this troubled generation, America is ready for yet another student-led revival.

The Western world has been retreating from the God of the Bible for over two hundred years. We have sown the wind and are reaping the whirlwind. The thinkers who led the rebellion are gone. Charles Darwin, the prophet of evolution, died in 1882. Karl Marx, the theorist of the Marxist revolutions and slaughters of the twentieth century, died in 1883. Julius Wellhauser, the founder of German higher criticism and modern liberal theology, died in 1918. Sigmund Freud, the father of godless psychology, died in 1939. John Maynard Keynes, the economist of the welfare state, died in 1946. John Dewey, the father of progressive secular education, died in 1952.

The ideas of these men have lingered long after their deaths and have tainted the thinking of whole generations. But God has providentially placed us in a time where we can not only expose the failures of their humanist dream, but offer a dynamic, intellectually valid, historically proven, and scripturally sound Christian faith. The vacuum left by the failure of the godless values of humanism must be filled. There exists a tension in modern culture as it awaits a new consensus. If Christian values are to prevail, then they will be championed by the children of godly parents, who have been prepared for the challenge of such a time in history.

Life at the close of the second millennium A.D. has much in common with that of the first century. As in the Roman era, a restive peace covers the world. As then, numerous philosophies and religions engage the attention of the masses, yet fail to offer real solutions to the problems of society. And in like manner, Christianity is on the outside of the major power centers in Western culture.

Like our first century counterparts, we can look forward with great anticipation to what God is going to do in the seventh millennium of recorded history. Just as early Christianity grew through parental leadership and education, we can train our children to rise up and have a transforming impact upon the next century. There is no more important task in the world than the daily discipleship of the world's future.

PART SEVEN

Appendixes

APPENDIX A

The Apostles' Creed

The basic creed of Reformed churches, as most familiarly known, is called the Apostles' Creed. It has received this title because of its great antiquity; it dates from very early times in the Church, a half century or so from the last writings of the New Testament.

> I believe in God, the Father Almighty,
> the Creator of heaven and earth,
> and in Jesus Christ,
> His only Son, our Lord:
> Who was conceived of the Holy Spirit,
> born of the Virgin Mary,
> suffered under Pontius Pilate,
> was crucified, died, and was buried.
> He descended into hell.
> The third day He arose again from the dead.
> He ascended into heaven
> and sits at the right hand of God the Father Almighty,
> whence He shall come to judge the living and the dead.
> I believe in the Holy Spirit,
> the holy *catholic church,
> the communion of saints,
> the forgiveness of sins,
> the resurrection of the body,
> and life everlasting.
> Amen.

---

*The word "catholic" refers not to the Roman Catholic Church,
but to the universal church of the Lord Jesus Christ.*

APPENDIX B

The Declaration of Independence
of The United States of America

IN CONGRESS, JULY 4, 1776,

THE UNANIMOUS DECLARATION OF THE THIRTEEN UNITED STATES OF AMERICA,

WHEN in the Course of human events, it becomes necessary for one people to dissolve the political bands which have connected them with another, and to assume, among the powers of the earth, the separate and equal station to which the Laws of Nature and of Nature's God entitle them, a decent respect to the opinions of mankind requires that they should declare the causes which impel them to the separation.——We hold these truths to be self-evident, that all men are created equal, that they are endowed by their Creator with certain unalienable Rights, that among these are Life, Liberty and the pursuit of Happiness.——That to secure these rights, Governments are instituted among Men, deriving their just powers from the consent of the governed,——That whenever any Form of Government becomes destructive of these ends, it is the Right of the People to alter or to abolish it, and to institute new Government, laying its foundation on such principles and organizing its powers in such form, as to them shall seem most likely to effect their Safety and Happiness. Prudence, indeed, will dictate that Governments long established should not be changed for light and transient causes; and accordingly all experience hath shewn, that mankind are more disposed to suffer, while evils are sufferable, than to right themselves by abolishing the forms to which they are accustomed. But when a long train of abuses and usurpations, pursuing invariably the same Object evinces a design to reduce them under absolute Despotism, it is their right, it is their duty, to throw off such Government, and to provide new Guards for their future security.——Such has been the patient sufferance of these Colonies; and such is now the necessity which constrains them to alter their former Systems of Government. The history of the present King of Great Britain is a history of repeated injuries and usurpations, all having in direct object the establishment of an absolute Tyranny over these States. To prove this, let Facts be submitted to a candid world.——He has refused his Assent to Laws, the most wholesome and necessary for the public good.——He has forbidden his Governors to pass Laws of immediate and pressing importance, unless suspended in their operation till his Assent should be obtained; and when so suspended, he has utterly neglected to attend to them.——He has refused to pass other Laws for the accommodation of large districts of people, unless those people would relinquish the right of Representation in the Legislature, a right inestimable to them and formidable to tyrants only.——He has called together legislative bodies at places unusual, uncomfortable, and distant from the depository of their public Records, for the sole purpose of fatiguing them into compliance with his measures.——He has dissolved Representative Houses repeatedly, for opposing with manly firmness his invasions on the rights of the people.——He has refused for a long time, after such dissolutions, to cause others to be elected; whereby the Legislative powers, incapable of Annihilation, have returned to the People at large for their exercise; the State remaining in the mean time exposed to all the dangers of invasion from without, and convulsions within.——He has endeavoured to prevent the population of these States; for that purpose obstructing the Laws of Naturalization of Foreigners; refusing to pass others to encourage their migration hither, and raising the conditions of new Appropriations of Lands.—— He has obstructed the Administration of Justice, by refusing his Assent to Laws for establishing Judiciary powers.——He has made Judges dependent on his Will alone, for the tenure of their offices, and the amount and payment of their salaries.——He has erected a multitude of New Offices, and sent hither swarms of Officers to harass our people, and eat out their substance.——He has kept among us, in times of peace, Standing Armies without the Consent of our legislatures.——He has affected to render the Military independent of and superior to the Civil power.——He has combined with others to subject us to a jurisdiction foreign to our constitution, and unacknowledged by our laws; giving his Assent to their Acts of pretended Legislation:——For quartering large bodies of armed troops among us:——For protecting them, by a mock Trial, from punishment for any Murders which they should commit on the Inhabitants of these States:——For cutting off our Trade with all parts of the world:——For imposing Taxes on us without our Consent:——For depriving us in many cases, of the benefits of Trial by Jury:——For transporting us beyond Seas to be tried for pretended offences:——For abolishing the free System of English Laws in a neighbouring Province, establishing therein an Arbitrary government, and enlarging its Boundaries so as to render it at once an example and fit instrument for introducing the same absolute rule into these Colonies:——For taking away our Charters, abolishing our most valuable Laws, and altering fundamentally the Forms of our Governments:——For suspending our own Legislatures and declaring themselves invested with power to legislate for us in all cases whatsoever.——He has abdicated Government here, by declaring us out of his Protection and waging War against us.——He has plundered our seas, ravaged our Coasts, burnt our towns, and destroyed the lives of our people.——He is at this time transporting large Armies of foreign Mercenaries to compleat the works of death, desolation and tyranny, already begun with circumstances of Cruelty & perfidy scarcely paralleled in the most barbarous ages, and totally unworthy the Head of a civilized nation.——He has constrained our fellow Citizens taken Captive on the high Seas to bear Arms against their Country, to become the executioners of their friends and Brethren, or to fall themselves by their Hands.——He has excited domestic insurrections amongst us and has endeavoured to bring on the inhabitants of our frontiers, the merciless Indian Savages, whose known rule of warfare, is an undistinguished destruction of all ages, sexes and conditions. In every stage of these Oppressions We have Petitioned for Redress in the most humble terms: Our repeated Petitions have been answered only by repeated injury. A Prince, whose character is thus marked by every act which may define a Tyrant, is unfit to be the ruler of a free people. Nor have We been wanting in attentions to our British brethren. We have warned them from time to time of attempts by their legislature to extend an unwarrantable jurisdiction over us. We have reminded them of the circumstances of our emigration and settlement here. We have appealed to their native justice and magnanimity, and we have conjured them by the ties of our common kindred to disavow these usurpations, which would inevitably interrupt our connections and correspondence. They too have been deaf to the voice of justice and of consanguinity. We must, therefore, acquiesce in the necessity, which denounces our Separation, and hold them, as we hold the rest of mankind, Enemies in War, in Peace Friends.——We, therefore, the Representatives of the united States of America, in General Congress, Assembled, appealing to the Supreme Judge of the world for the rectitude of our intentions, do, in the Name, and by Authority of the good People of these Colonies, solemnly publish and declare, That these United Colonies are, and of Right ought to be Free and Independent States; that they are Absolved from all Allegiance to the British Crown, and that all political connection between them and the State of Great Britain, is and ought to be totally dissolved; and that as Free and Independent States, they have full Power to levy War, conclude Peace, contract Alliances, establish Commerce, and to do all other Acts and Things which Independent States may of right do.——And for the support of this Declaration, with a firm reliance on the protection of divine Providence, we mutually pledge to each other our Lives, our Fortunes and our sacred Honor.

JOHN HANCOCK, President

Attested, CHARLES THOMSON, Secretary

New Hampshire
JOSIAH BARTLETT
WILLIAM WHIPPLE
MATTHEW THORNTON

Massachusetts-Bay
SAMUEL ADAMS
JOHN ADAMS
ROBERT TREAT PAINE
ELBRIDGE GERRY

Rhode Island
STEPHEN HOPKINS
WILLIAM ELLERY

Connecticut
ROGER SHERMAN
SAMUEL HUNTINGTON
WILLIAM WILLIAMS
OLIVER WOLCOTT

Georgia
BUTTON GWINNETT
LYMAN HALL
GEO. WALTON

Maryland
SAMUEL CHASE
WILLIAM PACA
THOMAS STONE
CHARLES CARROLL
 OF CARROLLTON

Virginia
GEORGE WYTHE
RICHARD HENRY LEE
THOMAS JEFFERSON
BENJAMIN HARRISON
THOMAS NELSON, JR.
FRANCIS LIGHTFOOT LEE
CARTER BRAXTON

New York
WILLIAM FLOYD
PHILIP LIVINGSTON
FRANCIS LEWIS
LEWIS MORRIS

Pennsylvania
ROBERT MORRIS
BENJAMIN RUSH
BENJAMIN FRANKLIN
JOHN MORTON
GEORGE CLYMER
JAMES SMITH
GEORGE TAYLOR
JAMES WILSON
GEORGE ROSS

Delaware
CAESAR RODNEY
GEORGE READ
THOMAS M'KEAN

North Carolina
WILLIAM HOOPER
JOSEPH HEWES
JOHN PENN

South Carolina
EDWARD RUTLEDGE
THOMAS HEYWARD, JR.
THOMAS LYNCH, JR.
ARTHUR MIDDLETON

New Jersey
RICHARD STOCKTON
JOHN WITHERSPOON
FRANCIS HOPKINSON
JOHN HART
ABRAHAM CLARK

Final Proclamation of Emancipation, 1863
January 1, 1863

Whereas, on the twenty-second day of September, in the year of our Lord one thousand eight hundred and sixty two, a proclamation was issued by the President of the United States, containing, among other things, the following, towit:

"That on the first day of January, in the year of our Lord one thousand eight hundred and sixty-three, all persons held as slaves within any State or designated part of a State, the people whereof shall then be in rebellion against the United States, shall be then, thenceforward, and forever free; and the Executive Government of the United States, including the military and naval authority thereof, will recognize and maintain the freedom of such persons, and will do no act or acts to repress such persons, or any of them, in any efforts they may make for their actual freedom.

"That the Executive will, on the first day of January aforesaid, by proclamation, designate the States and parts of States, if any, in which the people thereof, respectively, shall then be in rebellion against the United States; and the fact that any State, or the people thereof, shall on that day be, in good faith, represented in the Congress of the United States by members chosen thereto at elections wherein a majority of the qualified voters of such State shall have participated, shall, in the absence of strong countervailing testimony, be deemed conclusive evidence that such State, and the people thereof, are not then in rebellion against the United States."

Now, therefore I, Abraham Lincoln, President of the United States, by virtue of the power in me vested as Commander-in-Chief, of the Army and Navy of the United States in time of actual armed rebellion against authority and government of the United States, and as a fit and necessary war measure for suppressing said rebellion, do, on this first day of January, in the year of our Lord one thousand eight hundred and sixty three, and in accordance with my purpose so to do publicly proclaimed for the full period of one hundred days, from the day first above mentioned, order and designate as the States and parts of States wherein the people thereof respectively, are this day in rebellion against the United States, the following, towit:

Arkansas, Texas, Louisiana, (except the Parishes of St. Bernard, Plaquemines, Jefferson, St. Johns, St. Charles, St. James[,] Ascension, Assumption, Terrebonne, Lafourche, St. Mary, St. Martin, and Orleans, including the City of New-Orleans) Mississippi, Alabama, Florida, Georgia, South-Carolina, North-Carolina, and Virginia, (except the fortyeight counties designated as West Virginia, and also the counties of Berkley, Accomac, Northampton, Elizabeth-City, York, Princess Ann, and Norfolk, including the cities of Norfolk & Portsmouth [ )]; and which excepted parts are, for the present, left precisely as if this proclamation were not issued.

And by virtue of the power, and for the purpose aforesaid, I do order and declare that all persons held as slaves within said designated States, and parts of States, are, and henceforward shall be free; and that the Executive government of the United States, including the military and naval authorities thereof, will recognize and maintain the freedom of said persons.

And I hereby enjoin upon the people so declared to be free to abstain from all violence, unless in necessary self-defence; and I recommend to them that, in all cases when allowed, they labor faithfully for reasonable wages.

And I further declare and make known, that such persons of suitable condition, will be received into the armed service of the United States to garrison forts, positions, stations, and other places, and to man vessels of all sorts in said service.

And upon this act, sincerely believed to be an act of justice, warranted by the Constitution, upon military necessity, I invoke the considerate judgment of mankind, and the gracious favor of Almighty God....

APPENDIX D

Fundamental Orders of Connecticut
January 14-24, 1638-39

(In 1635-36, settlements were planted at Windsor, Wethersfield, and Hartford. In 1637 the three towns assumed the control of their own affairs, and in January, 1638-39, drew up the constitution known as the Fundamental Order of Connecticut—"the first written constitution known to history that created a government.")

Forasmuch as it hath pleased the Allmighty God by the wise disposition of his divyne providence so to Order and dispose of things that we the Inhabitants and Residents of Windsor, Harford and Wethersfield are now cohabiting and dwelling in and uppon the River of Conectecotte and the Lands thereunto adjoyneing; And well knowing where a people are gathered togather the word of God requires that to mayntayne the peace and union of such a people there should be an orderly and decent Government established according to God, to order and dispose of the affayres of the people at all seasons as occation shall require; doe therefore assotiate and conjoyne our selves to be as one Publike State or Commonwelth; and doe, for our selves and our Successors and such as shall be adjoyned to us att any tyme hereafter, enter into Comination and Confederation togather, to mayntayne and presearve the liberty and purity of the gospell of our Lord Jesus which we now professe, as also the disciplyne of the Churches, which according to the truth of the said gospell is now practised amongst us; As also in our Civell Affaires to be guided and governed according to such Lawes, Rules, Orders and decrees as shall be made, ordered & decreed, aks followeth....

APPENDIX E

The Gettysburg Address

Address at the dedication of the Gettysburg National Cemetery, November 19, 1863

Fourscore and seven years ago our fathers brought forth on this continent a new nation, conceived in liberty, and dedicated to the proposition that all men are created equal.

Now we are engaged in a great civil war, testing whether that nation, or any nation so conceived and so dedicated, can long endure. We are met on a great battlefield of that war. We have come to dedicate a portion of that field as a final resting place for those who here gave their lives that nation might live. It is altogether fitting and proper that we should do this.

But, in a larger sense, we cannot dedicate—we cannot consecrate—we cannot hallow—this ground. The brave men, living and dead, who struggled here, have consecrated it far above our poor power to add or detract. The world will little note nor long remember what we say here, but it can never forget what they did here. It is for us, the living, rather, to be dedicated here to the unfinished work which they who fought here have thus far so nobly advanced. It is rather for us to be here dedicated to the great task remaining before us—that from these honored dead we take increased devotion to that cause for which they gave the last full measure of devotion; that we here highly resolve that these dead shall not have died in vain, that this nation, under God, shall have a new birth of freedom; and that government of the people, by the people, and for the people, shall not perish from the earth.

APPENDIX F

Lincoln's Second Inaugural Address
March 4, 1865

Fellow countrymen: At this second appearing to take the oath of the presidential office, there is less occasion for an extended address than there was at the first. Then a statement, somewhat in detail, of a course to be pursued, seemed fitting and proper. Now, at the expiration of four years, during which public declarations have been constantly called forth on every point and phase of the great contest which still absorbs the attention and engrosses the energies of the nation, little that is new could be presented. The progress of our arms, upon which all else chiefly depends, is as well known to the public as to myself; and it is, I trust, reasonably satisfactory and encouraging to all. With high hope for the future, no prediction in regard to it is ventured.

On the occasion corresponding to this four years ago, all thoughts were anxiously directed to an impending civil war. All dreaded it—all sought to avert it. While the inaugural address was being delivered from this place, devoted altogether to saving the Union without war, insurgent agents were in the city seeking to destroy it without war—seeking to dissolve the Union, and divide effects, by negotiation. Both parties deprecated war; but one of them would make war rather than let the nation survive; and the other would accept war rather than let it perish. And the war came.

One-eighth of the whole population were colored slaves, not distributed generally over the Union, but localized in the Southern part of it. These slaves constituted a peculiar and powerful interest. All knew that this interest was, somehow, the cause of the war. To strengthen, perpetuate, and extend this interest was the object for which the insurgents would rend the Union, even by war; while the government claimed no right to do more than to restrict the territorial enlargement of it.

Neither party expected for the war the magnitude or the duration which it has already attained. Neither anticipated that the cause of the conflict might cease with, or even before, the conflict itself should cease. Each looked for an easier triumph, and a result less fundamental and astounding. Both read the same Bible, and pray to the same God; and each invokes his aid against the other. It may seem strange that any men should dare to ask a just God's assistance in wringing their bread from the sweat of other men's faces; but let us judge not, that we be not judged. The prayers of both could not be answered—that of neither has been answered fully.

The Almighty has his own purposes. "Woe unto the world because of offenses! for it must needs be that offenses come; but woe to that man by whom the offense cometh." If we shall suppose that American slavery is one of those offenses which, in the providence of God, must needs come, but which, having continued through his appointed time, he now wills to remove, and that he gives to both North and South this terrible war, as the woe due to those by whom the offense came, shall we discern therein any departure from those divine attributes which the believers in a living God always ascribe to him? Fondly do we hope—fervently do we pray—that this mighty scourge of war may speedily pass away. Yet, if God wills that it continue until all the wealth piled by the bondsman's two hundred and fifty years of unrequited toil shall be sunk, and until every drop of blood drawn by the lash shall be paid by another drawn with the sword, as was said three thousand years ago, so still it must be said, "The judgments of the Lord are true and righteous altogether."

With malice toward none; with charity for all; with firmness in the right, as God gives us to see the right, let us strive on to finish the work we are in; to bind up the nation's wounds; to care for him who shall have borne the battle, and for his widow, and his orphan—to do all which may achieve and cherish a just and lasting peace among ourselves, and with all nations.

APPENDIX G

Magna Carta (1215)

JOHN, by the grace of God King of England, Lord of Ireland, Duke of Normandy and Aquitaine, and Count of Anjou, to his archbishops, bishops, abbots, earls, barons, justices, foresters, sheriffs, stewards, servants, and to all his officials and loyal subjects, Greeting.

KNOW THAT BEFORE GOD, for the health of our soul and those of our ancestors and heirs, to the honour of God, the exaltation of the holy Church, and the better ordering of our kingdom, at the advice of our reverend fathers Stephen, archbishop of Canterbury, primate of all England, and cardinal of the holy Roman Church, Henry archbishop of Dublin, William bishop of London, Peter bishop of Winchester, Jocelin bishop of Bath and Glastonbury, Hugh bishop of Lincoln, Walter bishop of Coventry, Benedict bishop of Rochester, Master Pandulf subdeacon and member of the papal household, Brother Aymeric master of the knighthood of the Temple in England, William Marshal earl of Pembroke, William earl of Salisbury, William earl of Warren, William earl of Arundel, Alan de Galloway constable of Scotland, Warin Fitz Gerald, Peter Fitz Herbert, Hubert de Burgh seneschal of Poitou, Hugh de Neville, Matthew Fitz Herbert, Thomas Basset, Alan Basset, Philip Daubeny, Robert de Roppeley, John Marshal, John Fitz Hugh, and other loyal subjects:

(I) FIRST, THAT WE HAVE GRANTED TO GOD, and by this present charter have confirmed for us and our heirs in perpetuity, that the English Church shall be free, and shall have its rights undiminished, and its liberties unimpaired. That we wish this so to be observed, appears from the fact that of our own free will, before the outbreak of the present dispute between us and our barons, we granted and confirmed by charter the freedom of the Church's elections—a right reckoned to be of the greatest necessity and importance to it—and caused this to be confirmed by Pope Innocent III. This freedom we shall observe ourselves, and desire to be observed in good faith by our heirs in perpetuity.

TO ALL FREE MEN OF OUR KINGDOM we have also granted, for us and our heirs for ever, all the liberties written out below, to have and to keep for them and their heirs, of us and our heirs:
(2) If any earl, baron, or other person that holds lands directly of the Crown, for military service, shall die, and at his death his heir shall be of full age and owe a 'relief', the heir shall have his inheritance on payment of the ancient scale of 'relief'. That is to say, the heir or heirs of an earl shall pay £100 for the entire earl's barony, the heir or heirs of a knight 100S. at most for the entire knight's 'fee', and any man that owes less shall pay less, in accordance with the ancient usage of 'fees'.
(3) But if the heir of such a person is under age and a ward, when he comes of age he shall have his inheritance without 'relief' or fine.
(4) The guardian of the land of an heir who is under age shall take from it only reasonable revenues, customary dues, and feudal services. He shall do this without destruction or damage to men or property. If we have given the guardianship of the land to a sheriff, or to any person answerable to us for the revenues, and he commits destruction or damage, we will exact compensation from him, and the land shall be entrusted to two worthy and prudent men of the same 'fee', who shall be answerable to us for the revenues, or to the person to whom we have assigned them. If we have given or sold to anyone the guardianship of such land, and he causes destruction or damage, he shall lose the guardianship of it, and it shall be handed over to two worthy and prudent men of the same 'fee', who shall be similarly answerable to us.
(5) For so long as a guardian has guardianship of such land, he shall maintain the houses, parks, fish preserves, ponds, mills, and everything else pertaining to it, from the revenues of the land itself. When the heir comes of age, he shall restore the whole land to him, stocked with plough teams

and such implements of husbandry as the season demands and the revenues from the land can reasonably bear.

(6) Heirs may be given in marriage, but not to someone of lower social standing. Before a marriage takes place, it shall be made known to the heir's next-of-kin.

(7) At her husband's death, a widow may have her marriage portion and inheritance at once and without trouble. She shall pay nothing for her dower, marriage portion, or any inheritance that she and her husband held jointly on the day of his death. She may remain in her husband's house for forty days after his death, and within this period her dower shall be assigned to her.

(8) No widow shall be compelled to marry, so long as she wishes to remain without a husband. But she must give security that she will not marry without royal consent, if she holds her lands of the Crown, or without the consent of whatever other lord she may hold them of.

(9) Neither we nor our officials will seize any land or rent in payment of a debt, so long as the debtor has movable goods sufficient to discharge the debt. A debtor's sureties shall not be distrained upon so long as the debtor himself can discharge his debt. If, for lack of means, the debtor is unable to discharge his debt, his sureties shall be answerable for it. If they so desire, they may have the debtor's lands and debts until they have received satisfaction for the debt that they paid for him, unless the debtor can show that he has settled his obligations to them.

(10) If anyone who has borrowed a sum of money from Jews dies before the debt had been repaid, his heir shall pay no interest on the debt for so long as he remains under age, irrespective of whom he holds his lands. If such a debt falls into the hands of the Crown, it will take nothing except the principal sum specified in the bond.

(11) If a man dies owing money to Jews, his wife may have her dower and pay nothing towards the debt from it. If he leaves children that are under age, their needs may also be provided for on a scale appropriate to the size of his holding of lands. The debt is to be paid out of the residue, reserving the service due to his feudal lords. Debts owed to persons other than Jews are to be dealt with similarly.

(12) No 'scutage' or 'aid' may be levied in our kingdom without its general consent, unless it is for the ransom of our person, to make our eldest son a knight, and (once) to marry our eldest daughter. For these purposes only a reasonable 'aid' may be levied. 'Aids' from the city of London are to be treated similarly.

(13) The city of London shall enjoy all its ancient liberties and free customs, both by land and by water. We also will and grant that all other cities, boroughs, towns, and ports shall enjoy all their liberties and free customs.

(14) To obtain the general consent of the realm for the assessment of an 'aid'—except in the three cases above—or a 'scutage', we will cause the archbishops, bishops, abbots, earls, and greater barons to be summoned individually by letter. To those who hold lands directly of us we will cause a general summons to be issued, through the sheriffs and other officials, to come together on a fixed day (of which at least forty days notice shall be given) and at a fixed place. In all letters of summons, the cause of the summons will be stated. When a summons has been issued, the business appointed for the day shall go forward in accordance with the resolution of those present, even if not all those who were summoned have appeared.

(15) In future we will allow no one to levy an 'aid' from his free men, except to ransom his person, to make his eldest son a knight, and (once) to marry his eldest daughter. For these purposes only a reasonable 'aid' may be levied.

(16) No man shall be forced to perform more service for a knight's 'fee', or other free holding of land, than is due from it.

(17) Ordinary lawsuits shall not follow the royal court around, but shall be held in a fixed place.

(18) Inquests of *novel disseisin, mort d'ancestor*, and *darrein presentment* shall be taken only in their proper county court. We ourselves, or in our absence abroad our chief justice, will send two justices to each country four times a year, and these justices, with four knights of the county elected

by the county itself, shall hold the assizes in the country court, on the day and in the place where the court meets.

(19) If any assizes cannot be taken on the day of the county court, as many knights and freeholders shall afterwards remain behind, of those who have attended the court, as will suffice for the administration of justice, having regard to the volume of business to be done.

(20) For a trivial offence, a free man shall be fined only in proportion to the degree of his offence, and for a serious offence correspondingly, but not so heavily as to deprive him of his livelihood. In the same way, a merchant shall be spared his merchandise, and a husbandman the implements of husbandry, if they fall upon the mercy of a royal court. None of these fines shall be imposed except by the assessment on oath of reputable men of the neighbourhood.

(21) Earls and barons shall be fined only by their equals, and in proportion to the gravity of their offence.

(22) A fine imposed upon the lay property of a clerk in holy orders shall be assessed upon the same principles, without reference to the value of his ecclesiastical benefice.

(23) No town or person shall be forced to build bridges over rivers except those with an ancient obligation to do so.

(24) No sheriff, constable, coroners, or other royal officials are to hold lawsuits that should be held by the royal justices.

(25) Every country, hundred, wapentake, and tithing shall remain at its ancient rent, without increase, except the royal demesne manors.

(26) If at the death of a man who holds a lay 'fee' of the Crown, a sheriff or royal official produces royal letters patent of summons for a debt due to the Crown, it shall be lawful for them to seize and list movable goods found in the lay 'fee' of the dead man to the value of the debt, as assessed by worthy men. Nothing shall be removed until the whole debt is paid, when the residue shall be given over to the executors to carry out the dead man's will. If no debt is due to the Crown, all the movable goods shall be regarded as the property of the dead man, except the reasonable shares of his wife and children.

(27) If a free man dies intestate, his movable goods are to be distributed by his next-of-kin and friends, under the supervision of the Church. The rights of his debtors are to be preserved.

(28) No constable or other royal official shall take corn or other movable goods from any man without immediate payment, unless the seller voluntarily offers postponement of this.

(29) No constable may compel a knight to pay money for castleguard if the knight is willing to undertake the guard in person, or with reasonable excuse to supply some other fit man to do it. A knight taken or sent on military service shall be excused from castleguard for the period of this service.

(30) No sheriff, royal official, or other person shall take horses or carts for transport from any free man, without his consent.

(31) Neither we nor any royal official will take wood for our castle, or for any other purpose, without the consent of the owner.

(32) We will not keep the lands of people convicted of felony in our hand for longer than a year and a day, after which they shall be returned to the lords of the 'fees' concerned.

(33) All fish-weirs shall be removed from the Thames, the Medway, and throughout the whole of England, except on the sea coast.

(34) The writ called *precipe* shall not in future be issued to anyone in respect of any holding of land, if a free man could thereby be deprived of the right of trial in his own lord's court.

(35) There shall be standard measures of wine, ale, and corn (the London quarter), throughout the kingdom. There shall also be a standard width of dyed cloth, russett, and haberject, namely two ells within the selvedges. Weights are to be standardised similarly.

(36) In future nothing shall be paid or accepted for the issue of a writ of inquisition of life or limbs. It shall be given *gratis*, and not refused.

(37) If a man holds land of the Crown by 'fee-farm', 'socage', or 'burgage', and also holds land of someone else for knight's service, we will not have guardianship of his heir, nor of the land that belongs to the other person's 'fee', by virtue of the 'fee-farm', 'socage', or 'burgage', unless the 'fee-farm' owes knight's service. We will not have the guardianship of a man's heir, or of the land that he holds of someone else, by reason of any small property that he may hold of the Crown for a service of knives, arrows, or the like.

(38) In future no official shall place a man on trial upon his own unsupported statement, without producing credible witnesses to the truth of it.

(39) No free man shall be seized or imprisoned, or stripped of his rights or possessions, or outlawed or exiled, or deprived of his standing in any other way, nor will we proceed with force against him, or send others to do so, except by the lawful judgment of his equals or by the law of the land.

(40) To no one will we sell, to no one deny or delay right or justice.

(41) All merchants may enter or leave England unharmed and without fear, and may stay or travel within it, by land or water, for purposes of trade, free from all illegal exactions, in accordance with ancient and lawful customs. This, however, does not apply in time of war to merchants from a country that is at war with us. Any such merchants found in our country at the outbreak of war shall be detained without injury to their persons or property, until we or our chief justice have discovered how our own merchants are being treated in the country at war with us. If our own merchants are safe they shall be safe too.

(42) In future it shall be lawful for any man to leave and return to our kingdom unharmed and without fear, by land or water, preserving his allegiance to us, except in time of war, for some short period, for the common benefit of the realm. People that have been imprisoned or outlawed in accordance with the law of the land, people from a country that is at war with us, and merchants—who shall be dealt with as stated above—are excepted from this provision.

(43) If a man holds lands of any 'escheat' such as the 'honour' of Wallingford, Nottingham, Boulogne, Lancaster, or of other 'escheats' in our hand that are baronies, at his death his heir shall give us only the 'relief' and service that he would have made to the baron, had the barony been in the baron's hand. We will hold the 'escheat' in the same manner as the baron held it.

(44) People who live outside the forest need not in future appear before the royal justices of the forest in answer to general summonses, unless they are actually involved in proceedings or are sureties for someone who has been seized for a forest offence.

(45) We will appoint as justices, constables, sheriffs, or other officials, only men that know the law of the realm and are minded to keep it well.

(46) All barons who have founded abbeys, and have charters of English kings or ancient tenure as evidence of this, may have guardianship of them when there is no abbot, as is their due.

(47) All forests that have been created in our reign shall at once be disafforested. River-banks that have been enclosed in our reign shall be treated similarly.

(48) All evil customs relating to forests and warrens, foresters, warreners, sheriffs and their servants, or river-banks and their wardens, are at once to be investigated in every county by twelve sworn knights of the county, and within forty days of their enquiry the evil customs are to be abolished completely and irrevocably. But we, or our chief justice if we are not in England, are first to be informed.

(49) We will at once return all hostages and charters delivered up to us by Englishmen as security for peace or for loyal service.

(50) We will remove completely from their offices the kinsmen of Gerard de Athée, and in future they shall hold no offices in England. The people in question are Engelard de Cigogné, Peter, Guy, and Andrew de Chanceaux, Guy de Cigogné, Geoffrey de Martigny and his brothers, Philip Marc and his brothers, with Geoffrey his nephew, and all their followers.

(51) As soon as peace is restored, we will remove from the kingdom all the foreign knights, bowmen, their attendants, and the mercenaries that have come to it, to its harm, with horses and arms.

(52) To any man whom we have deprived or dispossessed of lands, castles, liberties, or rights, without the lawful judgement of his equals, we will at once restore these. In cases of dispute the matter shall be resolved by the judgement of the twenty-five barons referred to below in the clause for securing the peace [§ 61]. In cases, however, where a man was deprived or dispossessed of something without the lawful judgement of his equals by our father King Henry or our brother King Richard, and it remains in our hands or is held by others under our warranty, we shall have respite for the period commonly allowed to Crusaders, unless a lawsuit had been begun, or an enquiry had been made at our order, before we took the Cross as a Crusader. On our return from the Crusade, or if we abandon it, we will at once render justice in full.

(53) We shall have similar respite in rendering justice in connexion with forests that are to be disafforested, or to remain forests, when these were first afforested by our father Henry or our brother Richard; with the guardianship of lands in another person's 'fee', when we have hitherto had this by virtue of a 'fee' held of us for knight's service by a third party; and with abbeys founded in another person's 'fee', in which the lord of the 'fee' claims to own a right. On our return from the Crusade, or if we abandon it, we will at once do full justice to complaints about these matters.

(54) No one shall be arrested or imprisoned on the appeal of a woman for the death of any person except her husband.

(55) All fines that have been given to us unjustly and against the law of the land, and all fines that we have exacted unjustly, shall be entirely remitted or the matter decided by a majority judgement of the twenty-five barons referred to below in the clause for securing the peace [§ 61] together with Stephen, archbishop of Canterbury, if he can be present, and such others as he wishes to bring with him. If the archbishop cannot be present, proceedings shall continue without him, provided that if any of the twenty-five barons has been involved in a similar suit himself, his judgement shall be set aside, and someone else chosen and sworn in his place, as a substitute for the single occasion, by the rest of the twenty-five.

(56) If we have deprived or dispossessed any Welshmen of lands, liberties, or anything else in England or in Wales, without the lawful judgement of their equals, these are at once to be returned to them. A dispute on this point shall be determined in the Marches by the judgement of equals. English law shall apply to holdings of land in England, Welsh law to those in Wales, and the law of the Marches to those in the Marches. The Welsh shall treat us and ours in the same way.

(57) In cases where a Welshman was deprived or dispossessed of anything, without the lawful judgement of his equals, by our father King Henry or our brother King Richard, and it remains in our hands or is held by others under our warranty, we shall have respite for the period commonly allowed to Crusaders, unless a lawsuit has been begun, or an enquiry has been made at our order, before we took the Cross as a Crusader. But on our return from the Crusade, or if we abandon it, we will at once do full justice according to the laws of Wales and the said regions.

(58) We will at once return the son of Llywelyn, all Welsh hostages, and the charters delivered to us as security for the peace.

(59) With regard to the return of the sisters and hostages of Alexander, king of Scotland, his liberties and his rights, we will treat him in the same way as our other barons of England, unless it appears from the charters that we hold from his father, William, formerly king of Scotland, that he should be treated otherwise. This matter shall be resolved by the judgement of his equals in our court.

(60) All these customs and liberties that we have granted shall be observed in our kingdom in so far as concerns our own relations with our subjects. Let all men of our kingdom, whether clergy or laymen, observe them similarly in their relations with their own men.

(61) SINCE WE HAVE GRANTED ALL THESE THINGS for God, for the better ordering of our kingdom, and to allay the discord that has arisen between us and our barons, and since we desire that they shall be enjoyed in their entirety, with lasting strength, for ever, we give and grant to the barons the following security:

The barons shall elect twenty-five of their number to keep, and cause to be observed with all their might, the peace and liberties granted and confirmed to them by this charter.

If we, our chief justice, our officials, or any of our servants offend in any respect against any man, or transgress any of the articles of the peace or of this security, and the offence is made known to four of the said twenty-five barons, they shall come to us—or in our absence from the kingdom to the chief justice—to declare it and claim immediate redress. If we, or in our absence abroad the chief justice, make no redress within forty days, reckoning from the day on which the offence was declared to us or to him, the four barons shall refer the matter to the rest of the twenty-five barons, who may distrain upon and assail us in every way possible, with the support of the whole community of the land, by seizing our castles, lands, possessions, or anything else saving only our own person and those of the queen and our children, until they have secured such redress as they have determined upon. Having secured the redress, they may then resume their normal obedience to us.

Any man who so desires may take an oath to obey the commands of the twenty-five barons for the achievement of these ends, and to join with them in assailing us to the utmost of his power. We give public and free permission to take this oath to any man who so desires, and at no time will we prohibit any man from taking it. Indeed, we will compel any of our subjects who are unwilling to take it to swear it at our command.

If one of the twenty-five barons dies or leaves the country, or is prevented in any other way from discharging his duties, the rest of them shall choose another baron in his place, at their discretion, who shall be duly sworn in as they were.

In the event of disagreement among the twenty-five barons on any matter referred to them for decision, the verdict of the majority present shall have the same validity as a unanimous verdict of the whole twenty-five, whether these were all present or some of those summoned were unwilling or unable to appear.

The twenty-five barons shall swear to obey all the above articles faithfully, and shall cause them to be obeyed by others to the best of their power.

We will not seek to procure from anyone, either by our own efforts or those of a third party, anything by which any part of these concessions or liberties might be revoked or diminished. Should such a thing be procured, it shall be null void and we will at no time make use of it, either ourselves or through a third party.

(62) We have remitted and pardoned fully to all men any ill-will, hurt, or grudges that have arisen between us and our subjects, whether clergy or laymen, since the beginning of the dispute. We have in addition remitted fully, and for our own part have also pardoned, to all clergy and laymen any offences committed as a result of the said dispute between Easter in the sixteenth year of our reign [*i.e. 1215*] and the restoration of peace.

In addition we have caused letters patent to be made for the barons, bearing witness to this security and to the concessions set out above, over the seals of Stephen archbishop of Canterbury, Henry archbishop of Dublin, the other bishops named above, and Master Pandulf.

(63) IT IS ACCORDINGLY OUR WISH AND COMMAND that the English Church shall be free, and that men in our kingdom shall have and keep all these liberties, rights, and concessions, well and peaceably in their fulness and entirety for them and their heirs, of us and our heirs, in all things and all places for ever.

Both we and the barons have sworn that all this shall be observed in good faith and without deceit. Witness the abovementioned people and many others.

Given by our hand in the meadow that is called Runnymede, between Windsor and Staines, on the fifteenth day of June in the seventeenth year of our reign [*i.e. 1215: the new regnal year began on 28 May*].

APPENDIX H

The Mayflower Compact

November 11, 1620 [This was November 21, old-style calendar]

In name of God, Amen. We whose names are underwriten, the loyall subjects of our dread soveraigne Lord, King James, by ye grace of God, of Great Britaine, Franc, & Ireland king, defender of ye faith, &c., haveing undertaken, for ye glorie of God, and advancemente of ye Christian faith, and honour of our king & countrie, a voyage to plant ye first colonie in ye Northerne parts of Virginia, doe by these presents solemnly & mutualy in ye presence of God, and one of another, covenant & combine our selves togeather into a civill body politick, for our better ordering & preservation & furtherance of ye ends aforesaid; and by vertue hearof to enacte, constitute, and frame such just & equall lawes, ordinances, acts, constitutions, & offices, from time to time, as shall be thought most meete & convenient for ye generall good of ye Colonie, unto which we promise all due submission and obedience. In witnes wherof we have hereunder subscribed our names at Cap-Codd ye 11. of November, in ye year of ye raigne of our soveraigne lord, King James, of England, France, & Ireland ye eighteenth, and of Scotland ye fiftie fourth. Ano: Dom. 1620.

Mr. John Carver	Mr. Stephen Hopkins
Mr. William Bradford	Digery Priest
Mr. Edward Winslow	Thomas Williams
Mr. William Brewster	Gilbert Winslow
Isaac Allerton	Edmund Margesson
Miles Standish	Peter Brown
John Alden	Richard Bitteridge
John Turner	George Soule
Francis Eaton	Edward Tilly
James Chilton	John Tilly
John Craxton	Francis Cooke
John Billington	Thomas Rogers
Joses Fletcher	Thomas Tinker
John Goodman	John Ridgate
Mr. Samuel Fuller	Edward Fuller
Mr. Christopher Martin	Richard Clark
Mr. William Mullins	Richard Gardiner
Mr. William White	Mr. John Allerton
Mr. Richard Warren	Thomas English
John Howland	Edward Doten

Edward Liester

Ordinance of 1787

An Ordinance For The Government Of The Territory Of The
United States Northwest Of the River Ohio
(Northwest Ordinance)

Section 1

Be it ordained by the United States in Congress assembled, That the said territory, for the purpose of temporary government, be one district, subject, however, to be divided into two districts, as future circumstances may, in the opinion of Congress, make it expedient.

Section 2

[Relates to the descent and distribution of estates.]

Section 3

Be it ordained by the authority aforesaid, That there shall be appointed, from time to time, by Congress, a governor, whose commission shall continue in force for the term of three years, unless sooner revoked by Congress; he shall reside in the district, and have a freehold estate therein in one thousand acres of land, while in the exercise of his office.

Section 4

There shall be appointed from time to time, by Congress, a secretary, whose commission shall continue in force for four years, unless sooner revoked; he shall reside in the district and have a freehold estate therein, in five hundred acres of land, while in the exercise of his office. It shall be his duty to keep and preserve the acts and laws passed by the legislature, and the public records of the district, and the proceedings of the governor in his executive department, and transmit authentic copies of such acts and proceedings every six months to the Secretary of Congress. There shall also be appointed a court, to consist of three judges, any two of whom to form a court, who shall have a common-law jurisdiction, and reside in the district, and have each therein a freehold estate, in five hundred acres of land, while in the exercise of their offices; and their commissions shall continue in force during good behavior.

Section 5

The governor and judges, or a majority of them, shall adopt and publish in the district such laws of the original States, criminal and civil, as may be necessary, and best suited to the circumstances of the district, and report them to Congress from time to time, which laws shall be in force in the district until the organization of the general assembly therein, unless disapproved of by the Congress; but afterwards the legislature shall have authority to alter them as they shall think fit.

Section 6

The governor, for the time being, shall be commander-in-chief of the militia, appoint and commission all officers in the same below the rank of general officers; all general officers shall be appointed and commissioned by Congress.

Section 7

Previous to the organization of the general assembly the governor shall appoint such magistrates, and other civil officers, in each county or township, as he shall find necessary for the preservation of the peace and good order in the same. After the general assembly shall be organized the powers and duties of the magistrates and other civil officers shall be regulated and defined by the said assembly; but all magistrates and other civil officers, not herein otherwise directed, shall, during the continuance of this temporary government, be appointed by the governor.

Section 8

For the prevention of crimes and injuries, the laws to be adopted or made shall have force in all parts of the district, and for the execution of process, criminal and civil, the governor shall make proper divisions thereof; and he shall proceed, from time to time, as circumstances may require, to lay out the parts of the district in which the Indian titles shall have been extinguished, into countries and townships, subject, however, to such alterations as may thereafter be made by the legislature.

Section 9

So soon as there shall be five thousand free male inhabitants, of full age, in the district, upon giving proof thereof to the governor, they shall receive authority, with time and place, to elect representatives from their counties or townships, to represent them in the general assembly: *Provided,* That for every five hundred free male inhabitants there shall be one representative, and so on, progressively, with the number of free male inhabitants, shall the right of representation increase, until the number of representatives shall amount to twenty-five; after which the number of proportion of representatives, shall be regulated by the legislature: *Provided,* That no person be eligible or qualified to act as a representative, unless he shall have been a citizen of one of the United States three years, and be a resident in the district, or unless he shall have resided in the district three years; and, in either case, shall likewise hold in his own right, in fee simple, two hundred acres of land within the same: *Provided, also,* That a freehold in fifty acres of land in the district, having been a citizen of one of the States, and being resident in the district, or the like freehold and two years' residence in the district, shall be necessary to qualify a man as an elector of a representative.

Section 10

The representatives thus elected shall serve for the term of two years; and in case of the death of a representative, or removal from office, the governor shall issue a writ to the county or township, for which he was a member, to elect another in his stead, to serve for the residue of the term.

Section 11

The general assembly, or legislature, shall consist of the governor, legislative council, and a house of representatives. The legislative council shall consist of five members, to continue in office five years, unless sooner removed by Congress; any three of whom to be a quorum, and the members of the council shall be nominated and appointed in the following manner, to wit: As soon as representatives shall be elected the governor shall appoint a time and place for them to meet together, and when met they shall nominate ten persons, residents in the district, and each possessed of a freehold in five hundred acres of land, and return their names to Congress, five of whom Congress shall appoint and commission to service as aforesaid; and whenever a vacancy shall happen in the council, by death or removal from office, the house of representatives shall nominate two persons, qualified as aforesaid, for each vacancy, and return their names to Congress, one of whom Congress shall appoint and commission for the residue of the term; and every five years, four months at least before the expiration of the time of service of the members of council, the said house shall nominate ten persons, qualified as aforesaid, and return their names to Congress, five of whom Congress shall appoint and commission to serve as members of the council five years, unless sooner removed. And the governor, legislative council, and house of representatives shall have authority to make laws in all cases for the good government of the district, not repugnant to the principles and articles in this ordinance established and declared. And all bills, having passed by a majority in the house, and by a majority in the council, shall be referred to the governor for his assent; but no bill, or legislative act whatever, shall be of any force without his assent. The governor shall have power to convene, prorogue, and dissolve the general assembly when, in his opinion, it shall be expedient.

Section 12

(The governor and other officers to take an oath.) As soon as a legislature shall be formed in the district, the council and house assembled, in one room, shall have authority, by joint ballot, to elect a delegate to Congress who shall have a seat in Congress, with a right of debating, but not of voting, during this temporary government.

Section 13

And for extending the fundamental principles of civil and religious liberty, which form the basis whereon these republics, their laws and constitutions, are erected; to fix and establish those principles as the basis of all laws, constitutions, and governments, which forever hereafter shall be formed in the said territory; to provide, also, for the establishment of States, and permanent government therein, and for their admission to a share in the Federal councils on an equal footing with the original States, at as early periods as may be consistent with the general interest:

Section 14

It is hereby ordained and declared, by the authority aforesaid, that the following articles shall be considered as articles of compact, between the original States and the people and States in the said territory, and forever remain unalterable, unless by common consent, to wit:

Article I

No person, demeaning himself in a peaceable and orderly manner, shall ever be molested on account of his mode of worship, or religious sentiments, in the said territories.

Article II

The inhabitants of the said territory shall always be entitled to the benefits of the wit of *habeas corpus,* and of the trial by jury; of a proportionate representation of the people in the legislature, and of judicial proceedings according to the course of common law. All persons shall be bailable, unless for capital offences, where the proof shall be evident, or the presumption great. All fines shall be moderate; and no cruel or unusual punishments shall be inflicted. No man shall be deprived of his liberty or property, but by the judgment of his peers, or the law of the land, and should the public exigencies make it necessary, for the common preservation, to take any person's property, or to demand his particular services, full compensation shall be made for the same. And, in the just preservation of rights and property, it is understood and declared, that no law ought ever to be made or have force in the said territory, that shall, in any manner whatever, interfere with or affect private contracts, or engagements, bona fide, and without fraud previously formed.

Article III

Religion, morality, and knowledge being necessary to good government and the happiness of mankind, schools and the means of education shall forever be encouraged. The utmost good faith shall always be observed towards the Indians; their lands and property shall never be taken from them without their consent; and in their property, rights, and liberty they never shall be invaded or disturbed, unless in just and lawful wars authorized by Congress; but laws founded in justice and humanity shall, from time to time, be made, for preventing wrongs being done to them, and for preserving peace and friendship with them.

Article IV

The said territory, and the States which may be formed therein, shall forever remain a part of this confederacy of the United States of America, subject to the Articles of Confederation, and to such alterations therein as shall be constitutionally made; and to all acts and ordinances of the United States in Congress assembled, conformable thereto. The inhabitants and settlers in the said territory shall be subject to pay a part of the Federal debts, contracted, or to be contracted, and a proportional part of the expenses of government to be apportioned on them by Congress, according to the same common rule and measure by which apportionments thereof shall be made on the other States; and the taxes for paying their proportion shall be laid and levied by the authority and direction of the legislatures of the district, or districts, or new States, as in the original States, within the time agreed upon by the United States in Congress assembled. The legislatures of those districts, or new States, shall never interfere with the primary disposal of soil by the United States in Congress assembled, nor with any regulations Congress may find necessary for securing the title in such soil to the *bona fide* purchasers. No tax shall be imposed on lands the property of the United States; and in no case shall nonresident proprietors be taxed higher than residents. The navigable waters leading into the Mississippi and Saint Lawrence, and the carrying places between the same, shall be common highways, and forever free, as well to the inhabitants of the said territory as to the citizens of the United States, and those of any other States that may be admitted into the confederacy, without any tax, impost, or duty therefor.

Article V

There shall be formed in the said territory not less than three nor more than five States; and the boundaries of the States, as soon as Virginia shall alter her act of cession and consent to the same, shall become fixed and established as follows, to wit: the western State, in the said territory, shall be bounded by the Mississippi, the Ohio, and the Wabash Rivers; a direct line drawn from the Wabash and Post Vincents, due north, to the territorial line between the United States and Canada; and by the said territorial line to the Lake of the Woods and Mississippi. The middle State shall be bounded by the said direct line, the Wabash from Post Vincents to the Ohio, by the Ohio, by a direct line drawn due north from the mouth of the Great Miami to the said territorial line, and by the said territorial line. The eastern State shall be bounded by the last-mentioned direct line, the Ohio,

Pennsylvania, and the said territorial line: *Provided, however,* And it is further understood and declared, that the boundaries of these three States shall be subject so far to be altered, that, if Congress shall hereafter find it expedient, they shall have authority to form one or two States in that part of the said territory which lies north of an east and west line drawn through the southerly bend or extreme of Lake Michigan. And whenever any of the said States shall have sixty thousand free inhabitants therein, such State shall be admitted, by its delegates, into the Congress of the United States, on an equal footing with the original States, in all respects whatever; and shall be at liberty to form a permanent constitution and State government: *Provided,* The constitution and government, so to be formed, shall be republican, and in conformity to the principles contained in these articles, and, so far as it can be consistent with the general interest of the confederacy, such admission shall be allowed at an earlier period, and when there may be a less number of free inhabitants in the State than sixty thousand.

Article VI

There shall be neither slaver nor involuntary servitude in the said territory, otherwise than in the punishment of crimes, whereof the party shall have been duly convicted: Provided always, That any person escaping into the same, from whom labor or service is lawfully claimed in any one of the original States, such fugitive may be lawfully reclaimed, and conveyed to the person claiming his or her labor or service as aforesaid.

The Rights of Colonists
1772

(Adopted by the Boston Town Meeting)

Among the Natural Rights of the Colonists are these First. a Right to *Life*; Secondly to *Liberty*; thirdly to *Property*; together with the Right to support and defend them in the best manner they can—Those are evident Branches of, rather than deductions from the Duty of Self Preservation, commonly called the first Law of Nature—

All Men have a Right to remain in a State of Nature as long as they please: And in case of intollerable Oppression, Civil or Religious, to leave the Society they belong to, and enter into another.—

When Men enter into Society, it is by voluntary consent; and they have a right to demand and insist upon the performance of such conditions, And previous limitations as form an equitable original compact.—

Every natural Right not expressly given up or from the nature of a Social Compact necessarily ceded remains.—

All positive and civil laws, should conform as far as possible, to the Law of natural reason and equity.—

As neither reason requires, nor religion permits the contrary, every Man living in or out of a state of civil society, has a right peaceably and quietly to worship God according to the dictates of his conscience.....

The natural liberty of Men by entring into society is abridg'd or restrained so far only as is necessary for the Great end of Society the best good of the whole—

In the state of nature, every man is under God, Judge and sole Judge, of his own rights and the injuries done him: By entering into society, he agrees to an Arbiter or indifferent Judge between him and his neighbours; but he no more renounces his original right, than by taking a cause out of the ordinary course of law, and leaving the decision to Referees or indifferent Arbitrations....

"The natural liberty of man is to be free from any superior power on earth, and not to be under the will or legislative authority of man; but only to have the law of nature for his rule..."

In short it is the greatest absurdity to suppose it in the power of one or any number of men at the entering into society, to renounce their essential natural rights, or the means of preserving those rights when the great end of civil government from the very nature of its institution is for the support, protection and defence of those very rights: the principal of which as is before observed, are life, liberty and property. If men through fear, fraud or mistake, should in terms renounce and give up any essential natural right, the eternal law of reason and the great end of society, would absolutely vacate such renunciation; the right to freedom being *the gift* of God Almighty, it is not in the power of Man to alienate this gift, and voluntarily become a slave.....

A Common Wealth or state is a body politick or civil society of men, united together to promote their mutual safety and prosperity, by means of their union.

The *absolute Rights* of Englishman, and all freemen in or out of Civil society, are principally, *personal security personal liberty* and *private property.*

All Persons born in the British American Colonies are by the laws of God and nature, and by the Common law of England, *exclusive of all charters from the Crown,* well Entitled, and by the Acts of British Parliament are declared to be entitled to all natural essential, inherent & inseperable Rights Liberties and Privileges of Subjects born in Great Britian, or within the Realm. Among those Rights are the following; which no men or body of men, consistently with their own rights as men and citizens or members of society, can for themselves give up, or take away from others.

First, "The first fundamental positive law of all Commonwealths or States, is the establishing the legislative power; as the first fundamental natural law also, which is to govern even the legislative power itself, is the preservation of the Society."

Secondly, The Legislative has no right to absolute arbitrary power over the lives and fortunes of the people....

Thirdly, The supreme power cannot Justly take from any man, any part of his property without his consent, in person or by his Representative.—

These are some of the first principles of natural law & Justice, and the great Barriers of all free states, and of the British Constitution in particular. It is utterly irreconcileable to these principles, and to many other fundamental maxims of the common law, common sense and reason, that a British house of commons, should have a right, at pleasure, to give and grant the property of the Colonists.

The Ten Commandments
from the *New King James Version*

Exodus

20And God spoke all these words, saying:

2 "I *am* the Lord your God, who brought you out of the land Egypt, out of the house of bondage.

3 "You shall have no other gods before Me.

4 "You shall not make for yourself a carved image—any likeness of *anything* that is in heaven above, or that *is* in the earth beneath, or that is in the water under the earth;

5 you shall not bow down to them nor serve them. For I, the Lord your God, *am* a jealous God, visiting the iniquity of the fathers upon the children to the third and fourth *generations* of those who hate Me,

6 but showing mercy to thousands, to those who love Me and keep My commandments.

7 "You shall not take the name of the Lord your God in vain, for the Lord will not hold *him* guiltless who takes His name in vain.

8 "Remember the Sabbath day, to keep it holy.

9 Six days you shall labor and do all your work,

10 but the seventh day *is* the Sabbath to the Lord your God. *In it* you shall do no work: you, nor your son, nor your daughter, nor your male servant, nor your female servant, nor your cattle, nor your stranger who is within your gates.

11 For *in* six days the Lord made the heavens and the earth, the sea, and all that *is* in them, and rested on the seventh day. Therefore the Lord blessed the Sabbath day and hallowed it.

12 "Honor your father and your mother, that your days may be long upon the land which the Lord your God is giving you.

13 "You shall not murder.

14 "You shall not commit adultery.

15 "You shall not steal.

16 "You shall not bear false witness against your neighbor.

17 "You shall not covet your neighbor's house; you shall not covet your neighbor's wife, nor his male servant, nor female servant, nor his ox, nor his donkey, nor anything that *is* your neighbor's.

The Constitution of the United States of America, 1787

Preface

WE, THE PEOPLE of the United States, in Order to form a more perfect Union, establish Justice, insure domestic Tranquillity, provide for the common defence, promote the general Welfare, and secure the Blessings of Liberty to ourselves and our Posterity, do ordain and establish this Constitution for the United States of America.

Article I.

Section 1. All legislative Powers herein granted shall be vested in a Congress of the United States, which shall consist of a Senate and House of Representatives.

Section 2. The House of Representatives shall be composed of Members chosen every second Year by the People of the several States, and the Electors in each State shall have the Qualifications requisite for Electors of the most numerous Branch of the State Legislature.

No person shall be a Representative who shall not have attained to the Age of twenty-five Years, and been seven Years a Citizen of the United States, and who shall not, when elected, be an Inhabitant of that State in which he shall be chosen.

Representatives and direct Taxes shall be apportioned among the several States which may be included within this Union, according to their respective Numbers, which shall be determined by adding to the whole Number of free Persons, including those bound to Service for a Term of Years, and excluding Indians not taxed, three fifths of all other Persons. The actual Enumeration shall be made within three Years after the first Meeting of the Congress of the United States, and within every subsequent Term of ten Years, in such Manner as they shall by Law direct. The number of Representatives shall not exceed one for every thirty Thousand, but each State shall have at Least one Representative; and until such enumeration shall be made, the State of New Hampshire shall be entitled to chuse three, Massachusetts eight, Rhode-Island and Providence Plantations one, Connecticut five, New-York six, New Jersey four, Pennsylvania eight, Delaware one, Maryland six, Virginia ten, North Carolina five, South Carolina five, and Georgia three.

When vacancies happen in the Representation from any state, the Executive Authority thereof shall issue Writs of Election to fill such Vacancies.

The House of Representatives shall chuse their Speaker and other Officers; and shall have the sole Power of Impeachment.

Section 3. The Senate of the United States shall be composed of two Senators from each State, chosen by the Legislature thereof, for six Years; and each Senator shall have one Vote.

Immediately after they shall be assembled in Consequence of the first Election, they shall be divided as equally as may be into three Classes. The Seats of the Senators of the first Class shall be vacated at the expiration of the second Year, of the second Class at the expiration of the fourth Year, and of the third Class at the expiration of the sixth Year, so that one third may be chosen every second Year; and if Vacancies happen by Resignation, or otherwise, during the Recess of the Legislature of any State, the Executive thereof may make temporary Appointments until the next Meeting of the Legislature, which shall then fill such Vacancies.

No Person shall be a Senator who shall not have attained to the Age of thirty Years, and been nine Years a Citizen of the United States, and who shall not, when elected, be an Inhabitant of that State for which he shall be chosen.

The Vice President of the United States shall be President of the Senate, but shall have no Vote, unless they be equally divided.

The Senate shall chuse their other Officers, and also a President pro tempore, in the Absence of the Vice President, or when he shall exercise the Office of President of the United States.

The Senate shall have the sole Power to try all Impeachments. When sitting for that Purpose, they shall be on Oath or Affirmation. When the President of the United States is tried, the Chief Justice shall preside: And no Person shall be convicted without the Concurrence of two thirds of the Members present.

Judgment in Cases of Impeachment shall not extend further than to removal from Office, and disqualification to hold and enjoy any Office of honor, Trust or Profit under the United States: but the Party convicted shall nevertheless be liable and subject to Indictment, Trial, Judgment and Punishment, according to Law.

Section 4. The Times, Places and Manner of holding Elections for Senators and Representatives, shall be prescribed in each State by the Legislature thereof; but the Congress may at any time by Law make or alter such Regulations, except as to the Places of chusing Senators.

The Congress shall assemble at least once in every Year, and such Meeting shall be on the first Monday in December, unless they shall by Law appoint a different Day.

Section 5. Each House shall be the Judge of the Elections, Returns and Qualifications of its own Members, and a Majority of each shall constitute a Quorum to do Business; but a smaller Number may adjourn from day to day, and may be authorized to compel the Attendance of absent Members, in such Manner, and under such Penalties as each House may provide.

Each House may determine the Rules of its Proceedings, punish its Members for disorderly Behaviour, and, with the Concurrence of two thirds, expel a Member.

Each House shall keep a Journal of its Proceedings, and from time to time publish the same, excepting such Parts as may in their Judgment require Secrecy; and the Yeas and Nays of the Members of either House on any question shall, at the Desire of one fifth of those Present, be entered on the Journal.

Neither House, during the Session of Congress, shall, without the Consent of the other, adjourn for more than three days, nor to any other Place than that in which the two Houses shall be sitting.

Section 6. The Senators and Representatives shall receive a Compensation for their Services, to be ascertained by Law, and paid out of the Treasury of the United States. They shall in all Cases, except Treason, Felony and Breach of the Peace, be privileged from Arrest during their Attendance at the Session of their respective Houses, and in going to and returning from the same; and for any Speech or Debate in either House, they shall not be questioned in any other Place.

No Senator or Representative shall, during the Time for which he was elected, be appointed to any civil Office under the authority of the United States, which shall have been created, or the Emoluments whereof shall have been encreased during such time; and no Person holding any Office under the United States, shall be a Member of either House during his Continuance in Office.

Section 7. All Bills for raising Revenue shall originate in the House of Representatives; but the Senate may propose or concur with Amendments as on other Bills.

Every Bill which shall have passed the House of Representatives and the Senate, shall, before it becomes a Law, be presented to the President of the United States; If he approve he shall sign it, but if not he shall return it, with his Objections to that House in which it shall have originated, who shall enter the Objections at large on their Journal, and proceed to reconsider it. If after such Reconsideration two thirds of that house shall agree to pass the Bill, it shall be sent, together with the Objections, to the other House, by which it shall likewise be reconsidered, and if approved by two thirds of that House, it shall become a Law. But in all such Cases the Votes of both Houses shall be determined by yeas and Nays, and the Names of the Persons voting for and against the Bill shall be entered on the Journal of each House respectively. If any Bill shall not be returned by the President within ten Days (Sundays excepted) after it shall have been presented to him, the Same shall be a Law, in like Manner as if he had signed it, unless the Congress by their Adjournment prevent its Return, in which Case it shall not be a Law.

Every Order, Resolution, or Vote to which the Concurrence of the Senate and House of Representatives may be necessary (except on a question of Adjournment) shall be presented to the President of the United States; and before the Same shall take Effect, shall be approved by him, or being disapproved by him, shall be repassed by two thirds of the Senate and House of Representatives, according to the Rules and Limitations prescribed in the Case of a Bill.

Section 8. The Congress shall have Power to lay and collect Taxes, Duties, Imposts and Excises, to pay the Debts and provide for the common Defence and general Welfare of the United States; but all Duties, Imposts and Excises shall be uniform throughout the United States;

To borrow Money on the credit of the United States;

To regulate Commerce with foreign Nations, and among the several States, and with the Indian Tribes;

To establish an uniform Rule of Naturalization, and uniform Laws on the subject of Bankruptcies throughout the United States;

To coin Money, regulate the Value thereof, and of foreign Coin, and fix the Standard of Weights and Measures;

To provide for the Punishment of counterfeiting the Securities and current Coin of the United States;

To establish Post Offices and post Roads;

To promote the Progress of Science and useful Arts, by securing for limited Times to Authors and Inventors the exclusive Right to their respective Writings and Discoveries;

To constitute Tribunals inferior to the supreme Court;

To define and punish Piracies and Felonies committed on the high Seas, and Offenses against the Law of Nations;

To declare War, grant Letters of Marque and Reprisal, and make Rules concerning Captures on Land and Water;

To raise and support Armies, but no Appropriation of Money to that Use shall be for a longer term than two Years;

To provide and maintain a Navy;

To make Rules for the Government and Regulation of the land and naval Forces;

To provide for calling forth the Militia to execute the Laws of the Union, suppress Insurrections and repel Invasions;

To provide for organizing, arming, and disciplining, the Militia, and for governing such Part of them as may be employed in the Service of the United States, reserving to the States respectively, the Appointment of the Officers, and the Authority of training the Militia according to the discipline prescribed by Congress;

To exercise exclusive Legislation in all Cases whatsoever, over such District (not exceeding ten Miles square) as may, by Cession of particular States, and the Acceptance of Congress, become the Seat of the Government of the United States, and to exercise like Authority over all Places purchased by the Consent of the Legislature of the State in which the Same shall be, for the Erection of Forts, Magazines, Arsenals, dock-Yards, and other needful Buildings;—And

To make all Laws which shall be necessary and proper for carrying into Execution the foregoing Powers, and all other Powers vested by this Constitution in the Government of the United States, or in any Department or Officer thereof.

Section 9. The Migration or Importation of such Persons as any of the States now existing shall think proper to admit, shall not be prohibited by the Congress prior to the Year one thousand eight hundred and eight, but a Tax or Duty may be imposed on such Importation, not exceeding ten dollars for each Person.

The Privilege of the Writ of Habeas Corpus shall not be suspended, unless when in Cases of Rebellion or Invasion the public Safety may require it.

No Bill of Attainder or ex post facto Law shall be passed.

No Capitation, or other direct, Tax shall be laid, unless in Proportion to the Census or Enumeration herein before directed to be taken.

No Tax or Duty shall be laid on Articles exported from any State.

No Preference shall be given by any Regulation of Commerce or Revenue to the Ports of one State over those of another: nor shall Vessels bound to, or from, one State, be obliged to enter, clear, or pay Duties in another.

No Money shall be drawn from the Treasury, but in Consequence of Appropriations made by Law; and a regular Statement and Account of the Receipts and Expenditures of all public Money shall be published from time to time.

No Title of Nobility shall be granted by the United States: and no Person holding any Office of Profit or Trust under them, shall, without the Consent of the Congress, accept of any present, Emolument, Office, or Title, of any kind whatever, from any King, Prince, or foreign State.

Section 10. No State shall enter into any Treaty, Alliance, or Confederation; grant Letters of Marque and Reprisal; coin Money; emit Bills of Credit; make any Thing but gold and silver Coin a Tender in Payment of Debts; pass any Bill of Attainder, ex post facto Law, or Law impairing the Obligation of Contracts, or grant any Title of Nobility.

No State shall, without the Consent of the Congress, lay any Imposts or Duties on Imports or Exports, except what may be absolutely necessary for executing it's inspection Laws: and the net Produce of all Duties and Imposts, laid by any State on Imports or Exports, shall be for the Use of the Treasury of the United States; and all such Laws shall be subject to the Revision and Controul of the Congress.

No State shall, without the Consent of Congress, lay any Duty of Tonnage, keep Troops, or Ships of War in time of Peace, enter into any Agreement or Compact with another State, or with a foreign Power, or engage in War, unless actually invaded, or in such imminent Danger as will not admit of delay.

Article II.

Section 1. The executive Power shall be vested in a President of the United States of America. He shall hold his Office during the Term of four Years, and, together with the Vice President chosen for the same Term, be elected, as follows:

Each State shall appoint, in such Manner as the Legislature thereof may direct, a Number of Electors, equal to the whole Number of Senators and Representatives to which the State may be entitled in the Congress: but no Senator or Representative, or Person holding an Office of Trust or Profit under the United States, shall be appointed an Elector.

The Electors shall meet in their respective States, and vote by Ballot for two Persons, of whom one at least shall not lie an Inhabitant of the same State with themselves. And they shall make a List of all the Persons voted for, and of the Number of Votes for each; which List they shall sign and certify, and transmit sealed to the Seat of the Government of the United States, directed to the President of the Senate. The President of the Senate shall, in the Presence of the Senate and House of Representatives, open all the Certificates, and the Votes shall then be counted. The Person having the greatest Number of Votes shall be the President, if such Number be a Majority of the whole Number of Electors appointed; and if there be more than one who have such Majority, and have an equal Number of votes, then the House of Representatives shall immediately chuse by Ballot one of them for President; and if no Person have a Majority, then from the five highest on the List the said House shall in like Manner chuse the President. But in chusing the President, the Votes shall be taken by States, the Representation from each State having one Vote; a quorum for this Purpose shall consist of a Member or Members from two thirds of the States, and a Majority of all the States shall be necessary to a Choice. In every Case, after the Choice of the President, the Person having the greatest Number of Votes of the Electors shall be the Vice President. But if there should remain two or more who have equal Votes, the Senate shall chuse from them by Ballot the Vice President.

The Congress may determine the Time of chusing the Electors, and the Day on which they shall give their Votes; which Day shall be the same throughout the United States.

No Person except a natural born Citizen, or a Citizen of the United States, at the time of the Adoption of this Constitution, shall be eligible to the Office of President; neither shall any Person be eligible to that Office who shall not have attained to the Age of thirty five Years, and been fourteen Years a Resident within the United States.

In Case of the Removal of the President from Office, or of his Death, Resignation, or Inability to discharge the Powers and Duties of the said Office, the Same shall devolve on the Vice President, and the Congress may by Law provide for the Case of Removal, Death, Resignation or Inability, both of the President and Vice President, declaring what Officer shall then act as President, and such Officer shall act accordingly, until the Disability be removed, or a President shall be elected.

The President shall, at stated Times, receive for his Services, a Compensation, which shall neither be increased nor diminished during the Period for which he shall have been elected, and he shall not receive within that Period any other Emolument from the United States, or any of them.

Before he enters on the Execution of his Office, he shall take the following Oath or Affirmation:—"I do solemnly swear (or affirm) that I will faithfully execute the Office of President of the United States, and will to the best of my Ability, preserve, protect and defend the Constitution of the United States."

Section 2. The President shall be Commander in Chief of the Army and Navy of the United States, and of the Militia of the several States, when called into the actual Service of the United States; he may require the Opinion, in writing, of the principal Officer in each of the executive Departments, upon any Subject relating to the Duties of their respective Offices, and he shall have Power to grant Reprieves and Pardons for Offenses against the United States, except in Cases of Impeachment.

He shall have Power, by and with the Advice and Consent of the Senate, to make Treaties, provided two thirds of the Senators present concur; and he shall nominate, and by and with the Advice and Consent of the Senate, shall appoint Ambassadors, other public Ministers and Consuls, Judges of the supreme Court, and all other Officers of the United States, whose Appointments are not herein otherwise provided for, and which shall be established by Law: but the Congress may by Law vest the Appointment of such inferior Officers, as they think proper, in the President alone, in the Courts of Law, or in the Heads of Departments.

The President shall have Power to fill up all Vacancies that may happen during the Recess of the Senate, by granting Commissions which shall expire at the End of their next Session.

Section 3. He shall from time to time give to the Congress Information of the State of the Union, and recommend to their Consideration such Measures as he shall judge necessary and expedient; he may, on extraordinary Occasions, convene both Houses, or either of them, and in Case of Disagreement between them, with Respect to the Time of Adjournment, he may adjourn them to such Time as he shall think proper; he shall receive Ambassadors and other public Ministers; he shall take Care that the Laws be faithfully executed, and shall Commission all the Officers of the United States.

Section 4. The President, Vice President and all civil Officers of the United States, shall be removed from Office on Impeachment for, and Conviction of, Treason, Bribery, or other high Crimes and Misdemeanors.

Article III.

Section 1. The judicial Power of the United States, shall be vested in one supreme Court, and in such inferior Courts as the Congress may from time to time ordain and establish. The Judges, both of the supreme and inferior Courts, shall hold their Offices during good Behaviour, and shall, at stated Times, receive for their Services, a Compensation, which shall not be diminished during their Continuance in Office.

Section 2. The judicial Power shall extend to all Cases, in Law and Equity, arising under this Constitution, the Laws of the United States, and Treaties made, or which shall be made, under their Authority;—to all Cases affecting Ambassadors, other public Ministers and Consuls;—to all Cases of admiralty and maritime Jurisdiction;—to Controversies to which the United States shall be a Party;—to Controversies between two or more States;—between a State and Citizens of another State;—between Citizens of Different States;—between Citizens of the same State claiming Lands under Grants of different States, and between a State, or the Citizens thereof, and foreign States, Citizens or Subjects.

In all cases affecting Ambassadors, other public Ministers and Consuls, and those in which a State shall be Party, the supreme Court shall have original Jurisdiction. In all the other Cases before mentioned, the supreme Court shall have appellate Jurisdiction, both as to Law and Fact, with such Exceptions, and under such Regulations as the Congress shall make.

The Trial of all Crimes, except in Cases of Impeachment; shall be by Jury; and such Trial shall be held in the State where the said Crimes shall have been committed; but when not committed within any State, the Trial shall be at such Place or Places as the Congress may by Law have directed.

Section 3. Treason against the United States, shall consist only in levying War against them, or in adhering to their Enemies, giving them Aid and Comfort. No Person shall be convicted of Treason unless on the Testimony of two Witnesses to the same overt Act, or on Confession in open Court.

The Congress shall have Power to declare the Punishment of Treason, but no Attainder of Treason shall work Corruption of Blood, or Forfeiture except during the Life of the Person attainted.

Article IV.

Section 1. Full Faith and Credit shall be given in each State to the public Acts, Records, and judicial Proceedings of every other State; And the Congress may by general Laws prescribe the Manner in which such Acts, Records and Proceedings shall be proved, and the Effect thereof.

Section 2. The Citizens of each State shall be entitled to all Privileges and Immunities of Citizens in the several States.

A Person charged in any State with Treason, Felony, or other Crime, who shall flee from Justice, and be found in another State, shall on Demand of the executive Authority of the State from which he fled, be delivered up, to be removed to the State having Jurisdiction of the Crime.

No person held to Service or Labour in one State, under the Laws thereof, escaping into another, shall, in Consequence of any Law or Regulation therein, be discharged from such Service or Labour, But shall be delivered up on Claim of the Party to whom such Service or Labour may be due.

Section 3. New States may be admitted by the Congress into this Union; but no new State shall be formed or erected within the Jurisdiction of any other State; nor any State be formed by the Junction of two or more States, or Parts of States, without the Consent of the Legislatures of the States concerned as well as of the Congress. The Congress shall have Power to dispose of and make all needful Rules and Regulations respecting the Territory or other Property belonging to the United States; and nothing in this Constitution shall be so construed as to Prejudice any Claims of the United States, or of any particular State.

Section 4. The United States shall guarantee to every State in this Union a Republican Form of Government, and shall protect each of them against Invasion; and on Application of the Legislature, or of the Executive (when the Legislature cannot be convened) against domestic Violence.

Article V.

The Congress, whenever two thirds of both Houses shall deem it necessary, shall propose Amendments to this Constitution, or, on the Application of the Legislatures of two thirds of the several States, shall call a Convention for proposing Amendments, which, in either Case, shall be valid to all Intents and Purposes, as Part of this Constitution, when ratified by the Legislatures of three fourths of the several States, or by Conventions in three fourths thereof, as the one or the other Mode of Ratification may be proposed by the Congress; Provided that no Amendment which may be made prior to the Year One thousand eight hundred and eight shall in any Manner affect the first and fourth Clauses in the Ninth Section of the first Article; and that no State, without its Consent, shall be deprived of its equal Suffrage in the Senate.

Article VI.

All Debts contracted and Engagements entered into, before the Adoption of this Constitution, shall be as valid against the United States under this Constitution, as under the Confederation.

This Constitution, and the Laws of the United States which shall be made in Pursuance thereof; and all Treaties made, or which shall be made, under the Authority of the United States, shall be the supreme Law of the Land; and the Judges in every State shall be bound thereby, any Thing in the Constitution or Laws of any State to the Contrary notwithstanding.

The Senators and Representatives before mentioned, and the Members of the several State Legislatures, and all executive and judicial Officers, both of the United States and of the several States, shall be bound by Oath or Affirmation, to support this Constitution; but no religious Test shall ever be required as a Qualification to any Office or public Trust under the United States

Article VII.

The Ratification of the Conventions of nine States, shall be sufficient for the Establishment of this Constitution between the States so ratifying the Same.

Done in Convention by the Unanimous Consent of the States present the Seventeenth Day of September in the Year of our Lord one thousand seven hundred and Eighty seven and of the Independence of the United States of America the Twelfth In Witness whereof We have hereunto subscribed our Names,

George Washington—President
and deputy from Virginia

New Hampshire
  John Langdon
  Nicholas Gilman

Massachusetts
  Nathaniel Gorham
  Rufus King

Connecticut
  Wm. Saml. Johnson
  Roger Sherman

New York
  Alexander Hamilton

New Jersey
  Wil: Livingston
  David Brearley
  Wm. Paterson
  Jona: Dayton

Pennsylvania
  B. Franklin
  Thomas Mifflin
  Robt Morris
  Geo. Clymer
  Thos. FitzSimons
  Jared Ingersoll
  James Wilson
  Gouv Morris

Delaware
  Geo: Read
  Gunning Bedford jun
  John Dickinson
  Richard Basset
  Jaco: Broom

Maryland
  James McHenry
  Dan of St Thos. Jenifer
  Danl Carroll

Virginia
  John Blair—
  James Madison Jr.

North Carolina
  Wm. Blount
  Richd. Dobbs Spaight
  Hu Williamson

South Carolina
  J. Rutledge
  Charles C. Pinckney
  Charles Pinckney
  Pierce Butler

Georgia
  William Few
  Abr Baldwin

Attest William Jackson Secretary

Amendments to the Constitution
of the United States of America

Amendment I.

Congress shall make no law respecting an establishment of religion, or prohibiting the free exercise thereof; or abridging the freedom of speech or of the press, or the right of the people peaceably to assemble, and to petition the Government for a redress of grievances.

Amendment II.

A well regulated Militia, being necessary to the security of a free State, the right of the people to keep and bear Arms, shall not be infringed.

Amendment III.

No Soldier shall, in time of peace be quartered in any house, without the consent of the Owner, nor in time of war, but in a manner to be prescribed by law.

Amendment IV.

The right of the people to be secure in their persons, houses, papers, and effects, against unreasonable searches and seizures, shall not be violated, and no Warrants shall issue, but upon probable cause, supported by Oath or affirmation, and particularly describing the place to be searched, and the persons or things to be seized.

Amendment V.

No person shall be held to answer for a capital, or otherwise infamous crime, unless on a presentment or indictment of a Grand Jury, except in cases arising in the land or naval forces, or in the Militia, when in actual service in time of War or public danger; nor shall any person be subject for the same offence to be twice put in jeopardy of life or limb, nor shall be compelled in any criminal case to be a witness against himself, nor be deprived of life, liberty, or property, without due process of law; nor shall private property be taken for public use without just compensation.

Amendment VI.

In all criminal prosecutions, the accused shall enjoy the right to a speedy and public trial, by an impartial jury of the State and district wherein the crime shall have been committed; which district shall have been previously ascertained by law, and to be informed of the nature and cause of the accusation; to be confronted with the witness against him; to have compulsory process for obtaining witnesses in his favor, and to have the assistance of counsel for his defence.

Amendment VII.

In Suits at common law, where the value in controversy shall exceed twenty dollars, the right of trial by jury shall be preserved, and no fact tried by a jury shall be otherwise re-examined in any Court of the United States, then according to the rules of the common law.

Amendment VIII.

Excessive bail shall not be required, nor excessive fines imposed, nor cruel and unusual punishments inflicted.

Amendment IX.

The enumeration in the Constitution of certain rights shall not be construed to deny or disparage others retained by the people.

Amendment X.

The powers not delegated to the United States by the Constitution, nor prohibited by it to the States, are reserved to the States respectively, or to the people.

Amendment XI.

The Judicial power of the United States shall not be construed to extend to any suit in law or equity, commenced or prosecuted against one of the United States by Citizens of another State, or by Citizens or Subjects of any Foreign State.

Amendment XII.

The Electors shall meet in their respective states, and vote by ballot for President and Vice President, one of whom, at least, shall not be an inhabitant of the same state with themselves; they shall name in their ballots the person voted for as President, and in distinct ballots the person voted for as Vice-President, and they shall make distinct lists of all persons voted for as President, and of all persons voted for as Vice-President, and of the number of votes for each, which lists they shall sign and certify, and transmit sealed to the seat of the government of the United States, directed to the President of the Senate;—The President of the Senate shall, in the presence of the Senate and House of Representatives, open all the certificates and the votes shall then be counted;—The person having the greatest number of votes for President, shall be the President, if such number be a majority of the whole number of Electors appointed; and if no person have such majority, then from the persons having the highest numbers not exceeding three of the list of those voted for as President, the House of Representatives shall choose immediately, by ballot, the President. But in choosing the President, the votes shall be taken by states, the representation from each state having one vote; a quorum for this purpose shall consist of a member or members from two-thirds of the states, and a majority of all the states shall be necessary to a choice. And if the House of Representatives shall not choose a President whenever the right of choice shall evolve upon them, before the fourth day of March next following, then the Vice President shall act as President, as in the case of the death or other constitutional disability of the President—The person having the greatest number of votes as Vice-President, shall be the Vice-President, if such number be a majority of the whole number of Electors appointed, and if no person have a majority, then from the two highest numbers on the list, the Senate shall choose the Vice-President; a quorum for the purpose shall consist of two-thirds of the whole number of Senators, and a majority of the whole number shall be necessary to a choice. But no person constitutionally ineligible to the office of President shall be eligible to that of Vice-President of the United States.

Amendment XIII.

Section 1. Neither slavery nor involuntary servitude, except as punishment for crime whereof the party shall have been duly convicted, shall exist within the United States, or any place subject to their jurisdiction.

Section 2. Congress shall have power to enforce this article by appropriate legislation.

Amendment XIV.

Section 1. All persons born or naturalized in the United States and subject to the jurisdiction thereof, are citizens of the United States and of the State wherein they reside. No State shall make or enforce any law which shall abridge the privileges or immunities of citizens of the United States; nor shall any State deprive any person of life, liberty, or property, without due process of law; nor deny to any person within its jurisdiction the equal protection of the laws.

Section 2. Representatives shall be apportioned among the several States according to their respective numbers, counting the whole number of persons in each State, excluding Indians not taxed. But when the right to vote at any election for the choice of electors for President and Vice President of the United States, Representatives in Congress, the Executive and Judicial officers of a state, or the members of the Legislature thereof, is denied to any of the male inhabitants of such State, being twenty-one years of age, and citizens of the United States, or in any way abridged, except for participation in rebellion, or other crime, the basis of representation therein shall be reduced in the proportion which the number of such male citizens shall bear to the whole number of male citizens twenty-one years of age in such State.

Section 3. No person shall be a Senator or Representative in Congress, or elector of President and Vice President, or hold any office, civil or military, under the United States, or under any State, who, having previously taken an oath, as a member of Congress, or as an officer of the United States, or as a member of any State legislature, or as an executive or judicial officer of any State, to support the Constitution of the United States, shall have engaged in insurrection or rebellion against the same, or given aid or comfort to the enemies thereof. But Congress may by a vote of two-thirds of each House, remove such disability.

Section 4. The validity of the public debt of the United States, authorized by law, including debts incurred for payment of pensions and bounties for services in suppressing insurrection or rebellion, shall not be questioned. But neither the United States nor any State shall assume or pay any debt or obligation incurred in aid of insurrection or rebellion against the United States, or any claim for the loss or emancipation of any slave; but all such debts, obligations and claims shall be held illegal and void.

Section 5. The Congress shall have power to enforce, by appropriate legislation, the provisions of this article.

Amendment XV.

Section 1. The right of citizens of the United States to vote shall not be denied or abridged by the United States or by any State on account of race, color, or previous condition of servitude.

Section 2. The Congress shall have power to enforce this article by appropriate legislation.

Amendment XVI.

The Congress shall have power to lay and collect taxes on incomes, from whatever source derived, without apportionment among the several States, and without regard to any census or enumeration.

Amendment XVII.

The Senate of the United States shall be composed of two Senators from each State, elected by the people thereof, for six years; and each Senator shall have one vote. The electors in each State shall have the qualifications requisite for electors of the most numerous branch of the State legislatures.

When vacancies happen in the representation of any State in the Senate, the executive authority of such State shall issue writs of election to fill such vacancies: *Provided,* That the legislature of any State may empower the executive thereof to make temporary appointments until the people fill the vacancies by election as the legislature may direct.

This amendment shall not be so construed as to affect the election or term of any Senator chosen before it becomes valid as part of the Constitution.

Amendment XVIII.

Section 1. After one year from the ratification of this article the manufacture, sale, or transportation of intoxicating liquors within, the importation thereof into, or the exportation thereof from the United States and all territory subject to the jurisdiction thereof for beverage purposes is hereby prohibited.

Section 2. The Congress and the several States shall have concurrent powers to enforce this article by appropriate legislation.

Section 3. This article shall be inoperative unless it shall have been ratified as an amendment to the Constitution by the legislatures of the several States, as provided in the Constitution, within seven years from the date of the submission hereof to the States by the Congress.

Amendment XIX.

The right of citizens of the United States to vote shall not be denied or abridged by the United States or by any State on account of sex.

Congress shall have power to enforce this article by appropriate legislation.

Amendment XX.

Section 1. The terms of President and Vice President shall end at noon on the 20th day of January, and the terms of Senators and Representatives at noon on the 3d day of January, in the years in which such terms would have ended if this article had not been ratified; and the terms of their successors shall then begin.

Section 2. The Congress shall assemble at least once in every year, and such meeting shall begin at noon on the 3d day of January, unless they shall by law appoint a different day.

Section 3. If, at the time fixed for the beginning of the term of the President, the President elect shall have died, the Vice President elect shall become President. If a President shall not have been chosen before the time fixed for the beginning of his term, or if the President elect shall have failed to qualify, then the Vice President elect shall act as President until a President shall have qualified; and the Congress may by law provide for the case wherein neither a President elect nor a Vice President elect shall have qualified, declaring who shall then act as President, or the manner in which one who is to act shall be selected, and such person shall act accordingly until a President or Vice President shall have qualified.

Section 4. The Congress may by law provide for the case of the death of any of the persons from whom the House of Representatives may choose a President whenever the right of choice shall have devolved upon them and for the case of the death of any of the persons from whom the Senate may choose a Vice President whenever the right of choice shall have devovled upon them.

Section 5. Sections 1 and 2 shall take effect on the 15th day of October following the ratification of this article.

Section 6. This article shall be inoperative unless it shall have been ratified as an amendment to the Constitution by the legislatures of three-fourths of the several States within seven years from the date of its submission.

Amendment XXI.

Section 1. The eighteenth article of amendment to the Constitution of the United States is hereby repealed.

Section 2. The transportation or importation into any State, Territory, or possession of the United States for delivery or use therein of intoxicating liquors, in violation of the laws thereof, is hereby prohibited.

Section 3. This article shall be inoperative unless it shall have been ratified as an amendment to the Constitution by conventions in the several States, as provided in the Constitution, within seven years from the date of the submission hereof to the States by the Congress.

Amendment XXII.

Section 1. No person shall be elected to the office of the President more than twice, and no person who has held the office of President, or acted as President, for more than two years of a term to which some other person was elected President shall be elected to the office of President more than once. But this Article shall not apply to any person holding the office of President when this Article was proposed by the Congress, and shall not prevent any person who may be holding the office of President, or acting as President, during the term within which this Article becomes operative from holding the office of President or acting as President during the remainder of such term.

Section 2. This article shall be inoperative unless it shall have been ratified as an amendment to the Constitution by the legislatures of three-fourths of the several States within seven years from the date of its submission to the States by the Congress.

Amendment XXIII.

Section 1. The District constituting the seat of Government of the United States shall appoint in such manner as the Congress may direct:

A number of electors of President and Vice President equal to the whole number of Senators and Representatives in Congress to which the District would be entitled if it were a State, but in no event more than the least populous State; they shall be in addition to those appointed by the States, but they shall be considered, for the purposes of the election of President and Vice President, to be electors appointed by a State; and they shall meet in the District and perform such duties as provided by the twelfth article of amendment.

Section 2. The Congress shall have power to enforce this article by appropriate legislation.

Amendment XXIV.

Section 1. The right of citizens of the United States to vote in any primary or other election for President or Vice President, for electors for President or Vice President, or for Senator or Representative in Congress, shall not be denied or abridged by the United States or any State by reason of failure to pay any poll tax or other tax.

Section 2. The Congress shall have power to enforce this article by appropriate legislation.

Amendment XXV.

Section 1. In case of the removal of the President from office or of his death or resignation, the Vice President shall become President.

Section 2. Whenever there is a vacancy in the office of the Vice President, the President shall nominate a Vice President who shall take office upon confirmation by a majority vote of both Houses of Congress.

Section 3. Whenever the President transmits to the President pro tempore of the Senate and the Speaker of the House of Representatives his written declaration that he is unable to discharge the powers and duties of his office, and until he transmits to them a written declaration to the contrary, such powers and duties shall be discharged by the Vice President as Acting President.

Section 4. Whenever the Vice President and a majority of either the principal officers of the executive departments or of such other body as Congress may by law provide, transmit to the President pro tempore of the Senate and the Speaker of the House of Representatives their written declaration that the President is unable to discharge the powers and duties of his office, the Vice President shall immediately assume the powers and duties of the office as Acting President.

Thereafter, when the President transmits to the President pro tempore of the Senate and the Speaker of the House of Representatives his written declaration that no inability exists, he shall resume the powers and duties of his office unless the Vice President and a majority of either the principal officers of the executive department or of such other body as Congress may by law provide, transmit within four days to the President pro tempore of the Senate and the Speaker of the House of Representatives their written declaration that the President is unable to discharge the powers and duties of his office. Thereupon Congress shall decide the issue, assembling within forty-eight hours for that purpose if not in session. If the Congress, within twenty-one days after receipt of the latter written declaration, or, if Congress is not in session, within twenty-one days after Congress is required to assemble, determines by two-thirds vote of both Houses that the President is unable to discharge the powers and duties of his office, the Vice President shall continue to discharge the same as Acting President; otherwise, the President shall resume the powers and duties of his office.

Amendment XXVI.

Section 1. The right of citizens of the United States, who are eighteen years of age or older, to vote shall not be denied or abridged by the United States or by any State on account of age.

Section 2. The Congress shall have power to enforce this article by appropriate legislation.

Amendment XXVII.

No Law, varying the compensation for the services of the Senators and Representatives, shall take effect, until an election of Representatives shall have intervened.

Farewell Address of President George Washington

United States, September 19, 1796

Friends, and Fellow-Citizens:

The period for a new election of a Citizen, to Administer the Executive government of the United States, being not far distant, and the time actually arrived, when your thoughts must be employed in designating the person, who is to be cloathed with that important trust, it appears to me proper, especially as it may conduce to a more distinct expression of the public voice, that I should now apprise you of the resolution I have formed, to decline being considered among the number of those, out of whom a choice is to be made.

I beg you, at the same time, to do me the justice to be assured, that this resolution has not been taken, without a strict regard to all the considerations appertaining to the relation, which binds a dutiful citizen to his country, and that, in with drawing the tender of service which silence in my situation might imply, I am influenced by no diminution of zeal for your future interest, no deficiency of grateful respect for your past kindness; but am supported by a full conviction that the step is compatible with both.

The acceptance of, and continuance hitherto in, the office to which your Suffrages have twice called me, have been a uniform sacrifice of inclination to the opinion of duty, and to a deference for what appeared to be your desire. I constantly hoped, that it would have been much earlier in my power, consistently with motives, which I was not at liberty to disregard, to return to that retirement, from which I had been reluctantly drawn. The strength of my inclination to do this, previous to the last Election, had even led to the preparation of an address to declare it to you; but mature reflection on the then perplexed and critical posture of our Affairs with foreign Nations, and the unanimous advice of persons entitled to my confidence, impelled me to abandon the idea.

I rejoice, that the state of your concerns, external as well as internal, no longer renders the pursuit of inclination incompatible with the sentiment of duty, or propriety; and am persuaded whatever partially may be retained for my services, that in the present circumstances of our country, you will not disapprove my determination to retire.

The impressions, with which I first undertook the arduous trust, were explained on the proper occasion. In the discharge of this trust, I will only say, that I have, with good intentions, contributed towards the Organization and Administration of the government, the best exertions of which a very fallible judgment was capable. Not unconscious, in the outset, of the inferiority of my qualifications, experience in my own eyes, perhaps still more in the eyes of others, has strengthened the motives to diffidence of myself; and every day the encreasing weight of years admonishes me more and more, that the shade of retirement is as necessary to me as it will be welcome. Satisfied that if any circumstances have given peculiar value to my services, they were temporary, I have the consolation to believe, that while choice and prudence invite me to quit the political scene, patriotism does not forbid it.

I am looking forward to the moment, which is intended to terminate the career of my public life, my feelings do not permit me to suspend the deep acknowledgment of that debt of gratitude wch. I owe to my beloved country, for the many honors it has conferred upon me; still more for the stedfast confidence with which it has supported me; and for the opportunities I have thence enjoyed of manifesting my inviolable attachment, by services faithful and persevering, though in usefulness unequal to my zeal. If benefits have resulted to our country from these services, let it always be remembered to your praise, and as an instructive example in our annals, that, under circumstances in which the Passions agitated in every direction were liable to mislead, amidst appearances sometimes dubious, viscissitudes of fortune often discouraging, in situations in which not unfrequently want of Success has countenanced the spirit of criticism, the constancy of your support was the essential prop of the efforts, and a guarantee of the plans by which they were effected. Profoundly penetrated with this idea, I shall carry it with me to my grave, as a strong incitement to unceasing vows that Heaven may continue to you the choicest tokens of its beneficence; that your Union and brotherly affection may be perpetual; that the free constitution, which is the work of your hands, may be sacredly maintained; that its Administration in every department may be stamped with wisdom and Virtue; that, in fine, the happiness of the people of these States, under the auspices of liberty, may be made complete, by so careful a preservation and so prudent a use of this blessing as will acquire to them the glory of recommending it to the applause, the affection, and adoption of every nation which is yet a stranger to it.

Here, perhaps, I ought to stop. But a solicitude for your welfare, which cannot end but with my life, and the apprehension of danger, natural to that solicitude, urge me on an occasion like the present, to offer to you solemn contemplation, and to recommend to your frequent review, some sentiments; which are the result of much reflection, of no inconsiderable observation, and which appear to me all important to the permanency of your felicity as a People. These will be offered to you with the more freedom, as you can only see in them the disinterested warnings of a parting friend, who can possibly have no personal motive to biass his counsel. Nor can I forget, as an encouragement to it, your endulgent reception of my sentiments on a former and not dissimilar occasion.

Interwoven as is the love of liberty with every ligament of your hearts, no recommendation of mine is necessary to fortify or confirm the attachment.

The Unity of Government which constitutes you one people is also now dear to you. It is justly so; for it is a main Pillar in the Edifice of your real independence, the support of your tranquillity at home; your peace abroad; of your safety, of your prosperity; of that very Liberty which you so highly prize. But as it is easy to foresee, that from different causes and from different quarters, much pains will be taken, many artifices employed, to weaken in your minds, the conviction of this truth; as this is the point in your political fortress against which the batteries of internal and external enemies will be most constantly and actively (though often covertly and insidiously) directed, it is of infinite moment, that you should properly estimate the immense value of your national Union to your collective and individual happiness; that you should cherish a cordial, habitual and immoveable attachment to it; accustoming yourselves to think and speak of it as of the Palladium of your political safety and prosperity; watching for its preservation with jealous anxiety; discountenancing whatever may suggest even a suspicion that it can in any event be abandoned, and indignantly frowning upon the first dawning of every attempt to alienate any portion of our Country from the rest, or to enfeeble the sacred ties which now link together the various parts.

For this you have every inducement of sympathy and interest. Citizens by birth or choice, of a common country, that country has a right to concentrate your affections. The name of American, which belongs to you, in your national capacity, must always exalt the just pride of Patriotism, more than any appellation derived from local discriminations. With slight shades of difference, you have the same Religion, Manners, Habits and political Principles. You have in a common cause fought and triumphed together. The independence and liberty you possess are the work of joint councils, and joint efforts; of common dangers, sufferings and successes.

But these considerations, however powerfully they address themselves to your sensibility are greatly outweighed by those which apply more immediately to your Interest. Here every portion of our country finds the most commanding motives for carefully guarding and preserving the Union of the whole.

The *North*, in an unrestrained intercourse with the *South*, protected by the equals Laws of a common government, finds in the productions of the latter, great additional resources of Maritime and commercial enterprise and precious materials of manufacturing industry. The *South* in the same Intercourse, benefiting by the Agency of the *North*, sees its agriculture grow and its commerce expand. Turning partly into its own channels the seamen of the *North*, it finds its particular navigation envigorated; and while it contributes, in different ways, to nourish and increase the general mass of the National navigation, it looks forward to the production of a Maritime strength, to which itself is unequally adapted. The *East*, in a like intercourse with the *West*, already finds, and in the progressive improvement of interior communications, by land and water, will more and more find a valuable vent for the commodities which it brings from abroad, or manufactures at home. The *West* derives from the *East* supplies requisite to its growth and comfort, and what is perhaps of still greater consequence, it must of necessity owe the *secure* enjoyment of indispensable *outlets* for its own productions to the weight, influence, and the future Maritime strength of the Atlantic side of the Union, directed by an indissoluble community of Interest as *one Nation*. Any other tenure by which the *West* can hold this essential advantage, whether derived from its own separate strength, or from an apostate and unnatural connection with any foreign Power, must be intrinsically precarious.

While then every part of our country thus feels an immediate and particular Interest in Union, all the parts combined cannot fail to find in the united mass of means and efforts greater strength, greater resource, porportionably greater security from external danger, a less frequent interruption of their Peace by foreign Nations; and, what is of inestimable value! they must derive from Union an exemption of those broils and Wars between themselves, which so frequently afflict neighbouring countries not tied together by the same government; which their own rivalship alone would be sufficient to produce, but which opposite foreign alliances, attachments and intriegues would stimulate and imbitter. Hence likewise they will avoid the necessity of those overgrown Military establishments, which under any form of Government are inauspicious to liberty, and which are to be regarded as particularly hostile to Republican Liberty: In this sense it is, that your Union ought to be considered the main prop of your liberty, and that the love of the one ought to endear to you the preservation of the other.

These considerations speak a persuasive language to every reflecting and virtuous mind, and exhibit the continuance of the Union as a primary object of Patriotic desire. Is there a doubt, whether a common government can embrace so large a sphere? Let experience solve it. To listen to mere speculation in such a case were criminal. We are authorized to hope that a proper organization of the whole, with the auxiliary agency of governments for the respective Subdivisions, will afford a happy issue to the experiment. 'Tis well worth a fair and full experiment. With such powerful and obvious motives to Union, affecting all parts of our country, while experience shall not have demonstrated its impracticability, there will always be reason, to distrust the patriotism of those, who in any quarter may endeavor to weaken its bands.

In contemplating the causes wch. may disturb our Union, it occurs as matter of serious concern, that any ground should have been furnished for characterizing parties by *Geographical* discriminations: *Northern* and *Southern; Atlantic* and *Western*; whence designing men may endeavour to excite a belief that there is a real difference of local interests and views. One of the expedients of Party to acquire influence, within particular districts, is to misrepresent the opinions and aims of other Districts. You cannot shield yourselves too much against the jealousies and heart burnings which spring from these misrepresentations. They tend to render Alien to each other those who ought to be bound together by fraternal affection. The Inhabitants of our Western country have lately had a useful lesson on this head. They have seen, in the Negociation by the Executive, and in the unanimous ratification by the Senate, of the Treaty with Spain, and in the universal satisfaction at that event, throughout the United States, a decisive proof how unfounded were the suspicions propagated among them of a policy in the General Government and in the Atlantic States unfriendly to their Interests in regard to the Mississippi. They have been witness to the formation of two Treaties, that with G. Britain and that with Spain, which secure to them every thing they could desire, in respect to our Foreign relations, towards confirming their prosperity. Will it not be their wisdom to rely for the preservation of these advantages on the Union by wch. they were procured? Will they not henceforth be deaf to those advisers, if such there are, who would sever them from their Brethren and connect them with Aliens?

To the efficacy and permanency of Your Union, a Government for the whole is indispensable. No Alliances however strict between the parts can be an adequate substitute. They must inevitably experience the infractions and interruptions which all Alliances in all times have experienced. Sensible of this momentous truth, you have improved upon your first essay, by the adoption of a Constitution of Government, better calculated than your former for an intimate Union, and for the efficacious management of your common concerns. This government, the offspring of our own choice uninfluenced and unawed, adopted upon full investigation and mature deliberation, completely free in its principles, in the distribution of its powers, uniting security with energy, and containing within itself a provision for its own amendment, has a just claim to you confidence and your support. Respect for its authority, compliance with its Laws, acquiescence in its measures, are duties enjoined by the fundamental maxims of true Liberty. The basis of our political systems is the right of the people to make and to alter their Constitutions of Government. But the Constitution which at any time exists, 'til changed by an explicit and authentic act of the whole People, is sacredly obligatory upon all. The very idea of the power and the right of the People to establish Government presupposes the duty of every Individual to obey the established Government.

All obstructions to the execution of the Laws, all combinations and Associations, under whatever plausible character, with the real design to direct, controul, counteract, or awe the regular deliberation and action of the Constituted authorities are distructive of this fundamental principle and of fatal tendency. They serve to organize faction, to give it an artificial and extraordinary force; to put in the place of the delegated will of the Nation, the will of a party; often a small but artful and enterprizing minority of the Community; and, according to the alternate triumphs of different parties, to make the public administration the Mirror of the ill concerted and incongruous projects of faction, rather than the organ of consistent and wholesome plans digested by common councils and modefied by mutual interests. However combinations of Associations of the above description may now and then answer popular ends, they are likely, in the course of time and things, to become potent engines, by which cunning, ambitious and unprincipled men will be enabled to subvert the Power of the People, and to usurp for themselves the reins of Government; destroying afterwards the very engines which have lifted them to unjust dominion.

Towards the preservation of your Government and the permanency of your present happy state, it is requisite, not only that you steadily discountenance irregular oppositions to its acknowledged authority, but also that you resist with care the spirit of innovation upon its principles however specious the pretexts. one method of assault may be to effect, in the forms of the Constitution, alterations which will impair the energy of the system, and thus to undermine what cannot be directly overthrown. In all the changes to which you may be invited, remember that time and habit are at least as necessary to fix the true character of Governments, as of other human institutions; that experience is the surest standard, by which to test the real tendency of the existing Constitution of a country; that facility in charges upon the credit of mere hypotheses and opinion exposes to perpetual change, from the endless variety of hypotheses and opinion: and remember, especially, that for the efficient management of your common interests, in a country so extensive as ours, a Government of as much vigour as is consistent with the perfect security of Liberty is indispensable. Liberty itself will find in such a Government, with powers properly distributed and adjusted, its surest Guardian. It is indeed little else than a name, where the Government is too feeble to withstand the enterprises of faction, to confine each member of the Society within the limits prescribed by the laws and to maintain all in the secure and tranquil enjoyment of the rights of person and property.

I have already intimated to you the danger of Parties in the State, with particular reference to the founding of them on Geographical discriminations. Let me now take a more comprehensive view, and warn you in the most solemn manner against the baneful effects of the Spirit of Party, generally.

This spirit, unfortunately, is inseperable from our nature, having its root in the strongest passions of the human Mind. It exists under different shapes in all Governments, more or less stifled, controuled, or repressed; but, in those of the popular form it is seen in its greatest rankness and is truly their worst enemy.

The alternate domination of one faction over another, sharpened by the spirit of revenge natural to party dissention, which in different ages and countries has perpetuated the most horrid enormities, is itself a frightful despotism. But this leads at length to a more formal and permanent despotism. The disorders and miseries, which result, gradually incline the minds of men to seek security and repose in the absolute power of an Individual: and sooner or later the chief of some prevailing faction more able or more fortunate than his competitors, turns this disposition to the purposes of his own elevation, on the ruins of Public Liberty.

Without looking forward to an extremity of this kind (which nevertheless ought not to be entirely ought of sight) the common and continual mischiefs of the spirit of Party are sufficient to make it the interest and the duty of a wise People to discourage and restrain it.

It serves always to distract the Public Councils and enfeeble the Public administration. It agitates the Community with ill founded jealousies and false alarms, kindles the animosity of one part against another, foments occasionally riot and insurrection. It opens the door to foreign influence and corruption, which find a facilitated access to the government itself through the channels of party passions. Thus the policy and the will of one country, are subjected to the policy and will of another.

There is an opinion that parties in free countries are useful checks upon the Administration of the Government and serve to keep alive the spirit of Liberty. This within certain limits is probably true, and in Governments of a Monarchical cast Patriotism may look with endulgence, if not with favour, upon the spirit of party. But in those of the popular character, in Governments purely elective, it is a spirit not to be encouraged. From their natural tendency, it is certain there will always be enough of that spirit for every salutary purpose. And there being constant danger of excess, the effort ought to be, by force of public opinion, to mitigate and assuage it. A fire not to be quenched; it demands a uniform vigilance to prevent its bursting into a flame, lest instead of warming it should consume.

It is important, likewise, that the habits of thinking in a free Country should inspire caution in those entrusted with its administration, to confine themselves within their respective Constitutional spheres; avoiding in the exercise of the Powers of one department to encroach upon another. The spirit of encroachment tends to consolidate the powers of all the departments in one, and thus to create whatever the form of government, a real despotism. A just estimate of that love of power, and proneness to abuse it, which predominates in the human hear is sufficient to satisfy us of the truth of this position. The necessity of reciprocal checks in the exercise of political power; by dividing and distributing it into different depositories, and constituting each the Guardian of the Public Weal against invasions by the others, has been envinced by experiments ancient and modern; some of them in our country and under our own eyes. To preserve them must be as necessary as to institute them. If in the opinion of the People, the distribution or modification of the Constitutional powers be in any particular wrong, let it be corrected by an amendment in the way which the Constitution designates. But let there be no change by usurpation; for though this, in one instance, may be the instrument of good, it is the customary weapon by which free governments are destroyed. The precedent must always greatly overbalance in permanent evil any partial or transient benefit which the use can at any time yield.

Of all the dispositions and habits which lead to political prosperity, Religion and morality are indispensable supports. In vain would that man claim the tribute of Patriotism, who should labour to subvert these great Pillars of human happiness, these firmest props of the duties of Men and citizens. The mere Politician, equally with the pious man ought to respect and to cherish them.

A volume could not trace all their connections with private and public felicity. Let it simply be asked where is the security for property, for reputation, for life, if the sense of religious obligation desert the oaths, which are the instruments of investigation in Courts of Justice? And let us with caution indulge the supposition, that morality can be maintained without religion. Whatever may be conceded to the influence of refined education on minds of peculiar structure, reason and experience both forbid us to expect that National morality can prevail in exclusion of religious principle.

'Tis substantially true, that virtue or morality is a necessary spring of popular government. The rule indeed extends with more or less force to every species of free Government. Who that is a sincere friend to it, can look with indifference upon attempts to shake the foundation of the fabric

Promote then as an object of primary importance, Institutions for the general diffusion of knowledge. In proportion as the structure of a government gives force to public opinion, it is essential that public opinion should be enlightened.

As a very importance source of strength and security, cherish public credit. One method of preserving it is to use it as sparingly as possible: avoiding occasions of expence by cultivating peace, but remembering also that timely disbursements to prepare for danger frequently prevent much greater disbursements to repel it; avoiding likewise the accumulation of debt, not only by shunning occasions of expence, but by vigorous exertions in time of Peace to discharge the Debts which unavoidable wars may have occasioned, not ungenerously throwing upon posterity the burthen which we ourselves ought to bear. The execution of these maxims belongs to your Representatives, but it is necessary that public opinion should cooperate. To facilitate to them the performance of their duty, it is essential that you should practically bear in mind, that towards the payment of debts there must be Revenue; that to have Revenue there must be taxes; that no taxes can be devised which are not more or less inconvenient and unpleasant; that the intrinsic embarrassment inseperable for the selection of the proper objects (which is always a choice of difficulties) ought to be a decisive motive for candid construction of the Conduct of the Government in making it, and for a spirit of acquiescence in the measures for obtaining Revenue which the exigencies may at any time dictate.

Observe good faith and justice towds. all Nations. Cultivate peace and harmony with all. Religion and morality enjoin this conduct; and it can be that good policy does not equally enjoin it? It will worthy of a free, enlightened, and, at no distant period, a great Nation, to give to mankind the magnanimous and too novel example of a People always guided by an exalted justice and benevolence. Who can doubt that in the course of time and things the fruits of such a plan would richly repay any temporary advantages wch. might be lost by a steady adherence to it? Can it be, that Providence has not connected the permanent Felicity of a nation with its virtue? The experiment, at least, is recommended by every sentiment which ennobles human Nature. Alas! is it rendered impossible by its vices?

In the execution of such a plan nothing is more essential than that permanent, inveterate antipathies against particular Nations and passionate attachments for others should be excluded; and that in place of them, just and amicable feelings towards all should be cultivated. The Nation, which indulges towards another an habitual hatred, or an habitual fondness, is in some degree a slave. It is a slave to its animosity or to its affection, either of which is sufficient to lead it astray from its duty and its interest. Antipathy in one Nation against another, disposes each more readily to offer insult and injury, to lay hold of slight causes of umbrage, and to be haughty and intractable, when accidental or trifling occasions of dispute occur. Hence frequent collisions, obstinate envenomed and bloody contests. The Nation prompted by ill will and resentment sometimes impels to War the Government, contrary to the best calculations of policy. The Government sometimes participates in the national propensity, and adopts through passion what reason would reject; at other times, it makes the animosity of the Nation subservient to projects of hostility instigated by pride, ambition and other sinister and pernicious motives. The peace often, sometimes perhaps the Liberty, of Nations has been the victim.

So likewise, a passionate attachment of one Nation for another produces a variety of evils. Sympathy for the favourite nation, facilitating the illusion of an imaginary common interest, in cases where no real common interest exists, and infusing into one the enmities of the other betrays the former into a participation in the quarrels and Wars of the latter, without adequate inducement or justification. It leads also to concession to the favourite Nation of priviledges denied to others, which is apt doubly to injure the Nation making the concessions; by unnecessarily parting with what ought to have been retained; and by exacting jealously, ill will, and a disposition to retaliate, in the parties from whom eql. priviledges are withheld: And it gives to ambitious, corrupted, or deluded citizens (who devote themselves to the favourite Nation) facility to betray, or sacrifice the interests of their own country, without odium, sometimes even with popularity; gliding with the appearances of a virtuous sense of obligation a commendable deference for public opinion, or a laudable zeal for public good, the base or foolish compliances of ambition corruption or infatuation.

As avenues to foreign influence in innumerable ways, such attachments are particularly alarming to the truly enlightened and independent Patriot. How many opportunities do they afford to tamper with domestic factions, to practice the arts of seduction, to mislead public opinion, to influence or awe the public Councils! Such an attachment of a small or weak, towards a great and powerful Nation, dooms the former to be the satellite of the latter.

Against the insidious wiles of foreign influence (I conjure you to believe me fellow citizens) the jealousy of a free people ought to be *constantly* awake; since history and experience prove that foreign influence is one of the most baneful foes of Republican Government. But that jealousy to be useful must be impartial; else it becomes the instrument of the very influence to be avoided, instead of a defence against it. Excessive partiality for one foreign nation and excessive dislike of another, cause those whom they actuate to see danger only on one side, and serve to veil and even second the arts of influence on the other. Real Patriots, who may resist the intriegues of the favourite, are liable to become suspected and odious; while its tools and dupes usurp the applause and confidence of the people, to surrender their interests.

The Great rule of conduct for us, in regard to foreign Nations is in extending our commercial relations to have with them as little *political* connection as possible. So far we have already formed engagements let them be fulfilled, with perfect good faith. Here let us stop.

Europe has a set of primary interests, which to us have none, or a very remote relation. Hence she must be engaged in frequent controversies, the causes of which are essentially foreign to our concerns. Hence therefore it must be unwise in us to implicate ourselves, by artificial ties, in the ordinary vicissitudes of her politics, or the ordinary combinations and collisions of her friendships, or enmities:

Our detached and distant situation invites and enables us to pursue a different course. If we remain one People, under an efficient government, the period is not far off, when we may defy material injury from external annoyance; when we may take such an attitude as will cause the neutrality we may at any time resolve upon to be scrupulously respected; when belligerent nations, under the impossibility of making acquisitions upon us, will not lightly hazard the giving us provocation; when we may choose peace or war, as our interest guided by our justice shall Counsel.

Why forego the advantages of so peculiar a situation? Why quit our own to stand upon foreign ground? Why, by interweaving our destiny with that of any part of Europe, entangle our peace and prosperity in the toils of European Ambition, Rivalship, Interest, Humour or Caprice?

'Tis our true policy to steer clear of permanent Alliances, with any portion of the foreign world. So far, I mean, as we are now at liberty to do it, for let me not be understood as capable of patronising infidelity to existing engagements (I hold the maxim no less applicable to public than private affairs, that honesty is always the best policy). I repeat it therefore, let those engagements be observed in their genuine sense. But in my opinion, it is unnecessary and would be unwise to extend them.

Taking care always to keep ourselves, by suitable establishments, on a respectably defensive posture, we may safely trust to temporary alliances for extraordinary emergencies.

Harmony, liberal intercourse with all Nations, are recommended by policy, humanity and interest. But even our Commercial policy should hold an equal and impartial hand: neither seeking nor granting exclusive favours or preferences; consulting the natural course of things; diffusing and deversifying by gentle means the streams of Commerce, but forcing nothing; establishing with Powers so disposed; in order to give to trade a stable course, to define the rights of our Merchants, and to enable the Government to support them; conventional rules of intercourse, the best that present circumstances and mutual opinion will permit, but temporary, and liable to be from time to time abandoned or varied, as experience and circumstances shall dictate; constantly keeping in view, that 'tis folly in one Nation to look for disinterested favors from another; that it must pay with a portion of its Independence for whatever it may accept under that character; that by such acceptance, it may place itself in the condition of having given equivalents for nominal favours and yet of being reproached with ingratitude for not giving more. There can be no greater error than to expect, or calculate upon real favours from Nation to Nation. 'Tis an illusion which experience must cure, which a just pride ought to discard.

In offering to you, my Countrymen these counsels of an old and affectionate friend, I dare not hope they will make the strong and lasting impression, I could wish; that they will controul the usual current of the passions, or prevent our nation from running the course which has hitherto marked the Destiny of Nations: But if I may even flatter myself, that they may be productive of some partial benefit, some occasional good; that they may now and then recur to moderate the fury of party spirit, to warn against the mischiefs of foreign Intriegue, to guard against the Impostures of pretended patriotism; this hope will be a full recompence for the solicitude for your welfare, by which they have been dictated.

How far in the discharge of my Official duties, I have been guided by the principles which have been delineated, the public Records and other evidences of my conduct must Witness to You and to the world. To myself, the assurance of my own conscience is, that I have at least believed myself to be guided by them.

In relation to the still subsisting War in Europe, my Proclamation of the 22d. of April 1793 is the index to my Plan. Sanctioned by your approving voice and by that of your Representatives in both Houses of Congress, the spirit of that measure has continually governed me; uninfluenced by any attempts to deter or divert me from it.

After deliberate examination with the aid of the best lights I could obtain I was well satisfied that our Country, under all the circumstances of the case, had a right to take, and was bound in duty and interest, to take a Neutral position. Having taken it, I determined, as far as should depend upon me, to maintain it, with moderation, perseverence and firmness.

The considerations, which respect the right to hold this conduct, it is not necessary on this occasion to detail. I will only observe, that according to my understanding of the matter, the right, so far from being denied by any of the Belligerent Powers has been virtually admitted by all.

The duty of holding a Neutral conduct may be inferred, without any thing more, from the obligation which justice and humanity impose on every Nation, in cases in which it is free to act, to maintain inviolate the relations of Peace and amity towards other Nations.

The inducements of interest for observing that conduct will best be referred to your own reflections and experience. With me, a predominant motive has been to endeavour to gain time to our country to settle and mature its yet recent institutions, and to progress without interruption, to that degree of strength and consistency, which is necessary to give it, humanly speaking, the command of its own fortunes.

Though in reviewing the incidents of my Administration, I am unconscious of internal error, I am nevertheless too sensible of my defects not to think it probable that I may have committed many errors. Whatever they may be I fervently beseech the Almighty to avert or mitigate the evils to which they may tend. I shall also carry with me the hope that my Country will never cease to view them with indulgence; and that after forty five years of my life dedicated to its Service, with an upright zeal, the faults of incompetent abilities will be consigned to oblivion, as myself must soon be to the Mansions of rest.

Relying on its kindness in this as in other things, and actuated by that fervent love towards it, which is so natural to a Man, who views in it the native soil of himself and his progenitors for several Generations; I anticipate with pleasing expectation that retreat, in which I promise myself to realize, without alloy, the sweet enjoyment of partaking, in the midst of my fellow Citizens, the benign influence of good Laws under a free Government, the ever favourite object of my heart, and the happy reward, as I trust, of our mutual cares, labours and dangers.

The Rules Of Civility And Decent Behavior In Company And Conversation

From George Washington's Personal Notebook

1 Every action done in company ought to be with some sign of respect to those that are present.

2 When in company, put not your hands to any part of the body not usually discovered.

3 Show nothing to your friend that may affright him.

4 In the presence of others, sing not to yourself with a humming voice, or drum with your fingers or feet.

5 If you cough, sneeze, sigh, or yawn, do it not loud but privately, and speak not in your yawning, but put your handkerchief or hand before your face and turn aside.

6 Sleep not when others speak; sit not when others stand; speak not when you should hold your peace; walk not on when others stop.

7 Put not off your clothes in the presence of others, nor go out your chamber half dressed.

8 At play and at fire, it's good manners to give place to the last comer, and affect not to speak louder than ordinary.

9 Spit not into the fire, nor stoop low before it; neither put your hands into the flames to warm them, nor set your feet upon the fire, especially if there be meat before it.

10 When you sit down, keep your feet firm and even; without putting one on the other or crossing them.

11 Shift not yourself in the sight of others, nor gnaw your nails.

12 Shake not the head, feet, or legs; roll not the eyes; lift not one eyebrow higher than the other, wry not the mouth, and bedew no man's face with your spittle by [approaching too near] him [when] you speak.

13 Kill no vermin, or fleas, lice, ticks, etc. in the sight of others; if you see any filth or thick spittle put your foot dexterously upon it; if it be upon the clothes of your companions, put it off privately, and if it be upon your own clothes, return thanks to him who puts it off.

14 Turn not your back to others, especially in speaking; jog not the table or desk on which another reads or writes; lean not upon anyone.

15 Keep your nails clean and short, also your hands and teeth clean, yet without showing any great concern for them.

16 Do not puff up the cheeks, loll not out the tongue with the hands, or beard, thrust out the lips, or bite them, or keep the lips too open or too close.

17 Be no flatterer, neither play with any that delight not to be played withal.

18 Read no letter, books, or papers in company, but when there is a necessity for the doing of it, you must ask leave; come not near the books or writings of another so as to read them unless desired, or give your opinion of them unasked; also look not nigh when another is writing a letter.

19 Let your countenance be pleasant but in serious matters somewhat grave.

20 The gestures of the body must be suited to the discourse you are upon.

21 Reproach none for the infirmities of nature, nor delight to put them that have in mind of thereof.

22 Show not yourself glad at the misfortune of another though he were your enemy.

23 When you see a crime punished, you may be inwardly pleased; but [   ] show pity to the suffering offender.

24 [damaged manuscript]

25 Superfluous compliments and all affectation of ceremonies are to be avoided, yet where due they are not to be neglected.

26 In putting off your hat to persons of distinction, as noblemen, justices, churchmen, etc., make a reverence, bowing more or less according to the custom of the better bred, and quality of the persons; among your equals expect not always that they should begin with you first; but to pull off the hat when there is no need is affectation, in the manner of saluting and resaluting in word keep to the most usual custom.

27 'Tis ill manners to bed one more eminent than yourself be covered, as well as not to do it to whom it is due. Likewise he that makes too much haste to put on his hat does not well, yet he ought to put it on at the first, or at most the second time of being asked; now what is herein spoken, of qualification in behavior or saluting, ought also to be observed in taking of place and sitting down for ceremonies without bounds are troublesome.

28 If any one come to speak to you while you are [are] sitting, stand up, though he be your inferior, and when you present seats, let it be to everyone according to his degree.

29 When you meet with one of greater quality than yourself, stop, and retire, especially if it be at a door or any straight place, to give way for him to pass.

30 If walking the highest place in most countries seems to be on the right hand; therefore place yourself on the left of him whom you desire to honor: but if three walk together the middle place is the most honorable; the wall is usually given to the most worthy if two walk together.

31 If anyone far surpasses others, either in age, estate, or merits [and] would give place to a meaner than himself, the same ought not to accept it, s[ave he offer] it above once or twice.

32 To one that is your equal, or not much inferior, you are to give the chief place in your lodging, and he to whom it is offered ought at the first to refuse it, but at the second to accept though not without acknowledging his own unworthiness.

33 They that are in dignity or in office have in all places precedency, but whilst they are young, they ought to respect those that are their equals in birth or other qualities, though they have no public charge.

34 It is good manners to prefer them to whom we speak before ourselves, especially if they be above us, with whom in no sort we ought to begin.

35 Let your discourse with men of business be short and comprehensive.

36 Artificers and persons of low degree ought not to use many ceremonies to lords or others of high degree, but respect and highly honor them, and those of high degree ought to treat them with affability and courtesy, without arrogance.

37 In speaking of men of quality do not lean nor look them full in the face, nor approach to near them at left. Keep a full pace from them.

38 In visiting the sick, do not presently play the physician if you be not knowing therein.

39 In writing or speaking, give to every person his due title according to his degree and the custom of the place.

40 Strive not with your superior in argument, but always submit your judgment to others with modesty.

41 Undertake not to teach your equal in the art himself professes; it [   ] of arrogance.

42 [damaged manuscript]; and same with a clown and a prince.

43 Do not express joy before one sick in pain, for that contrary passion will aggravate his misery.

44 When a man does all he can, though it succeed not well, blame not him that did it.

45 Being to advise or reprehend any one, consider whether it ought to be in public or in private, and presently or at some other time; in what terms to do it; and in reproving show no signs of cholor but do it with all sweetness and mildness.

46 Take all admonitions thankfully in what time or place soever given, but afterwards not being culpable take a time and place convenient to let him [him] know it that gave them.

47 Mock not nor jest at any thing of importance. Break no jests that are sharp, biting; and if you deliver any thing witty and pleasant, abstain from laughing thereat yourself.

48 Wherein [wherein] you reprove another be unblameable yourself; for example is more prevalent than precepts.

49 Use no reproachful language against any one; neither curse nor revile.

50 Be not hasty to believe flying reports to the disparagement of any.

51 Wear not your clothes foul, or ripped, or dusty, but see they be brushed once every day at least and take heed that you approach not to any uncleanness.

52 In your apparel be modest and endeavor to accommodate nature, rather than to procure admiration; keep to the fashion of your equals, such as are civil and orderly with respect to time and places.

53 Run not in the streets, neither go too slowly, nor with mouth open; go not shaking of arms, nor upon the toes, nor in a dancing [damaged manuscript].

54 Play not the peacock, looking everywhere about you, to see if you be well decked, if your shoes fit well, if your stockings sit neatly and clothes handsomely.

55 Eat not in the streets, nor in your house, out of season.

56 Associate yourself with men of good quality if you esteem your own reputation; for 'tis better to be alone than in bad company.

57 In walking up and down in a house, only with one in company if he be greater than yourself, at the first give him the right hand and stop not till he does and be not the first that turns, and when you do turn let it be with your face towards him; if he be a man of great quality walk not with him cheek by jowl but somewhat behind him but yet in such a manner that me may easily speak to you.

58 Let your conversation be without malice or envy, for 'tis a sign of a tractable and commendable nature, and in all causes of passion permit reason to govern.

59 Never express anything unbecoming, nor act against the rules before your inferiors.

60 Be not immodest in urging your friends to discover a secret.

61 Utter not base and frivolous things among grave and learned men, nor very difficult questions or subjects among the ignorant, or things hard to be believed; stuff not your discourse with sentences among your betters nor equals.

62 Speak not of doleful things in a time of mirth or at the table; speak not of melancholy things or death and wounds, and if others mention them, change if you can the discourse; tell not your dreams, but to your intimate friend.

63 A man ought not to value himself of his achievements or rare qualities [damaged manuscript] virtue or kindred.

64 Break not a jest where none take pleasure in mirth; laugh not alone, nor at all without occasion; deride no man's misfortune though there seem to be some cause.

65 Speak not injurious words neither in jest nor earnest; scoff at none although they give occasion.

66 Be not forward but friendly and courteous, the first to salute, hear, and answer; and be not pensive when it's a time to converse.

67 Detract not from others, neither be excessive in commanding.

68 Go not thither, where you know not whether you shall be welcome or not; give not advice [without] being asked, and when desired do it briefly.

69 If two contend together take not the part of either unconstrained, and be not obstinate in your own opinion; in things indifferent be of the major side.

70 Reprehend not the imperfections of others, for that belongs to parents, masters, and superiors.

71 Gaze not on the marks or blemishes of others and ask not how they came. What you may speak in secret to your friend, deliver not before others.

72 Speak not in an unknown tongue in company but in your own language and that as those of quality do and not as the vulgar; sublime matters treat seriously.

73 Think before you speak; pronounce not imperfectly, nor bring out your words too hastily, but orderly and distinctly.

74 When another speaks, be attentive yourself; and disturb not the audience. If any hesitate in his words, help him not nor prompt him without desired; interrupt him not, nor answer him till his speech has ended.

75 In the midst of discourse [damaged manuscript] but if you perceive any stop because of [damaged manuscript]; to proceed: If a person of quality comes in while you're conversing, it's handsome to repeat what was said before.

76 While you are talking, point not with your finger at him of whom you discourse, nor approach too near him to whom you talk especially to his face.

77 Treat with men at fit times about business and whisper not in the company of others.

78 Make no comparisons and if any of the company be commended for any brave act of virtue, commend not another for the same.

79 Be not apt to relate news if you know not the truth thereof. In discoursing of things you have heard, name not your author always; a secret discover not.

80 Be not tedious in discourse or in reading unless you find the company pleased therewith.

81 Be not curious to know the affairs of others, neither approach those that speak in private.

82 Undertake not what you cannot perform but be careful to keep your promise.

83 When you deliver a matter do it without passion and with discretion, however mean the person be you do it to.

84 When your superiors talk to anybody hear not neither speak nor laugh.

85 In company of those of higher quality than yourself, speak not 'til you are asked a question, then stand upright, put off your hat and answer in few words.

86 In disputes, be not so desirous to overcome as not to give liberty to each one to deliver his opinion and submit to the judgment of the major part, specially if they are judges of the dispute.

87 [damaged manuscript] as becomes a man grave, settled, and attentive [damaged manuscript] [pre]dict not at every turn what others say.

88 Be not diverse in discourse; make not many digressions; nor repeat often the same manner of discourse.

89 Speak not evil of the absent, for it is unjust.

90 Being set at meat scratch not, neither spit, cough, or blow your nose except there's a necessity for it.

91 Make no show of taking great delight in your victuals; feed not with greediness; eat your bread with a knife; lean not on the table; neither find fault with what you eat.

92 Take no salt nor cut bread with your knife greasy.

93 Entertaining anyone at table it is decent to present him with meat; undertake not to help others undesired by the master.

94 If you soak bread in the sauce, let it be no more than what you put in your mouth at a time and blow not your broth at the table; let it stay till cools of itself.

95 Put not your meat to your mouth with your knife in your hand; neither spit forth the stones of any fruit pie upon a dish nor cast anything under the table.

96 It's unbecoming to heap much to one's meat; keep your fingers clean; when foul wipe them on a corner of your table napkin.

97 Put not another bite into your mouth till the former be swallowed; let not your morsels be too big.

98 Drink not nor talk with your mouth full; neither gaze about you while you are a drinking.

99 Drink not too leisurely nor yet too hastily. Before and after drinking wipe your lips; breathe not then or ever with too great a noise, for it is an evil.

100 Cleanse not your teeth with the table cloth napkin, fork, or knife; but if others do it, let it be done without a peep to them.

101 Rinse not your mouth in the presence of others.

102 It is not of use to call upon the company often to eat; nor need you drink to others every time you drink.

103 In company of your betters be not [damaged manuscript] than they are; lay not your arm but [damaged manuscript].

104 It belongs to the chiefest in company to unfold his napkin and fall to meat first; be he ought then to begin in time and to dispatch with dexterity that the slowest may have time allowed him.

105 Be not angry at table whatever happens and if you have reason to be so, show it not but on a cheerful countenance especially if there be strangers, for good humor makes one dish of meat and whey.

106 Set not yourself at the upper of the table but if it be your due, or that the master of the house will have it so, contend not, lest you should trouble the company.

107 If others talk at table be attentive but talk not with meat in your mouth.

108 When you speak of God or his Attributes, let it be seriously; reverence, honor and obey your natural parents although they be poor.

109 Let your recreations be manful not sinful.

110 Labor to keep alive in your breast that little spark of celestial fire called conscience.

APPENDIX O
The Westminster Shorter Catechism

Q. 1. What is the chief end of man?

A. Man's chief end is to glorify God, (a) and to enjoy him forever (b).

    (a). Ps. 86:9; Isa. 60:21; Rom. 11:36; I Cor. 6:20; 10:31; Rev. 4:11
    (b). Ps. 16:5–11; 144:15; Isa. 12:2; Luke 2:10; Phil. 4:4; Rev. 21:3–4

Q. 2. What rule hath God given to direct us how we may glorify and enjoy him?

A. The Word of God, which is contained in the Scriptures of the Old and New Testaments, (a) is the only rule to direct us how we may glorify and enjoy him (b).

    (a). Matt. 19:4–5 with Gen. 2:24; Luke 24:27, 44; I Cor. 2:13; 14:37; II Pet.1:20–21; 3:2, 15–16
    (b). Deut. 4:2; Ps. 19:7–11; Isa. 18:20; John 15:11; 20:30–31; Acts 17:11; II Tim. 3:15–17; I John 1:4

Q. 3. What do the Scriptures principally teach?

A. The Scriptures principally teach what man is to believe concerning God, (a) and what duty God requires of man (b).

    (a). Gen. 1:1; John 5:39; 20:31; Rom. 10:17; II Tim. 3:15
    (b). Deut. 10:12–13; Josh. 1:8; Ps. 119:105; Mic. 6:8; II Tim. 3:16–17

Q. 4. What is God?

A. God is a Spirit (a), infinite (b), eternal (c), and unchangeable (d) in his being (e), wisdom (f), power (g), holiness (h), justice (i), goodness (j), and truth (k).

    (a). Deut. 4:15–19; Luke 24:39; John 1:18; 4:24; Acts 17:29
    (b). I Kings 8:27; Ps. 139:7–10; 145:3; 147:5; Jer. 23:24; Rom. 11:33–36
    (c). Deut. 33:27; Ps. 90:2; 102:12, 24–27; Rev. 1:4, 8
    (d). Ps. 33:11; Mal. 3:6; Heb. 1:12; 6:17–18; 13:8; Jas. 1:17
    (e). Ex. 3:14; Ps. 115:2–3; I Tim. 1:17; 6:15–16
    (f). Ps. 104:24; Rom. 11:33–34; Heb. 4:13; I John 3:20
    (g). Gen. 17:1; Ps. 62:11; Jer. 32:17; Mat. 19:26; Rev. 1:8
    (h). Heb. 1:13; I Pet. 1:15–16; I John 3:3, 5; Rev. 15:4
    (i). Gen. 18:25; Ex. 34:6–7; Deut. 32:4; Ps. 96:13; Rom. 3:5, 26
    (j). Ps. 103:5; 107:8; Matt. 19:17; Rom. 2:4
    (k). Ex. 34:6; Deut. 32:4; Ps. 86:15; 117:2; Heb. 6:18

Q. 5. Are there more Gods than one?

A. There is but one only (a), the living and true God (b).

    (a). Deut. 6:4; Isa. 44:6; 45:21–22; I Cor. 8:4–6
    (b). Jer. 10:10; John 17:3; I Thess. 1:9; I John 5:20

Q. 6. How many persons are there in the Godhead?

A. There are three persons in the Godhead; the Father, the Son, and the Holy Ghost (a); and these three are one God, the same in substance, equal in power and glory (b).

    (a). Matt. 3:16–17; 28:19; II Cor. 13:14; I Pet. 1:2
    (b). Ps. 45:6; John 1:1; 17:5; Acts 5:3–4; Rom. 9:5; Col. 2:9; Jude 24–25

Q. 7. What are the decrees of God?

A. The decrees of God are, his eternal purpose, according to the counsel of his will, whereby, for his own glory, he hath foreordained whatsoever comes to pass (a).

    (a). Ps. 33:11; Isa. 14:24; Acts 2:23; Eph. 1:11–12

Q. 8. How doth God execute his decrees?

A. God executeth his decrees in the works of creation and providence (a).

    (a). Ps. 148:8; Isa. 40:26; Dan. 4:35; Acts 4:24–28; Rev. 4:11

Q. 9. What is the work of creation?

A. The work of creation is, God's making all things of nothing, by the word of his power (a), in the space of six days, and all very good (b).

    (a). Gen. 1:1; Ps. 33:6, 9; Heb. 11:3
    (b). Gen. 1:31

Q. 10. How did God create man?

A. God created man male and female, after his own image (a), in knowledge (b), righteousness, and holiness (c), with dominion over the creatures (d).

    (a). Gen. 1:27
    (b). Col. 3:10
    (c). Eph. 4:24
    (d). Gen. 1:28; see Ps. 8

Q. 11. What are God's works of providence?

A. God's works of providence are, his most holy (a), wise (b), and powerful (c) preserving (d) and governing (e) all his creatures, and all their actions (f).

    (a). Ps. 145:17
    (b). Ps. 104:24
    (c). Heb. 1:3
    (d). Neh. 9:6
    (e). Eph. 1:19–22
    (f). Ps. 36:6; Prov. 16:33; Matt. 10:30

Q. 12. What special act of providence did God exercise toward man in the estate wherein he was created?

A. When God had created man, he entered into a covenant of life with him, upon condition of perfect obedience; forbidding him to eat of the tree of the knowledge of good and evil, upon pain of death (a).

   (a). Gen. 2:16–17; Jas. 2:10

Q. 13. Did our first parents continue in the estate wherein they were created?

A. Our first parents, being left to the freedom of their own will, fell from the estate wherein they were created, by sinning against God (a).

   (a). Gen. 3:6–8, 13; II Cor. 11:3

Q. 14. What is sin?

A. Sin is any want of conformity unto, or transgression of, the law of God (a).

   (a). Lev. 5:17; Jas. 4:17; I John 3:4

Q. 15. What was the sin whereby our first parents fell from the estate wherein they were created?

A. The sin whereby our first parents fell from the estate wherein they were created, was their eating the forbidden fruit (a).

   (a). Gen. 3:6

Q. 16. Did all mankind fall in Adam's first transgression?

A. The covenant being made with Adam (a), not only for himself, but for his posterity; all mankind, descending from him by ordinary generation, sinned in him, and fell with him, in his first transgression (b).

   (a). Gen. 2:16–17; Jas. 2:10
   (b). Rom. 5:12–21; I Cor. 15:22

Q. 17. Into what estate did the fall bring mankind?

A. The fall brought mankind into an estate of sin and misery (a).

   (a). Gen. 3:16–19, 23; Rom. 3:16; 5:12; Eph. 2:1

Q. 18. Wherein consists the sinfulness of that estate whereinto man fell?

A. The sinfulness of that estate whereinto man fell, consists in the guilt of Adam's first sin (a), the want of original righteousness (b), and the corruption of his whole nature (c), which is commonly called original sin; together with all actual transgressions which proceed from it (d).

(a). Rom. 5:12, 19
(b). Rom. 3:10; Col. 3:10; Eph. 4:24
(c). Ps. 51:5; John 3:6; Rom. 3:18; 8:7–8; Eph. 2:3
(d). Gen. 6:5; Ps. 53:1–3; Matt. 15:19; Rom. 3:10–18, 23; Gal. 5:19–21; Jas. 1:14–15

Q. 19. What is the misery of that estate whereinto man fell?

A. All mankind by their fall lost communion with God (a), are under his wrath (b) and curse (c), and so made liable to all miseries in this life (d), to death (e) itself, and to the pains of hell forever (f).

(a). Gen. 3:8, 24; John 8:34, 42, 44; Eph. 2:12; 4:18
(b). John 3:36; Rom. 1:18; Eph. 2:3; 5:6
(c). Gal. 3:10; Rev. 22:3
(d). Gen. 3:16–19; Job 5:7; Ecc. 2:22–23; Rom. 8:18–23
(e). Ezek. 18:4; Rom. 5:12; 6:23
(f). Matt. 25:41, 46; II Thess. 1:9; Rev. 14:9–11

Q. 20. Did God leave all mankind to perish in the estate of sin and misery?

A. God having, out of his mere good pleasure, from all eternity, elected some to everlasting life (a,) did enter into a covenant of grace, to deliver them out of the estate of sin and misery, and to bring them into an estate of salvation by a Redeemer (b).

(a). Acts 13:48; Eph. 1:4–5; II Thess. 2:13–14
(b). Gen. 3:15; 17:7; Ex. 19:5–6; Jer. 31:31–34; Matt. 20:28; I Cor. 11:25; Heb. 9:15

Q. 21. Who is the Redeemer of God's elect?

A. The only Redeemer of God's elect is the Lord Jesus Christ (a), who, being the eternal Son of God (b), became man (c) and so was, and continueth to be, God and man in two distinct natures, and one person, forever (d).

(a). John 14:6; Acts 4:12; I Tim. 2:5–6
(b). Ps. 2:7; Matt. 3:17; 17:5; John 1:18
(c). Isa. 9:6; Matt. 1:23; John 1:14; Gal. 4:4
(d). Acts 1:11; Heb. 7:24–25

Q. 22. How did Christ, being the Son of God, become man?

A. Christ, the Son of God, became man, by taking to himself a true body, and a reasonable soul (a), being conceived by the power of the Holy Ghost, in the womb of the Virgin Mary, and born of her (b) yet without sin (c).

(a). Phil. 2:7; Heb. 2:14, 17
(b). Luke 1:27, 31, 35
(c). II Cor. 5:21; Heb. 4:15; 7:26; I John 3:5

Q. 23. What offices doth Christ execute as our Redeemer?

A. Christ, as our Redeemer, executeth the offices of a prophet (a), of a priest (b), and of a king (c), both in his estate of humiliation and exaltation.

(a). Deut. 18:18; Acts 2:33; 3:22–23; Heb. 1:1–2
(b). Heb. 4:14–15; 5:5–6
(c). Isa. 9:6–7; Luke 1:32–33; John 18:37; I Cor. 15:25

Q. 24. How doth Christ execute the office of a prophet?

A. Christ executeth the office of a prophet, in revealing to us, by his Word (a) and Spirit (b,) the will of God for our salvation (c).

(a). Luke 4:18–19, 21; Acts 1:1–2; Heb. 2:3
(b). John 15:26–27; Acts 1:8; I Pet. 1:11
(c). John 4:41–42; 20:30–31

Q. 25. How doth Christ execute the office of a priest?

A. Christ executeth the office of a priest, in his once offering up of himself a sacrifice to satisfy divine justice (a), and reconcile us to God (b); and in making continual intercession for us (c).

(a). Isa. 53; Acts 8:32–35; Heb. 9:26–28; 10:12
(b). Rom. 5:10–11; II Cor. 5:18; Col. 1:21–22
(c). Rom. 8:34; Heb. 7:25; 9:24

Q. 26. How doth Christ execute the office of a king?

A. Christ executeth the office of a king, in subduing us to himself, in ruling and defending us (a), and in restraining and conquering all his and our enemies (b).

(a). Ps. 110:3; Matt. 28:18–20; John 17:2; Col. 1:13
(b). Ps. 2:6–9; 110:1–2; Matt. 12:28; I Cor. 15:24–26; Col. 2:15

Q. 27. Wherein did Christ's humiliation consist?

A. Christ's humiliation consisted in his being born, and that in a low condition (a), made under the law (b), undergoing the miseries of this life (c), the wrath of God (d), and the cursed death of the cross (e); in being buried, and continuing under the power of death for a time (f).

(a). Luke 2:7; II Cor. 8:9; Gal. 4:4
(b). Gal. 4:4
(c). Isa. 53:3; Luke 9:58; John 4:6; 11:35; Heb. 2:18
(d). Ps. 22:1 (Matt. 27:46); Isa. 53:10; I John 2:2
(e). Gal. 3:13; Phil. 2:8
(f). Matt. 12:40; I Cor. 15:3–4

Q. 28. Wherein consisteth Christ's exaltation?

A. Christ's exaltation consisteth in his rising again from the dead on the third day (a), in ascending up into heaven (b), in sitting at the right hand (c) of God the Father, and in coming to judge the world at the last day (d).

(a). I Cor. 15:4
(b). Ps. 68:18; Acts 1:11; Eph. 4:8
(c). Ps. 110:1; Acts 2:33–34; Heb. 1:3
(d). Matt. 16:27; Acts 17:31

Q. 29. How are we made partakers of the Redemption purchased by Christ?

A. We are made partakers of the Redemption purchased by Christ, by the effectual application of it to us by his Holy Spirit (a).

(a). Titus 3:4–7

Q. 30. How doth the Spirit apply to us the Redemption purchased by Christ?

A. The Spirit applieth to us the Redemption purchased by Christ, by working faith in us (a), and thereby uniting us to Christ in our effectual calling (b).

(a). Rom. 10:17; I Cor. 2:12–16; Eph. 2:8; Phil. 1:29
(b). John 15:5; I Cor. 1:9; Eph. 3:17

Q. 31. What is effectual calling?

A. Effectual calling is the work of God's Spirit, whereby, convincing us of our sin and misery, enlightening our minds in the knowledge of Christ (a), and renewing our wills (b), he doth persuade and enable us to embrace Jesus Christ (c), freely offered to us in the gospel (d).

(a). Acts 26:18; I Cor. 2:10, 12; II Cor. 4:6; Eph. 1:17–18
(b). Deut. 30:6; Ezk. 36:26–27; John 3:5; Titus 3:5
(c). John 6:44–45; Acts 16:14
(d). Isa. 45:22; Matt. 11:28–30; Rev. 22:17

Q. 32. What benefits do they that are effectually called partake of in this life?

A. They that are effectually called do in this life partake of justification, adoption, and sanctification, and the several benefits which in this life do either accompany or flow from them (a).

(a). Rom. 8:30; I Cor. 1:30; 6:11; Eph. 1:5

Q. 33. What is justification?

A. Justification is an act of God's free grace (a), wherein he pardoneth all our sins (b), and accepteth us as righteous in his sight (c), only for the righteousness of Christ imputed to us (d), and received by faith alone (e).

(a). Rom. 3:24
(b). Rom. 4:6–8; II Cor. 5:19
(c). II Cor. 5:21
(d). Rom. 4:6, 11; 5:19
(e). Gal. 2:16; Phil. 3:9

Q. 34. What is adoption?

A. Adoption is an act of God's free grace (a), whereby we are received into the number, and have a right to all the privileges, of the sons of God (b).

    (a). I John 3:1
    (b). John 1:12; Rom. 8:17

Q. 35. What is sanctification?

A. Sanctification is the work of God's free grace (a), whereby we are renewed in the whole man after the image of God (b), and are enabled more and more to die unto sin, and live unto righteousness (c).

    (a). Ezk. 36:27; Phil. 2:13; II Thess. 2:13
    (b). II Cor. 5:17; Eph. 4:23–24; I Thess. 5:23
    (c). Ezek. 36:25–27; Rom. 6:4, 6, 12–14; II Cor. 7:1; I Pet. 2:24

Q. 36. What are the benefits which in this life do accompany or flow from justification, adoption, and sanctification?

A. The benefits which in this life do accompany or flow from justification, adoption, and sanctification, are, assurance of God's love (a), peace of conscience (b), joy in the Holy Ghost (c), increase of grace (d), and perseverance therein to the end (e).

    (a). Rom. 5:5
    (b). Rom. 5:1
    (c). Rom. 14:17
    (d). II Pet. 3:18
    (e). Phil. 1:6; I Pet. 1:5

Q. 37. What benefits do believers receive from Christ at death?

A. The souls of believers are at their death made perfect in holiness (a), and do immediately pass into glory (b); and their bodies, being still united to Christ (c), do rest in their graves till the resurrection (d).

    (a). Heb. 12:23
    (b). Luke 23:43; II Cor. 5:6, 8; Phil. 1:23
    (c). I Thess. 4:14
    (d). Dan. 12:2; John 5:28–29; Acts 24:15

Q. 38. What benefits do believers receive from Christ at the resurrection?

A. At the resurrection, believers being raised up in glory (a), shall be openly acknowledged and acquitted in the day of judgment (b), and made perfectly blessed in the full enjoying of God (c) to all eternity (d).

    (a). I Cor. 15:42–43
    (b). Matt. 25:33–34, 46
    (c). Rom. 8:29; I John 3:2
    (d). Ps. 16:11; I Thess. 4:17

Q. 39. What is the duty which God requireth of man?

A. The duty which God requireth of man, is obedience to his revealed will (a).

   (a). Deut. 29:29; Mic. 6:8; I John 5:2–3

Q. 40. What did God at first reveal to man for the rule of his obedience?

A. The rule which God at first revealed to man for his obedience, was the moral law (a).

   (a). Rom. 2:14–15; 10:5

Q. 41. Wherein is the moral law summarily comprehended?

A. The moral law is summarily comprehended in the Ten Commandments (a).

   (a). Deut. 4:13; Matt. 19:17–19

Q. 42. What is the sum of the Ten Commandments?

A. The sum of the Ten Commandments is, To love the Lord our God with all our heart, with all our soul, with all our strength, and with all our mind; and our neighbour as ourselves (a).

   (a). Matt. 22:37–40

Q. 43. What is the preface to the Ten Commandments?

A. The preface to the Ten Commandments is in these words, I am the Lord thy God, which have brought thee out of the land of Egypt, out of the house of bondage (a).

   (a). Ex. 20:2; Deut. 5:6

Q. 44. What doth the preface to the Ten Commandments teach us?

A. The preface to the Ten Commandments teacheth us, That because God is the Lord, and our God, and Redeemer, therefore we are bound to keep all his commandments (a).

   (a). Luke 1:74–75; I Pet. 1:14–19

Q. 45. Which is the First Commandment?

A. The First Commandment is, Thou shalt have no other gods before me (a).

   (a). Ex. 20:3; Deut. 5:7

Q. 46. What is required in the First Commandment?

A. The First Commandment requireth us to know and acknowledge God to be the only true God, and our God; and to worship and glorify him accordingly (a).

   (a). I Chron. 28:9; Isa. 45:20–25; Matt. 4:10

Q. 47. What is forbidden in the First Commandment?

A. The First Commandment forbiddeth the denying (a), or not worshipping and glorifying the true God as God (b), and our God (c); and the giving of that worship and glory to any other, which is due to him alone (d).

   (a). Ps. 14:1
   (b). Rom. 1:20–21
   (c). Ps. 81:10–11
   (d). Ezek. 8:16–18; Rom. 1:25

Q. 48. What are we specially taught by these words, "before me," in the First Commandment?

A. These words, before me, in the First Commandment teach us, that God, who seeth all things, taketh notice of, and is much displeased with, the sin of having any other God (a).

   (a). Deut. 30:17–18; Ps. 44:20–21; Ezek. 8:12

Q. 49. Which is the Second Commandment?

A. The Second Commandment is, Thou shalt not make unto thee any graven image, or any like-ness of anything that is in heaven above, or that is in the earth beneath, or that is in the water under the earth: thou shalt not bow down thy self to them, nor serve them: for I the Lord thy God am a jealous God, visiting the iniquity of the fathers upon the children unto the third and fourth gener-ation of them that hate me; and showing mercy unto thousands of them that love me, and keep my commandments (a).

   (a). Ex. 20:4–6; Deut. 5:8–10

Q. 50. What is required in the Second Commandment?

A. The Second Commandment requireth the receiving, observing, and keeping pure and entire, all such religious worship and ordinances as God hath appointed in his Word (a).

   (a). Deut. 12:32; Matt. 28:20

Q. 51. What is forbidden in the Second Commandment?

A. The Second Commandment forbiddeth the worshipping of God by images (a), or any other way not appointed in his Word (b).

   (a). Deut. 4:15–19; Rom. 1:22–23
   (b). Lev. 10:1–2; Jer. 19:4–5; Col. 2:18–23

Q. 52. What are the reasons annexed to the Second Commandment?

A. The reasons annexed to the Second Commandment are, God's sovereignty over us (a), his pro-priety in us (b), and the zeal he hath to his own worship (c).

   (a). Ps. 95:2–3, 6–7; 96:9–10

(b). Ex. 19:5; Ps. 45:11; Isa. 54:5
(c). Ex. 34:14; I Cor. 10:22

Q. 53. Which is the Third Commandment?

A. The Third Commandment is, Thou shalt not take the name of the Lord thy God in vain; for the Lord will not hold him guiltless that taketh his name in vain (a).

(a). Ex. 20:7; Deut. 5:11

Q. 54. What is required in the Third Commandment?

A. The Third Commandment requireth the holy and reverend use of God's names, titles (a), attributes (b), ordinances (c), Word (d), and works (e).

(a). Deut. 10:20; Ps. 29:2; Matt. 6:9
(b). I Chron. 29:10–13; Rev. 15:3–4
(c). Acts 2:42; I Cor. 11:27–28
(d). Ps. 138:2; Rev. 22:18–19
(e). Ps. 107:21–22; Rev. 4:11

Q. 55. What is forbidden in the Third Commandment?

A. The Third Commandment forbiddeth all profaning or abusing of anything whereby God maketh himself known (a).

(a). Lev. 19:12; Matt. 5:33–37; Jas. 5:12

Q. 56. What is the reason annexed to the Third Commandment?

A. The reason annexed to the Third Commandment is, that however the breakers of this commandment may escape punishment from men, yet the Lord our God will not suffer them to escape his righteous judgment (a).

(a). Deut. 28:58–59; I Sam. 3:13; 4:11

Q. 57. Which is the Fourth Commandment?

A. The Fourth Commandment is, Remember the Sabbath day, to keep it holy. Six days shalt thou labor, and do all thy work; but the seventh day is the Sabbath of the Lord thy God: in it thou shalt not do any work, thou, nor thy son, nor thy daughter, thy manservant, nor thy maidservant, nor thy cattle, nor thy stranger that is within thy gates. For in six days the Lord made heaven and earth, the sea, and all that in them is, and rested the seventh day: wherefore the Lord blessed the Sabbath day, and hallowed it (a).

(a). Ex. 20:8–11; Deut. 5:12–15

Q. 58. What is required in the Fourth Commandment?

A. The Fourth Commandment requireth the keeping holy to God such set times as he hath appointed in his Word; expressly one whole day in seven, to be a holy Sabbath to himself (a).

(a). Ex. 31:13, 16–17

Q. 59. Which day of the seven hath God appointed to be the weekly Sabbath?

A. From the beginning of the world to the Resurrection of Christ, God appointed the seventh day of the week to be the weekly Sabbath (a); and the first day of the week ever since, to continue to the end of the world, which is the Christian Sabbath (b).

 (a). Gen. 2:2–3; Ex. 20:11
 (b). Mark 2:27–28; Acts 20:7; I Cor. 16:2; Rev. 1:10

Q. 60. How is the Sabbath to be sanctified?

A. The Sabbath is to be sanctified by a holy resting all that day, even from such worldly employments and recreations as are lawful on other days (a); and spending the whole time in the public and private exercises of God's worship (b), except so much as is to be taken up in the works of necessity and mercy (c).

 (a). Ex. 20:10; Neh. 13:15–22; Isa. 58:13–14
 (b). Ex. 20:8; Lev. 23:3; Luke 4:16; Acts 20:7
 (c). Matt. 12:1–13

Q. 61. What is forbidden in the Fourth Commandment?

A. The Fourth Commandment forbiddeth the omission or careless performance of the duties required, and the profaning the day by idleness, or doing that which is in itself sinful, or by unnecessary thoughts, words, or works, about our worldly employments or recreations (a).

 (a). Neh. 13:15–22; Isa. 58:13–14; Amos 8:4–6

Q. 62. What are the reasons annexed to the Fourth Commandment?

A. The reasons annexed to the Fourth Commandment are, God's allowing us six days of the week for our own employments (a), his challenging a special propriety in the seventh, his own example, and his blessing the Sabbath day (b).

 (a). Ex. 20:9; 31:15; Lev. 23:3
 (b). Gen. 2:2–3; Ex. 20:11; 31:17

Q. 63. Which is the Fifth Commandment?

A. The Fifth Commandment is, Honour thy father and thy mother; that thy days may be long upon the land which the Lord thy God giveth thee (a).

 (a). Ex. 20:12; Deut. 5:16

Q. 64. What is required in the Fifth Commandment?

A. The Fifth Commandment requireth the preserving the honor, and performing the duties, belonging to everyone in their several places and relations, as superiors, inferiors, or equals (a).

(a). Rom. 13:1, 7; Eph. 5:21–22, 24; 6:1, 4–5, 9; I Pet. 2:17

Q. 65. What is forbidden in the Fifth Commandment?

A. The Fifth Commandment forbiddeth the neglecting of, or doing anything against, the honor and duty which belongeth to everyone in their several places and relations (a).

(a). Matt. 15:4–6; Rom. 13:8

Q. 66. What is the reason annexed to the Fifth Commandment?

A. The reason annexed to the Fifth Commandment is, a promise of long life and prosperity (as far as it shall serve for God's glory and their own good) to all such as keep this commandment (a).

(a). Ex. 20:12; Deut. 5:16; Eph. 6:2–3

Q. 67. Which is the Sixth Commandment?

A. The Sixth Commandment is, Thou shalt not kill (a).

(a). Ex. 20:13; Deut. 5:17

Q. 68. What is required in the Sixth Commandment?

A. The Sixth Commandment requireth all lawful endeavors to preserve our own life, and the life of others (a).

(a). Eph. 5:28–29

Q. 69. What is forbidden in the Sixth Commandment?

A. The Sixth Commandment forbiddeth the taking away of our own life, or the life of our neighbour, unjustly, or whatsoever tendeth thereunto (a).

(a). Gen. 9:6; Matt. 5:22; I John 3:15

Q. 70. Which is the Seventh Commandment?

A. The Seventh Commandment is, Thou shalt not commit adultery (a).

(a). Ex. 20:14; Deut. 5:18

Q. 71. What is required in the Seventh Commandment?

A. The Seventh Commandment requireth the preservation of our own and our neighbour's chastity, in heart, speech, and behavior (a).

(a). I Cor. 7:2–3, 5; I Thess. 4:3–5

Q. 72. What is forbidden in the Seventh Commandment?

A. The Seventh Commandment forbiddeth all unchaste thoughts, words, and actions (a).

(a). Matt. 5:28; Eph. 5:3–4

Q. 73. Which is the Eighth Commandment?

A. The Eighth Commandment is, Thou shalt not steal (a).

(a). Ex. 20:15; Deut. 5:19

Q. 74. What is required in the Eighth Commandment?

A. The Eighth Commandment requireth the lawful procuring and furthering the wealth and outward estate of ourselves and others (a).

(a). Lev. 25:35; Eph. 4:28b; Phil. 2:4

Q. 75. What is forbidden in the Eighth Commandment?

A. The Eighth Commandment forbiddeth whatsoever doth, or may, unjustly hinder our own, or our neighbour's, wealth or outward estate (a).

(a). Prov. 28:19ff; Eph. 4:28a; II Thess. 3:10; I Tim. 5:8

Q. 76. Which is the Ninth Commandment?

A. The Ninth Commandment is, Thou shalt not bear false witness against thy neighbour (a).

(a). Ex. 20:16; Deut. 5:20

Q. 77. What is required in the Ninth Commandment?

A. The Ninth Commandment requireth the maintaining and promoting of truth between man and man, and of our own and our neighbour's good name (a), especially in witness bearing (b).

(a). Zech. 8:16; Acts 25:10; III John 12
(b). Prov. 14:5, 25

Q. 78. What is forbidden in the Ninth Commandment?

A. The Ninth Commandment forbiddeth whatsoever is prejudicial to truth, or injurious to our own, or our neighbour's, good name (a).

(a). Lev. 19:16; Ps. 15:3; Prov. 6:16–19; Luke 3:14

Q. 79. Which is the Tenth Commandment?

A. The Tenth Commandment is, Thou shalt not covet thy neighbour's house, thou shalt not covet thy neighbour's wife, nor his manservant, nor his maidservant, nor his ox, nor his ass, nor anything that is thy neighbour's (a).

(a). Ex. 20:17; Deut. 5:21

Q. 80. What is required in the Tenth Commandment?

A. The Tenth Commandment requireth full contentment with our own condition (a), with a right and charitable frame of spirit toward our neighbour, and all that is his (b).

   (a). Ps. 34:1; Phil. 4:11; ITim. 6:6; Heb. 13:5
   (b). Luke 15:6, 9, 11–32; Rom. 12:15; Phil. 2:4

Q. 81. What is forbidden in the Tenth Commandment?

A. The Tenth Commandment forbiddeth all discontentment with our own estate (a), envying or grieving at the good of our neighbour, and all inordinate motions and affections to anything that is his (b).

   (a). I Cor. 10:10; Jas. 3:14–16
   (b). Gal. 5:26; Col. 3:5

Q. 82. Is any man able perfectly to keep the commandments of God?

A. No mere man, since the fall, is able in this life perfectly to keep the commandments of God, but doth daily break them in thought, word, and deed (a).

   (a). Gen. 8:21; Rom. 3:9ff, 23

Q. 83. Are all transgressions of the law equally heinous?

A. Some sins in themselves, and by reason of several aggravations, are more heinous in the sight of God than others (a).

   (a). Ezek. 8:6, 13, 15; Matt. 11:20–24; John 19:11

Q. 84. What doth every sin deserve?

A. Every sin deserveth God's wrath and curse, both in this life, and that which is to come (a).

   (a). Matt. 25:41; Gal. 3:10; Eph. 5:6; Jas. 2:10

Q. 85. What doth God require of us, that we may escape his wrath and curse, due to us for sin?

A. To escape the wrath and curse of God, due to us for sin, God requireth of us faith in Jesus Christ, repentance unto life (a), with the diligent use of all the outward means whereby Christ communicateth to us the benefits of Redemption (b).

   (a). Mark 1:15; Acts 20:21
   (b): Acts 2:38; I Cor. 11:24–25; Col. 3:16

Q. 86. What is faith in Jesus Christ?

A. Faith in Jesus Christ is a saving grace (a), whereby we receive and rest upon him alone for salvation, as he is offered to us in the gospel (b).

(a). Eph. 2:8–9; cf. Rom. 4:16
(b). John 20:30–31; Gal. 2:15–16; Phil. 3:3–11

Q. 87. What is repentance unto life?

A. Repentance unto life is a saving grace (a), whereby a sinner, out of a true sense of his sin, and apprehension of the mercy of God in Christ (b), doth, with grief and hatred of his sin, turn from it unto God (c), with full purpose of, and endeavour after, new obedience (d).

(a). Acts 11:18; II Tim. 2:25
(b). Ps. 51:1–4; Joel 2:13; Luke 15:7, 10; Acts 2:37
(c). Jer. 31:18–19; Luke 1:16–17; I Thess. 1:9
(d). II Chron. 7:14; Ps. 119:57–64; Matt. 3:8; II Cor. 7:10

Q. 88. What are the outward and ordinary means whereby Christ communicateth to us the benefits of Redemption?

A. The outward and ordinary means whereby Christ communicateth to us the benefits of Redemption are, his ordinances, especially the Word, sacraments, and prayer; all which are made effectual to the elect for salvation (a).

(a). Matt. 28:18–20; Acts 21:41, 42

Q. 89. How is the Word made effectual to salvation?

A. The Spirit of God maketh the reading, but especially the preaching of the Word, an effectual means of convincing and converting sinners, and of building them up in holiness and comfort, through faith, unto salvation (a).

(a). Neh. 8:8–9; Acts 20:32; Rom. 10:14–17; II Tim. 3:15–17

Q. 90. How is the Word to be read and heard, that it may become effectual to salvation?

A. That the Word may become effectual to salvation, we must attend thereunto with diligence, preparation, and prayer (a); receive it with faith and love, lay it up in our hearts, and practice it in our lives (b).

(a). Deut. 6:6ff; Ps. 119:18; I Pet. 2:1–2
(b). Ps. 119:11; II Thess. 2:10; Heb. 4:2; Jas. 1:22–25

Q. 91. How do the sacraments become effectual means of salvation?

A. The sacraments become effectual means of salvation, not from any virtue in them, or in him that doth administer them; but only by the blessing of Christ, and the working of his Spirit in them that by faith receive them (a).

(a). I Cor. 3:7; cf. I Cor. 1:12–17

Q. 92. What is a sacrament?

A. A sacrament is a holy ordinance instituted by Christ (a); wherein, by sensible signs, Christ, and the benefits of the new covenant, are represented, sealed, and applied to believers (b).

  (a). Matt. 28:19; 26:26–28; Mark 14:22–25; Luke 22:19–20; I Cor. 1:22–26
  (b). Gal. 3:27; I Cor. 10:16–17

Q. 93. Which are the sacraments of the New Testament?

A. The sacraments of the New Testament are, Baptism (a), and the Lord's Supper (b).

  (a). Matt. 28:19
  (b). I Cor 11:23–26

Q. 94. What is Baptism?

A. Baptism is a sacrament, wherein the washing with water in the name of the Father, and of the Son, and of the Holy Ghost (a), doth signify and seal our ingrafting into Christ, and partaking of the benefits of the covenant of grace, and our engagement to be the Lord's (b).

  (a). Matt. 28:19
  (b). Acts 2:38–42; 22:16; Rom. 6:3–4; Gal. 3:26–27; I Pet. 3:21

Q. 95. To whom is Baptism to be administered?

A. Baptism is not to be administered to any that are out of the visible church, till they profess their faith in Christ, and obedience to him (a); but the infants of such as are members of the visible church are to be baptized (b).

  (a). Acts. 2:41; 8:12, 36, 38; 18:8
  (b). Gen. 17:7, 9–11; Acts 2:38–39; 16:32–33; Col. 2:11–12

Q. 96. What is the Lord's Supper?

A. The Lord's Supper is a sacrament, wherein, by giving and receiving bread and wine, according to Christ's appointment, his death is showed forth (a); and the worthy receivers are, not after a corporal and carnal manner, but by faith, made partakers of his body and blood, with all his benefits, to their spiritual nourishment, and growth in grace (b).

  (a). Luke 22:19–20; I Cor. 11:23–26
  (b). I Cor. 10:16–17

Q. 97. What is required for the worthy receiving of the Lord's Supper?

A. It is required of them that would worthily partake of the Lord's Supper, that they examine themselves of their knowledge to discern the Lord's body, of their faith to feed upon him, of their repentance, love, and new obedience; lest, coming unworthily, they eat and drink judgment to themselves (a).

  (a). I Cor. 11:27–32

Q. 98. What is prayer?

A. Prayer is an offering up of our desires unto God (a), for things agreeable to his will (b), in the name of Christ (c), with confession of our sins (d), and thankful acknowledgement of his mercies (e).

    (a). Ps. 10:17; 62:8; Matt. 7:7–8
    (b). I John 5:14
    (c). John 16:23–24
    (d). Ps. 32:5–6; Dan. 9:4–19; I John 1:9
    (e). Ps. 103:1–5; 136; Phil. 4:6

Q. 99. What rule hath God given for our direction in prayer?

A. The whole Word of God is of use to direct us in prayer (a); but the special rule of direction is that form of prayer which Christ taught his disciples, commonly called The Lord's Prayer (b).

    (a). I John 5:14
    (b). Matt. 6:9–13

Q. 100. What doth the preface of the Lord's Prayer teach us?

A. The preface of the Lord's Prayer, which is, Our Father which art in heaven, teacheth us to draw near to God with all holy reverence (a) and confidence (b), as children to a father (c), able and ready to help us (d); and that we should pray with and for others (e).

    (a). Ps. 95:6
    (b). Eph. 3:12
    (c). Matt. 7:9–11, cf. Luke 11:11–13; Rom. 8:15
    (d). Eph. 3:20
    (e). Eph. 6:18; I Tim. 2:1–2

Q. 101. What do we pray for in the first petition?

A. In the first petition, which is, Hallowed be thy name, we pray, that God would enable us, and others, to glorify him in all that whereby he maketh himself known (a); and that he would dispose all things to his own glory (b).

    (a). Ps. 67:1–3; 99:3; 100:3–4
    (b). Rom. 11:33–36; Rev. 4:11

Q. 102. What do we pray for in the second petition?

A. In the second petition, which is, Thy kingdom come, we pray, that Satan's kingdom may be destroyed (a); and that the kingdom of grace may be advanced (b), ourselves and others brought into it, and kept in it (c); and that the kingdom of glory may be hastened (d).

    (a). Matt. 12:25–28; Rom. 16:20; I John 3:8
    (b). Ps. 72:8–11; Matt. 24:14; I Cor. 15:24–25
    (c). Ps. 119:5; Luke 22:32; II Thess. 3:1–5
    (d). Rev. 22:20

Q. 103. What do we pray for in the third petition?

A. In the third petition, which is, Thy will be done in earth, as it is in heaven, we pray, that God, by his grace, would make us able and willing to know, obey, and submit to his will in all things (a), as the angels do in heaven (b).

(a). Ps. 19:14; 119; I Thess. 5:23; Heb. 13:20–21
(b). Ps. 103:20–21; Heb. 1:14

Q. 104. What do we pray for in the fourth petition?

A. In the fourth petition, which is, Give us this day our daily bread, we pray that of God's free gift we may receive a competent portion of the good things of this life, and enjoy his blessing with them (a).

(a). Prov. 30:8–9; Matt. 6:31–34; Phil. 4:11, 19; I Tim. 6:6–8

Q. 105. What do we pray for in the fifth petition?

A. In the fifth petition, which is, And forgive us our debts, as we forgive our debtors, we pray that God, for Christ's sake, would freely pardon all our sins (a); which we are the rather encouraged to ask, because by his grace we are enabled from the heart to forgive others (b).

(a). Ps. 51:1–2, 7, 9; Dan. 9:17–19; I John 1:7
(b). Matt. 18:21–35; Eph. 4:32; Col. 3:13

Q. 106. What do we pray for in the sixth petition?

A. In the sixth petition, which is, And lead us not into temptation, but deliver us from evil, we pray, that God would either keep us from being tempted to sin (a), or support and deliver us when we are tempted (b).

(a). Ps. 19:13; Matt. 26:41; John 17:15
(b). Luke 22:31–32; I Cor. 10:13; II Cor. 12:7–9; Heb. 2:18

Q. 107. What doth the conclusion of the Lord's Prayer teach us?

A. The conclusion of the Lord's Prayer, which is, For thine is the kingdom, and the power, and the glory, forever, Amen. teacheth us to take our encouragement in prayer from God only (a), and in our prayers to praise him, ascribing kingdom, power, and glory to him (b); and, in testimony of our desire, and assurance to be heard, we say, Amen (c).

(a). Dan. 9:4, 7–9, 16–19; Luke 18:1, 7–8
(b). I Chron. 29:10–13; I Tim. 1:17; Rev. 5:11–13
(c). I Cor. 14:16; Rev. 22:20

(Note: The Westminster Catechism was used extensively in colonial America. There is a Baptist version of the shorter catechism available, as well as various catechisms for different denominations. Check with your church or pastor for further information.)

QUESTION ANSWERS

Geography: Setting the Stage

1. To fill the earth with His glory.
2. The protection of England by the English Channel and the influence of weather on the outcome of wars.
3. Pollution and the depletion of natural resources are two.
4. It is a "circle," or "sphere."

Act One: The Drama of Ancient History

1. Some answers may be: the Israelites wandering in the wilderness rather than taking the Promised Land; the Israelites' later worship of Baal; conquests for world dominion, such as those led by Alexander, Napoleon, and Lenin.
2. Great cities, architecture, arithmetic, geometry, and astronomy.
3. Greek: modeled after man; Christian: made man in His own image. Greek: immoral; Christian: perfect.
4. Augustus (Octavius); Tiberius.
5. See Exodus 20:117.
6. Idolatry; tyranny; slavery; unjust government; persecution of the followers of God.
7. Jesus
8. The Bible

Act Two: The Middle Ages and the Renaissance

1. Prayer; Bible study; the Holy Spirit; wise counsel; learning from history.
2. Barbarian attacks; the conversion of barbarians to Christianity.
3. The Magna Carta; the Declaration of Independence, the U. S. Constitution, and the Bill of Rights.
4. The Crusades, the Great Schism, and the Plague.
5. John Wycliffe; he translated the Bible into English.
6. Humanism
7. Using the Renaissance to revive an interest in the classical languages and in the searching out of early manuscripts; provoking a spirit of inquiry and the questioning of the authority of the Roman Church; popularizing the use of movable type printing; providing in the Renaissance an obvious contrast to the biblical faith declared in Scripture.

Act Three: The Foundations of European Liberty

1. No
2. They felt the Church was hypocritical and in need of change.
3. Evangelism
4. Martin Luther
5. William Tyndale
6. John Knox
7. The Netherlands; Scotland; France.

Act Four: The American Expression of Liberty

1. For material prosperity and freedom, which would attract others; the corruption of their children by Dutch moral laxity; the fear of a Spanish offensive in the Netherlands; to spread the Gospel.

2. Jamestown
3. Puritans
4. The arrival of much-needed and prayed-for rain.
5. Thomas Hooker.
6. The Great Awakening
6. American pastors
7. Lexington, Massachusetts; 19 April 1775.

Act Five: The Birth of a Nation

1. The French Revolution
2. See *The American Revolution vs. The French Revolution* section.
3. Christ's birth.
4. Idleness
5. John Calvin
6. Prayer
7. The Bill of Rights.
8. The Bible.
9. In a democracy, all the people rule; in a representative government, the people choose their representatives, who rule on their behalf. America has a representative government.
10. Legislative, executive, and judicial; to preserve the liberty of citizens.

The Christian History of Black America

1. They are important in remembering the history of black Americans.
2. The founders did not rely on God for its solution, and instead compromised with pro-slavery ideas.
3. George Liele; David George; Richard Allen.
4. Galatians 3:28 and Philemon 1516.

Act Six: The Drama of Modern History

1. Religion and morality.
2. It determines a society's view of man, and thus its view of government.
3. The Trinity
4. Transcendentalism, cults, Darwinism, liberal theology.
5. Not confronting humanism; causing intolerance and bigotry.
6. The Bible.
7. Horace Mann and John Dewey.
8. Charitable organizations.
9. Stewardship of private property; the nobility of work; divine calling; tithing; honesty; savings and investment; creativity; optimism.
10. State government and self-government.
11. Legal cases.

Crime: Its Causes and Cures

1. The ability of Americans to govern themselves.
2. Religion
3. Environmental influences
4. Man's sin nature.
5. To punish the wicked and reward the righteous.

6. The Gospel; Christian charity; a restoration of civil government to its proper role; the reestablishment of the family's authority.
7. By the election of godly leaders.

Worldview Expression in Art

1. God's created order.
2. They are both concerned with the "eternal and spiritual."
3. To defend against false sentiment with just sentiments.
4. Flat and emotionless; perfectly proportioned; panicked emotionalism.
5. In catacombs.
6. Cathedrals.
7. See *The Renaissance* section.
8. Through painting scenes and themes from the Bible.
9. Portraying average people.
10. The Enlightenment and the romantic movement.
11. The degradation of the figure and reality.
12. It is impossible to live in such a world as man has created, which the art depicts.

Worldview Expression in Literature

1. It trains the mind to think.
2. Evaluate worldviews.
3. The Bible.
4. The Middle Ages; drama.
5. The Scientific Revolution; through orderly, simple writing.
6. See *The Age of Man* section.
7. The meaninglessness of life without absolutes.
8. Offer the hope of salvation through Christ.

Faith and Music

1. Psalms
2. Order; peace; instruction; relaxation; thankfulness; excitement & praise to God; and worship.
3. George Friderick Handel
4. Franz Joseph Haydn
5. Ludwig van Beethoven
6. Franz Peter Schubert

Faith and Science

1. Jesus Christ
2. Sir Isaac Newton
3. No
4. That there are some big gaps in the theory of evolution. The fossil record itself shows mass extinctions followed by the creation of new species, appearing without any trace of evolutionary development.
5. The theory of evolution maintains that organisms move from the simple to the complex, opposite of what the second law of thermodynamics states.
6. Crime, the 'victim' mentality, animal rights debate, human sexuality, the in-built sinfulness of man and his rebellion against God's authority.

Myths and Legends

1. Refer to the CD-ROMs.
2. To explain life.
3. The flood and creation stories.
4. Its basis is in historical and revealed truth.

Christian Leadership

1. John Wesley was an evangelist; Charles Wesley, a Christian songwriter.
2. George Whitefield
3. Jonathan Edwards
4. Charles G. Finney
5. Dwight L. Moody
6. Charles Spurgeon
7. Billy Sunday
8. When he chose to believe God's Word was true and that he would always believe it and preach it.

Preparing the Christian Student for College

1. Humanism
2. The Bible.
3. Know God; know God's Word; associate with God's people; know God's world.
4. The Ten Commandments; the Apostles' Creed; the Westminster Confession of Faith.
5. It makes it easier for students to be influenced by humanistic ideas.
6. Revivalistic piety.
7. God-oriented and man-oriented.
8. See the *Non-Christian Worldviews* section.
9. Vision; have a plan for their lives.
10. See *The Final Step* section.

NOTES

Quotations from the Jewish and Christian Scriptures are taken
from the *New King James Version.*

Part One: A Biblical Plan for Godly Education

1. Matt. 19:14.
2. Perry Miller and Thomas Johnson, *The Puritans* (New York: American Literary Service, 1938) 11.
3. Quoted in Marshall Foster and Mary-Elaine Swanson, *The American Covenant: The Untold Story* (Thousand Oaks, CA: Mayflower Institute, 1992) 8–9.
4. Paul Johnson, *Intellectuals* (New York: Harper & Row, 1988) 1.
5. William J. Bennett, *The Index of Leading Cultural Indicators,* Vol. 1 (March 1993) Heritage Foundation.
6. Thomas Sowell, *Inside American Education* (New York: Free Press, 1993) 3.
7. Francis A. Schaeffer, *How Should We Then Live?* (Wheaton, IL: Crossway, 1976) 19.
8. Stephen K. McDowell and Mark A. Belilies, *Liberating the Nations* (Charlottesville, VA: Providence Foundation, 1993) 104.
9. R.L. Dabney, *On Secular Education* (Moscow, ID: Ransom, 1989) 17.
10. Philip Schaff, *The Person of Christ* (New York: Doran, 1913) 137–138.
11. Philip Schaff, *The Person of Christ: The Miracle of History* (Boston: The American Tract Society) 323, 328.
12. Ps. 127:3–4.
13. Prov. 22:6.
14. Deut. 6:4.
15. Deut. 6:5.
16. Rom. 5:8.
17. Douglas Wilson, *Recovering the Lost Tools of Learning: An Approach to Distinctively Christian Education* (Wheaton, IL: Crossway, 1991) 48.
18. Deut. 6:6–7.
19. Deut. 7:8–9.
20. Heb. 10:16; Jer. 31:33.
21. Deut. 6:10–12.
22. Deut. 7:9.
23. Gen. 18:17–19.
24. William J. Federer, *America's God and Country Encyclopedia of Quotations* (Coppell, TX: Fame, 1994) 676.
25. Verna M. Hall, ed., *The Bible and the Constitution of the United States of America* (San Francisco: Foundation for American Christian Education, 1983) 4.
26. John 8:32.
27. 2 Tim. 3:16.
28. Heb. 5:14.
29. Verna M. Hall, ed., *The Christian History of the Constitution of the United States of America* (San Francisco: Foundation for American Christian Education, 1975) xiv.
30. John Naisbitt and Patricia Aburdene, *Megatrends 2000* (New York: Morrow, 1990) 303.

Part Two: God's Historical Drama

Geography: Setting the Stage

1. Quoted in Rosalie J. Slater, *Teaching and Learning America's Christian History* (San Francisco: Foundation for American Christian Education, 1984) 142.

2. Alexis de Tocqueville, *Democracy in America* (New York: Doubleday, 1969) 30.

3. Gen. 1:28.

4. Matt. 28:18–20.

5. Loren Cunningham, "Fill the Earth," *Target Earth*, ed. Frank Kaleb Jansen, (Pasadena, CA: Global Mapping Int'l, 1989) 101.

6. Quoted in Gary DeMar, *God and Government: Issues in Biblical Perspective*, Vol. 2 (Atlanta, GA: American Vision, 1984) 210.

7. Quoted in Gary DeMar and Fred Douglas Young, *A New World in View* (Atlanta: American Vision, 1996) 78.

8. Job 38:4–11; 40:3–5.

9. Quoted in Slater 142.

10. Isa. 11:9.

Act One: The Drama of the Ancient World

1. Gen. 10:8.

2. Exod. 20:4–5.

3. Loren Cunningham, "Fill the Earth," *Target Earth*. Frank Kaleb Jansen, ed. (Pasadena, CA: Global Mapping, 1989) 101.

4. Isa. 8:12-13.

5. Quoted in Marshall Foster and Mary-Elaine Swanson, *The American Covenant: The Untold Story* (Thousand Oaks, CA: Mayflower Institute, 1992) 31.

6. Quoted in Foster 31.

7. Josh McDowell, *Evidence that Demands a Verdict* (Campus Crusade for Christ, 1972) 68.

8. 2 Pet. 1:16.

9. Prov. 2:6–8.

10. Quoted in Foster 30.

11. Verna Hall and Rosalie J. Slater, *The Bible and the Constitution of the United States of America* (San Francisco: Foundation for American Christian Education, 1983) 18.

12. 1 Cor. 15:25.

13. Rom. 14:11.

14. Rousas J. Rushdoony, *World History Notes* (Fairfax, VA: Thoburn Press, 1974) 3–4.

15. Gen. 6:5

16. Gen. 12:1–3

17. Quoted in Foster 68.

18. Matt. 1:20–21.

19. Matt. 28:18.

20. Rev. 1:5

21. McDowell 198.

22. Eph. 1:21.

23. Matt. 28:18–20.

24. John 21:25.

25. William J. Federer, *America's God and Country Encyclopedia of Quotations* (Coppell, TX, Fame, 1994) 463.

26. Matthew Henry, *Commentary on the Whole Bible* (Old Tappan, NJ: Revell) 446.

27. Otto Scott, *The Great Christian Revolution* (Windsor, NY: Reformer Library, 1994) 1.

28. Noah Webster's 1828 Dictionary.

29. James Dale Davidson and Lord William Rees-Mogg, *The Great Reckoning* (New York: Summit, 1991) 51.

30. John Eidsmoe, *Christianity and the Constitution* (Grand Rapids, MI: Baker, 1987) 52.

31. Eidsmoe 71.

32. Eidsmoe 72.

33. James Madison, *The Federalist, No. 10* (New York: Tudor, 1937) 67.

34. John Carey, ed., *Eyewitness to History* (New York: Avon, 1987) 15.

35. Rom. 2:14–15.

36. Josh. 1:8.

37. Ps. 76:10.

38. Gen. 50:20.

39. John Foxe, *Foxe's Christian Martyrs of the World* (San Antonio, TX: Mantle) 98–99.

Act Two: The Middle Ages and the Renaissance

1. James Dale Davidson and Lord William Rees-Mogg, *The Great Reckoning* (New York: Summit, 1991) 29.

2. John C. Ridpath, *A Cloud of Witnesses* (Portland, OR: American Heritage Ministries, 1987) 164.

3. 1 Cor. 10:11–12.

4. Quoted in Davidson 235.

5 Sharon Camp and Joseph Spiedel, "Quality of Life Index," *Target Earth*. Frank Kaleb Jansen, ed. (Pasadena, CA: Global Mapping Int'l, 1989) 90–91.

6. Quoted in *Mayflower Institute Journal*, Vol. 10, No. 9 (October 1995) 2.

7. Quoted in Louis B. Wright, *Magna Carta and the Tradition of Liberty* (Washington, DC: American Revolution Bicentennial Administration, 1976) 54–55.

8. Quoted in Wright 58.

9. Niccolo Machiavelli, *The Prince,* Ch. 18.

10. Isa. 28:13.

Act Three: The European Foundations of Liberty

1. Quoted in Kay Brigham, *Christopher Columbus* (Barcelona: Clie, 1990) 39.

2. Quoted in *Brigham* 85.

3. William Bradford, *History of the Plymouth Settlement* (Portland, OR: American Heritage, 1988) 21.

4. James M. Kittleson, "The Breakthrough," *Christian History* (Issue 34) 15.

5. Robert D. Linder, "Allies or Enemies," *Christian History* (Issue 39) 44.

6. Tony Lane, "A Man for All People: Introducing William Tyndale," *Christian History* (Issue 16) 7.

7. S. M. Houghton, *Sketches from Church History* (Carlisle, PA: Banner of Truth Trust, 1980) 124.

8. Jock Purves, *Fair Sunshine* (Carlisle, PA: Banner of Truth Trust, 1990) 106.

9. Purves 39–40.

10. Purves 47.

11. Charles Carleton Coffin, *The Story of Liberty* (Gainesville, FL: Maranatha, 1987) 335.

12. Coffin 335.

Act Four: The American Expression of Liberty

1. Wilson, George F. *Saints and Strangers* (Orleans, MA: Parnassus, 1983) 7.

2. William Bradford, *History of the Plymouth Settlement* (Portland, OR: American Heritage, 1988) 21.

3. William Bradford, *Of Plymouth Plantation,* Samuel Eliot Morrison, ed. (New York: Modern Library, 1967) 81.

4. Bradford, Plantation, 81.

5. Bradford, Settlement, 115–116.

6. Bradford, Plantation, 145.

7. Quoted in Marshall Foster and Mary-Elaine Swanson, *The American Covenant: The Untold Story* (Thousand Oaks, CA: Mayflower Institute, 1992) 92.

8. John Fiske, *The Beginnings of New England, or The Puritan Theocracy in its Relation to Civil and Religious Liberty* (New York: Houghton, 1900) 102.

9. H. Sheldon Smith, Robert T. Handy, and Lefferts A Loetscher, *American Christianity: An Historical Interpretation with Representative Documents* (New York: Scribners, 1960) 100–101.

10. Verna M. Hall, *The Christian History of the Constitution of the United States of America* (San Francisco, CA: Foundation for American Christian Education, 1975) 250–251.

11. John Fiske, *Beginnings of New England*, 1889. Quoted in Verna M. Hall, *The Christian History of the Constitution of the United States of America* (San Francisco, CA: Foundation for American Christian Education, 1978) 252.

12. Hall 252.

13. George Washington, *The Writings of George Washington*, Vol. 1, 252.

14. Washington, *Writings*, Vol. 30, 427.

15. Quoted in *Mayflower Institute Journal*, 10.10 (Nov 95) 3.

16. Wrong, George M. *The Conquest of New France* (New Haven: University Press, 1918) 82–91.

17. Thomas Prince, *Mr. Prince's Thanksgiving Sermon on the Salvation of God in 1746* (Boston: D. Henchman, 1746) 21.

18. Prince 27.

19. Prince 28.

20. Quoted in Verna M. Hall, *Christian History of the American Revolution* (San Francisco: Foundation for American Christian Education, 1976) 51.

21. Prince 29.

22. Hall, *Revolution*, 51.

23. Jonathan Edwards, "Sinners in the Hands of an Angry God," *Jonathan Edwards* (New York: American Book Company, 1935) 155–172.

24. John Whitehead, *The American Dream* (Westchester, IL: Crossway, 1987) 37.

25. Harry S. Stout, *The New England Soul: Preaching and Religious Culture in Colonial New England* (New York: Oxford University Press, 1986) 3–4.

26. Cushing Strout, *The New Heavens and the New Earth* (New York: Harper, 1974) 59.

27. George Bancroft, *Bancroft's History of the United States*, Vol. VII, Third Edition (Boston: Little & Brown, 1838) 274.

28. Hall 407.

Act Five: The Birth of a Nation

1. Quoted in Margaret Brown Klapthor and Howard Alexander Morrison, *George Washington: A Figure Upon the Stage* (Washington, D.C.: Smithsonian Institute, 1982) 188.

2. Gary T. Amos, *Defending the Declaration* (Brentwood, TN: Wolgemuth, 1989) 33.

3. John Quincy Adams, July 4, 1837, oration on the sixty-first anniversary of the Declaration of Independence (Newburyport, MA: Charles Whipple, 1837).

4. Daniel J. Elazar, "From Biblical Covenant To Modern Federalism: The Federal Theology Bridge," *Workshop on Covenant and Politics* (Philadelphia, PA: Center for the Study of Federalism, Temple University, 1980) 17.

5. John Fiske, *The American Revolution*, 2 Vols. (Boston: Houghton, 1898) Vol. 1, 212.

6. Mercy Otis Warren, *History of the Rise, Progress, and Termination of the American Revolution*, Vol. 1 (Indianapolis, IN: Liberty Classics, 1988).

7. Warren 291.

8. Warren 191.

9. Prov. 24:15–16.

10. William J. Johnson, *George Washington the Christian* (Mott Media, 1976) 103.

11. William Hosmer, "Remember Our Bicentennial—1781," *Foundation for Christian Self-Government Journal* (June 1981) 5.

12. George Washington, *The Writings of George Washington*, Vol. 23, 343.

13. Fred L. Holmes, *George Washington Traveled This Way* (Boston: Page, 1935) 161.

14. M. E. Bradford, *A Worthy Company* (Marlborough, NH: Plymouth Rock Foundation, 1982) viii.

15. John Eidsmoe, *Christianity and the Constitution* (Grand Rapids, MI: Baker, 1987) 18.

16. William Bradford, *History of the Plymouth Settlement* (Portland, OR: American Heritage, 1988) 7.

17. James Madison, *Notes of Debate in the Federal Convention of 1787* (New York: Norton, 1987) 210.

18. James Madison, *The Federalist*, No. 10 (New York: Tudor, 1937) 67.

19. Quoted in Marshall Foster and Mary-Elaine Swanson, *The American Covenant: The Untold Story* (Thousand Oaks, CA: Mayflower Institute, 1992) 139.

20. John Bartlett, *Bartlett's Familiar Quotations* (Boston: Little, 1980) 615.

21. Quoted in Cleon W. Skousen, *The Making of America* (Washington, D.C.: National Center for Constitutional Studies, 1985) 234.

22. Quoted in William J. Federer, *America's God and Country Encyclopedia of Quotations* (Coppell, TX: Fame, 1994) 411.

23. John Fiske, *The Critical Period of American History: 1783–1789* (New York: Houghton, 1898) 239.

24. Bradford 21.

25. Washington, Vol. 30, 11.

The Christian History of Black America

1. John Quincy Adams, July 4, 1837, oration on the sixty-first anniversary of the Declaration of Independence (Newburyport, MA: Charles Whipple, 1837).

2. Quoted in Marshall Foster and Mary-Elaine Swanson, *The American Covenant: The Untold Story* (Thousand Oaks, CA: Mayflower Institute, 1992) 142.

3. Phillis Wheatley, *Poems* (Bedford, MA: Applewood, 1969) 48.

4. Earle E. Cairns, *Christianity through the Centuries* (Grand Rapids, MI: Zondervan, 1967) 457–58.

Act Six: The Drama of Modern History

1. George Washington, *George Washington: A Collection*. W. B. Allen, ed. (Indianapolis, IN: Liberty, 1988) 514.

2. Washington 522–23.

3. Washington 520–21.

4. Washington 521–22.

5. K. M. Tanikkar, *A Survey of Indian History*, (Bombay: Asia Publishing House, 1963) 222.

6. Quoted in Peter Marshall and David Manuel, *From Sea to Shining Sea* (Grand Rapids, MI: Revell, 1986) 49.

7. John 8:31–32.

8. John Eidsmoe, *Christianity and the Constitution* (Grand Rapids, MI: Baker, 1987) 22-3.

9. Benjamin Rush, *Essays, Literary, Moral, and Philosophical* (Philadelphia, PA: Thomas & Samuel Bradford, 1798) 112.

10. Paul Vitz, *Censorship: Evidence of Bias in Our Children's Textbooks* (Ann Arbor: Servant, 1986) 11, 16.

11. Quoted in Marvin Olasky, *The Tragedy of American Compassion* (Wheaton, IL: Crossway, 1992) 43.

12. Quoted In Olasky 22.

13. John Charles Ryle, *The Upper Room* (London: Banner of Truth [1888]1990) 60.

14. Quoted in D. James Kennedy and Jerry Newcombe, *What if Jesus Had Never Been Born?* (Nashville, TN: Nelson, 1994) 112.

15. George Gilder, Microcosm (New York: Simon, 1989) 11.

16. Gilder 361.

17. George Gilder, *Wealth and Poverty* (New York: Basic, 1981) 73.

18. Quoted in Verna M. Hall, *The Christian History of the American Revolution* (San Francisco: Foundation for American Christian Education, 1976) 20.

19. Herb Titus, *God, Man, and Law: The Biblical Principles* (Oak Brook, IL: Institute in Basic Life Principles, 1994) 5.

20. Quoted in John W. Whitehead, *The Second American Revolution* (Elgin, IL: Cook, 1982) 67–8.

21. Thomas Jefferson, *Jefferson's Letters*. Wilson Whitman, ed. (Eau Claire, WI: Hale, 1900) 338.

22. Robert H. Bork, *Slouching Towards Gomorrah* (New York: Harper, 1996) 319.

23. Paul Johnson, *Intellectuals* (New York: Harper, 1988) 342.

24. John Winthrop, *The Winthrop Papers,* Vol. 2 (Boston: Massachusetts Historical Society) 292–295.

Crime: Its Causes and Its Cures

1. Quoted in William J. Federer, ed., *America's God and Country Encyclopedia of Quotations,* (Coppell, TX: FAME Pub, 1994) 411.

2. Quoted in *Federer* 205.

3. William J. Bennett, *The Index of Leading Cultural Indicators* Vol. 1 (March 93).

4. Robert H. Bork, *Slouching Towards Gomorrah* (New York: Harper, 1996) 165.

5. Bennett 1.

6. Mark 7:20–23.

7. Horace Mann, Quoted in John Eidsmoe, *God and Caesar* (Westchester, IL: Crossway, 1984) 194.

8. Quoted in Marvin Olasky, *The Tragedy of American Compassion* (Wheaton, IL: Crossway, 1992) 6.

9. John Eidsmoe, *God and Caesar* (Westchester, IL: Crossway, 1984) 196.

10. Bork 170.

11. Charles Colson, cited in Eidsmoe 237.

12. Eidsmoe 197.

13. Quoted in Cleon W. Skousen, *The Making of America* (Washington, D.C.: National Center for Constitutional Studies, 1985) 234.

14. H. R. Warfel, *Noah Webster, Schoolmaster to America* (New York: Octagon, 1966) 181.

15. Isa. 58:12.

16. Daniel Webster, *The Works of Daniel Webster,* Vol. 1 (Boston: Little, Brown & Company, 1853) 48.

Part Three: Academic Disciplines That Manifest God's Principles

Worldview Expression in Art

1. Saint Augustine, *Confessions,* trans. R. S. Pine-Coffin (London: Penguin, 1961) 281.

2. Augustine 256.

3. Augustine 340-341.

4. Cynthia Pearl Maus, *Christ and the Fine Arts* (New York: Harper, 1938) 8.

5. C. S. Lewis, *The Abolition of Man* (New York: Macmillan, 1947).

6. Franky Schaeffer, *A Time for Anger* (Westchester, IL: Crossway, 1982) 147.

Worldview Expression in Literature

1. Gene Edward Veith Jr., *Reading Between the Lines* (Wheaton, IL: Crossway, 1990) 169–170.

2. Veith 29.

3. Veith 154.

4. D. James Kennedy, *What if Jesus Had Never Been Born?* (Nashville, TN: Nelson, 1994) 178.

5. Susan V. Gallagher and Roger Lundin, *Literature Through the Eyes of Faith* (San Francisco: Harper, 1989) 10.

6. Veith 45.

Faith and Science

1. Henry M. Morris, *The Long War Against God* (Grand Rapids, MI: Baker, 1990) 256.
2. David Raup, "Conflicts Between Darwin and Paleontology," *Field Museum of Natural History Bulletin,* January 1979, 25.
3. Paul Davies, *Superforce* (New York: Simon and Schuster, 1984) 233.
4. Walter T. Brown Jr., *In the Beginning* (Phoenix: Center for Scientific Creation, 1986) 20.
5. Michael Denton, *Evolution: A Theory in Crisis* (Bethesda, MD: Adler and Adler, 1986) 109.
6. Dean Kenyon, "Going Beyond the Naturalistic Mindset in Origin-of-Life Research," *Origins Research,* Spring/Summer 1989, 15.
7. H. P. Yockey, "Self Organization Origin of Life Scenarios and Information Theory," *Journal of Theoretical Biology,* Vol. 91 (1981), 29.
8. Brown 3.
9. Wolfgang Smith, *Teilhardism and the New Religion* (Rockford, IL: Tan Books, 1988) 5.
10. Denton 77.
11. Paul Amos Moody, *Introduction to Evolution* (New York: Harper and Row, 1970) 497.
12. Quoted in Norman Macbeth, *Darwin Retired* (Boston: Gambit, 1971) 101.
13. Luther D. Sunderland, *Darwin's Enigma* (San Diego: Master Books, 1984) 148.
14. Denton 64–5.
15. Evolutionist Stephen J. Gould, "Evolution's Erratic Pace," *Natural History,* Vol. 86 (May 1977) 14.
16. Denton 290.
17. Philosopher of Science Karl Popper, *Unended Quest* (La Salle, IL: Open Court, 1990) 168.

Myths & Legends

1. 1 Cor. 1:18.
2. Donna Rosenberg, *World Mythology: An Anthology of Great Myths and Epics,* 2d. ed. (1995) xv–xvi.
3. Josh McDowell, *Evidence that Demands a Verdict* (Campus Crusade for Christ, 1972) 367–8.
4. Frank S. Mead, ed., *The Encyclopedia of Religious Quotations* (Old Tappan, NJ: Revell, 1976) 90.
5. C.S. Lewis, *Mere Christianity* (New York; MacMillan, 1952) 41.

Part Five: Preparing for the Twenty-first Century

1. Allan Bloom, *The Closing of the American Mind* (New York: Simon & Schuster, 1987) 25.
2. For a good analysis of political correctness, see Thomas Sowell's *Inside American Education,* chapter 7.
3. E. R. Norman, *Imprimis* (April 1981)
4. Robert Flood, *The Rebirth of America* (Philadelphia: DeMoss Foundation, 1986) 127.
5. William Bradford, *The Plymouth Settlement* (San Antonio, TX: Mantle) 21.
6. James C. Dobson and Gary L. Bauer, *Children at Risk: The Bettle for the Hearts and Minds of Our Kids* (Dallas, TX: Word, 1990) 19–20.
7. Ps. 119:11, 98–99.
8. Thomas Sowell, *Inside American Education* (New York: Free Press, 1993) 178.
9. Sowell 178.
10. James Dale Davidson and Lord William Rees-Mogg, *The Great Reckoning* (New York: Summit Books, 1991) 26.
11. Sowell 2.
12. John Whitehead, *The Second American Revolution* (Elgin, IL: Cook, 1982) 39–40.
13. John C. Whitcomb and Henry M. Morris, *The Genesis Flood* (Phillipsburg, NJ: Presbyterian and Reformed, 1995) 440–41.

14. Whitehead 36.
15. Francis A. Schaeffer, *A Christian Manifesto* (Westchester, IL: Crossway, 1981) 23.
16. Isa. 14:12.
17.Gen. 3:5.
18. Schaeffer 24.
19. David A. Noebel, *Understanding the Times* (Manitou Springs, CO: Summit, 1991) 19.
20. Quoted in Gary DeMar, *Surviving College Successfully.* (Brentwood, TN: Wolgemuth, 1988) 93.
21. Schaeffer 54.
22. 1 Cor. 10:20.
23. David A. Noebel, *Understanding the Times* (Manitou Springs, CO: Summit, 1991) 14.
24. John 10:10b.
25. George Barna, *What Americans Believe* (Ventura, CA: Regal, 1991) 298.

Part Six: Conclusion

1. Robin Kane Fox, *Pagans and Christians* (San Francisco: Harper, 1986) 331.
2. Prov. 22:6

GLOSSARY

abolitionist A person who favors the outlawing of slavery.

aesthetic (also *esthetic*) Relating to an appreciation of beauty and nature.

anarchists People who oppose government or authority and usually try to overthrow it through violence.

animism The belief that the spirit is separate from the body.

apostasy The repudiation of a religious faith or previously held belief or loyalty.

appellate Relating to an appeal, or the power of a court to review the judgment of a lower court.

atheist A person who does not believe that any god exists.

autonomous Self-sufficient, able to act without help from other people or God.

axiom A statement that is the logical beginning point for deduction which cannot be arrived at as the result of prior deduction.

barbarism The actions or behaviors of a barbarian, or a backward, savage person.

bellwethers Indications of patterns or trends.

bowers A shelter formed from trees and vines that are intertwined.

Buddhism A religion of central and eastern Asia, founded in India in the sixth century B.C. by Buddha. It teaches that right thinking and self-denial will enable the soul to reach Nirvana, a state of release from misdirected desire.

Byzantine In art, similar to the style of the Byzantine Empire, with lush colors, intricate work, and religious themes.

capitalism An economic system in which ownership is public or private and prices, distribution of goods, and rates of production are determined by competition.

chimerical Imaginary; unreal; ridiculous.

conquistadores Those who conquer; specifically, the Spaniards who explored and conquered the Americas in the sixteenth century.

cuneiform An ancient form of writing, consisting of wedge-shaped characters, found primarily in Middle Eastern civilizations.

Darwinist A person who supports the teachings of Charles Darwin, particularly his theory of evolution.

Decalogue The Ten Commandments.

deist One who holds to the philosophy of deism, specifically that God is not involved with the world. The deist relies on reason more than revealed truth.

democracy A term originating in ancient Greece to describe a form of government in which the people share in directing the activities of the state.

despotic Characteristic of a despot, or a ruler who has absolute power.

dilettantes A person who follows art or science only for amusement and in a superficial way.

Druidism The religion and beliefs of Druids, or Celtic priests.

egalitarianism A belief in treating all people in a society equally, especially with regard to social, political, and economic rights.

elitist One who advocates government or control by an elite, the group or part of a group selected or regarded as the finest, best, most distinguished, most powerful, etc.

esthetic See *aesthetic.*

extrapolation   To arrive at conclusions or results by hypothesizing from known facts or observations.

feudalism   The dominant political, economic, and social system of medieval Europe, in which society was strictly divided into classes: the landholding nobility, an influential and sometimes powerful clergy, and the peasantry, or serfs.

gendarmes   In France, soldiers who make up an armed police force.
genocide   The systematic extermination of a group of people.
gourd   A herbaceous, vine-bearing plant; for example, a cucumber or a melon.

Hellenistic   Describing the period in ancient Greek history and culture following the death of Alexander the Great and before the rise of the Roman Empire.
heresy   A religious belief opposed to the orthodox doctrines of a church.
Hessians   During the American Revolution, German mercenaries who fought for the British.
Hinduism   The religion of most of the people of India that accepts the Veda as its sacred scriptures and has produced the caste system of social classification.
humanism   A modern, nontheistic, rationalist movement that holds that man is capable of self-fulfillment, ethical conduct, etc., without recourse to the supernatural.
hypocrisy   Pretending to be something one is not or believing what one does not.
hypothesis   An unproved supposition tentatively accepted to explain certain facts or to provide a basis for further investigation.

ideologies   Systems or ways of belief.
idolatry   The worship of idols or other physical objects as gods.
immutable   That which cannot be altered.

Judaism   The religious beliefs and practices of the Jews, who accept the Torah—the Old Testament—as their divinely revealed teachings and believe in a single God.
jurisprudence   A body of law.

largesse   Generosity.
lexicographer   Someone who writes or edits a dictionary.
lintel   In architecture, a horizontal structure that carries the load above an opening.

macroevolution   Large-scale and long-range evolution involving the appearance of new genera, families, etc., of organisms.
Magnificat   The canticle, or liturgical song, of the Virgin Mary.
Marxist   One who advocates Karl Marx's political philosophy of communism, in which the state controls the means of production and distribution, rationing the produce and profits among the citizens. Marx theorized that the state would eventually become unnecessary and wither away, but this has not occurred in any communist state.
materialist   A person who supports the philosophy of materialism, or that reality and worth are based on material objects.
mentor   A wise advisor who trains a pupil in his own philosophies.
messianic   Relating to a messiah, or an idealistic, crusading leader.
metaphysical   Not perceived by the senses; characteristic of studies such as theology and psychology as opposed to history and biology.

microevolution Small-scale hereditary in organisms through mutations and recombinations, resulting in the formation of slightly different varieties.

millennium One thousand years.

monotheism The belief in one god.

Mormonism An offshoot of Christianity founded by Joseph Smith, who claimed that the Book of Mormon had been revealed to him. The Mormons belong to the Church of Jesus Christ of Latter-Day Saints, based in Salt Lake City, Utah.

multiculturalism Supporting and studying all different cultures and groups equally, frequently emphasizing cultures that have been ignored in the past.

mutation A sudden variation in some inheritable characteristic of an individual, animal, or plant.

natural selection The process supposed by Darwin's theory of evolution, in which organisms possessing certain attributes reproduced more successfully, causing over time a shift in the characteristics of a species.

naturalistic Applied realism and objectivity in work of art and literature, without moral judgment the material depicted.

nihilistic From the Latin nihil for "nothing." Believing that nothing has purpose.

Nineveh Ancient capital of Assyria.

oligarchy A form of government in which the power rests in a small number of individuals, who are usually corrupt.

paleontology The branch of biology that deals with prehistoric forms of life through the study of plant and animal fossils.

pandemic Describing something, such as a disease, that covers a large geographic area and affects a high percentage of its population.

Pandora In Greek mythology, Pandora was a woman who was forbidden by the gods to open a box that they had sent down to Earth. When her curiosity got the best of her, she opened the box and unleashed evils on the world.

paradigm In science, a model, pattern, or ideal theory, from which perspective phenomena are explained.

philosophes French writers of the Enlightenment; for example, Jean-Jacques Rousseau.

pluralism The belief that truth does not exist except inasmuch as an individual believes something to be true, and that therefore, all opinions, beliefs, and doctrines are to be allowed the same degree of credibility.

polygamy The practice of being married to more than one spouse simultaneously.

polytheistic Describing a religion that professes the existence of multiple gods.

providence The actions of God in history; the intervention of God on behalf of His people or person.

relativism The idea that values are not universally applicable in all times or in all places, but that they differ from society to society, from person to person.

revisionism The philosophy that the interpretation of historical occurrences should be revised to fit contemporary sensibilities.

secular Nonreligious, worldly.

Separatists Pilgrims; those who sought to separate themselves from the Church of England during the sixteenth and seventeenth centuries.

serf In the Middle Ages, a person who was bound to the feudal manner and the wishes of his lord.

skeptic A person who habitually doubts, questions, or suspends judgment on matters generally accepted.

Talmudists Those who specialize in the Talmud, or the principal books of Jewish tradition and law.

tariffs Taxes imposed by a country on imported or exported goods.

tithe A tenth of one's income, given in support of a religious institution.

tract In some masses, a verse of Scripture that is used between the gradual and the Gospel.

transcendentalism A philosophy that maintains the importance of transcendent reality, or a reality that relies on nature and is based on deductive reasoning. American authors Henry David Thoreau and Ralph Waldo Emerson were noted proponents of this philosophy.

tyranny A government in which all of the power is in the hands of a single ruler.

Unitarianism A religious denomination that considers itself Christian, but denies the doctrine of the Trinity, maintaining that God exists in one person. Its emphasis, however, is not on doctrine, but on freedom of individual belief and world unity.

vassals In the Middle Ages, occupants of a feudal manor who were above the class of serfs, but below that of lords. A vassal was under the protection and guidance of a lord, whom he had vowed to serve.

INDEX

Notes

ALSO FROM ZANE PUBLISHING

LEARNING GUIDES

The Reference Companion to Zane Publishing's Titles

The Learning Guides is a 480-page book detailing the titles featured in the Zane Home Library, Zane Special Interest, and Zane Reference series. Families will learn the outstanding educational content of these titles through:

Learning objectives	**Study Questions**
Title Features	**Glossary terms**

Most Zane titles are part of a series, using a pedagogical approach designed to reinforce or supplement classroom learning…assist homeschoolers teaching a curriculum…help a student write a report or prepare for a test…and empower parents to actively participate in their child's education.

Zane Publishing is committed to producing educational and reference titles that educate, elevate, and enlighten.

Zane Publishing, Inc.
1950 Stemmons, Suite 4044
Dallas, Texas 75207-3109

Phone: 214-800-6000
Fax: 214-800-6090
Website: http://www.zane.com